taste of home.
the ULTIMATE
Comfort
FOOD
COOKBOOK

taste of home
the ULTIMATE
Comfort
FOOD
COOKBOOK

VICE PRESIDENT, EDITOR-IN-CHIEF:	Catherine Cassidy
VICE PRESIDENT, EXECUTIVE EDITOR/BOOKS:	Heidi Reuter Lloyd
CREATIVE DIRECTOR:	Howard Greenberg
FOOD DIRECTOR:	Diane Werner, RD
SENIOR EDITOR/BOOKS:	Mark Hagen
EDITOR:	Christine Rukavena
ASSOCIATE CREATIVE DIRECTOR:	Edwin Robles Jr.
ART DIRECTOR:	Jessie Sharon
CONTENT PRODUCTION MANAGER:	Julie Wagner
LAYOUT DESIGNER:	Nancy Novak
COPY CHIEF:	Deb Warlaumont Mulvey
COPY EDITOR:	Alysse Gear
RECIPE ASSET SYSTEM MANAGER:	Coleen Martin
RECIPE TESTING AND EDITING:	Taste of Home Test Kitchen
FOOD PHOTOGRAPHY:	Taste of Home Photo Studio
COVER PHOTOGRAPHER:	Dan Roberts
COVER FOOD STYLIST:	Alynna Malson
COVER SET STYLIST:	Dee Dee Jacq
ADMINISTRATIVE ASSISTANT:	Barb Czysz

VICE PRESIDENT, GENERAL MANAGER, RDA MILWAUKEE:	Lisa Karpinski
VICE PRESIDENT/BOOK MARKETING:	Dan Fink
CREATIVE DIRECTOR/CREATIVE MARKETING:	Jim Palmen

The Reader's Digest Association, Inc.

PRESIDENT AND CHIEF EXECUTIVE OFFICER:	Robert E. Guth
PRESIDENT, NORTH AMERICA:	Dan Lagani

Front cover: Meatball Sub Casserole (p. 120), Italian Shepherd's Pie (p. 119), Tropical BBQ Chicken (p. 150), Ham Mac and Cheese (p. 127), Edna's Ho Ho Cake (p. 289).

Back cover: Turkey Potpies (p. 111), Sausage Mac Supper (p. 54), Roasted Chicken with Rosemary (p. 105), Cloverleaf Rolls (p. 233).

International Standard Book Number (10): 0-89821-951-5
International Standard Book Number (13): 978-0-89821-951-7
Library of Congress Control Number: 2011931582

Printed in USA.

For other Taste of Home books and products, visit ShopTasteofHome.com

TABLE OF CONTENTS

introduction..4

appetizers & munchies.....................................6

stovetop suppers 32

casseroles & oven entrees 84

from the slow cooker...................................134

side dishes 170

bakeshop favorites 214

rich & creamy desserts 274

index 310

PICTURED: RUSTIC AUTUMN FRUIT TART, PAGE 257

GO AHEAD—indulge in our biggest-ever

For some, nothing says comfort food like creamy mac 'n' cheese, bubbling potpie or even pizza loaded with favorite toppings. For others, it's a wedge of chocolate cake, creamy milkshakes or freshly baked bread. Whatever comfort food means to you, you're sure to find it in this enormous collection of 468 Taste of Home readers' beloved recipes! *The Ultimate Comfort Food Cookbook* has it all!

TREASURED CLASSICS.

Savor family-favorite classics such as hot shredded beef, homemade potato salad and pretty deviled eggs. Thrill your loved ones with warm sticky buns, the perfect layer cake or a beautiful berry pie. Rekindle fond childhood memories with satisfying chili dogs and frosty homemade fudge pops. Fuel up the sports fans in your house with yummy pub foods such as nachos, sliders, spicy wings and hot spinach dip.

Our tempting assortment is loaded with delicious memories just waiting to be made!

CONTEMPORARY DELIGHTS.

If you've ever enjoyed crispy coffee-shop biscotti, admired an antipasto platter laden with meats, olives and cheeses, or savored a chewy fresh-cooked bagel and wondered if you could ever whip up amazing creations like these at home, now you can!

Explore fresh takes on old favorites with carrot cake doughnuts, meat loaf gyros and a gorgeous loaf of rosemary focaccia that's table-ready in just 25 minutes. It simply couldn't be easier to surprise (and satisfy) your family with the hearty delights they crave most.

BUSY COOKS, REJOICE!

Buttery, hot cinnamon rolls in just 20 minutes from mixing to munching? It's true! With this amazing collection, you can enjoy scrumptious homemade comfort food anytime. In fact, more than 100 delicious foods are ready to serve in just 30 minutes or less. And 55 hearty recipes even use the slow cooker for fuss-free meals that always fit your schedule.

FAVORITES FROM HOME COOKS.

Almost every selection in this book comes from the personal recipe files of home cooks just like you. And because every recipe was tested and approved by our experts in the Taste of Home Test Kitchen, you're guaranteed delicious results every time. So go ahead, flip through *The Ultimate Comfort Food Cookbook* and find a new family favorite today!

collection of amazing COMFORT FOOD!

CHAPTER ONE

appetizers & munchies

PICTURED LEFT TO RIGHT: HAM AND CHEESE PARTY CALZONES, PAGE 13 • FRENCH ONION CHEESE FONDUE, PAGE 14
FESTIVE FETA CHEESE BALL, PAGE 16 • PICKLED SHRIMP, PAGE 27

cathy tang
REDMOND, WASHINGTON

These fun, filling pretzels with a mild Southwestern kick are the perfect snack for watching football games. And they'll score just as high with adults as kids!

RAPID MIXING METHOD

In the rapid mixing method for yeast doughs, flour, yeast and other dry ingredients are combined, and then a hot liquid (120° to 130°) is added. Quick-rise or regular active dry yeast may be used with this mixing method.

southwest pretzels

PREP: 30 min. + standing | **BAKE:** 25 min.

    4 cups all-purpose flour
    1 tablespoon sugar
    1 package (1/4 ounce) quick-rise yeast
1-1/2 teaspoons salt
    1 teaspoon dried minced onion
1/2 teaspoon chili powder
1/4 teaspoon ground cumin
1/4 teaspoon cayenne pepper
1-1/2 cups warm water (120° to 130°)
    1 egg, lightly beaten
Coarse salt
Salsa con queso dip

In a large bowl, combine 2 cups flour, sugar, yeast, salt, minced onion and spices. Add water. Beat just until moistened. Stir in enough remaining flour to form a soft dough.

Turn onto a floured surface; knead until smooth and elastic, about 4-6 minutes. Cover and let rest for 10 minutes. Divide dough into 16 equal portions; roll each into a 15-in. rope. Cover and let rest 10 minutes longer.

Twist into pretzel shapes. Place on greased baking sheets; brush with egg. Bake at 350° for 15 minutes. Brush again with egg; sprinkle with coarse salt. Bake 10-13 minutes longer or until golden brown. Remove to wire racks. Serve pretzels warm with the dip.

YIELD: 16 pretzels.

dawn onuffer
CRESTVIEW, FLORIDA

There's no faster way to get a party started than with these bacon-wrapped poppers. Make them ahead and bake just before serving. Even the hot-pepper intolerant will want to give them a try.

sweet & spicy jalapeno poppers

PREP/TOTAL TIME: 30 min.

    6 jalapeno peppers
    4 ounces cream cheese, softened
    2 tablespoons shredded cheddar cheese
    6 bacon strips, halved widthwise
1/4 cup packed brown sugar
    1 tablespoon chili seasoning

Cut jalapenos in half lengthwise and remove seeds; set aside. In a small bowl, beat cheeses until blended. Spoon into pepper halves. Wrap a half-strip of bacon around each pepper half.

Combine brown sugar and chili seasoning; coat peppers with sugar mixture. Place in a greased 15-in. x 10-in. x 1-in. baking pan.

Bake at 350° for 18-20 minutes or until bacon is firm.

YIELD: 1 dozen.

EDITOR'S NOTE: Wear disposable gloves when cutting hot peppers; the oils can burn skin. Avoid touching your face.

smoky potato rounds

PREP: 15 min. | **BAKE:** 55 min.

> 2 large baking potatoes
> 1/3 cup barbecue sauce
> 1/2 cup shredded cheddar cheese
> 6 bacon strips, cooked and crumbled
> 1/2 cup sour cream
> 3 green onions, thinly sliced

Scrub and pierce potatoes. Bake at 375° for 45 minutes or until almost tender.

When cool enough to handle, cut each potato widthwise into 1/2-in. slices. Place on a greased baking sheet. Brush with barbecue sauce; sprinkle with cheese and bacon.

Bake for 8-10 minutes or until potatoes are tender and cheese is melted. Top with sour cream and onions.

YIELD: 1-1/2 dozen.

rebecca dozier
KOUTS, INDIANA

I love potato skins but decided to change up the flavor by topping them with barbecue sauce. Once the potatoes are baked, these appetizers come together in a hurry.

cyndi fynaardt
OSKALOOSA, IOWA

*Here's an awesome update
of classic pigs in a blanket.
A yummy mixture of pork
and beef gets wrapped up in
from-scratch pastry dough.
Bet you can't eat just one!*

pigs in a blanket

PREP: 45 min. | BAKE: 35 min.

  3 cups all-purpose flour
  1 tablespoon sugar
  2 teaspoons baking powder
1/2 cup shortening
1/2 cup cold butter
  1 cup milk
 10 crushed Zwieback *or* Holland rusks
    (1-1/4 cups)
1/4 teaspoon salt
1/4 teaspoon pepper
1-3/4 pounds ground beef
1-3/4 pounds bulk pork sausage
Dijon mustard, optional

In a large bowl, combine the flour, sugar and baking
powder. Cut in shortening and butter until mixture
resembles coarse crumbs. Gradually add milk,
tossing with a fork until dough forms a ball. Divide
dough into three portions. Refrigerate until chilled.

For filling, in a large bowl, combine the Zwieback
crumbs, salt and pepper. Crumble beef and pork
over mixture and mix well. Shape rounded
tablespoonfuls of meat mixture into 3-in. logs.

On a floured surface, knead one portion of
dough 8-10 times. Roll dough to 1/8-in. thickness; cut
with a floured 3-in. round cutter.

Place one log in the center of each circle. Brush
edges of dough with water; fold dough over filling
and pinch edges to seal. Reroll scraps. Repeat with
remaining dough and filling.

Place on greased racks in shallow baking pans.
Bake at 350° for 35-40 minutes or until a meat
thermometer reads 160°. Serve appetizers with
mustard if desired.

YIELD: about 4-1/2 dozen.

pineapple ham pizzas

PREP/TOTAL TIME: 10 min.

- 2 English muffins, split and toasted
- 2 tablespoons barbecue sauce
- 2 ounces sliced deli ham, cut into strips
- 1 snack-size cup (4 ounces) pineapple tidbits, well drained
- 2 slices (1 ounce *each*) Swiss cheese, quartered

Place English muffins cut side up on a broiler pan. Spread with barbecue sauce; top with ham, pineapple and cheese. Broil 4-6 in. from the heat for 2-3 minutes or until cheese is melted.

YIELD: 4 pizzas.

vicky priestley
ALUM CREEK, WEST VIRGINIA

Whip up these barbecue Hawaiian pizzas as a quick after-school snack. Prepared on English muffins, the cheesy treats are something that kids of all ages will think are special.

creamy olive-bacon dip

PREP/TOTAL TIME: 15 min.

- 1 cup (8 ounces) sour cream
- 12 bacon strips, cooked and crumbled
- 3/4 cup mayonnaise
- 3/4 cup shredded cheddar cheese
- 2 cans (2-1/4 ounces *each*) sliced ripe olives, drained
- 1 medium tomato, seeded and chopped
- Bagel chips *or* assorted crackers

In a large bowl, combine the first six ingredients. Refrigerate until serving. Serve dip with bagel chips or crackers.

YIELD: 3 cups.

kari caven
POST FALLS, IDAHO

When I had just 15 minutes to prepare something for a party, I combined the ingredients I had on hand and came up with a cheesy dip. I knew the recipe was a keeper when I took home a nearly empty bowl.

tomato nacho dip

PREP/TOTAL TIME: 15 min.

- 1 can (4 ounces) chopped green chilies
- 1/2 cup chopped onion
- 2 tablespoons butter
- 2 tablespoons all-purpose flour
- 1/2 cup milk
- 1-1/2 cups (6 ounces) cubed process American cheese (Velveeta)
- 1 cup (4 ounces) shredded Monterey Jack cheese
- 1/2 cup chopped fresh tomato
- Tortilla chips

In a 1-1/2-qt. microwave-safe dish, combine chilies, onion and butter. Cover and microwave on high for 45 seconds or until butter is melted. Stir in flour until smooth. Gradually stir in milk until blended.

Cook, uncovered, on high for 30-60 seconds or until thickened. Add the cheeses and tomato. Microwave, uncovered, at 70% power for 1-2 minutes or until cheese is melted. Serve dip with tortilla chips.

YIELD: 2-2/3 cups.

EDITOR'S NOTE: This recipe was tested in a 1,100-watt microwave.

rhonda mckee
GREENSBURG, KANSAS

A friend gave me the recipe for this simple dip that gets its zip from canned green chilies. It's a snap to heat up in the microwave.

linda lane
BENNINGTON, VERMONT

I started preparing mini burgers several years ago as a way to use up bread crusts accumulating in my freezer. Their tiny size makes them irresistible.

mini burgers with the works

PREP/TOTAL TIME: 30 min.

1/4 pound ground beef

3 slices process American cheese

4 slices white bread (heels of loaf recommended)

2 tablespoons prepared Thousand Island salad dressing

2 pearl onions, thinly sliced

4 baby dill pickles, thinly sliced

3 cherry tomatoes, thinly sliced

Shape the beef into twelve 1-in. patties. Place on a microwave-safe plate lined with paper towels. Cover with another paper towel; microwave patties on high for 1 minute until a thermometer reads 160° and juices run clear. Cut each slice of cheese into fourths; set aside.

Using a 1-in. round cookie cutter, cut out six circles from each slice of bread. Spread half of the bread circles with dressing. Layer with burgers, cheese, onions, pickles and tomatoes. Top with remaining bread circles; secure with toothpicks.

YIELD: 1 dozen.

EDITOR'S NOTE: This recipe was tested in a 1,100-watt microwave.

kevalyn henderson
HAYWARD, WISCONSIN

These fall-off-the-bone-tender wings have just the right amount of heat. The cool blue cheese sauce creates the perfect flavor combination for dipping.

spicy chicken wings

PREP: 25 min. + marinating | BAKE: 2 hours

1 cup reduced-sodium soy sauce

2/3 cup sugar

2 teaspoons salt

2 teaspoons grated orange peel

2 garlic cloves, minced

1/2 teaspoon pepper

3 pounds frozen chicken wingettes and drumettes, thawed

3 teaspoons chili powder

3/4 teaspoon cayenne pepper

3/4 teaspoon hot pepper sauce

BLUE CHEESE DIP:

1 cup mayonnaise

1/2 cup blue cheese salad dressing

1/3 cup buttermilk

2 teaspoons Italian salad dressing mix

In a small bowl, combine the soy sauce, sugar, salt, orange peel, garlic and pepper. Pour half of the marinade into a large resealable plastic bag. Add the chicken; seal bag and turn to coat. Refrigerate for 1 hour. Cover and refrigerate remaining marinade.

Drain wings and discard marinade. Transfer wings to a greased 13-in. x 9-in. baking dish. Cover and bake at 325° for 1-1/2 hours or until chicken juices run clear.

Using tongs, transfer wings to a greased 15-in. x 10-in. x 1-in. baking pan. In a small bowl, combine the chili powder, cayenne, pepper sauce and reserved marinade. Drizzle over wings.

Bake, uncovered, for 30 minutes, turning once. In a small bowl, whisk the dip ingredients. Serve dip with wings.

YIELD: 2 dozen (1-3/4 cups dip).

ham and cheese party calzones

PREP: 20 min. | **BAKE:** 20 min.

shelby marino
NEPTUNE BEACH, FLORIDA

2 tubes (13.8 ounces *each*) refrigerated pizza crust
1 cup ricotta cheese
4 to 6 ounces sliced pepperoni
2 cups diced fully cooked ham
2 cups (8 ounces) shredded part-skim mozzarella cheese
Shredded Parmesan cheese, optional
Dried basil, optional
Spaghetti sauce, warmed

Unroll one pizza crust on a greased baking sheet; roll out into a 14-in. x 11-in. rectangle. Spread half of the ricotta cheese lengthwise on half of the dough to within 1 in. of the edges.

Sprinkle with half of the pepperoni, ham and mozzarella cheese. Fold dough over filling; press edges firmly to seal. Repeat with remaining crust and filling ingredients.

Bake at 400° for 20-25 minutes or until golden brown. Sprinkle with Parmesan cheese and basil if desired. Cut into slices. Serve with spaghetti sauce.

YIELD: 2 calzones (7 servings each).

This sort of bundled-up pizza is something I concocted one evening when I had leftover baked ham and needed to fix something quickly. My husband loved it—and so did all his friends when he brought some to work to share.

cathy ostrawski
AMHERST, NEW YORK

Here's a three-ingredient fondue that's quick to stir together. It is just perfect for company, but any leftovers are great over potatoes or pasta!

french onion cheese fondue

PREP/TOTAL TIME: 15 min.

1 can (10-3/4 ounces) condensed cheddar cheese soup, undiluted

1 carton (8 ounces) French onion dip

2 cups (8 ounces) shredded cheddar cheese

1 loaf (1 pound) French bread, cubed, *or* assorted fresh vegetables

In a large saucepan, combine soup and dip. Add cheese. Cook and stir over medium-low heat until cheese is melted; keep warm. Serve with bread cubes or vegetables.

YIELD: 3 cups.

brie phyllo cups

PREP/TOTAL TIME: 20 min.

- 1 package (1.9 ounces) frozen miniature phyllo tart shells
- 3 tablespoons crushed gingersnaps
- 6 ounces Brie cheese, rind removed, cubed
- 1/4 cup spreadable fruit of your choice

Place the tart shells on an ungreased baking sheet. Sprinkle about 1/2 teaspoon gingersnap crumbs into each shell; top with Brie and spreadable fruit.

Bake the phyllo cups at 325° for 5 minutes or until cheese is melted.

YIELD: 15 appetizers.

brenda little
BOISE, IDAHO

Mini phyllo shells from the freezer section hurry along these elegant cups. They look fancy and taste delicious, but they are a snap to put together for a special occasion.

pizza egg rolls

PREP: 35 min. | COOK: 10 min.

- 1 pound bulk Italian sausage
- 3/4 cup diced green pepper
- 1 garlic clove, minced
- 1 can (15 ounces) crushed tomatoes
- 1/4 cup tomato paste
- 1/2 teaspoon salt
- 1/2 teaspoon dried oregano
- 1/4 teaspoon sugar
- 1/8 teaspoon dried rosemary, crushed
- Dash pepper
- 8 ounces cubed part-skim mozzarella cheese
- 13 egg roll wrappers
- 1 egg, lightly beaten
- Oil for frying

In a large skillet, cook sausage and green pepper over medium heat until meat is no longer pink. Add garlic; cook 1 minute longer. Drain. Stir in the tomatoes, tomato paste and seasonings. Bring to a boil. Reduce heat; cover and simmer for 10 minutes. Uncover and simmer 10 minutes longer. Remove from the heat; cool for 20 minutes. Stir in cheese.

Place 1/3 cup sausage mixture in the center of each egg roll wrapper. Fold bottom corner over filling; fold sides toward center over filling. Brush remaining corner with egg; roll up tightly to seal.

In an electric skillet or deep-fat fryer, heat 1 in. of oil to 375°. Fry egg rolls in batches for 1-2 minutes on each side or until golden brown. Drain egg rolls on paper towels.

YIELD: 13 egg rolls.

tammy schill
OMAHA, NEBRASKA

My husband and kids love these very nontraditional egg rolls. Their crisp wrappers and flavorful pizza filling make them taste so good!

cinde ryan
GIG HARBOR, WASHINGTON

I created my feta and bacon cheese ball when I was asked to bring an appetizer to a party. Everyone loved it! It is so pretty, people will really think you've fussed.

SHAPE A CHEESE BALL MESS-FREE

To keep hands and countertop clean, spoon mixture for the cheese ball onto a piece of plastic wrap. Working from the underside of the wrap, pat the mixture into a ball.

sandra twait
TAMPA, FLORIDA

My husband was in the Air Force so we've entertained guests in many parts of the world. I acquired this recipe while in California. It's one of my best appetizers for a special occasion.

festive feta cheese ball

PREP: 10 min. + chilling

- 2 packages (8 ounces *each*) cream cheese, softened
- 1/2 cup crumbled feta cheese
- 2 teaspoons ranch salad dressing mix
- 1/4 cup shredded Parmesan cheese
- 1/4 cup crumbled cooked bacon
- 1/2 teaspoon dill weed
- Assorted crackers

In a large bowl, beat cream cheese until fluffy. Add feta cheese and dressing mix; mix well. Shape mixture into a ball.

In a small bowl, combine the Parmesan cheese, bacon and dill weed; roll cheese ball in Parmesan mixture. Wrap tightly in plastic wrap. Refrigerate for at least 1 hour or until firm. Serve with crackers.

YIELD: 2 cups.

brie in puff pastry

PREP: 15 min. | BAKE: 20 min. + standing

- 1 round (13.2 ounces) Brie cheese
- 1/2 cup crumbled blue cheese
- 1 sheet frozen puff pastry, thawed
- 1/4 cup apricot jam
- 1/2 cup slivered almonds, toasted
- 1 egg, lightly beaten
- Assorted crackers

Slice Brie horizontally in half. Sprinkle one cut side of Brie with blue cheese; top with remaining Brie. On a lightly floured surface, roll out pastry into a 14-in. square. Cut off corners to make a circle. Spread jam to within 1 in. of pastry edge; sprinkle with nuts. Place Brie on top; fold pastry over the cheese and pinch edges to seal.

Place seam side down on an ungreased baking sheet. Brush top and sides of pastry with egg. Bake at 400° for 20 minutes or until pastry is golden brown. Immediately remove from the baking sheet. Let stand for 1 hour before serving. Serve cheese with crackers.

YIELD: 10 servings.

antipasto platter

PREP: 10 min. + chilling

- 1 jar (24 ounces) pepperoncinis, drained
- 1 can (15 ounces) garbanzo beans *or* chickpeas, rinsed and drained
- 2 cups halved fresh mushrooms
- 2 cups halved cherry tomatoes
- 1/2 pound provolone cheese, cubed
- 1 can (6 ounces) pitted ripe olives, drained
- 1 package (3-1/2 ounces) sliced pepperoni
- 1 bottle (8 ounces) Italian vinaigrette dressing

Lettuce leaves

In a large bowl, combine the peppers, beans, mushrooms, tomatoes, cheese, olives and pepperoni. Pour vinaigrette over mixture and toss to coat.

Refrigerate for at least 30 minutes or overnight. Arrange on a lettuce-lined platter. Serve antipasto with toothpicks.

YIELD: 14-16 servings.

teri lindquist
GURNEE, ILLINOIS

We have company often, and antipasto is one of our favorite crowd-pleasers. It's a satisfying change from the usual chips and dip.

betsy hedeman
TIMONIUM, MARYLAND

These scrumptious crab cakes won First Place at the National Hard Crab Derby in Crisfield, Maryland. I entered them on a whim after trying many crab cake recipes for my family.

seasoned crab cakes

PREP: 20 min. + chilling | **COOK:** 10 min.

3 cans (6 ounces *each*) crabmeat, drained, flaked and cartilage removed

1 cup cubed bread

2 eggs

3 tablespoons mayonnaise

3 tablespoons half-and-half cream

1 tablespoon lemon juice

1 tablespoon butter, melted

1-1/2 teaspoons seafood seasoning

1 teaspoon Worcestershire sauce

1 teaspoon salt

1/2 cup dry bread crumbs

1/2 cup canola oil

In a large bowl, combine crab and bread cubes. In another bowl, whisk the eggs, mayonnaise, cream, lemon juice, butter, seafood seasoning, Worcestershire sauce and salt. Add to crab mixture and mix gently (mixture will be moist).

Place bread crumbs in a shallow dish. Drop crab mixture by 1/3 cupfuls into crumbs; shape each into a 3/4-in.-thick patty. Carefully turn to coat. Cover and refrigerate for at least 2 hours.

In a large skillet, cook crab cakes in oil for 4-5 minutes on each side or until golden brown and crispy. Drain on paper towels.

YIELD: 8 crab cakes.

savory ham cheesecake

PREP: 35 min. | **BAKE:** 1 hour + chilling

    3 cups oyster crackers, crushed
    1 cup grated Parmesan cheese
    1/3 cup butter, melted
FILLING:
    4 packages (8 ounces *each*) cream
      cheese, softened
    4 eggs, lightly beaten
    2 cups finely chopped fully cooked ham
    2 cups (8 ounces) shredded Swiss cheese
    1/3 cup minced chives
    1/4 cup minced fresh basil
    1/4 teaspoon salt
    1/4 teaspoon white pepper
  Assorted crackers

In a large bowl, combine the cracker crumbs, Parmesan cheese and melted butter. Set aside 1/4 cup for topping. Press remaining crumb mixture onto the bottom and 2 in. up the sides of a greased 9-in. springform pan. Refrigerate the crust for at least 30 minutes.

In a large bowl, beat cream cheese until smooth. Add eggs; beat on low speed just until combined (mixture will be thick). Add the ham, Swiss cheese, chives, basil, salt and pepper; beat just until combined. Pour into crust. Sprinkle with reserved crumb mixture.

Place pan on a baking sheet. Bake at 325° for 60-70 minutes or until filling is almost set. Turn oven off. Leave cheesecake in oven with door ajar for 30 minutes.

Cool cheesecake on a wire rack for 10 minutes. Carefully run a knife around edge of pan to loosen; cool 1 hour longer. Refrigerate overnight. Remove sides of pan. Serve chilled or at room temperature with crackers.

YIELD: 24-30 servings.

shannon soper
WEST BEND, WISCONSIN

My mom was the best cook—everything she made was special. She served her elegant cheesecake on Sunday following a Saturday ham dinner. Now my family loves it, too!

fat rascals

PREP/TOTAL TIME: 20 min.

    1/2 cup all-purpose flour
    1/4 teaspoon baking powder
  Salt and pepper to taste
    2 cups (8 ounces) shredded American *or*
      cheddar cheese
    1 cup mashed potatoes
    2 eggs, lightly beaten
    1/2 cup milk
  Oil for deep-fat frying

In a large bowl, combine the flour, baking powder, salt and pepper. Combine cheese, mashed potatoes, eggs and milk; stir into dry ingredients.

In an electric skillet or deep fryer, heat 2 in. of oil to 375°. Drop batter by rounded tablespoonfuls, a few at a time, into hot oil. Fry until golden brown, about 1-1/2 minutes on each side. Drain on paper towels. Serve immediately.

YIELD: about 2 dozen.

noami giddis
GRAWN, MICHIGAN

Here is the all-time-favorite Saturday night snack at our house. My family very deliberately leaves some mashed potatoes in the bowl during dinner so that I can make this yummy specialty the next day!

pizza cups

PREP/TOTAL TIME: 30 min.

    1 pound spicy *or* mild pork sausage
    1 jar (14 ounces) pizza sauce
    2 tablespoons ketchup
    1/4 teaspoon garlic powder
    2 tubes (10 ounces *each*) refrigerated
      biscuits
  Shredded part-skim mozzarella cheese
  Grated Parmesan cheese

In a large skillet, cook sausage over medium heat until no longer pink; drain. Stir in the pizza sauce, ketchup and garlic powder; set aside.

Press biscuits into 20 well-greased muffin cups. Spoon 1 or 2 tablespoons of the meat sauce into each biscuit; top with mozzarella cheese and sprinkle with Parmesan cheese.

Bake at 350° for 10 to 15 minutes or until the pizza cups are golden brown. (Refrigerate or freeze any remaining meat sauce.)

YIELD: 20 pizza cups.

suzanne mckinley
LYONS, GEORGIA

These snacks couldn't be quicker. I make the miniature pizzas often since my girls frequently have friends over. Even their big brother loves the tasty no-fuss cups!

To keep a summer kitchen cool, we suggest preparing pizzas on the grill! A variety of ingredients tops flour tortillas for three terrific pizzeria-inspired tastes.

appetizer pizzas

PREP: 30 min. | GRILL: 10 min.

    9 flour tortillas (6 inches)
    3 tablespoons olive oil

TRADITIONAL PIZZAS:

    1/3 cup chopped pepperoni
    3/4 cup shredded Colby-Monterey Jack
      cheese
    1 jar (14 ounces) pizza sauce

MEDITERRANEAN PIZZAS:

    1/2 cup chopped seeded tomato
    1/3 cup sliced ripe olives
    3/4 cup crumbled feta cheese
    1/4 cup thinly sliced green onions
    1 carton (7 ounces) hummus

MARGHERITA PIZZAS:

    9 thin slices tomato
    1 package (8 ounces) small fresh
      mozzarella cheese balls, sliced
    1 tablespoon minced fresh basil
    1 cup prepared pesto

Brush one side of each tortilla with oil. Place oiled side down on grill rack. Grill, uncovered, over medium heat for 2-3 minutes or until puffed. Brush tortillas with oil; turn and top with pizza toppings.

FOR TRADITIONAL PIZZAS: Top three grilled tortillas with pepperoni and cheese. Cover and grill for 2-3 minutes or until cheese is melted. Cut into wedges; serve with pizza sauce.

FOR MEDITERRANEAN PIZZAS: Top three grilled tortillas with tomato, olives, feta cheese and onions. Cover and grill them for 2-3 minutes or until the cheese is heated through. Cut into wedges and serve with hummus.

FOR MARGHERITA PIZZAS: Top three grilled tortillas with tomato slices, mozzarella cheese and basil. Cover and grill for 2-3 minutes or until cheese is melted. Cut into wedges; serve with pesto.

YIELD: 9 appetizer pizzas.

My mother-in-law gave me the recipe for her delightful taffy apple dip. It tastes like the real thing! The whole family will love it.

taffy apple dip

PREP/TOTAL TIME: 10 min.

    1 package (8 ounces) cream cheese,
      softened
    3/4 cup packed brown sugar
    1 tablespoon vanilla extract
    1/2 cup chopped peanuts
    6 apples, cut into wedges

In a small bowl, beat the cream cheese, brown sugar and vanilla until smooth. Sprinkle the mixture with nuts. Serve with apple wedges.

YIELD: 6 servings.

mexican chicken meatballs

PREP: 20 min. | BAKE: 15 min.

1/2 cup egg substitute
1 can (4 ounces) chopped green chilies
1 cup crushed cornflakes
1 cup (4 ounces) shredded reduced-fat Mexican cheese blend
1/2 teaspoon seasoned salt
1/4 teaspoon cayenne pepper
1 pound ground chicken
Salsa, optional

In a large bowl, combine the first six ingredients. Crumble chicken over mixture and mix well. Shape into 1-in. balls. Place on baking sheets coated with cooking spray.

Bake at 375° for 12-15 minutes or until a meat thermometer reads 165° and juices run clear, turning occasionally. Serve with salsa if desired.

YIELD: about 5 dozen.

katrina lopes
LYMAN, SOUTH CAROLINA

These low-fat meatballs taste fabulous on their own, but if you want to take things up a notch, serve them with a dip made of hot Velveeta cheese and a little salsa.

**taste of home
test kitchen**

Kids and adults alike will love the fun of mini burgers. Juiced up with pickle relish and topped with cheese, these sliders will disappear in no time flat! You can even top them with decorative cheese cutouts for the different holidays.

party time mini cheeseburgers

PREP/TOTAL TIME: 30 min.

1 egg, lightly beaten
2 tablespoons dill pickle relish
2 tablespoons ketchup
2 teaspoons Worcestershire sauce
2 teaspoons prepared mustard
1/4 cup quick-cooking oats
1/4 teaspoon pepper
1/8 teaspoon garlic powder
1 pound ground beef
3 to 4 slices process American cheese
10 dinner rolls, split

In a large bowl, combine the first eight ingredients. Crumble beef over mixture and mix well. Shape into 10 patties.

Broil 3-4 in. from the heat for 4-6 minutes on each side or until a thermometer reads 160° and juices run clear.

Meanwhile, cut out 10 decorative shapes from cheese slices using a 1-in. cutter. Immediately place on burgers; serve on rolls.

YIELD: 10 servings.

mini bbq chicken pizzas

PREP/TOTAL TIME: 25 min.

- 1 medium onion, chopped
- 2 teaspoons olive oil
- 1-1/2 cups shredded cooked chicken
- 2/3 cup barbecue sauce
- 1 can (4 ounces) chopped green chilies
- 1-1/2 teaspoons garlic powder
- 1/4 teaspoon pepper
- 6 whole wheat English muffins, split
- 1-1/2 cups (6 ounces) shredded part-skim mozzarella cheese

In a large nonstick skillet, saute onion in oil until tender. Stir in the chicken, barbecue sauce, chilies, garlic powder and pepper. Spread over muffin halves; sprinkle with cheese.

Place the pizzas on baking sheets; broil 4-6 in. from the heat for 2-3 minutes or until heated through and cheese is melted.

YIELD: 1 dozen.

deborah forbes
FORT WORTH, TEXAS

Here is a budget-friendly snack that's perfect for almost any time of day. Or turn the little pizzas into a quick weeknight dinner by adding a salad.

SNACK SMART
English muffin pizzas make satisfying snacks, and many of them freeze well. Freeze unused portions until firm and then wrap individually for a quick and easy bite when you need it.

cheddar crab bites

PREP/TOTAL TIME: 25 min.

- 1 jar (8 ounces) sharp cheddar cheese spread
- 1 package (8 ounces) imitation crabmeat, chopped
- 1/2 cup butter, melted
- 1 teaspoon Worcestershire sauce
- 1/8 teaspoon garlic powder
- 6 English muffins, split

In a small bowl, combine the cheese spread, crab, butter, Worcestershire sauce and garlic powder. Spread over muffin halves.

Place in two ungreased 15-in. x 10-in. x 1-in. baking pans. Bake at 400° for 10-12 minutes or until golden brown. Cut each muffin half into quarters. Serve appetizers warm.

YIELD: 4 dozen.

elaine anderson
NEW GALILEE, PENNSYLVANIA

Our guests always love these toasty little treats. The appetizers also freeze well, so I often save some for us to snack on while watching our favorite movies.

orange-glazed smokies

PREP/TOTAL TIME: 15 min.

- 1 cup packed brown sugar
- 1 tablespoon all-purpose flour
- 1/4 cup thawed orange juice concentrate
- 2 tablespoons prepared mustard
- 1 tablespoon cider vinegar
- 1 package (16 ounces) miniature smoked sausages

In a large microwave-safe bowl, combine the first five ingredients. Add sausages; stir to coat.

Cover and microwave on high for 3-4 minutes or until bubbly, stirring three times.

YIELD: about 4 dozen.

EDITOR'S NOTE: This recipe was tested in a 1,100-watt microwave.

judy wilson
SUN CITY WEST, ARIZONA

I can whip up these tasty sausages in a matter of minutes for parties, and the tangy citrus sauce is an instant conversation starter.

kaitlyn benito
EVERETT, WASHINGTON

Fancy-looking and filling, these sensational appetizers are a lot easier to make than they look. With just a few ingredients, they're really a breeze!

prosciutto pinwheels

PREP: 20 min. | **BAKE:** 15 min.

1 sheet frozen puff pastry, thawed
1/4 cup sweet hot mustard
1/4 pound sliced prosciutto *or* deli ham, chopped
1/2 cup shredded Parmesan cheese

Unfold puff pastry. Spread mustard over pastry to within 1/2 in. of edges. Sprinkle with prosciutto and cheese. Roll up one side to the middle of the dough; roll up the other side so the two rolls meet in the center. Using a serrated knife, cut into 1/2-in. slices.

Place on greased baking sheets. Bake at 400° for 11-13 minutes or until puffed and golden brown. Serve warm.

YIELD: 20 appetizers.

peggy allen
PASADENA, CALIFORNIA

I serve shrimp cocktail for every special occasion and on big-game days. It's always popular.

shrimp cocktail

PREP: 30 min. + chilling

3 quarts water
1 small onion, sliced
1/2 medium lemon, sliced
2 sprigs fresh parsley
1 tablespoon salt
5 whole peppercorns
1/4 teaspoon dried thyme
1 bay leaf
3 pounds uncooked large shrimp, peeled and deveined (tails on)

SAUCE:

1 cup chili sauce
2 tablespoons lemon juice
2 tablespoons prepared horseradish
4 teaspoons Worcestershire sauce
1/2 teaspoon salt
Dash cayenne pepper

In a Dutch oven, combine the first eight ingredients. Bring to a boil. Add the shrimp. Reduce heat; simmer, uncovered, for 4-5 minutes or until shrimp turn pink.

Drain the shrimp and immediately rinse them in cold water. Refrigerate for 2-3 hours. In a small bowl, combine the sauce ingredients. Refrigerate until serving.

Arrange shrimp on a serving platter; serve with cocktail sauce.

YIELD: about 6 dozen (1-1/4 cups sauce).

easy buffalo chicken dip

PREP/TOTAL TIME: 30 min.

1 package (8 ounces) reduced-fat cream cheese
1 cup (8 ounces) reduced-fat sour cream
1/2 cup Louisiana-style hot sauce
3 cups shredded cooked chicken breast
Assorted crackers

In a large bowl, beat the cream cheese, sour cream and hot sauce until smooth; stir in chicken.

Transfer to an 8-in. square baking dish coated with cooking spray. Cover and bake at 350° for 18-22 minutes or until dip is heated through. Serve warm with crackers.

YIELD: 4 cups.

janice foltz
HERSHEY, PENNSYLVANIA

Guys and gals will simply devour this delicious dip with shredded chicken throughout. The spicy kick makes it perfect TV-night food. Add celery sticks for color, if you like.

beatrice vetrano
LANDENBERG, PENNSYLVANIA

Rich Italian sausage filling makes a delicious hot appetizer that's always the hit of the party. You can't go wrong with a classic stuffed mushroom.

sausage-stuffed mushrooms

PREP: 25 min. | BAKE: 20 min.

12 to 15 large fresh mushrooms
2 tablespoons butter, *divided*
2 tablespoons chopped onion
1 tablespoon lemon juice
1/4 teaspoon dried basil
Salt and pepper to taste
4 ounces bulk Italian sausage
1 tablespoon chopped fresh parsley
2 tablespoons dry bread crumbs
2 tablespoons grated Parmesan cheese

Remove stems from the mushrooms. Chop stems finely; set mushroom caps aside. Place stems in paper towels and squeeze to remove any liquid.

In a large skillet, heat 1-1/2 tablespoons butter. Cook stems and onion until tender. Add the lemon juice, basil, salt and pepper; cook until almost all the liquid has evaporated. Cool.

In a large bowl, combine the mushroom mixture, sausage and parsley; stuff reserved mushroom caps. Combine crumbs and cheese; sprinkle over tops. Dot each with remaining butter.

Place in a greased baking pan. Bake at 400° for 20 minutes or until sausage is no longer pink, basting occasionally with pan juices. Serve hot.

YIELD: 12-15 servings.

pickled shrimp

PREP: 45 min. + marinating

1/3 cup olive oil

1/4 cup red wine vinegar

1 tablespoon tomato paste

1-1/2 teaspoons sugar

1-1/2 teaspoons celery seed

1 garlic clove, minced

1/2 teaspoon coarsely ground pepper

1/4 teaspoon salt

1/4 teaspoon ground mustard

1/8 teaspoon crushed red pepper flakes

1/8 teaspoon hot pepper sauce

1 pound cooked large shrimp, peeled and deveined

1 small onion, thinly sliced and separated into rings

2 bay leaves

In a large resealable plastic bag, combine the first 11 ingredients; add the shrimp, onion and bay leaves. Seal bag and turn to coat; refrigerate mixture for up to 24 hours.

Drain and discard marinade and bay leaves. Serve shrimp with toothpicks.

YIELD: about 1-1/2 dozen.

kathi nelson
YORBA LINDA, CALIFORNIA

I appreciate an easy make-ahead appetizer, especially during the hectic holiday season. You'll find the flavors are extraordinary.

MAKE-AHEAD MENU

For an easy yet comforting make-ahead appetizer menu, team the pickled shrimp with Brie cheese, toasted baguette slices and the bruschetta topping found on page 29.

spinach artichoke dip

PREP/TOTAL TIME: 25 min.

1 package (10 ounces) frozen chopped spinach, thawed

1/4 cup chopped onion

1 tablespoon butter

4 ounces cream cheese, softened

1/4 cup heavy whipping cream

1 can (14 ounces) water-packed artichoke hearts, rinsed, drained and chopped

1 cup (4 ounces) shredded Monterey Jack cheese

1/2 cup shredded part-skim mozzarella cheese

1/2 cup shredded Swiss cheese

1/4 teaspoon cayenne pepper

1/8 teaspoon pepper

1/2 cup shredded Parmesan cheese

Assorted crackers

Cook spinach according to package directions for microwave; drain and squeeze dry. Set aside. Place onion and butter in a small microwave-safe bowl. Cover and microwave at 70% power for 2-3 minutes or until onion is tender, stirring once; set aside.

In a large bowl, beat cream cheese and whipping cream until smooth. Fold in the spinach, artichokes, cheeses, cayenne, pepper and onion mixture.

Transfer to a greased 9-in. microwave-safe pie plate. Sprinkle with Parmesan cheese. Microwave, uncovered, on high for 4-5 minutes or until bubbly. Serve with crackers.

YIELD: about 3-1/2 cups.

EDITOR'S NOTE: This recipe was tested in a 1,100-watt microwave.

suzanne zick
MAIDEN, NORTH CAROLINA

No one will ever guess that this crowd-pleasing dip was made in the microwave! It is so creamy, rich and good. Serve tortilla chips instead of crackers if you prefer.

kelly alaniz
EUREKA, CALIFORNIA

The subtle flavors of mustard and onion make deviled eggs a favorite at my house. If you like, garnish each egg half with a little fresh parsley.

delightful deviled eggs

PREP/TOTAL TIME: 20 min.

  6 hard-cooked eggs
  2 tablespoons mayonnaise
1-1/2 teaspoons grated onion
1-1/2 teaspoons sweet pickle relish
  1/2 teaspoon spicy brown mustard
  1/4 teaspoon salt
  1/8 teaspoon crushed red pepper flakes
  1/8 teaspoon pepper

Slice eggs in half lengthwise. Remove yolks; set whites aside. In a small bowl, mash yolks. Stir in the mayonnaise, onion, relish, mustard, salt, pepper flakes and pepper.

Pipe or spoon filling into egg whites. Refrigerate until serving.

YIELD: 1 dozen.

christine smoot
CHILDRESS, TEXAS

Just three ingredients are needed for these speedy meatballs. They're so deliciously different, you'll never have leftovers! I catered my daughter's wedding and served them as appetizers. Also try them with rice as a main dish.

easy meatballs

PREP/TOTAL TIME: 15 min.

1 package (12 ounces) frozen fully cooked Italian meatballs, thawed
1 cup barbecue sauce
1/2 cup sweet-and-sour sauce

Place the meatballs in a 3-qt. microwave-safe dish; cover and microwave on high for 3-4 minutes or until heated through. In a small microwave-safe bowl, combine the sauces; cover and heat on high for 2-3 minutes or until heated through.

Pour over meatballs; cover and microwave on high for 1-2 minutes, stirring occasionally.

YIELD: 2 dozen.

EDITOR'S NOTE: This recipe was tested in a 1,100-watt microwave.

janice freeman
KEWANEE, ILLINOIS

For a wonderfully thick and yummy dip, I simply add softened cream cheese to the recipe on the envelope of dressing mix.

creamy ranch dip

PREP/TOTAL TIME: 10 min.

2 cups (16 ounces) sour cream
1 package (8 ounces) cream cheese, softened
2 envelopes ranch salad dressing mix
Fresh vegetables, crackers *or* chips

In a small bowl, beat the sour cream, cream cheese and ranch dressing mix on medium speed until smooth. Transfer to a serving bowl; refrigerate until serving. Serve with vegetables, crackers or chips.

YIELD: 3 cups.

olive & roasted pepper bruschetta

PREP/TOTAL TIME: 15 min.

- 1/2 cup grated Romano cheese
- 1/2 cup chopped pitted green olives
- 1/2 cup chopped roasted sweet red peppers
- 2 teaspoons olive oil
- 1/2 teaspoon dried basil
- 16 slices French bread baguette (1/2 inch thick), toasted

In a small bowl, combine first five ingredients. Top each bread slice with 1 tablespoon olive mixture.

YIELD: 16 appetizers.

jennifer mathis
HILTON HEAD, SOUTH CAROLINA

I've tried many versions of bruschetta but I think this version contains the perfect blend of ingredients. It's super easy, and you can even make the topping well in advance.

nancy horsburgh
EVERETT, ONTARIO

Allspice adds a slightly sweet, spicy twist to typical barbecue meatballs. Because it uses ingredients you probably have on hand, this recipe is one that you'll turn to time and again.

glazed meatballs

PREP: 30 min. | COOK: 15 min.

  2 eggs, lightly beaten
2/3 cup milk
  1 tablespoon prepared horseradish
1-1/4 cups soft bread crumbs
1-1/2 pounds ground beef
  1 cup water
1/2 cup chili sauce
1/2 cup ketchup
1/4 cup maple syrup
1/4 cup soy sauce
1-1/2 teaspoons ground allspice
1/2 teaspoon ground mustard

In a large bowl, combine the eggs, milk, horseradish and bread crumbs. Crumble beef over mixture and mix well. Shape into 1-1/2-in. balls.

Place meatballs on a greased rack in a shallow baking pan. Bake at 375° for 15-20 minutes or until meat is no longer pink; drain.

In a large saucepan, combine the remaining ingredients. Bring to a boil; add the meatballs. Reduce heat; cover and simmer for 15 minutes or until heated through, stirring occasionally.

YIELD: about 3-1/2 dozen.

SAUCY MEATBALLS: Omit glaze ingredients. In a large saucepan, combine the 1-3/4 cups ketchup, 1 jar (12 ounces) jelly and 1 cup chopped onion. Cook and stir over medium heat for 3-5 minutes or until jelly is melted. Transfer meatballs to a greased 13-in. x 9-in. baking dish. Pour sauce over meatballs. Bake, uncovered, 20 minutes longer or until sauce is bubbly.

CRANBERRY MEATBALLS: Omit glaze ingredients. In a saucepan, combine 1 can (16 ounces) whole-berry cranberry sauce, 1 bottle (12 ounces) chili sauce, 1 tablespoon brown sugar, 1 tablespoon each brown sugar, prepared mustard and lemon juice and 2 minced garlic cloves. Bring to a boil. Reduce heat; simmer for 10 minutes, stirring occasionally. Pour over meatballs; serve warm.

stromboli ladder loaf

PREP: 25 min. + rising | **BAKE:** 20 min. + standing

1-1/2 cups water (70° to 80°)
2 tablespoons canola oil
1 teaspoon lemon juice
2 tablespoons nonfat dry milk powder
2 tablespoons sugar
1 teaspoon salt
4 cups bread flour
3 teaspoons active dry yeast

FILLING:

3/4 cup pizza sauce
1 package (3-1/2 ounces) sliced pepperoni
2 cups (8 ounces) shredded part-skim mozzarella cheese
1/2 cup grated Parmesan cheese
1 egg white
1 tablespoon water

In bread machine pan, place first eight ingredients in the order suggested by manufacturer. Select dough setting (check dough after 5 minutes of mixing; add 1-2 tablespoons of water or flour if needed). When cycle is completed, turn dough onto a lightly floured surface. Roll into a 15-in. x 12-in. rectangle. Place on a greased baking sheet.

Spread pizza sauce in a 3-in.-wide strip lengthwise down the center of dough to within 2 in. of ends. Arrange pepperoni over sauce; sprinkle with cheeses. On each long side, cut 1-in.-wide strips about 2-1/2 in. toward the center. Starting at one end, fold alternating strips at an angle across filling. Pinch ends to seal.

Beat egg white and water; brush over dough. Bake at 425° for 20-25 minutes or until golden brown. Let stand for 10 minutes before cutting.

YIELD: 1 loaf (2 pounds).

EDITOR'S NOTE: We recommend you do not use a bread machine's time-delay feature for this recipe.

chrystie wear
OAK RIDGE, NORTH CAROLINA

I whip up homemade dough in my bread maker for this tasty filled pizza. For variety, add veggies to the filling or even make a Reuben-style stromboli with Thousand Island dressing, corned beef, sauerkraut and Swiss cheese.

fun-on-the-run snack mix

PREP/TOTAL TIME: 5 min.

2 cups Wheat Chex
2 cups miniature fish-shaped crackers
2 cups pretzel sticks
1 cup salted peanuts
1 cup dried cranberries

In a large bowl, combine the cereal, crackers, pretzels, peanuts and cranberries. Store in an airtight container.

YIELD: 8 cups.

carrie hubbard
BUENA VISTA, COLORADO

The kids love my snack mix and have no idea they're eating cranberries. It's a great healthy nibble for car rides, hikes and picnics.

chicken chili nachos

PREP/TOTAL TIME: 25 min.

1 pound boneless skinless chicken breasts, cubed
1 can (10 ounces) diced tomatoes and green chilies, undrained
1 can (16 ounces) kidney beans, rinsed and drained
1 can (16 ounces) chili beans, undrained
1 teaspoon paprika
1 teaspoon ground cumin
1/2 teaspoon cayenne pepper
1 package (13-1/2 ounces) tortilla chips
1-1/2 cups (6 ounces) shredded Mexican cheese blend

In a large skillet coated with cooking spray, cook chicken until no longer pink. Add tomatoes; cook over medium-high heat for 3 minutes or until tomato juice is reduced. Stir in the beans, paprika, cumin and cayenne; cook for 5 minutes or until heated through.

Arrange the tortilla chips on two large microwave-safe plates; sprinkle each with 1/4 cup cheese. Top with chicken mixture and remaining cheese. Microwave, uncovered, on high for 25-30 seconds or until cheese is melted.

YIELD: 8 servings.

karen horning
ROCKFORD, ILLINOIS

Spicy nachos with plenty of chicken, cheese and two kinds of beans make a fun and filling munchie.

CHAPTER TWO

stovetop suppers

PICTURED LEFT TO RIGHT: BOHEMIAN POT ROAST, PAGE 38 • FRIED CHICKEN WITH PAN GRAVY, PAGE 39
PESTO SCALLOPS VERMICELLI, PAGE 40 • FAMILY-PLEASING SLOPPY JOES, PAGE 58

sandra anderson
NEW YORK, NEW YORK

Back when we used farm-fresh ingredients, our foods didn't need much embellishment to make them look and taste wonderful.

classic fried chicken

PREP: 10 min. | **COOK:** 45 min.

1-1/2 cups all-purpose flour
1-1/2 teaspoons salt
1/2 teaspoon garlic powder
1/2 teaspoon pepper
1 broiler/fryer chicken (2-1/2 to 3 pounds), cut up
Canola oil

In a large resealable plastic bag, combine first four ingredients. With paper towels, pat chicken dry; add to bag, a few pieces at a time. Seal bag and shake chicken to coat.

In a large skillet over medium-high heat, heat 1/2 in. of oil; fry chicken until browned on all sides. Reduce heat; cover and cook for 30-35 minutes or until juices run clear, turning occasionally. Uncover and cook 5 minutes longer. Drain on paper towels.

YIELD: 6 servings.

carmen edwards
MIDLAND, TEXAS

This stovetop favorite is tasty and filling. It's easy to prepare, even after a long day at work.

beef macaroni skillet

PREP: 15 min. | **COOK:** 30 min.

1/2 pound lean ground beef (90% lean)
1/3 cup chopped onion
1/4 cup chopped green pepper
1-1/2 cups spicy hot V8 juice
1/2 cup uncooked elbow macaroni
1 teaspoon Worcestershire sauce
1/4 teaspoon pepper

In a large skillet, cook the beef, onion and green pepper over medium heat until meat is no longer pink; drain. Stir in the remaining ingredients. Bring to a boil. Reduce heat; cover and simmer for 15-20 minutes or until macaroni is tender.

YIELD: 2 servings.

GROUND BEEF SAVES TIME

When I'm browning ground beef for a recipe, I cook extra. When it's cooked, I take out a few cups, cool it and put it in a heavy-duty plastic bag in the freezer. On a day when time gets away from me, I defrost the cooked ground beef in the microwave and combine it with other easy ingredients for a quick and hearty dinner.
—PAM H.
GOSHEN, INDIANA

turkey reubens

PREP/TOTAL TIME: 10 min.

4 slices pumpernickel *or* rye bread

2 tablespoons Thousand Island salad dressing

6 ounces sliced deli smoked turkey

1/2 cup sauerkraut, rinsed and well drained

2 slices Swiss cheese

2 teaspoons butter, softened

Spread two slices of bread with salad dressing. Layer with turkey, sauerkraut and cheese; top with remaining bread. Butter outsides of sandwiches.

In a large skillet, toast sandwiches for 3-4 minutes on each side or until heated through.

YIELD: 2 servings.

jo ann dalrymple

CLAREMORE, OKLAHOMA

I have always enjoyed Reuben sandwiches, and I tried them with smoked turkey a few years ago. These are good to make in summer when you don't want to heat up the kitchen.

al robbins

CHANDLER, ARIZONA

After experimenting with many different versions, I came up with this super-delicious tuna mac recipe. My family simply can't get enough of it.

tuna veggie macaroni

PREP/TOTAL TIME: 25 min.

1-1/4 cups uncooked elbow macaroni

5 ounces process cheese (Velveeta), cubed

1/2 cup milk

2 cups frozen peas and carrots, thawed

1 can (5 ounces) white water-packed tuna, drained

1/4 teaspoon dill weed

In a saucepan, cook the macaroni according to package directions; drain. Add cheese and milk; stir until cheese is melted. Stir in the vegetables, tuna and dill; heat through.

YIELD: 3 servings.

pasta sausage supper

PREP/TOTAL TIME: 25 min.

- 1 package (16 ounces) uncooked penne pasta
- 1 pound smoked kielbasa *or* Polish sausage, cut into 1/4-inch slices
- 1 medium green pepper, julienned
- 1 medium sweet red pepper, julienned
- 1 medium onion, halved and sliced
- 1 tablespoon canola oil
- 1 jar (26 ounces) meatless spaghetti sauce, warmed

Cook pasta according to package directions.

Meanwhile, in large skillet, saute the sausage, peppers and onion in oil until sausage is browned and vegetables are crisp-tender.

Drain pasta; divide among six serving plates. Top each serving with the warmed spaghetti sauce and the sausage mixture.

YIELD: 6 servings.

taste of home test kitchen

Here's a swift stovetop entree featuring sliced kielbasa and bright bell pepper strips. While the pasta is cooking, it's a breeze to saute the meat and veggies and warm the jarred spaghetti sauce.

dilly salmon patties

PREP/TOTAL TIME: 25 min.

- 2 eggs, lightly beaten
- 1 medium onion, finely chopped
- 1/4 cup mashed potato flakes
- 1/4 cup seasoned bread crumbs
- 1 garlic clove, minced
- 1/4 teaspoon dill weed
- 1/4 teaspoon pepper
- 1/8 teaspoon celery salt
- 1 can (14-3/4 ounces) salmon, drained, bones and skin removed
- 1 teaspoon olive oil

In a small bowl, combine the first eight ingredients. Crumble salmon over mixture and mix well. Shape into four patties.

In a large nonstick skillet coated with cooking spray, cook patties in oil over medium heat for 5 minutes on each side or until browned.

YIELD: 4 servings.

aerial ryan
ACRA, NEW YORK

Here's a quick and easy recipe with great dill flavor! I like to serve these light and tender patties with a crisp side salad.

mollie fry
RALEIGH, NORTH CAROLINA

My mother would buy the ham for this recipe and make a batch of sauce on Saturday. Then after church on Sunday, our hungry family would be able to have a fast meal.

barbecue ham sandwiches

PREP/TOTAL TIME: 25 min.

    1 cup plus 2 tablespoons chili sauce
  3/4 cup packed brown sugar
  1/2 cup plus 1 tablespoon water
  3/4 teaspoon prepared mustard
  1/4 to 1/2 teaspoon chili powder
  1/8 teaspoon ground cloves
1-1/2 pounds shaved fully cooked ham
    6 hamburger buns, split and toasted

In a large saucepan, combine the first six ingredients. Cook, uncovered, over low heat for 15 minutes. Stir in ham; heat through. Using a slotted spoon, serve on buns.

YIELD: 6 servings.

vera melvin
ST. ANN, MISSOURI

This dish got its name because my husband is of Bohemian descent and he absolutely loves this pot roast! I appreciate that it's so easy to prepare. You can get this one-pot supper cooking, then practically forget about it until it's time for dinner.

bohemian pot roast

PREP: 5 min. | COOK: 2-1/4 hours

1/4 cup all-purpose flour
1/4 teaspoon pepper
  1 boneless beef chuck pot roast (2 to 3 pounds)
  2 tablespoons canola oil
  1 cup water
  1 can (14-1/2 ounces) diced tomatoes
  1 teaspoon caraway seeds

  1 envelope onion soup mix
  2 bay leaves

GRAVY:
1/4 cup cold water
  3 tablespoons all-purpose flour

In a large resealable plastic bag, combine the flour and pepper. Add beef and turn to coat. In a Dutch oven, brown roast over medium heat in oil on all sides. Drain.

Stir in the water, tomatoes, caraway seeds, onion soup mix and bay leaves. Bring to boil. Reduce heat; cover tightly and simmer 2-3 hours or until roast is tender.

Remove roast to a serving platter; keep warm. Let stand for 5 minutes before slicing. Discard bay leaves. For gravy, combine water and flour until smooth. Add to the cooking liquid; bring to a boil. Cook and stir for 1-2 minutes or until thickened. Slice roast and serve with gravy.

YIELD: 6-8 servings.

fried chicken with pan gravy

PREP: 15 min. | COOK: 45 min.

1 cup all-purpose flour
3/4 teaspoon salt
1/4 teaspoon dried thyme
1/4 teaspoon rubbed sage
1/4 teaspoon pepper
1 broiler/fryer chicken (3-1/2 to 4 pounds),
   cut up
Oil for frying
GRAVY:
2 tablespoons all-purpose flour
1/8 teaspoon salt
1-1/3 cups 2% milk

In a large resealable plastic bag, combine the first five ingredients. Add chicken, a few pieces at a time, and shake to coat.

In a large skillet over medium-high heat, heat 1/4 in. of oil; fry chicken until browned on all sides. Reduce heat; cover and cook for 30-35 minutes or until juices run clear, turning occasionally. Uncover and cook 5 minutes longer. Remove chicken to paper towels and keep warm.

Pour off excess fat from the skillet, reserving the browned bits and 2 tablespoons drippings. Stir in flour and salt until blended; gradually add the milk. Bring to a boil; cook and stir for 1-2 minutes or until thickened. Serve with chicken.

YIELD: 6 servings (1-1/2 cups gravy).

HERBED FRIED CHICKEN WITH GRAVY: Omit the sage. Add 1 teaspoon each dried tarragon, oregano, paprika and ground mustard, and 1/2 teaspoon each onion powder and garlic powder to the flour mixture. Proceed as directed.

ginny werkmeister
TILDEN, NEBRASKA

Mom's traditional fried chicken always cooked up golden brown and crispy. Drizzled with the pan gravy, this dish is real comfort food.

marilyn lustgarten
WENTZVILLE, MISSOURI

Quick and easy with a gourmet flavor, tender bay scallops shine in a simple sauce made with pesto and white wine.

pesto scallops vermicelli

PREP/TOTAL TIME: 15 min.

    4 ounces uncooked vermicelli
    2 tablespoons butter
  1/2 teaspoon garlic powder
  1/4 teaspoon dried oregano
  1/8 teaspoon pepper
  1/2 pound bay scallops
    2 tablespoons white wine *or* chicken
      broth
    3 tablespoons prepared pesto

Cook vermicelli according to package directions. Meanwhile, in a large skillet, melt butter. Stir in the garlic powder, oregano and pepper. Add scallops and wine; cook and stir over medium heat for 5-6 minutes or until scallops are firm and opaque.

    Reduce heat to low. Stir in pesto; heat through. Drain vermicelli; toss with scallop mixture.

YIELD: 2 servings.

gnocchi with hearty meat sauce

PREP/TOTAL TIME: 30 min.

- 1 package (16 ounces) potato gnocchi
- 1 package (19-1/2 ounces) Italian turkey sausage links, casings removed
- 1 large green pepper, cut into 1-inch pieces
- 1 large sweet red pepper, cut into 1-inch pieces
- 1/4 cup dry red wine *or* reduced-sodium chicken broth
- 1 can (14-1/2 ounces) diced tomatoes, undrained
- 1 can (8 ounces) no-salt-added tomato sauce
- 2 tablespoons tomato paste
- 2 teaspoons brown sugar

Cook gnocchi according to package directions. Meanwhile, crumble the sausage into a large nonstick skillet; add peppers. Cook over medium heat until meat is no longer pink and peppers are tender; drain.

Add wine; cook and stir for 2 minutes. Stir in the tomatoes, tomato sauce, tomato paste and brown sugar; heat through. Drain the gnocchi; serve with meat sauce.

YIELD: 6 servings.

EDITOR'S NOTE: Look for potato gnocchi in the pasta or frozen foods section.

taste of home test kitchen

When time's at a premium, this hearty, full-flavored meat sauce can turn packaged gnocchi into something special.

kielbasa cabbage skillet

PREP/TOTAL TIME: 25 min.

- 1/2 cup chopped onion
- 1/2 cup chopped green pepper
- 1 to 2 teaspoons butter
- 1/2 pound smoked kielbasa *or* Polish sausage, cut into 1/2-inch slices
- 1/2 small head cabbage, coarsely chopped (about 3 cups)
- 1/4 cup chicken broth *or* water

Salt to taste, optional
Pepper to taste

In a large skillet, saute onion and green pepper in butter until crisp-tender. Add sausage; cook and stir until browned. Add the cabbage, broth, salt if desired and pepper. Cover and cook 10-12 minutes or until cabbage is tender.

YIELD: 2 servings.

I microwaved potatoes + added them to the peppers+onions to fry. good

sue engle
IRVING, TEXAS

This easy, quick-to-fix recipe has long been a staple at my house because it tastes so good.

CABBAGE POINTERS

When buying cabbage, look for heads with crisp-looking leaves that are firmly packed. The head should feel heavy for its size. Store cabbage tightly wrapped in a plastic bag in the refrigerator for up to 2 weeks. Remove the core, rinse and blot dry just before using. A 1-1/2-pound cabbage will yield about 8 cups shredded.

catherine braley
BARBOURSVILLE,
WEST VIRGINIA

We host lots of hay rides, picnics, hot dog roasts and ice cream socials on our farm, and these chili dogs never fail to please. There's always someone who fills a paper cup with the sauce and eats it straight.

farmhouse chili dogs

PREP: 15 min. | COOK: 30 min.

1 pound ground beef
1 medium onion, chopped
1 can (10-3/4 ounces) condensed tomato soup, undiluted
1/2 cup water
3 tablespoons ketchup
1 tablespoon sugar
1-1/2 teaspoons chili powder
8 hot dogs
8 hot dog buns, split
Shredded cheddar cheese, optional

In a large skillet, cook beef and onion over medium heat until meat is no longer pink; drain. Stir in the soup, water, ketchup, sugar and chili powder; bring to a boil. Reduce heat; simmer, uncovered, for 20 minutes or until thickened.

Cook hot dogs according to package directions. Place in buns; top with meat sauce. Sprinkle with cheese if desired.

YIELD: 8 servings.

mike kirschbaum
CARY, NORTH CAROLINA

My wife, Jennie, is a wonderful cook who's generally skeptical about my kitchen experiments. But she likes my pasta creation so much that she always gives me kitchen privileges so I can make it for our family!

southwest bean and chicken pasta

PREP/TOTAL TIME: 25 min.

3 cups uncooked mostaccioli
1/4 cup chopped onion
1/4 cup chopped sweet red pepper
1 tablespoon canola oil
1/2 teaspoon minced garlic
1 can (10-3/4 ounces) condensed nacho cheese soup, undiluted

1 package (9 ounces) ready-to-use Southwestern chicken strips
3/4 cup water
1 can (15 ounces) black beans, rinsed and drained
1/4 cup shredded Monterey Jack cheese, optional

Cook the mostaccioli according to package directions. Meanwhile, in a large skillet, saute onion and red pepper in oil until tender. Add garlic; cook 1 minute longer. Stir in the soup, chicken and water. Bring to a boil. Reduce heat; cover and simmer for 8 minutes.

Stir in beans; heat through. Drain mostaccioli; transfer to a serving bowl and top with chicken mixture. Sprinkle with cheese if desired.

YIELD: 6 servings.

confetti mac 'n' cheese

PREP/TOTAL TIME: 25 min.

1-1/2 cups uncooked elbow macaroni
2 cups chopped zucchini
1/2 cup chopped onion
2 tablespoons canola oil
1 can (14-1/2 ounces) diced tomatoes, drained
1 can (10-3/4 ounces) condensed cheddar cheese soup, undiluted
2 cups (8 ounces) shredded cheddar cheese
1/2 cup milk

1/2 teaspoon dried basil
1/2 teaspoon prepared mustard

Cook macaroni according to package directions. Meanwhile, in a large saucepan, saute zucchini and onion in oil until tender. Stir in the tomatoes, soup, cheese, milk, basil and mustard.

Cook, uncovered, over medium heat for 6-7 minutes or until cheese is melted, stirring often. Drain macaroni; toss with vegetable cheese sauce.

YIELD: 4 servings.

debbie amacher
AMHERST, NEW YORK

My gang just loves this rich and comforting dish. As long as the kids don't realize it contains zucchini, they'll keep on eating it!

mary lou koskella
PRESCOTT, ARIZONA

One evening, we had unexpected company. Since I had some of these meatballs left over in the freezer, I warmed them up as appetizers. Everyone raved! This classic recipe makes a big batch and is perfect for entertaining.

big-batch spaghetti 'n' meatballs

PREP: 30 min. | **COOK:** 1 hour 50 min.

1-1/2 cups chopped onion
2 tablespoons olive oil
3 garlic cloves, minced
3 cups water
1 can (29 ounces) tomato sauce
2 cans (12 ounces *each*) tomato paste
1/3 cup minced fresh parsley
1 tablespoon dried basil
1 tablespoon salt
1/2 teaspoon pepper

MEATBALLS:

4 eggs, lightly beaten
2 cups soft bread cubes (1/4-inch pieces)
1-1/2 cups milk
1 cup grated Parmesan cheese
3 garlic cloves, minced
1 tablespoon salt
1/2 teaspoon pepper
3 pounds ground beef
2 tablespoons canola oil
Hot cooked spaghetti

In a Dutch oven over medium heat, saute onion in oil. Add garlic; cook 1 minute longer. Add the water, tomato sauce and paste, parsley, basil, salt and pepper; bring to a boil. Reduce heat; cover and simmer for 50 minutes.

In a large bowl, combine the first seven meatball ingredients. Crumble beef over mixture and mix well. Shape into 1-1/2-in. balls.

In a large skillet over medium heat, brown meatballs in oil until no longer pink; drain. Add to sauce; bring to a boil. Reduce the heat; cover and simmer for 1 hour or until flavors are blended, stirring occasionally. Serve with spaghetti.

YIELD: 12-16 servings.

apricot ham steak

PREP/TOTAL TIME: 10 min.

> 4 boneless fully cooked ham steaks (5 ounces *each*)
> 2 tablespoons butter, *divided*
> 1/2 cup apricot preserves
> 1 tablespoon cider vinegar
> 1/4 teaspoon ground ginger
> Dash salt

In a large skillet, cook ham in 1 tablespoon butter over medium heat until lightly browned on each side and heated through.

Meanwhile, in a small saucepan, combine the preserves, vinegar, ginger, salt and remaining butter. Cook over medium heat until heated through. Serve with ham.

YIELD: 4 servings.

taste of home test kitchen

Ham is a versatile menu item that's a favorite of country cooks. One of the best ways to serve ham slices is topped off with a slightly sweet glaze, like our apricot version.

steak and rice roll-ups

PREP: 25 min. | COOK: 1-1/4 hours

> 1 cup finely chopped fresh mushrooms
> 2 green onions, finely chopped
> 1/4 cup finely chopped green pepper
> 2 tablespoons butter
> 1-1/2 cups cooked long grain rice
> 2 tablespoons diced pimientos
> 1/4 teaspoon dried thyme
> 1/4 teaspoon dried marjoram
> 2 pounds beef top round steak (1/2 inch thick)
> 2 tablespoons canola oil
> 2 tablespoons plus 1 teaspoon onion soup mix
> 1 cup water

In a large skillet, saute the mushrooms, onions and pepper in butter until tender. Transfer the mixture to a small bowl; stir in the rice, pimientos, thyme and marjoram.

Cut steak into six pieces; flatten to 1/2-in. thickness. Spread evenly with mushroom mixture; roll up and secure with toothpicks.

In the same skillet, brown the roll-ups in oil on all sides. Add the soup mix and water; cover and simmer for 1 to 1-1/4 hours or until meat is tender, occasionally spooning cooking liquid over roll-ups.

Thicken cooking juices if desired; serve with roll-ups. Discard toothpicks.

YIELD: 6 servings.

elaine selander
LITTLETON, COLORADO

My steak roll-ups have been a favorite family recipe since I started making them in the 1960s. They make any meal special.

joanne schlabach
SHREVE, OHIO

These Italian-style sloppy joes are just great. The filling can be kept hot until everyone is settled and all set to eat.

pizza joes

PREP/TOTAL TIME: 30 min.

- 1 pound lean ground beef (90% lean)
- 1 can (15 ounces) pizza sauce
- 1 teaspoon dried oregano
- 1/2 medium onion
- 1/2 medium green pepper
- 1 ounce sliced pepperoni
- 6 hamburger buns, split
- 1/2 cup shredded mozzarella cheese
- 1/2 cup sliced fresh mushrooms

In a large skillet, brown ground beef until no pink remains; drain. Stir in sauce and oregano.

In a food processor, combine the onion, pepper, pepperoni; cover and process until chopped. Add to beef mixture. Simmer 20-25 minutes or until vegetables are tender. Spoon mixture onto buns. Top with cheese and mushrooms.

YIELD: 6 servings.

karen adams
CLEVELAND, TENNESSEE

Quick-cooking turkey breast slices make it easy to prepare a satisfying meal in minutes. I've also flattened boneless skinless chicken breast halves in place of the turkey.

turkey scallopini

PREP/TOTAL TIME: 20 min.

- 1 package (17.6 ounces) turkey breast cutlets
- 1/4 cup all-purpose flour
- 1/8 teaspoon salt
- 1/8 teaspoon pepper
- 1 egg
- 2 tablespoons water
- 1 cup soft bread crumbs
- 1/2 cup grated Parmesan cheese
- 1/4 cup butter, cubed

Minced fresh parsley

Flatten turkey to 1/4-in. thickness. In a shallow bowl, combine the flour, salt and pepper. In another bowl, beat egg and water. In a third shallow bowl, combine bread crumbs and cheese.

Dredge the turkey in the flour mixture, then dip it in the egg mixture and coat with crumbs. Let stand for 5 minutes.

Melt butter in a large skillet over medium-high heat; cook turkey for 2-3 minutes on each side or until meat is no longer pink and coating is golden brown. Sprinkle with parsley.

YIELD: 4 servings.

pizza spaghetti

PREP: 20 min. | COOK: 30 min.

- 1/2 pound lean ground beef (90% lean)
- 1/2 pound Italian turkey sausage links, casings removed, crumbled
- 1/2 cup chopped sweet onion
- 4 cans (8 ounces *each*) no-salt-added tomato sauce
- 3 ounces sliced turkey pepperoni
- 1 tablespoon sugar
- 2 teaspoons minced fresh parsley *or* 1/2 teaspoon dried parsley flakes
- 2 teaspoons minced fresh basil *or* 1/2 teaspoon dried basil
- 9 ounces uncooked whole wheat spaghetti
- 3 tablespoons grated Parmesan cheese

In a large nonstick skillet, cook the beef, sausage and onion over medium heat until beef is no longer pink and sausage is browned; drain.

Stir in the tomato sauce, pepperoni, sugar, parsley and basil. Bring to a boil. Reduce heat; simmer, uncovered, for 20-25 minutes or until thickened. Meanwhile, cook spaghetti according to package directions.

Drain spaghetti; toss with sauce. Sprinkle each serving with cheese.

YIELD: 6 servings.

robert smith
LAS VEGAS, NEVADA

The idea for this recipe came to me when I saw someone dip a slice of pizza into a pasta dish. My wife and kids love it and so do my friends!

stephanie homme
BATON ROUGE, LOUISIANA

Moist and tender pork chops are treated to a sweet, light cranberry glaze in this weeknight-friendly entree. It's one of my husband's favorites and quite suitable for company, too.

pork chops with cranberry sauce

PREP/TOTAL TIME: 30 min.

6 boneless pork loin chops (4 ounces each)

1/4 teaspoon coarsely ground pepper

1/8 teaspoon salt

2 teaspoons cornstarch

1 cup cranberry-apple juice

2 teaspoons honey

3/4 cup dried cranberries

1 tablespoon minced fresh tarragon

1 tablespoon minced fresh parsley

3 cups hot cooked brown rice

Sprinkle pork chops with pepper and salt. In a large nonstick skillet coated with cooking spray, cook chops over medium heat for 3-4 minutes on each side or until lightly browned. Remove chops and keep warm.

In a small bowl, combine the cornstarch, juice and honey until smooth. Add to pan, stirring to loosen browned bits. Stir in the cranberries, tarragon and parsley. Bring to a boil; cook 2 minutes longer or until thickened and bubbly.

Return pork to the pan. Reduce heat; cover and simmer for 4-6 minutes or until a thermometer reads 145°. Let stand for 5 minutes before serving. Serve with rice.

YIELD: 6 servings.

bacon cheeseburger pasta

PREP/TOTAL TIME: 20 min.

8 ounces uncooked penne pasta
1 pound ground beef
6 bacon strips, diced

1 can (10-3/4 ounces) condensed tomato soup, undiluted
1 cup (4 ounces) shredded cheddar cheese
Barbecue sauce and prepared mustard, optional

Cook pasta according to package directions. Meanwhile, in a large skillet, cook beef over medium heat until no longer pink; drain and set aside.

In the same skillet, cook the bacon until crisp; remove with a slotted spoon to paper towels to drain. Discard the drippings. Drain the pasta; add to the skillet. Stir in the soup, beef and bacon; heat through.

Remove from the heat and sprinkle with cheese. Cover and let stand for 2-3 minutes or until the cheese is melted. Serve with barbecue sauce and mustard if desired.

YIELD: 4-6 servings.

melissa stevens
ELK RIVER, MINNESOTA

I try to make foods that are not only kid friendly, but are also easy to reheat since my husband works long hours and often eats later than our children. If you like, use reduced-fat cheese and ground turkey for a lighter version.

crunchy ham and cheese

PREP/TOTAL TIME: 25 min.

1 tablespoon butter, softened
4 slices white bread
1 tablespoon Dijon mustard
4 slices process American cheese
2 slices deli ham (1 ounce *each*)
1/2 medium tomato, thinly sliced
2 eggs
2 tablespoons 2% milk
1/8 teaspoon onion powder
1 cup crushed ridged potato chips

Butter one side of each slice of bread. Spread mustard over the unbuttered side of two slices; layer each with one slice of cheese, ham, tomato, remaining cheese and remaining bread, buttered side up.

In a shallow bowl, whisk the eggs, milk and onion powder. Place potato chips in another bowl. Dip each sandwich into egg mixture, then coat with potato chips.

In a large nonstick skillet or griddle coated with cooking spray, toast sandwiches for 4 minutes on each side or until golden brown.

YIELD: 2 servings.

karen wolf
NILES, ILLINOIS

Crushed potato chips put the crunch in this appetizing variation of ham and cheese. Serve this layered sandwich with a bowl of soup, and you'll have one of the best comfort-food meals of your life.

margery bryan
MOSES LAKE, WASHINGTON

Here's a dish that's pure comfort food to my husband and me— it's our favorite. I've shared the recipe with many friends over the years.

EASY GREEN ONIONS

Instead of using a knife, I recently found that snipping green onions with a pair of kitchen scissors takes only a few seconds. It doesn't dirty a cutting board, either.
—KRISTY B.
KELOWNA, BRITISH COLUMBIA

paula wray
FREDERICK, MARYLAND

Laced with a refreshing splash of lemon, my special shrimp entree couldn't be much simpler to prepare. You really can make an easy and satisfying meal just for yourself!

cubed steak stroganoff

PREP/TOTAL TIME: 30 min.

2 tablespoons all-purpose flour
1/4 teaspoon salt
2 beef cubed steaks (6 ounces *each*)
1 to 2 tablespoons canola oil
1 can (4 ounces) mushroom stems and pieces, drained
3 green onions, thinly sliced
2/3 cup water
1 teaspoon beef bouillon granules
1/8 teaspoon pepper
7 to 8 tablespoons sour cream
Hot cooked egg noodles

In a large resealable plastic bag, combine the flour and salt. Add cubed steaks, one at a time. Seal bag and shake to coat.

In a large skillet, cook the steaks in oil over medium heat for 4-5 minutes on each side or until browned and tender. Remove and keep warm.

In the same skillet, saute mushrooms and onions until tender. Add water, bouillon and pepper; cook and stir until mixture comes to a boil, scraping up browned bits from bottom of pan. Reduce heat; stir in sour cream and heat through (do not boil). Return meat to pan; heat through. Serve with noodles.

YIELD: 2 servings.

easy shrimp scampi

PREP/TOTAL TIME: 25 min.

2 ounces uncooked linguine
1 small garlic clove, minced
1 tablespoon butter
1 tablespoon olive oil
1 tablespoon lemon juice

1/8 teaspoon Italian seasoning
6 cooked large shrimp, peeled and deveined

Cook linguine according to package directions. Meanwhile, in a small nonstick skillet, cook garlic in butter and oil until golden. Stir in the lemon juice, Italian seasoning and shrimp; heat through. Drain linguine; toss with shrimp mixture.

YIELD: 1 serving.

breaded chicken strips

PREP/TOTAL TIME: 25 min.

1/2 cup seasoned bread crumbs

2 tablespoons grated Parmesan cheese

1/2 teaspoon garlic salt

1/4 teaspoon paprika

1/4 teaspoon pepper

1/2 cup all-purpose flour

1/4 cup 2% milk

2 tablespoons beaten egg

2 boneless skinless chicken breasts
(5 ounces *each*), cut into 1-inch strips

1/4 cup canola oil

In a large resealable plastic bag, combine the first five ingredients. Place flour in a shallow bowl. In another shallow bowl, whisk milk and egg. Coat chicken in flour, then dip in egg mixture. Place in bag; seal and shake to coat.

In a large skillet, cook chicken in oil over medium heat for 2-3 minutes on each side or until chicken is no longer pink. Drain on paper towels.

YIELD: 2 servings.

**taste of home
test kitchen**
GREENDALE, WISCONSIN

We created tender, golden brown chicken strips that are tasty and just right for two. Enjoy them stuffed into a tortilla, served on a bed of lettuce or just plain!

karin woodbury
OCALA, FLORIDA

I found this recipe when I first started experimenting with herbs and rubs to flavor meats. It quickly became a family favorite. The fancy, flavorful onions make tenderloin steaks even more special.

peppered filets & balsamic red onions

PREP: 10 min. | COOK: 35 min.

2 teaspoons olive oil, *divided*
2 large red onions, cut into 1/2-inch slices
1 teaspoon salt, *divided*
2 tablespoons balsamic vinegar
1/2 teaspoon sugar
2 teaspoons coarsely ground pepper
1-1/2 teaspoons dried thyme
4 beef tenderloin steaks (4 ounces *each*)

Heat 1 teaspoon oil in a large nonstick skillet coated with cooking spray; add onions. Cook and stir over medium heat for 25-30 minutes or until tender and browned. Stir in 1/2 teaspoon salt, vinegar and sugar. Remove and keep warm.

Combine the pepper, thyme and remaining salt; rub over steaks. In the same skillet, cook steaks for 4-7 minutes on each side or until meat reaches desired doneness (for medium-rare, a thermometer should read 145°; medium, 160°; well-done, 170°). Serve with onions.

YIELD: 4 servings.

deluxe macaroni dinner

PREP/TOTAL TIME: 30 min.

- 1/2 pound ground beef
- 1 small onion, chopped
- 2 garlic cloves, minced
- 10 cups water
- 1 package (14 ounces) deluxe four-cheese macaroni and cheese dinner
- 2 cups chopped fresh broccoli

In a large skillet over medium heat, cook beef and onion until meat is no longer pink. Add garlic; cook 1 minute longer. Drain.

In a large saucepan, bring water to a boil. Add macaroni; cook for 5 minutes. Add broccoli; cook 4-5 minutes longer or until macaroni and broccoli are tender. Drain, reserving 1/4 cup cooking liquid. Place contents of cheese sauce mix in saucepan. Stir in the macaroni mixture, beef mixture and reserved liquid; heat through.

YIELD: 4-6 servings.

michele odstrcilek
LEMONT, ILLINOIS

When I serve my dressed-up macaroni, there are never leftovers. The recipe starts with a convenient boxed mix and includes plenty of good-for-you broccoli.

sweet cherry pork chops

PREP: 20 min. | **COOK:** 15 min.

- 4 boneless pork chops (3/4 inch thick and 4 ounces each)
- 1 tablespoon canola oil
- 1 cup orange juice
- 3/4 cup pitted sweet cherries, halved
- 2 green onions, sliced
- 1/4 cup cherry preserves
- 4 teaspoons cornstarch
- 3 tablespoons cold water
- Hot cooked rice

In a large skillet, brown pork chops in oil on both sides; drain. Add the orange juice, cherries and onions to skillet; bring to a boil. Reduce heat; simmer, uncovered, for 4-6 minutes or until a thermometer reads 145°. Remove chops and keep warm.

Stir preserves into pan juices. Combine cornstarch and cold water until smooth; stir into pan juices. Bring to a boil; cook and stir for 1-2 minutes or until thickened. Serve with pork and rice.

YIELD: 4 servings.

shannon mink
COLUMBUS, OHIO

I make pork chops often, so I like to experiment with different ideas. I dreamed up these yummy chops using ingredients that I had on hand. The cherry-orange sauce makes them special enough for guests.

margaret peschke
HADLEY, NEW YORK

Looking for a heartwarming meal-in-one on a chilly autumn evening? Try my hearty stew. It's both quick and economical.

italian beef stew

PREP: 20 min. | COOK: 1 hour

- 3/4 pound beef cubed steak, chopped
- 1 cup water
- 1 can (8 ounces) tomato sauce
- 1 small potato, peeled and cubed
- 1/2 cup sliced fresh carrot
- 1/2 small onion, cut into thin wedges
- 1/2 small sweet red pepper, chopped
- 1 tablespoon onion soup mix
- 1/2 teaspoon Italian seasoning
- 1/4 teaspoon garlic powder
- 1/2 cup frozen peas

In a large saucepan coated with cooking spray, brown meat over medium heat for 5 minutes. Stir in the water, tomato sauce, potato, carrot, onion, red pepper, soup mix, Italian seasoning and garlic powder. Bring to a boil. Reduce heat; simmer, uncovered, for 45 minutes.

Stir in peas; simmer 5-10 minutes longer or until vegetables are tender.

YIELD: 2 servings.

a. jean sheppard
FRANKLIN, NORTH CAROLINA

Because my husband loves sausage and this hearty entree is so easy to make, I prepare it often. My sister shared the recipe with me long ago.

sausage mac supper

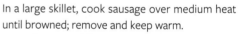

PREP/TOTAL TIME: 25 min.

- 1/2 pound smoked kielbasa *or* Polish sausage, cut into 1/4-inch slices
- 1 small onion, chopped
- 1/4 cup chopped celery
- 1/4 cup chopped green pepper
- 1 tablespoon butter
- 1 can (8 ounces) tomato sauce
- 1/2 teaspoon chili powder
- 1/8 teaspoon pepper
- 2 cups cooked elbow macaroni
- 1/4 cup shredded cheddar cheese

In a large skillet, cook sausage over medium heat until browned; remove and keep warm.

In the same skillet, saute the onion, celery and green pepper in butter until tender. Add the tomato sauce, chili powder and pepper. Stir in macaroni and sausage; heat through.

Sprinkle with the cheese; cook until the cheese is melted.

YIELD: 2 servings.

garlic-butter steak

PREP/TOTAL TIME: 20 min.

   1 beef flatiron steak *or* boneless top
      sirloin steak (3/4 pound)
 1/8 teaspoon salt
 1/8 teaspoon pepper
   2 tablespoons butter, softened, *divided*
   1 teaspoon minced fresh parsley
 1/2 teaspoon minced garlic
 1/4 teaspoon reduced-sodium soy sauce

Sprinkle steak with salt and pepper. In a large skillet, cook the steak in 1 tablespoon butter over medium-high heat for 4-6 minutes on each side or until the meat reaches desired doneness (for medium-rare, thermometer should read 145°; medium, 160°; well-done, 170°). Let stand for 5 minutes before slicing.

In a small bowl, combine the parsley, garlic, soy sauce and remaining butter. Serve with steak.

YIELD: 2 servings.

lily julow
GAINESVILLE, FLORIDA

Here's a restaurant-quality way to prepare steak that is sure to become a staple at your house.

frankie allen mann
WARRIOR, ALABAMA

With fresh peaches and sweet caramelized onions, these pork chops are sure to be a hit. Even finicky eaters will enjoy these sweet and tender chops.

peachy pork chops

PREP/TOTAL TIME: 25 min.

- 1 cup chopped onion
- 1 tablespoon canola oil
- 4 pork rib chops (1/2 inch thick and 6 ounces each)
- 1/2 teaspoon salt
- 1/2 teaspoon dried thyme
- 1/2 cup chopped peeled fresh peaches *or* frozen unsweetened sliced peaches, thawed and chopped
- 1/4 cup sugar
- 2 tablespoons white vinegar
- 1/4 teaspoon pepper

In a large skillet, saute onion in oil for 4-5 minutes or until crisp-tender. Remove and keep warm. Sprinkle both sides of pork chops with salt and thyme; add to skillet. Cover and cook for 6-7 minutes on each side or until a thermometer reads 145°. Remove and keep warm.

In the same skillet, combine the peaches, sugar, vinegar and pepper. Bring to a boil. Reduce heat; cook and stir for 2-3 minutes or until thickened. Return pork and onion to the pan; heat through.

YIELD: 4 servings.

glazed pork medallions

PREP/TOTAL TIME: 25 min.

- 1 pork tenderloin (3/4 pound)
- 1/8 teaspoon salt
- 3 tablespoons reduced-sugar orange marmalade
- 1 teaspoon cider vinegar
- 1 teaspoon Worcestershire sauce
- 1/4 teaspoon minced fresh gingerroot
- Dash crushed red pepper flakes

Cut pork into 1-in. slices and flatten them to 1/4-in. thickness; sprinkle with salt.

In a large nonstick skillet coated with cooking spray, cook pork in batches over medium-high heat until meat is tender. Reduce heat to low; return all meat to the pan. Combine the remaining ingredients; pour over pork and turn to coat. Heat through.

YIELD: 2 servings.

michele flagel
SHELLSBURG, IOWA

A deliciously elegant entree that's less than a half-hour away—it may seem hard to believe, but it's true! A sweet and savory sauce lends a hint of Asian flavor to tender pork medallions.

PORK TENDERLOIN

Pork tenderloin is a versatile cut. Because it's so tender, it's great cut into cubes for kabobs, medallions for sauteing and strips for stir-frying. You can also roast a whole tenderloin in just 30 minutes.

meatless chili mac

PREP: 15 min. | COOK: 25 min.

- 1 large onion, chopped
- 1 medium green pepper, chopped
- 1 tablespoon olive oil
- 1 garlic clove, minced
- 2 cups water
- 1-1/2 cups uncooked elbow macaroni
- 1 can (16 ounces) mild chili beans, undrained
- 1 can (15-1/2 ounces) great northern beans, rinsed and drained
- 1 can (14-1/2 ounces) diced tomatoes, undrained
- 1 can (8 ounces) tomato sauce
- 4 teaspoons chili powder
- 1 teaspoon salt
- 1 teaspoon ground cumin
- 1/2 cup fat-free sour cream

In a Dutch oven, saute onion and green pepper in oil until tender. Add garlic; cook 1 minute longer. Stir in the water, macaroni, beans, tomatoes, tomato sauce, chili powder, salt and cumin.

Bring to a boil. Reduce heat; cover and simmer for 15-20 minutes or until macaroni is tender. Top each serving with 1 tablespoon sour cream.

YIELD: 8 servings.

cindy ragan
NORTH HUNTINGDON, PENNSYLVANIA

I came across this recipe in a newspaper years ago and it's been popular at our house ever since. It's fast and flavorful and appeals to all ages.

tricia buss
TELFORD, PENNSYLVANIA

My sister-in-law prepared these hearty sandwiches that are filled with chicken, mushrooms and pepperoni. My husband loved them so much, I just had to ask for the recipe!

italian chicken pockets

PREP/TOTAL TIME: 15 min.

3/4 pound boneless skinless chicken breast, cubed
2 tablespoons olive oil
1 medium green pepper, chopped
1 cup sliced fresh mushrooms
1 package (3-1/2 ounces) sliced pepperoni
1 cup spaghetti sauce
3 pita breads (6 inches), halved and warmed
Grated Parmesan cheese, optional

IIn a large skillet, cook chicken over medium heat in oil until no longer pink. Add green pepper and mushrooms; cook until tender, stirring occasionally. Add pepperoni and spaghetti sauce; heat through.

Spoon into pita bread halves. Sprinkle with cheese if desired.

YIELD: 6 servings.

patricia ringle
EDGAR, WISCONSIN

My grandchildren love these sandwiches. I like the recipe because it can be made ahead of time and keeps well in a slow cooker until the family is ready to eat.

family-pleasing sloppy joes

PREP: 10 min. | COOK: 45 min.

2 pounds ground beef
1 large onion, chopped
1-1/4 cups ketchup
1/2 cup water
1 tablespoon brown sugar
1 tablespoon white vinegar
1/2 teaspoon salt
1/2 teaspoon ground mustard
1/2 teaspoon chili powder
1/4 teaspoon ground allspice
8 sandwich buns, split

In a Dutch oven, cook beef and onion over medium heat until meat is no longer pink; drain. Stir in the ketchup, water, brown sugar, vinegar, salt, mustard, chili powder and allspice. Bring to a boil. Reduce heat; simmer, uncovered, for 35-40 minutes or until heated through.

Just before serving, spoon about 1/2 cup meat mixture onto each bun.

YIELD: 8 servings.

prosciutto-pepper pork chops

PREP/TOTAL TIME: 20 min.

> 4 boneless pork loin chops (4 ounces each)
> 1/8 teaspoon garlic powder
> 1/8 teaspoon pepper
> 2 teaspoons canola oil
> 4 thin slices prosciutto *or* deli ham
> 1/2 cup julienned roasted sweet red peppers
> 2 slices reduced-fat provolone cheese, cut in half

Sprinkle pork chops with garlic powder and pepper. In a large nonstick skillet, cook the chops in oil over medium heat for 4-5 minutes on each side or until a thermometer reads 145°.

Top each pork chop with the prosciutto, red peppers and cheese. Cover and cook for 1-2 minutes or until the cheese is melted. Let stand for 5 minutes before serving.

YIELD: 4 servings.

donna prisco
RANDOLPH, NEW JERSEY

Here's a dish that's easy, fast and—most importantly—delicious. It's easy to make for two, six, or even eight. Serve these pork chops with pasta salad for a light and satisfying meal.

mrs. priscilla gilbert

INDIAN HARBOR BEACH,
FLORIDA

*Here is a good, hearty
salmon dish that's quick
and simple to prepare. My
husband and I love salmon
and this is one of our
favorites. It's creamy and
classic, nicely seasoned and
very rich.*

salmon mornay

PREP/TOTAL TIME: 25 min.

> 4 salmon fillets (6 ounces *each*)
> 1 teaspoon lemon-pepper seasoning, *divided*
> 3 tablespoons butter, *divided*
> 1-1/2 teaspoons all-purpose flour
> 1/8 teaspoon salt
>
> Dash pepper
>
> Dash cayenne pepper
> 1/4 cup 2% milk
> 1/4 cup heavy whipping cream
> 1/4 cup shredded Swiss cheese

Sprinkle salmon with 1/2 teaspoon lemon pepper. In a large skillet, cook salmon in 2 tablespoons butter for 4-6 minutes on each side or until fish flakes easily with a fork.

Meanwhile, in a small saucepan, melt remaining butter. Stir in the flour, salt, pepper, cayenne and remaining lemon pepper until blended. Gradually add milk and cream. Bring to a boil; cook and stir for 1-2 minutes or until thickened. Remove from heat; stir in the cheese until melted. Serve with salmon.

YIELD: 4 servings.

smoked sausage pasta

PREP/TOTAL TIME: 20 min.

2-2/3 cups uncooked tricolor spiral pasta
1 pound smoked sausage, cut into 1/4-inch slices
1-1/2 cups sliced fresh carrots
1 cup coarsely chopped green pepper
1 small onion, halved and sliced
1 tablespoon canola oil
1 can (2-1/4 ounces) sliced ripe olives, drained
1/2 cup Italian salad dressing

Cook pasta according to package directions. Meanwhile, in a large skillet, saute the sausage, carrots, green pepper and onion in oil until sausage is browned and vegetables are tender.

Drain pasta; place in a large bowl. Add sausage mixture and olives. Drizzle with dressing and toss to coat. Serve warm or chilled.

YIELD: 4 servings.

jasen guillermo
TUCSON, ARIZONA

One of the things I like most about this recipe is that you can chill the leftovers and have them as an equally delicious pasta salad later in the week.

spicy pepper steak

PREP: 15 min. | COOK: 45 min.

1/2 pound beef top round steak, cut into thin strips
1/4 teaspoon salt
1/4 teaspoon pepper
1 tablespoon canola oil
1 medium green pepper, julienned
1/4 cup chopped onion
1 garlic clove, minced
1 teaspoon beef bouillon granules
3/4 cup hot water
1 can (10 ounces) diced tomatoes and green chilies
2 tablespoons cornstarch
1/4 cup cold water
Hot cooked noodles, optional

Sprinkle beef with salt and pepper. In a large skillet, cook beef in oil until no longer pink; remove and keep warm. In the same skillet, saute green pepper and onion until tender. Add garlic; cook 1 minute longer.

Dissolve bouillon in hot water; stir into skillet with tomatoes. Return beef to the pan; bring to a boil. Reduce heat; cover and simmer for 30-35 minutes or until meat is tender.

Combine cornstarch and cold water; stir into meat mixture. Bring to a boil; cook and stir for 2 minutes or until thickened. Serve the steak mixture with noodles if desired.

YIELD: 2 servings.

ladonna reed
PONCA CITY, OKLAHOMA

My surprisingly spicy pepper steak has a bit of Southwestern flair from the green chilies. The recipe is economical and convenient.

jackie hannahs
FOUNTAIN, MICHIGAN

Here is a delicious classic. You'll love what the light and crispy batter does for your fresh catch.

MILD FISH FLAVOR

To get rid of fishy flavors with just about any type of fish, I refrigerate the fillets in milk for 30-90 minutes before cooking. This makes the fish's flavor a lot more mild.

—SANDY F.
OLIVIA, MINNESOTA

lemon-batter fish

PREP/TOTAL TIME: 25 min.

1-1/2 cups all-purpose flour, *divided*
1 teaspoon baking powder
3/4 teaspoon salt
1/2 teaspoon sugar
1 egg, lightly beaten
2/3 cup water
2/3 cup lemon juice, *divided*
2 pounds perch *or* walleye fillets, cut into serving-size pieces
Oil for frying
Lemon wedges, optional

In a shallow bowl, combine 1 cup flour, baking powder, salt and sugar; set aside. Combine the egg, water and 1/3 cup lemon juice; stir into the dry ingredients until smooth.

In separate shallow bowls, place remaining lemon juice and remaining flour. Dip fillets in lemon juice, then flour and coat with the batter.

In a large skillet, over medium-high heat, heat 1 in. of oil. Fry fish, a few fillets at a time, for 2-3 minutes on each side or until golden brown and fish flakes easily with a fork. Drain on paper towels. Garnish with lemon if desired.

YIELD: 5 servings.

change-of-pace burgers

nita smith
BELLEFONTE, PENNSYLVANIA

Please the whole family with an all-American meal. These burgers are filled with a tantalizing blend of vegetables and offer a great new way to serve up a classic at home.

PREP/TOTAL TIME: 20 min.

1/4 cup finely chopped onion
1/4 cup finely chopped green pepper
3 tablespoons chopped fresh mushrooms
3 tablespoons chili sauce
1 pound ground beef

4 hamburger buns, split
Ketchup and mustard, optional

In a large bowl, combine the onion, green pepper, mushrooms and chili sauce. Crumble beef over mixture and mix well. Shape into four patties.

In a large skillet, cook patties over medium heat for 5-6 minutes on each side or until a thermometer reads 160° and juices run clear. Serve on buns with ketchup and mustard if desired.

YIELD: 4 servings.

shrimp 'n' noodle bowls

PREP/TOTAL TIME: 25 min.

    8 ounces uncooked angel hair pasta
    1 pound cooked small shrimp
    2 cups broccoli coleslaw mix
    6 green onions, thinly sliced
  1/2 cup minced fresh cilantro
  2/3 cup reduced-fat sesame ginger salad
         dressing

Cook pasta according to package directions; drain and rinse in cold water. Transfer to a large bowl. Add the shrimp, coleslaw mix, onions and cilantro. Drizzle with dressing; toss to coat. Cover and refrigerate until serving.

YIELD: 6 servings.

mary bergfeld
EUGENE, OREGON

Here's a great quick meal that feels like it came from a restaurant. Cooked shrimp, bagged slaw and bottled dressing reduce the time needed to get it on the table.

joy bilbey
HOLT, MICHIGAN

Here's a no-hassle dinner to serve your family. Caesar salad dressing and Parmesan cheese give the pasta an authentic taste without added work.

chicken caesar pasta

PREP/TOTAL TIME: 30 min.

3 quarts water
2-1/2 cups uncooked tricolor spiral pasta
1-1/2 cups cut fresh asparagus (1-inch pieces)
1-1/2 pounds boneless skinless chicken breasts, cut into 1-inch pieces
2 teaspoons olive oil
2 large tomatoes, chopped
2/3 cup reduced-fat Caesar vinaigrette
3 green onions, chopped
3 tablespoons grated Parmesan cheese

In a Dutch oven, bring water to a boil. Add pasta. Return to a boil; cook for 4 minutes. Add asparagus; cook 6-8 minutes longer or until pasta and asparagus are tender.

Meanwhile, in a large nonstick skillet, saute the chicken in oil until no longer pink. Remove from the heat.

Drain pasta mixture. Add the chicken, tomatoes and vinaigrette; cook over low heat until heated through. Sprinkle with onions and cheese.

YIELD: 6 servings.

rosemary lamb chops

PREP/TOTAL TIME: 20 min.

    2 teaspoons dried rosemary, crushed
    1 teaspoon dried thyme
    1/2 teaspoon salt
    1/4 teaspoon pepper
    1/4 cup olive oil
    8 lamb loin chops (1 inch thick and
        6 ounces each)

Combine rosemary, thyme, salt and pepper. Pour oil over both sides of chops; rub with herb mixture.

In a large skillet, cook chops over medium heat for 6-7 minutes on each side or until meat reaches desired doneness (for medium-rare, a thermometer should read 145°; medium, 160°; well-done, 170°).

YIELD: 4 servings.

beth tomlinson
MORGANTOWN,
WEST VIRGINIA

Lamb chops make a meal feel extra-special, but they're fast and easy to prepare. I serve them on special occasions, although they are quick enough for a weeknight dinner. Perfectly seasoned with rosemary and thyme, these chops are sure to impress guests.

spaghetti 'n' meatballs for 2

PREP: 15 min. | COOK: 20 min.

    1 egg, beaten
    3 tablespoons Italian-seasoned bread
        crumbs
    2 tablespoons chopped onion
    1 tablespoon grated Parmesan cheese
    1/8 teaspoon pepper
    1/4 pound ground beef
    1/4 pound bulk Italian sausage
    1 jar (14 ounces) spaghetti sauce or 1-1/2
        cups homemade spaghetti sauce
Hot cooked spaghetti
Additional Parmesan cheese, optional

In a large bowl, combine the first five ingredients. Crumble the meat over mixture and mix well. Shape into 2-in. meatballs.

In a large skillet, brown meatballs over medium heat until a thermometer reads 160°; drain. Add spaghetti sauce; bring to a boil. Reduce heat; simmer, uncovered, for 20-30 minutes or until heated through. Serve with spaghetti; sprinkle with cheese if desired.

YIELD: 2 servings.

david stierheim
PITTSBURGH, PENNSYLVANIA

When I was a teenager, I cooked dinner every night for our family of four. Over the years, I have perfected these meatballs to suit my family's tastes. I also reduced the recipe to serve two people. It's easy to modify this recipe and make it your own!

marilyn paradis
WOODBURN, OREGON

Slices of tender pork are served in a tangy sauce. Cranberries give the dish a festive yuletide touch.

DRIED CRANBERRIES

Slightly sweet dried cranberries are a tasty snack by the handful, or a perfect addition to savory entrees, stuffings, salads, breads or trail mixes.

ronda weirich
PLAINS, KANSAS

This ravioli has a gourmet-sounding name because it uses a classic Italian pairing of rich Alfredo sauce and crispy cooked bacon. This tempting recipe uses just five ingredients!

charlotte giltner
MESA, ARIZONA

I like to serve my mac and cheese with a salad and crusty bread. It's a satisfying meal that feels upscale but will fit just about any budget.

cranberry-dijon pork

PREP/TOTAL TIME: 20 min.

- 1 pork tenderloin (3/4 pound)
- 1 tablespoon olive oil
- 1/2 cup reduced-sodium beef broth, *divided*
- 2 tablespoons dried cranberries
- 1-1/2 teaspoons Dijon mustard
- 1 tablespoon thawed orange juice concentrate
- 1 teaspoon cornstarch

Cut tenderloin into 12 slices; flatten to 1/4-in. thickness. In a large skillet, brown pork on both sides over medium heat in oil. Add 1/4 cup of beef broth; reduce heat. Cover and simmer for 4-6 minutes or until tender. Remove meat to a serving dish and keep warm. In the same skillet, add the cranberries, mustard and remaining broth. Combine orange juice concentrate and cornstarch until smooth; gradually add to broth mixture. Bring to a boil; cook and stir for 1-2 minutes or until thickened. Serve with pork.

YIELD: 4 servings.

ravioli carbonara

PREP/TOTAL TIME: 25 min.

- 1 package (16 ounces) frozen cheese ravioli
- 8 bacon strips, diced
- 1 cup prepared Alfredo sauce
- 1/4 cup milk
- 2 to 3 teaspoons dried basil
Pepper to taste

Cook ravioli according to package directions. Meanwhile, in a large skillet, cook bacon over medium heat until crisp. Remove to paper towels; drain, reserving 2 teaspoons drippings.

Stir Alfredo sauce, milk and basil into drippings; heat through. Drain the ravioli; add to sauce and toss to coat. Sprinkle with bacon and pepper.

YIELD: 3 servings.

bistro mac & cheese

PREP/TOTAL TIME: 30 min.

- 1 package (16 ounces) uncooked elbow macaroni
- 3 tablespoons butter
- 3 tablespoons all-purpose flour
- 2-1/2 cups 2% milk
- 1 teaspoon salt
- 1/2 teaspoon onion powder
- 1/2 teaspoon pepper
- 1/4 teaspoon garlic powder
- 1 cup (4 ounces) shredded part-skim mozzarella cheese
- 1 cup (4 ounces) shredded cheddar cheese
- 1 package (3 ounces) cream cheese, softened
- 1/2 cup crumbled Gorgonzola cheese
- 1/2 cup sour cream

Cook macaroni according to package directions. Meanwhile, in a Dutch oven, melt butter. Stir in flour until smooth. Gradually stir in milk and seasonings. Bring to a boil; cook and stir for 2 minutes or until sauce is thickened.

Reduce heat; add cheeses and stir until melted. Stir in sour cream. Drain macaroni; stir into sauce.

YIELD: 8 servings.

pizza pork chops

PREP/TOTAL TIME: 30 min.

2 cups sliced fresh mushrooms

2 tablespoons butter

4 boneless pork loin chops (4 ounces each)

1/4 teaspoon salt

1/4 teaspoon pepper

2 tablespoons olive oil

2 cups marinara *or* spaghetti sauce

16 slices pepperoni

1 cup (4 ounces) shredded part-skim mozzarella cheese

In a large skillet, saute mushrooms in butter until tender. Remove and keep warm. Sprinkle pork chops with salt and pepper. In the same skillet, brown chops in oil on both sides; drain.

Add marinara sauce; bring to a boil. Reduce heat; simmer, uncovered, for 4-5 minutes on each side or until a thermometer reads 145°. Layer pork with pepperoni, mushrooms and cheese. Remove from the heat. Cover and let stand for 5 minutes before serving.

YIELD: 4 servings.

vance werner jr.

FRANKLIN, WISCONSIN

Pepperoni and mozzarella cheese punch up pork chops with a taste that diners of all ages are sure to love. I like to dress up this speedy supper by using portobello mushrooms and serving the chops with fresh broccoli or green beans.

diane zalewski
FREEHOLD, NEW JERSEY

My children absolutely love this scrumptious pork entree. I garnish it with orange slices and parsley for a pretty presentation.

pork medallions in orange sauce

PREP: 15 min. | **COOK:** 25 min.

1/2 cup orange juice
1/4 cup sherry *or* reduced-sodium chicken broth
2 tablespoons ketchup
1 tablespoon light corn syrup
1 teaspoon grated orange peel
1 pork tenderloin (1 pound), cut into 1/2-inch slices
1/4 to 1/2 teaspoon dried rosemary, crushed
1/4 teaspoon salt
1/8 teaspoon pepper
1-1/2 teaspoons canola oil

In a small bowl, combine the orange juice, sherry or broth, ketchup, corn syrup and orange peel; set mixture aside.

Flatten pork to 1/4-in. thickness; sprinkle with rosemary, salt and pepper. In a large nonstick skillet, brown pork in oil. Remove and keep warm.

Pour juice mixture into the skillet, stirring to loosen browned bits. Bring to a boil. Reduce heat; simmer, uncovered, for 10-15 minutes or until liquid is reduced to 1 cup. Return pork to the pan; cover and simmer for 4-5 minutes or until tender.

YIELD: 4 servings.

pork in mustard sauce

PREP/TOTAL TIME: 30 min.

4 boneless pork chops (about 2 pounds)
2 tablespoons butter

Salt and pepper to taste
2 to 3 tablespoons Dijon mustard
1/4 cup chopped onion
1-1/2 teaspoons minced fresh tarragon *or* 1/2 teaspoon dried tarragon
Hot cooked noodles
3/4 cup sour cream
1 teaspoon browning sauce, optional

In a large skillet, brown pork chops on both sides in butter. Season with salt and pepper. Add the mustard, onion and tarragon; cover and simmer for 4-6 minutes or until a thermometer reads 145°.

Place noodles on a serving platter. Arrange pork over noodles; keep warm. Add sour cream and browning sauce to the skillet if desired; heat through (do not boil). Serve with pork and noodles.

YIELD: 4 servings.

cheryl mutch
EDMONTON, ALBERTA

I like to add a little zip to plain pork chops with my mustard sauce. This is a wonderful entree to make for company—it looks fancy but isn't difficult to fix.

pizzeria burgers

PREP/TOTAL TIME: 30 min.

3/4 cup pizza sauce, *divided*
1/4 cup dry bread crumbs
1/4 teaspoon dried oregano
1 teaspoon salt
Dash pepper
1-1/2 pounds ground beef
1/4 pound bulk pork sausage
6 slices part-skim mozzarella cheese
6 sandwich rolls, split

In a large bowl, combine 1/2 cup pizza sauce, bread crumbs, oregano, salt and pepper. Crumble beef and sausage over mixture and mix well. Shape into six patties.

In a large skillet, cook patties over medium heat for 5-7 minutes on each side or until a thermometer reads 160° and juices run clear. Top with remaining pizza sauce and cheese. Cover and cook 2 minutes longer or until cheese is melted. Serve on rolls.

YIELD: 6 servings.
MAMA MIA BURGERS: Substitute bulk Italian sausage and sliced provolone cheese for the pork sausage and mozzarella cheese.

amy lapointe
NORTH FOND DU LAC, WISCONSIN

When my children were teens, they requested these delicious burgers every week. I like making them because they actually don't take much work to prepare. Kids of all ages will love them!

debbie carlson
SAN DIEGO, CALIFORNIA

You can't beat this comforting recipe to please the family and go easy on the budget. It's a classic, satisfying meatless entree.

budget macaroni and cheese

PREP/TOTAL TIME: 20 min.

   1 package (7 ounces) elbow macaroni
   3 tablespoons butter
   3 tablespoons all-purpose flour
   1/4 teaspoon salt
Dash pepper
   1 cup milk
   1 cup (4 ounces) shredded cheddar cheese

Cook the macaroni according to package directions. Meanwhile, in a large saucepan, melt butter over medium-low heat. Add the flour, salt and pepper; stir until smooth; gradually add milk. Bring to a boil; cook and stir for 2 minutes or until thickened. Remove from the heat; stir in cheese until melted.

   Drain macaroni. Add to the cheese mixture; toss to coat.

YIELD: 4 servings.

blanche stevens
ANDERSON, INDIANA

My quick-to-fix dish looks special and tastes absolutely delicious. A delightful mushroom sauce nicely complements the juicy beef. I like to serve it with toasted French bread.

mushroom beef tenderloin

PREP/TOTAL TIME: 20 min.

   3/4 pound fresh mushrooms, sliced
   5 tablespoons butter, *divided*
   2 teaspoons all-purpose flour
   1 teaspoon salt
   1/4 teaspoon pepper

   1 cup heavy whipping cream
   1 tablespoon minced fresh parsley
   6 beef tenderloin steaks (1-1/2 inches thick and 6 ounces *each*)

In a large skillet, saute mushrooms in 3 tablespoons butter for 6-8 minutes or until tender. Stir in the flour, salt and pepper until blended. Gradually add the cream. Bring to a gentle boil; cook and stir for 1-2 minutes or until thickened. Stir in parsley; set aside and keep warm.

   Meanwhile, in another large skillet, heat the remaining butter over medium-high heat. Cook steaks for 6-7 minutes on each side or until the meat reaches desired doneness (for medium-rare, a thermometer should read 145°; medium, 160°; well-done, 170°). Serve with the mushroom sauce.

YIELD: 6 servings.

shrimp piccata pasta

PREP/TOTAL TIME: 20 min.

  6 ounces uncooked spaghetti
  2 shallots, chopped
  1 tablespoon olive oil
  1 pound uncooked medium shrimp,
    peeled and deveined
  1 jar (3 ounces) capers, drained
  3 tablespoons lemon juice
1/2 teaspoon garlic powder

Cook spaghetti according to package directions. Meanwhile, in a large nonstick skillet, saute shallots in oil until tender. Add the shrimp, capers, lemon juice and garlic powder; cook and stir for 5-6 minutes or until shrimp turn pink.

Drain spaghetti; toss with shrimp mixture.

YIELD: 4 servings.

carole bess white
PORTLAND, OREGON

Want a quick, easy and flavorful way to serve shrimp? A light and tangy sauce spiked with capers makes it an instant classic.

rita brower

EXETER, CALIFORNIA

Tired of the same-old, same-old meals for dinner? Try something new tonight! A sweet and tangy relish of cranberries and pineapple tops these hearty ham steaks, adding lots of flavor and color.

pineapple cranberry ham

PREP/TOTAL TIME: 25 min.

   4 boneless fully cooked ham steaks
      (6 ounces *each*)
1-1/2 teaspoons canola oil
   1/2 cup jellied cranberry sauce
   1/2 cup undrained crushed pineapple
     3 tablespoons brown sugar
   1/8 teaspoon ground cloves

Cut each ham steak in half. In a large skillet over medium heat, cook ham in oil in batches for 3-5 minutes on each side or until browned and heated through. Set aside and keep warm.

Meanwhile, in a small saucepan, mash the cranberry sauce; stir in the remaining ingredients. Bring to a boil; cook and stir for 3-5 minutes or until slightly thickened. Serve with ham.

YIELD: 4 servings.

chicken fried steak

PREP/TOTAL TIME: 25 min.

- 1/2 pound beef top sirloin steak (1/2 inch thick)
- 1/4 cup all-purpose flour
- 1/4 cup seasoned bread crumbs
- 1 egg
- 2 teaspoons water
- 3 tablespoons canola oil

COUNTRY GRAVY:

- 2 tablespoons all-purpose flour
- 1-1/4 cups 2% milk
- 1/4 teaspoon salt
- 1/4 teaspoon white pepper

Flatten steak to 1/4-in. thickness. Cut into two serving-size pieces. Place flour and bread crumbs in separate shallow bowls. In another shallow bowl, whisk egg and water. Coat steaks with flour, then dip into egg mixture and coat with crumbs.

In a large skillet, cook steaks in oil over medium heat for 1-2 minutes on each side or until meat reaches desired doneness. Remove the steaks and keep warm.

For gravy, stir flour into pan drippings until blended, loosening browned bits. Gradually stir in milk. Bring to a boil over medium heat; cook and stir for 2 minutes or until thickened. Season with salt and pepper. Serve with steaks.

YIELD: 2 servings.

judy yackey
KALISPELL, MONTANA

I've been the chief cook ever since I moved in with my father. With its crispy coating, this Southern specialty is his favorite.

PRESTO PAN GRAVY

When pan-frying pork chops or chicken, I use undiluted cream soup as gravy. After removing the meat, I cook the soup and enough water to make it the consistency we like. We like cream of mushroom soup with pork chops and cream of chicken soup with chicken.

—CAROL P.
ARKOMA, OKLAHOMA

dad's swedish meatballs

PREP: 30 min. | COOK: 35 min.

- 1 egg, lightly beaten
- 1/2 cup milk
- 1 cup soft bread crumbs
- 1/2 cup finely chopped onion
- 1 teaspoon salt
- 1/4 teaspoon ground nutmeg
- 1/4 teaspoon pepper
- 1 pound ground beef
- 1/2 pound ground pork
- 1/4 cup butter, cubed

DILL CREAM SAUCE:

- 2 tablespoons all-purpose flour
- 1 cup heavy whipping cream
- 1 cup beef broth
- 1 teaspoon salt
- 1/2 teaspoon dill seed

In a large bowl, combine the first seven ingredients. Crumble beef and pork over mixture and mix well. Shape into 1-1/2-in. balls. In a large skillet, cook meatballs in butter in batches until a thermometer reads 160°. Remove and keep warm.

In a small bowl, combine the sauce ingredients until blended. Stir into the skillet. Bring to a boil; cook and stir for 2 minutes or until thickened. Serve with meatballs.

YIELD: 6 servings.

michelle lizotte
CUMBERLAND, RHODE ISLAND

My father used to make these tender meatballs every year for Christmas when I was a kid. Now I carry on the tradition, and everyone still loves them.

lisa bleich

FLAGSTAFF, ARIZONA

Apple juice and onions come together for a delicious, old-fashioned way to flavor pork chops. This is a satisfying main dish with noodles or roasted potatoes.

apple-onion pork chops

PREP/TOTAL TIME: 30 min.

- 1/4 cup all-purpose flour
- 1/2 teaspoon plus 1/8 teaspoon salt, *divided*
- 1/4 teaspoon plus 1/8 teaspoon pepper, *divided*
- 4 boneless pork loin chops (6 ounces each)
- 2 tablespoons butter
- 1 small onion, sliced and separated into rings
- 1 cup apple juice
- 1 tablespoon cornstarch
- 1 tablespoon cold water
- 1/4 teaspoon browning sauce, optional

In a large resealable plastic bag, combine the flour, 1/2 teaspoon salt and 1/4 teaspoon pepper; add pork chops. Seal bag and shake to coat. In a large skillet, brown chops on both sides in butter.

Add the onion and apple juice. Bring to a boil. Reduce heat; cover and simmer for 4-6 minutes or until a thermometer reads 145°. Remove the pork chops and keep them warm. Let stand for 5 minutes before serving.

Combine cornstarch and water until smooth; stir into skillet. Bring to a boil; cook and stir for 1 minute or until thickened. Stir in remaining salt and pepper and browning sauce if desired. Serve with pork chops.

YIELD: 4 servings.

vicki didier

MACHESNEY PARK, ILLINOIS

When it's just my husband and me for dinner, I rely on this easy favorite. It tastes like old-fashioned tuna casserole, but a packaged mix makes it really quick to prepare.

tuna alfredo

PREP/TOTAL TIME: 20 min.

- 1 package (4.4 ounces) quick-cooking Alfredo noodles and sauce mix
- 1 can (6 ounces) tuna, drained and flaked
- 1 tablespoon chopped green onion

Prepare noodles and sauce mix according to the package directions. Stir in the tuna and onion; heat mixture through.

YIELD: 2-3 servings.

helen bridges

WASHINGTON, VIRGINIA

Golden brown potatoes give simple ham a tasty touch. Not only do the potatoes pick up the flavor of the ham, but they are crispy and look beautiful! Just add veggies or a salad and dinner's done.

country ham and potatoes

PREP/TOTAL TIME: 30 min.

- 2 pounds fully cooked sliced ham (about 1/2 inch thick)
- 2 to 3 tablespoons butter
- 1-1/2 pounds potatoes, peeled, quartered and cooked

Snipped fresh parsley

In a large heavy skillet, brown ham over medium-high heat in butter on both sides until heated through. Move ham to one side of the skillet; brown potatoes in drippings until tender. Sprinkle potatoes with parsley.

YIELD: 6 servings.

tacos in a bowl

PREP/TOTAL TIME: 25 min.

1/2 pound lean ground beef (90% lean)
2 tablespoons finely chopped onion
3/4 cup canned diced tomatoes, drained
2 tablespoons taco seasoning
1 cup water
1 package (3 ounces) ramen noodles
1/4 cup shredded cheddar *or* Mexican cheese blend
1/4 cup crushed tortilla chips, optional

In a small skillet, cook beef and onion over medium heat until meat is no longer pink; drain. Stir in the tomatoes, taco seasoning and water. Bring to a boil. Add ramen noodles (discard seasoning packet or save for another use). Cook and stir for 3-5 minutes or until noodles are tender.

Spoon into serving bowls; sprinkle with cheese and tortilla chips if desired.

YIELD: 2 servings.

sue schoening
SHEBOYGAN, WISCONSIN

Here is an easy skillet dish that's perfect for a busy weeknight. Garnish it with sour cream and salsa for added Southwestern flare.

fay strait
WAUKEE, IOWA

These are my family's favorite! My kids will eat anything we roll up in the yummy homemade wraps. The original recipe called for all white flour and a lot of salt. I added whole wheat flour and cut back on the salt to make them healthier.

super flatbread wraps

PREP: 40 min. + rising | **COOK:** 15 min.

- 1/2 teaspoon active dry yeast
- 1/2 cup warm water (110° to 115°)
- 1 teaspoon olive oil
- 1/2 teaspoon salt
- 1/3 cup whole wheat flour
- 1 cup all-purpose flour

FILLING:

- 1 beef flank steak (1 pound)
- 1/2 teaspoon salt
- 1/4 teaspoon pepper
- 1 tablespoon canola oil
- 1 cup shredded lettuce
- 1/4 cup sliced ripe olives
- 2 tablespoons crumbled feta cheese

In a small bowl, dissolve yeast in warm water. Add the oil, salt, whole wheat flour and 3/4 cup all-purpose flour; beat on medium speed for 3 minutes. Stir in enough remaining flour to form a firm dough.

Turn onto a lightly floured surface; knead until smooth and elastic, about 6-8 minutes. Place in a large bowl coated with cooking spray, turning once to coat the top. Cover and let rise in a warm place until doubled, about 45 minutes.

Punch dough down. Turn onto a lightly floured surface; divide into four portions. Roll each into an 8-in. circle.

Heat a large nonstick skillet coated with cooking spray over medium heat; add a portion of dough. Cook for 30-60 seconds or until bubbles form on top. Turn and cook until the second side is golden brown. Remove and keep warm. Repeat with remaining dough, adding cooking spray as needed.

Sprinkle steak with salt and pepper. In a large skillet over medium-high heat, cook steak in oil for 6-8 minutes on each side or until meat reaches desired doneness (for medium-rare, a thermometer should read 145°; medium, 160°; well-done, 170°).

Let stand for 5 minutes before cutting steak thinly across the grain. Serve on warm flatbreads with lettuce, olives and cheese.

YIELD: 4 servings.

the **ULTIMATE COMFORT FOOD** cookbook

salmon cakes

PREP/TOTAL TIME: 30 min.

- 2 eggs
- 1/4 cup heavy whipping cream
- 1/4 cup cornmeal
- 2 tablespoons sliced green onions
- 2 tablespoons all-purpose flour
- 1/4 teaspoon baking powder

Pinch pepper

- 1/2 teaspoon salt, optional
- 1 can (14-3/4 ounces) salmon, drained, bones and skin removed
- 1 to 2 tablespoons butter

In a small bowl, beat eggs. Stir in the cream, cornmeal, green onions, flour, baking powder, pepper and salt if desired. Flake salmon into bowl; blend gently.

Melt butter in a large nonstick skillet or griddle over medium heat. Drop salmon mixture by 1/3 cupfuls into butter. Fry in batches for 5 minutes on each side or until lightly browned. Serve hot.

YIELD: 3-4 servings (six patties).

imogene hutton
BROWNWOOD, TEXAS

Salmon was a special treat for us on Sundays when we were growing up. We ate these cakes fast as Mama could fry them—she couldn't get them off the griddle fast enough!

italian stew

PREP: 15 min. | **COOK:** 1 hour

- 1 pound bulk Italian sausage
- 1 small onion, chopped
- 1 garlic clove, minced
- 3 cups beef broth
- 1 can (14-1/2 ounces) stewed tomatoes, cut up
- 1 can (8 ounces) tomato sauce
- 1 medium carrot, thinly sliced
- 1 teaspoon dried basil
- 1 teaspoon dried oregano
- 1 package (9 ounces) refrigerated cheese tortellini
- 1 small zucchini, sliced
- 1/3 cup chopped green pepper
- 2 tablespoons minced fresh parsley

Grated Parmesan cheese

In a large saucepan, cook sausage and onion over medium heat until meat is no longer pink and onion is tender. Drain. Add garlic; cook 1 minute longer.

Stir in the broth, tomatoes, tomato sauce, carrot, basil and oregano. Bring to a boil. Reduce heat; simmer, uncovered, for 30 minutes.

Gently stir in the tortellini, zucchini, green pepper and parsley. Cover and simmer for 20-25 minutes or until tortellini is tender. Serve with Parmesan cheese.

YIELD: 6-8 servings (2 quarts).

lorinda pearson
GREEN VALLEY, ARIZONA

Sausage, tortellini, veggies and herbs make a rich, satisfying meal that's different from typical stews showcasing meat and potatoes. It's a hearty one-dish meal that's simple to prepare.

barbara kemmer
ROHNERT PARK, CALIFORNIA

This recipe makes just the right amount for my husband and me. I like the idea of cooking it all in one pan, which makes cleanup a breeze.

FRESH GARLIC SUBSTITUTES

When you don't have fresh garlic, substitute 1/4 teaspoon of garlic powder for each clove the recipe requires. Also consider using jarred minced garlic from the produce section. Use 1/2 teaspoon jarred garlic for each clove that the recipe requires.

hamburger mac skillet

PREP/TOTAL TIME: 30 min.

1/2 pound ground beef
1/4 cup chopped onion
1/4 cup chopped green pepper
1 garlic clove, minced
1 can (11-1/2 ounces) tomato juice
1/2 cup uncooked elbow macaroni
1 teaspoon Worcestershire sauce
3/4 teaspoon salt
1/8 teaspoon pepper

In a large skillet, cook the beef, onion and green pepper over medium heat until meat is no longer pink. Add garlic; cook 1 minute longer. Drain.

Add the tomato juice, macaroni, Worcestershire sauce, salt and pepper; bring to a boil. Reduce heat; cover and simmer for 20 minutes or until macaroni is tender.

YIELD: 2 servings.

janet les
CHILLIWACK,
BRITISH COLUMBIA

Dijon mustard and honey create a sweet and subtly tangy sauce that perfectly complements lean pork tenderloin.

honey mustard pork

PREP/TOTAL TIME: 30 min.

1 pound pork tenderloin, cut into thin strips
1 tablespoon canola oil
1 cup reduced-sodium beef broth, *divided*

1/4 cup honey
1 tablespoon Dijon mustard
1 tablespoon cornstarch
2 tablespoons cold water
Hot cooked long grain and wild rice, optional

In a large nonstick skillet, brown pork in oil on all sides. Add 1/2 cup broth. Bring to a boil. Reduce heat; cover and simmer for 10 minutes or until meat is tender. Remove pork with a slotted spoon and keep warm.

Stir in the honey, mustard and remaining broth. Combine cornstarch and water until smooth. Gradually stir into the pan. Bring to a boil; cook and stir for 2 minutes or until thickened. Return pork to the pan; heat through. Serve with rice if desired.

YIELD: 4 servings.

beef stew for 2

PREP: 30 min. + marinating | **COOK:** 1 hour

1-1/2 cups dry red wine *or* beef broth, *divided*

   3 tablespoons lemon juice

   2 teaspoons reduced-sodium soy sauce

   2 teaspoons Worcestershire sauce

1/2 pound beef stew meat, cut into 1-inch cubes

   2 teaspoons olive oil

   1 small onion, chopped

   3 garlic cloves, minced

2-1/2 cups beef broth, *divided*

   2 small potatoes, cut into 1-inch cubes

   2 medium carrots, cut into 1-inch slices

   1 cup sliced baby portobello mushrooms

   2 fresh thyme sprigs

1/8 teaspoon cayenne pepper

   2 teaspoons cornstarch

In a large resealable plastic bag, combine 1 cup wine, lemon juice, soy sauce and Worcestershire sauce; add the beef. Seal bag and turn to coat; refrigerate for 8 hours or overnight.

Drain and discard marinade. In a large saucepan, brown beef in oil. Remove meat and set aside. In the same pan, saute onion until tender. Add garlic; cook 1 minute longer. Add 2 cups beef broth and remaining wine. Return meat to pan.

Bring to a boil. Reduce heat; cover and simmer for 30 minutes. Add potatoes, carrots, mushrooms, thyme and cayenne. Bring to a boil. Reduce heat; cover and simmer for 30 minutes or until vegetables and beef are tender. Discard the thyme sprigs.

In a small bowl, combine the cornstarch and remaining beef broth until smooth. Gradually stir into stew. Bring to a boil; cook and stir for 2 minutes or until thickened.

YIELD: 2 servings.

roger slivon
GENESEE DEPOT, WISCONSIN

You will love this rich and satisfying stew with its little kick of cayenne. It's perfect for a chilly day.

krissy black

MT. VERNON, OHIO

Family and friends love my healthy take on chili mac. I use power foods: tomatoes, black beans, olive oil and whole wheat pasta... here is comfort food to feel good about!

chili mac

PREP/TOTAL TIME: 30 min.

- 2 cups uncooked whole wheat elbow macaroni
- 1 pound lean ground turkey
- 1 small onion, chopped
- 2 to 3 jalapeno peppers, seeded and chopped
- 2 teaspoons olive oil
- 2 garlic cloves, minced
- 1 can (15 ounces) black beans, rinsed and drained
- 1 can (14-1/2 ounces) diced tomatoes, undrained
- 1 can (8 ounces) tomato sauce
- 1 to 2 tablespoons hot pepper sauce
- 2 to 3 teaspoons chili powder
- 1 teaspoon ground cumin
- 1/4 teaspoon cayenne pepper
- 1/4 teaspoon pepper
- 3/4 cup shredded reduced-fat cheddar cheese

Cook macaroni according to package directions. Meanwhile, in a large nonstick skillet coated with cooking spray, cook the turkey, onion and jalapenos in oil over medium heat until meat is no longer pink. Add garlic; cook 1 minute longer. Drain.

Add the beans, tomatoes, tomato sauce, pepper sauce and seasonings. Drain macaroni; stir into turkey mixture. Cook over medium-low heat for 5 minutes or until heated through.

Sprinkle with cheese. Remove from the heat; cover and let stand until cheese is melted.

YIELD: 6 servings.

EDITOR'S NOTE: Wear disposable gloves when cutting hot peppers; the oils can burn skin. Avoid touching your face.

pork chops with mushroom gravy

PREP: 25 min. | **COOK:** 1-3/4 hours

1/2 cup all-purpose flour, *divided*
1/2 cup seasoned bread crumbs, *divided*
4 pork chops (1/2 inch thick)
2 tablespoons canola oil
1 medium onion, sliced
2 garlic cloves, minced
1/4 teaspoon pepper
3 cups water
2 tablespoons beef bouillon granules
1 teaspoon browning sauce, optional
2 bay leaves
1 jar (4-1/2 ounces) sliced mushrooms, drained
1/2 cup cold water

In a large resealable plastic bag, combine half of the flour and bread crumbs; add pork chops, a few at a time. Seal bag and toss to coat.

In a large skillet over medium heat, brown pork chops on both sides in oil. Add the onion, garlic, pepper and water. Stir in the bouillon, browning sauce if desired and bay leaves; bring to a boil. Reduce heat; cover and simmer for 1-1/2 hours or until pork is tender.

Discard bay leaves. Remove pork to serving platter and keep warm. Add mushrooms to skillet. Combine cold water and remaining flour until smooth; stir into pan juices. Bring to a boil, stirring constantly until thickened and bubbly. Stir in the remaining bread crumbs. Serve with pork chops.

YIELD: 4 servings.

nancy schilling
BERKELEY SPRINGS,
WEST VIRGINIA

Even people who think that pork is dry enjoy these tender pork chops, prepared with what my grandmother called her "moist meat" cooking method. I serve them with mashed potatoes, peas and cranberry sauce.

tuna noodle skillet

PREP/TOTAL TIME: 30 min.

2 jars (16 ounces *each*) Alfredo sauce
1 can (14-1/2 ounces) chicken broth
1 package (16 ounces) wide egg noodles
1 package (10 ounces) frozen peas
1/4 teaspoon pepper
1 can (12 ounces) solid white water-packed tuna, drained and flaked

In a large skillet over medium heat, bring Alfredo sauce and broth to a boil. Add noodles; cover and cook for 7-8 minutes.

Reduce heat; stir in peas and pepper. Cover and cook 4 minutes longer or until noodles are tender. Stir in tuna; heat through.

YIELD: 6 servings.

ruth simon
BUFFALO, NEW YORK

Savor the comforting flavor of tuna noodle casserole in minutes with this creamy stovetop version. It's easy to make with convenient ingredients like frozen peas and bottled Alfredo sauce.

cassie dion
SOUTH BURLINGTON,
VERMONT

*It's fun to make turkey a
different way, and you can't
beat this recipe's creamy,
cheesy sauce. It's perfect for
company and easy on the
budget, too.*

turkey pasta supreme

PREP/TOTAL TIME: 20 min.

3/4 pound uncooked turkey breast
2 tablespoons butter
2 garlic cloves, minced
1-1/4 cups heavy whipping cream
2 tablespoons minced fresh basil *or*
  2 teaspoons dried basil
1/4 cup grated Parmesan cheese
Dash pepper
3 to 4 cups hot cooked pasta

Cut turkey into 2-in. x 1/4-in. pieces. In a large skillet,
saute turkey in butter until turkey is browned and
no longer pink, about 6 minutes. Add garlic; cook 1
minute longer.

Add the cream, basil, cheese and pepper; bring
mixture to a boil. Reduce heat; simmer for 3 minutes,
stirring frequently.

Stir in pasta and toss to coat.

YIELD: 4 servings.

edith landinger
LONGVIEW, TEXAS

*This yummy dish is loaded
with ground beef, pasta,
veggies and cheddar cheese,
and it comes together in a
jiffy. It's perfect comfort
food for a busy day.*

stovetop hamburger casserole

PREP/TOTAL TIME: 25 min.

1 package (7 ounces) small pasta shells
1-1/2 pounds ground beef
1 large onion, chopped
3 medium carrots, chopped
1 celery rib, chopped
3 garlic cloves, minced
3 cups cubed cooked red potatoes
1 can (15-1/4 ounces) whole kernel corn,
  drained
2 cans (8 ounces *each*) tomato sauce
1-1/2 teaspoons salt
1/2 teaspoon pepper
1 cup (4 ounces) shredded cheddar
  cheese

Cook pasta according to package directions.
Meanwhile, in a large skillet, cook beef and onion
over medium heat until meat is no longer pink;
drain. Add carrots and celery; cook and stir for 5
minutes or until vegetables are crisp-tender. Add
garlic; cook 1 minute longer.

Stir in the potatoes, corn, tomato sauce, salt and
pepper; heat through. Drain pasta and add to skillet;
toss to coat. Sprinkle with cheese. Cover and cook
until cheese is melted.

YIELD: 6 servings.

my favorite burger

PREP/TOTAL TIME: 25 min.

1/4 cup grated onion
1/2 teaspoon garlic powder
1/4 teaspoon salt
1/4 teaspoon pepper
1 pound lean ground beef (90% lean)
1 cup sliced fresh mushrooms
1/2 cup sliced sweet onion
4 kaiser rolls, split
4 ounces fat-free cream cheese
2 bacon strips, cooked and crumbled

In a large bowl, combine the onion, garlic powder, salt and pepper. Crumble beef over mixture and mix well. Shape into four patties.

In a large skillet over medium heat, cook burgers for 4-6 minutes on each side or until a thermometer reads 160° and juices run clear.

Meanwhile, in a small skillet coated with cooking spray, cook and stir mushrooms and onion over medium heat until onion is golden brown.

Spread rolls with cream cheese; top with burgers and mushroom mixture. Sprinkle with bacon.

YIELD: 4 servings.

kris swihart
PERRYSBURG, OHIO

After having a burger similar to this at a diner years ago, I tried to lighten it up without losing the great flavors. Now I can enjoy one more often without feeling guilty!

CHAPTER THREE

casseroles & oven entrees

angela spengler
CLOVIS, NEW MEXICO

There's a little bit of Deutschland in every slice of this quick, creative pizza. If you like sausage and 'kraut, you'll love this dish!

german oktoberfest pizza

PREP/TOTAL TIME: 25 min.

- 1 tube (13.8 ounces) refrigerated pizza crust
- 1 pound smoked kielbasa *or* Polish sausage, cut into 1/4-in. slices
- 2 teaspoons butter
- 2 cups leftover *or* refrigerated mashed potatoes
- 1 cup sauerkraut, rinsed and well drained
- 1 cup (4 ounces) shredded cheddar cheese
- 1 teaspoon caraway seeds

Unroll dough into a greased 15-in. x 10-in. x 1-in. baking pan; flatten dough and build up edges slightly. Bake at 425° for 8-10 minutes or until crust is light golden brown.

Meanwhile, in a large skillet, saute kielbasa in butter until browned. Spread mashed potatoes over crust. Layer with sauerkraut, kielbasa, cheese and caraway seeds. Bake for 10-15 minutes or until golden brown.

YIELD: 6 pieces.

diane nemitz
LUDINGTON, MICHIGAN

A day without pasta is a like a day without sunshine! Loaded with vegetables, Italian seasonings and cheeses, vegetarian ziti is sure to brighten your day.

four-cheese baked ziti

PREP: 30 min. | BAKE: 10 min.

- 1 cup chopped onion
- 1/2 cup chopped green pepper
- 1/2 cup shredded carrots
- 2 garlic cloves, minced
- 2 cans (14-1/2 ounces *each*) Italian diced tomatoes
- 1 can (15 ounces) crushed tomatoes
- 1 cup vegetable broth
- 1/8 teaspoon crushed red pepper flakes
- 8 ounces uncooked ziti *or* small tube pasta
- 1 cup (8 ounces) part-skim ricotta cheese
- 1/2 cup shredded provolone cheese
- 1/4 cup loosely packed basil leaves, thinly sliced
- 1 cup (4 ounces) shredded part-skim mozzarella cheese
- 1/4 cup grated Parmesan cheese

In a large nonstick skillet coated with cooking spray, cook the onion, green pepper and carrots until crisp-tender. Add garlic; cook 1 minute longer. Stir in the tomatoes, broth and pepper flakes; bring to a boil. Reduce heat and simmer mixture, uncovered, for 15 minutes.

Cook ziti according to package directions; drain. Stir in the vegetable mixture, ricotta cheese, provolone cheese and basil.

Transfer to a 13-in. x 9-in. baking dish coated with cooking spray. Sprinkle with mozzarella and Parmesan cheeses. Bake, uncovered, at 425° for 10-15 minutes or until heated through and cheese is melted.

YIELD: 8 servings.

south-of-the-border quiche

PREP: 20 min. | **BAKE:** 35 min. + standing

- 2 unbaked pastry shells (9 inches)
- 2 teaspoons chili powder
- 1 teaspoon ground cumin
- 1-1/2 cups (6 ounces) shredded cheddar cheese
- 1-1/2 cups (6 ounces) shredded Monterey Jack cheese
- 1 cup (4 ounces) shredded sharp cheddar cheese
- 8 eggs, lightly beaten
- 2 cups half-and-half cream
- 2 cans (4 ounces *each*) chopped green chilies
- 2 cans (2-1/4 ounces *each*) sliced ripe olives, drained
- 1/4 cup chopped green onions
- 2 tablespoons minced fresh cilantro
- 1/2 teaspoon salt
- 1/2 teaspoon pepper

Salsa and sour cream, optional

Line unpricked pastry shells with a double thickness of heavy-duty foil. Bake at 400° for 5 minutes. Remove foil; bake 5 minutes longer.

Sprinkle chili powder and cumin over shells; sprinkle with cheeses. In a large bowl, whisk the eggs, cream, chilies, olives, onions, cilantro, salt and pepper. Pour evenly over cheeses.

Cover and freeze one quiche for up to 3 months. Cover edges of remaining quiche loosely with foil; place on a baking sheet. Bake at 400° for 35-40 minutes or until a knife inserted near the center comes out clean. Let stand for 10 minutes before cutting. Serve with salsa and sour cream if desired.

TO USE FROZEN QUICHE: Remove from the freezer 30 minutes before baking (do not thaw). Cover edges of crust loosely with foil; place on a baking sheet. Bake at 400° for 55-60 minutes or until a knife inserted near the center comes out clean. Let stand for 10 minutes before cutting.

YIELD: 2 quiches (6 servings each).

paula marchesi
LENHARTSVILLE, PENNSYLVANIA

When the entire family gets together for a holiday brunch, I make several of these, and there are never any leftovers. It's my most-requested quiche.

**taste of home
test kitchen**

*Here is a fantastic five-
ingredient recipe that takes
almost no time to prep for
the oven.*

oregano roasting chicken

PREP: 10 min. | **BAKE:** 2-1/4 hours

1/4 cup butter, melted
1 envelope Italian salad dressing mix
2 tablespoons lemon juice
1 roasting chicken (6 to 7 pounds)
2 teaspoons dried oregano

In a small bowl, combine the butter, salad dressing mix and lemon juice. Place chicken on a rack in an ungreased roasting pan. Spoon butter mixture over the chicken.

Cover and bake at 350° for 45 minutes. Uncover chicken; sprinkle with oregano. Bake, uncovered, for 1-1/2 to 1-3/4 hours or until a meat thermometer reads 180°.

YIELD: 6 servings.

creole meat loaf

PREP: 15 min. | **BAKE:** 1-1/4 hours + standing

1 can (5 ounces) evaporated milk
1 egg, lightly beaten
1/2 cup chopped green pepper
1/4 cup chopped onion
1/2 cup coarsely crushed saltine crackers
1 teaspoon salt
1 teaspoon ground mustard
1/4 teaspoon pepper
1-1/2 pounds lean ground beef (90% lean)

SAUCE:

1 can (10-3/4 ounces) condensed tomato soup, undiluted
2 tablespoons ketchup
1/2 teaspoon horseradish

In a large bowl, combine the milk, egg, green pepper and onion. Stir in the crackers, salt, mustard and pepper. Crumble beef over mixture and mix well. Pat into an ungreased 8-in. x 4-in. loaf pan.

Bake, uncovered, at 350° for 1-1/4 hours or until no pink remains in the meat and a thermometer reads 160°. Drain.

Let loaf stand in pan for 10 minutes. Meanwhile, in a small saucepan, combine the sauce ingredients. Cook until heated through. Turn loaf out onto a serving platter. Spoon 1/2 cup hot sauce over loaf; serve remaining sauce with meat loaf.

YIELD: 6 servings.

linda kornelson
EMPRESS, ALBERTA

We may live in Canada, but the flavor of this meat loaf says "New Orleans!" It's one of the best ways I know to enjoy bell peppers when they are in season.

pizza carbonara

PREP/TOTAL TIME: 30 min.

1 tube (13.8 ounces) refrigerated pizza crust
1/3 cup finely chopped onion
1 tablespoon butter
2 garlic cloves, minced
1 tablespoon all-purpose flour
1/8 teaspoon white pepper
1 cup milk
1/4 teaspoon chicken bouillon granules
1/4 cup grated Parmesan cheese
1/2 pound sliced bacon, cooked and crumbled
1-1/2 cups (6 ounces) shredded Monterey Jack cheese
3 green onions, thinly sliced

Unroll pizza crust. Press onto a greased 12-in. pizza pan and build up edges slightly. Prick thoroughly with a fork. Bake at 425° for 7-10 minutes or until lightly browned.

Meanwhile, in a large saucepan, saute onion in butter until tender. Add garlic; cook 1 minute longer. Stir in flour and pepper until blended. Gradually add milk and bouillon. Bring to a boil; cook and stir for 2 minutes or until thickened. Reduce heat; stir in Parmesan cheese until blended. Spread over hot crust. Sprinkle with bacon, Monterey Jack cheese and green onions.

Bake at 425° for 8-12 minutes or until cheese is melted. Let stand for 5 minutes before cutting.

YIELD: 4-6 servings.

sherry keethler
LAKE ST. LOUIS, MISSOURI

Convenient refrigerated pizza crust is dressed up with a creamy Parmesan sauce and a topping of Monterey Jack cheese, bacon and green onions. It's a deliciously different addition to any pizza party.

THRIFTY PIZZA

Pizza is a great way to use up leftovers. Recently, I topped a ready-made pizza crust with leftover spaghetti sauce, some leftover taco meat, chopped onion and Parmesan and mozzarella cheeses. It was a hit!
—KAREN M.
SCHAUMBURG, ILLINOIS

carol poindexter
NORRIDGE, ILLINOIS

Try my ravioli, which is so loaded with rich-tasting roasted peppers that no one will miss the extra fat or calories. I serve it with a green salad and homemade Italian herb bread.

roasted pepper ravioli bake

PREP: 25 min. + standing | **BAKE:** 30 min.

 2 each medium green, sweet red and yellow peppers
 1 package (25 ounces) frozen cheese ravioli
 1 tablespoon olive oil
 1 teaspoon sugar
1/4 teaspoon salt
 2 cups meatless spaghetti sauce
 4 ounces sliced part-skim mozzarella cheese

Place peppers on a broiler pan. Broil 4 in. from the heat until skins blister, about 6-8 minutes. With tongs, rotate peppers a quarter turn. Broil and rotate until all sides are blistered and blackened. Immediately place peppers in a bowl; cover and let stand for 15-20 minutes.

Meanwhile, cook ravioli according to package directions; drain. Peel off and discard charred skin from peppers. Remove stems and seeds. Finely chop peppers; drain. In a large bowl, combine the peppers, oil, sugar and salt.

Spread 1-1/2 cups spaghetti sauce in a 13-in. x 9-in. baking dish coated with cooking spray. Layer with ravioli, pepper mixture and cheese. Top with remaining spaghetti sauce.

Cover and bake at 350° for 15 minutes. Uncover; bake 15-20 minutes longer or until heated through.

YIELD: 8 servings.

sue mackey
JACKSON, WISCONSIN

My husband loves these fluffy dumplings with plenty of gravy poured over them. The basil adds just the right touch of flavor, making our whole house smell so good while this dish is baking.

chicken and dumpling casserole

PREP: 30 min. | **BAKE:** 40 min.

1/2 cup chopped onion
1/2 cup chopped celery
1/4 cup butter, cubed
 2 garlic cloves, minced
1/2 cup all-purpose flour
 2 teaspoons sugar
 1 teaspoon salt
 1 teaspoon dried basil
1/2 teaspoon pepper
 4 cups chicken broth
 1 package (10 ounces) frozen green peas
 4 cups cubed cooked chicken

DUMPLINGS:
 2 cups biscuit/baking mix
 2 teaspoons dried basil
2/3 cup 2% milk

In a large saucepan, saute onion and celery in butter until tender. Add garlic; cook 1 minute longer. Stir in the flour, sugar, salt, basil and pepper until blended. Gradually add broth; bring to a boil. Cook and stir for 1 minute or until thickened; reduce heat. Add peas and cook for 5 minutes, stirring constantly. Stir in chicken. Pour into a greased 13-in. x 9-in. baking dish.

For the dumplings, in a small bowl, combine the baking mix and basil. Stir in milk with a fork until moistened. Drop by tablespoonfuls into 12 mounds over chicken mixture.

Bake, uncovered, at 350° for 30 minutes. Cover and bake 10 minutes longer or until a toothpick inserted in a dumpling comes out clean.

YIELD: 6-8 servings.

cornmeal oven-fried chicken

PREP: 20 min. | **BAKE:** 40 min.

- 1/2 cup dry bread crumbs
- 1/2 cup cornmeal
- 1/3 cup grated Parmesan cheese
- 1/4 cup minced fresh parsley *or* 4 teaspoons dried parsley flakes
- 3/4 teaspoon garlic powder
- 1/2 teaspoon salt
- 1/2 teaspoon onion powder
- 1/2 teaspoon dried thyme
- 1/2 teaspoon pepper
- 1/2 cup buttermilk
- 1 broiler/fryer chicken (3 to 4 pounds), cut up, skin removed
- 1 tablespoon butter, melted

In a large resealable plastic bag, combine the first nine ingredients. Place the buttermilk in a shallow bowl. Dip chicken in buttermilk, then add to bag, a few pieces at a time, and shake to coat.

Place in a 13-in. x 9-in. baking pan coated with cooking spray. Bake at 375° for 10 minutes; drizzle with butter. Bake 30-40 minutes longer or until juices run clear.

YIELD: 6 servings.

deb williams
PEORIA, ARIZONA

A coating of cornmeal and Parmesan cheese really perks up fried chicken. It's a crisp and tasty variation from the usual.

edie despain
LOGAN, UTAH

I rate my deep-dish double-crust pizza as excellent. Favorite fillings are tucked inside, and a bright red tomato sauce tops the pie.

chicago-style stuffed pizza

PREP: 30 min. + rising | **BAKE:** 30 min.

  1 teaspoon active dry yeast
  1 cup warm water (110° to 115°)
  2 teaspoons sugar
  2 tablespoons canola oil
1-1/2 teaspoons salt
2-1/2 to 3 cups all-purpose flour
  1/2 cup yellow cornmeal
  1/2 pound bulk Italian sausage
  1 small green pepper, diced
  1 small onion, diced
  3 garlic cloves, peeled and sliced
  2 cups (8 ounces) shredded part-skim
    mozzarella cheese
  1/3 cup chopped pepperoni
  1/4 cup grated Parmesan cheese
  1 teaspoon dried oregano
  1/4 cup tomato sauce

In a large bowl, dissolve yeast in warm water. Add the sugar; let stand for 5 minutes. Add oil and salt. Add 1-1/2 cups flour and cornmeal; beat until smooth. Stir in enough remaining flour to form a soft dough.

Turn onto a floured surface; knead until smooth and elastic, about 4-5 minutes. Place in a greased bowl; turn once to grease top. Cover and let rise in a warm place until doubled, about 1 hour.

Punch dough down; let rest for 5 minutes. Divide into two portions, one slightly larger than the other. On a lightly floured surface, roll out larger portion to a 12-in. circle. Press onto the bottom and up the sides of a greased 10-in. ovenproof skillet.

In a large skillet, cook the sausage, green pepper and onion over medium heat until meat is no longer pink. Add garlic; cook 1 minute longer. Drain. Stir in the mozzarella cheese, pepperoni, Parmesan cheese and oregano. Add to prepared crust.

On a lightly floured surface, roll remaining dough into an 11-in. circle. Place over pizza; seal edges. Cut four slits in top. Bake at 375° for 30-35 minutes or until crust is golden brown. Spread with tomato sauce.

YIELD: 8 slices.

the **ULTIMATE COMFORT FOOD** cookbook

family-style turkey potpie

PREP: 20 min. | **BAKE:** 45 min.

- 3 cups all-purpose flour
- 1 teaspoon baking powder
- 1/2 teaspoon salt
- 1/2 cup cold butter, cubed
- 3/4 to 1 cup cold water
- 4 cups cubed cooked turkey
- 2 cups (8 ounces) shredded Monterey Jack cheese
- 1 can (10-3/4 ounces) condensed cream of chicken soup, undiluted
- 1 cup (8 ounces) sour cream
- 1 small onion, finely chopped
- 1 can (4 ounces) chopped green chilies
- 2 green onions, sliced

In a large bowl, combine the flour, baking powder and salt. Cut in butter until crumbly. Gradually add water, tossing with a fork until dough forms a ball. Turn onto a lightly floured surface; knead 10-12 times or until smooth.

Set aside a third of the dough. Roll remaining dough into a 15-in. x 11-in. rectangle. Transfer to an ungreased 11-in. x 7-in. baking dish.

In a large bowl, combine the turkey, cheese, soup, sour cream, onion, chilies and green onions. Spoon into crust. Roll out reserved dough; make a lattice crust. Place over filling; trim, seal and flute edges. Cover edges loosely with foil.

Bake at 400° for 45-50 minutes or until crust is golden brown and filling is bubbly.

YIELD: 6 servings.

karen ann bland
GOVE, KANSAS

Despite our last name, we like spicy, flavorful foods like this hearty potpie seasoned with zesty green chilies and cheese.

ham-noodle bake

PREP: 10 min. | **BAKE:** 30 min.

- 1/4 cup butter, cubed
- 1/4 cup all-purpose flour
- 1/2 teaspoon salt
- 1/8 teaspoon pepper
- 2-1/2 cups milk
- 3 to 4 teaspoons prepared horseradish
- 1 tablespoon prepared mustard
- 6 cups cooked wide egg noodles
- 2 cups cubed fully cooked ham
- 1 cup cubed cheddar cheese
- 1/2 cup soft bread crumbs, toasted

In a large saucepan over medium heat, melt butter. Stir in the flour, salt and pepper until smooth. Gradually add milk. Bring to a boil. Cook and stir for 2 minutes or until thickened and bubbly. Add horseradish and mustard; mix well. Stir in the noodles, ham and cheese.

Pour into a greased 2-1/2-qt. baking dish. Cover and bake at 350° for 20 minutes. Uncover; sprinkle with bread crumbs. Bake 10-15 minutes longer or until bubbly and heated through.

YIELD: 4-6 servings.

mary richards
ELLENDALE, MINNESOTA

My husband and I build up an appetite after a long day doing chores on the farm, and a hot, creamy casserole really hits the spot.

pam west
ERNUL, NORTH CAROLINA

My nursing career keeps me busy, so easy recipes that taste great are important to me. I came up with this one by combining items I had on hand.

chicken 'n' corn bread dressing

PREP: 15 min. | **BAKE:** 30 min.

2 celery ribs, chopped
1 large onion, chopped
1/4 cup butter, cubed
2 eggs
2 cups buttermilk
1 can (10-1/2 ounces) condensed chicken broth, undiluted
2 packages (8-3/4 ounces *each*) corn bread/muffin mix
1 can (8-1/4 ounces) cream-style corn
2 teaspoons poultry seasoning
1/2 teaspoon salt
1/2 teaspoon pepper
5 cups seasoned stuffing croutons

3 cans (5 ounces *each*) white chicken, drained
1 medium potato, peeled and diced

In a large skillet, saute celery and onion in butter until tender; set aside. In a large bowl, whisk the eggs, buttermilk and broth. Add the muffin mixes, corn, poultry seasoning, salt and pepper; mix well. Stir in the croutons, chicken, potato and celery mixture until blended.

Transfer to a greased 13-in. x 9-in. baking dish. Bake, uncovered, at 375° for 30-35 minutes or until a thermometer reads 160°.

YIELD: 10-12 servings.

taste of home test kitchen

Thyme, sage and marjoram blend beautifully with apple cider and maple syrup in this heartwarming recipe. The maple butter can be prepared 1 to 2 days in advance.

maple-butter turkey with gravy

PREP: 40 min. + chilling | **BAKE:** 3 hours + standing

2 cups apple cider *or* juice
1/3 cup maple syrup
3/4 cup butter, cubed
2 tablespoons minced fresh thyme *or* 2 teaspoons dried thyme
1 tablespoon minced fresh sage *or* 1 teaspoon dried sage leaves
2 teaspoons dried marjoram
1 teaspoon salt
1 teaspoon pepper

1 turkey (14 to 16 pounds)
2 to 2-1/2 cups chicken broth
3 tablespoons all-purpose flour

For maple butter, in a small heavy saucepan, bring cider and syrup to a boil. Cook until reduced to 1/2 cup, about 20 minutes. Remove from the heat; stir in the butter, thyme, sage, marjoram, salt and pepper. Transfer to a bowl; cover and refrigerate until set.

With fingers, carefully loosen the skin from both sides of turkey breast. Rub 1/2 cup maple butter under turkey skin. Refrigerate remaining maple butter. Skewer turkey openings; tie drumsticks together. Place on a rack in a roasting pan. Cover with foil and bake at 325° for 2 hours.

Brush the top with 1/3 cup maple butter. Bake turkey, uncovered, 1 to 1-1/2 hours longer or until a thermometer reads 180°, basting occasionally with pan drippings. (Cover loosely with foil if turkey browns too quickly.) Remove turkey to a serving platter and keep warm. Cover and let stand for 20 minutes before carving.

Pour drippings and loosened brown bits into a 4-cup measuring cup. Skim and discard fat. Add enough broth to drippings to measure 3 cups. In a large saucepan, combine flour and broth mixture until smooth. Stir in remaining maple butter. Bring to a boil; cook and stir for 2 minutes or until thickened. Serve with turkey.

YIELD: 14-16 servings (3-1/3 cups gravy).

chicken lasagna rolls

PREP: 20 min. | **BAKE:** 45 min.

1 small onion, chopped

3 tablespoons butter

3 tablespoons all-purpose flour

1 can (14-1/2 ounces) chicken broth

1 cup milk

1-1/2 cups (6 ounces) shredded Monterey Jack cheese

3 cups diced cooked chicken

6 cups frozen chopped broccoli, thawed and drained

2 eggs, lightly beaten

3/4 cup dry bread crumbs

1 jar (6-1/2 ounces) diced pimientos, drained

1/4 cup minced fresh parsley

1/2 teaspoon salt, optional

12 lasagna noodles, cooked and drained

In a large saucepan, saute onion in butter until tender. Stir in flour until blended. Gradually add broth and milk. Bring to a boil; cook and stir for 2 minutes or until thickened. Remove from the heat; stir in cheese. Pour 1/3 cup each into two greased 8-in. square baking dishes; set aside.

In a large bowl, combine 1 cup cheese sauce, chicken, broccoli, eggs, bread crumbs, pimientos, parsley and salt if desired. Spread about 1/2 cup over each noodle. Roll up jelly-roll style, beginning with a short side; secure ends with toothpicks. Place in baking dishes. Top with remaining cheese sauce.

Cover and freeze one casserole for up to 3 months. Cover and bake second casserole at 350° for 40 minutes or until a thermometer reads 160°. Uncover; bake 5 minutes longer or until bubbly. Discard toothpicks.

TO USE FROZEN CASSEROLE: Thaw in the refrigerator for 8 hours or overnight. Bake roll-ups as directed.

YIELD: 2 casseroles (3 servings each).

darlene brenden
SALEM, OREGON

I roll a cheesy mixture of chicken and broccoli into lasagna noodles, making enough for two dinners. It's nice to have a pan of these roll-ups in the freezer for unexpected company.

LASAGNA NOODLE SOUP

Whenever I have lasagna noodles left in the box, I use them in homemade soup. I break them into small pieces since they will expand a fair amount during cooking.
—SANDY J.
CHETEK, WISCONSIN

pat habiger
SPEARVILLE, KANSAS

This golden casserole with fluffy dumplings is a favorite of our field hands when I take it out to serve them during harvest. It really satisfies.

swiss steak with dumplings

PREP: 25 min. | **BAKE:** 70 min.

2 pounds beef top round steak
1/3 cup all-purpose flour
2 tablespoons canola oil
2 cans (10-3/4 ounces *each*) condensed cream of chicken soup, undiluted
1-1/3 cups water
1/2 teaspoon salt
1/8 teaspoon pepper

DUMPLINGS:

1/2 cup dry bread crumbs
5 tablespoons butter, melted, *divided*
1-1/3 cups all-purpose flour
2 teaspoons baking powder
1/2 teaspoon salt
1/4 teaspoon poultry seasoning
2/3 cup milk

Cut steaks into six or eight pieces. Place flour in a large resealable bag. Add beef, a few pieces at a time, and shake to coat. In a large skillet, brown meat in oil on both sides. Transfer to a greased 2-1/2-qt. baking dish.

In the same skillet, combine the soup, water, salt and pepper; bring to a boil, stirring occasionally. Pour over steak. Cover and bake at 350° for 50-60 minutes or until meat is tender.

For dumplings, combine bread crumbs and 2 tablespoons butter in a small bowl; set aside. In another bowl, combine the flour, baking powder, salt and poultry seasoning. Stir in milk and remaining butter just until moistened.

Drop by rounded tablespoonfuls into the crumb mixture; roll until coated. Place dumplings over steak. Bake, uncovered, at 425° for 20-30 minutes or until dumplings are lightly browned and a toothpick inserted near the center comes out clean.

YIELD: 6-8 servings.

holiday corn 'n' turkey casserole

PREP: 20 min. | **BAKE:** 25 min.

1 small onion, finely chopped
1/4 cup butter, cubed
1/4 cup all-purpose flour
3/4 teaspoon salt
1/2 teaspoon ground mustard
1/2 teaspoon pepper
3/4 cup milk
2 cups frozen corn, thawed
1 package (9 ounces) frozen broccoli cuts, thawed and chopped
2 cups cubed cooked turkey
1 cup (4 ounces) shredded cheddar cheese
2 eggs, lightly beaten
1/3 cup sliced almonds

In a large saucepan, saute onion in butter until tender. Combine the flour, salt, mustard and pepper; stir into onion mixture until blended. Gradually add milk. Bring to a boil over medium heat. Cook and stir for 2 minutes or until thickened. Remove from the heat.

In a large bowl, combine the corn, broccoli, turkey and cheese. Whisk eggs into onion mixture. Pour over turkey mixture; stir until combined.

Transfer to a greased 1-1/2-qt. baking dish. Sprinkle with almonds. Bake, uncovered, at 350° for 25-30 minutes or until a thermometer reads 160°.

YIELD: 8 servings.

edie despain
LOGAN, UTAH

My family looks forward to the tasty, nutritious casserole I make using leftover holiday turkey each year. I like how quickly it comes together.

citrus-baked cornish hens

PREP: 10 min. | **BAKE:** 1-1/4 hours

4 Cornish game hens (20 to 24 ounces each)
SAUCE:
1/4 cup apricot preserves
2 tablespoons grated onion
1 tablespoon butter
1 tablespoon Dijon mustard
1 garlic clove, minced
Juice and grated peel of 1 lemon
Juice and grated peel of 1 orange

Tie legs of hens together; turn wing tips under backs. In a small saucepan, combine all the sauce ingredients. Simmer 5 minutes. Spoon half of the sauce over hens.

Place hens breast side up on a rack in a large roasting pan. Bake at 350° for about 1-1/4 hours or until meat juices run clear, brushing occasionally with remaining sauce.

YIELD: 4 servings.

mary-lynne mason
JANESVILLE, WISCONSIN

Here's a sensational entree that's worthy of a special occasion. The mustard and citrus provide a double zing of sumptuous flavor.

terri keenan
TUSCALOOSA, ALABAMA

If you like foods with Southwestern flair, taco lasagna just might become a new favorite. There are never any leftovers when I take it to potlucks.

taco lasagna

PREP: 20 min. | **BAKE:** 25 min.

1 pound ground beef
1/2 cup chopped green pepper
1/2 cup chopped onion
2/3 cup water
1 envelope taco seasoning
1 can (15 ounces) black beans, rinsed and drained
1 can (14-1/2 ounces) Mexican diced tomatoes, undrained
6 flour tortillas (8 inches)
1 can (16 ounces) refried beans
3 cups (12 ounces) shredded Mexican cheese blend

In a large skillet, cook the beef, green pepper and onion over medium heat until meat is no longer pink; drain. Add water and taco seasoning; bring to a boil. Reduce heat; simmer, uncovered, for 2 minutes. Stir in black beans and tomatoes. Simmer, uncovered, for 10 minutes.

Place two tortillas in a greased 13-in. x 9-in. baking dish. Spread with half of the refried beans and the beef mixture; sprinkle with 1 cup cheese. Repeat layers. Top with the remaining tortillas and cheese.

Cover and bake at 350° for 25-30 minutes or until heated through and cheese is melted.

YIELD: 9 servings.

marva vandivier
BATTLE GROUND, WASHINGTON

I actually created this recipe when I was a girl. Since then, I've found it's a good way to use up the second pastry when I make a one-crust pie. When I tell my husband, "It's chicken potpie tonight," he lights up and thinks I've worked in the kitchen all day!

chicken vegetable potpie

PREP: 20 min. | **BAKE:** 50 min.

2 medium carrots, sliced
1 medium potato, peeled and cubed
1 small onion, chopped
1 celery rib, chopped
1 can (10-3/4 ounces) condensed cream of chicken soup, undiluted
1 cup cubed cooked chicken
1/2 cup frozen peas, thawed
Pastry for single-crust pie (9 inches)

Place the carrots, potato, onion and celery in a large saucepan and cover with water. Reduce heat; cover and cook for 15-20 minutes or until tender. Drain. Stir in soup and chicken. Gently stir in peas.

Pour into a greased 1-1/2-qt. deep baking dish. Roll out pastry to fit top of dish; place over filling. Trim, seal and flute edges. Cut slits in pastry.

Bake at 350° for 50 minutes or until crust is golden and filling is bubbly.

YIELD: 2 servings.

roasted chicken with sausage stuffing

PREP: 20 min. | **BAKE:** 2-1/2 hours

julie ann schmidt
AURORA, ILLINOIS

Looking for an attractive main dish with down-home country flavor? Friends and family will be thrilled when you put this impressive chicken on the table.

- 1/2 pound bulk pork sausage
- 1/2 cup chopped onion
- 1/2 cup chopped celery
- 1/2 cup diced sweet red pepper
- 1 tablespoon butter
- 5 cups unseasoned stuffing croutons
- 1/4 cup minced fresh parsley
- 1-1/2 teaspoons minced fresh tarragon *or* 1/2 teaspoon dried tarragon
- 1 teaspoon poultry seasoning
- 1/2 teaspoon salt
- 1/4 teaspoon pepper
- 1-1/2 to 2 cups chicken broth, *divided*
- 1 roasting chicken (6 to 7 pounds)

In a large skillet, cook the sausage, onion, celery and red pepper in butter until sausage is no longer pink and vegetables are crisp-tender; do not drain.

Place croutons in a large bowl; add sausage mixture. Stir in the parsley, tarragon, poultry seasoning, salt and pepper. Stir in enough broth until stuffing is moistened and holds together.

Just before baking, loosely stuff chicken. Place with breast side up on a rack in a shallow roasting pan. Pour 1/2 cup broth around chicken.

Bake, uncovered, at 325° for 2-1/2 to 3 hours or until a thermometer reads 180° for chicken and 165° for stuffing, basting occasionally with pan juices.

YIELD: 6 servings.

jackie smulski
LYONS, ILLINOIS

Turn to this recipe when you want a tuna casserole that's a bit different—the horseradish adds a little kick of unexpected flavor.

tuna 'n' pea casserole

PREP: 20 min. | **BAKE:** 40 min.

8 ounces uncooked egg noodles

2 cans (10-3/4 ounces *each*) condensed cream of mushroom soup, undiluted

1/2 cup mayonnaise

1/2 cup 2% milk

2 to 3 teaspoons prepared horseradish

1/2 teaspoon dill weed

1/8 teaspoon pepper

1 cup frozen peas, thawed

1 can (4 ounces) mushroom stems and pieces, drained

1 small onion, chopped

1 jar (2 ounces) diced pimientos, drained

2 cans (6 ounces *each*) tuna, drained and flaked

1/4 cup dry bread crumbs

1 tablespoon butter, melted

Cook noodles according to package directions. Meanwhile, in a large bowl, combine the soup, mayonnaise, milk, horseradish, dill and pepper. Stir in the peas, mushrooms, onion, pimientos and tuna.

Drain noodles; stir into soup mixture. Transfer to a greased 2-qt. baking dish. Toss bread crumbs and butter; sprinkle over the top.

Bake, uncovered, at 375° for 40-45 minutes or until bubbly.

YIELD: 6 servings.

cordon bleu casserole

PREP: 25 min. | BAKE: 25 min.

- 2 cups cubed fully cooked ham
- 4 cups cubed cooked turkey
- 1 cup (4 ounces) shredded Swiss cheese
- 1 large onion, chopped
- 1/3 cup butter, cubed
- 1/3 cup all-purpose flour
- 1/8 teaspoon ground mustard
- 1/8 teaspoon ground nutmeg
- 1-3/4 cups milk

TOPPING:

- 1-1/2 cups soft bread crumbs
- 1/2 cup shredded Swiss cheese
- 1/4 cup butter, melted

In a large nonstick skillet, cook ham for 4-5 minutes or until browned; drain and pat dry. In a greased 2-qt. baking dish, layer the turkey, cheese and ham; set aside.

In a large saucepan, saute onion in butter until tender. Stir in the flour, mustard and nutmeg until blended. Gradually stir in milk. Bring to a boil; cook and stir for 2 minutes or until thickened. Pour over the ham.

Combine topping ingredients; sprinkle over the top. Bake, uncovered, at 350° for 25-30 minutes or until golden brown and bubbly.

YIELD: 6 servings.

joyce paul
QU'APPELLE, SASKATCHEWAN

I often roast a turkey just to have leftovers for this creamy casserole. It makes for a pretty presentation at potluck dinners.

homemade fish sticks

PREP/TOTAL TIME: 25 min.

- 1/2 cup all-purpose flour
- 1 egg, beaten
- 1/2 cup dry bread crumbs
- 1/2 teaspoon salt
- 1/2 teaspoon paprika
- 1/2 teaspoon lemon-pepper seasoning
- 3/4 pound cod fillets, cut into 1-inch strips
- Butter-flavored cooking spray

Place flour and egg in separate shallow bowls. In another shallow bowl, combine bread crumbs and seasonings. Dip fish in the flour, then egg, then roll in the crumb mixture.

Place on a baking sheet coated with cooking spray. Spritz fish sticks with butter-flavored spray. Bake at 400° for 10-12 minutes or until fish flakes easily with a fork, turning once.

YIELD: 2 servings.

jennifer rowland
ELIZABETHTOWN, KENTUCKY

I'm a nutritionist and needed a healthy fish fix. Moist inside and crunchy outside, these are great with oven fries or roasted veggies and low-fat homemade tartar sauce.

PURCHASING FISH

When buying fresh fish fillets, look for firm flesh that has a moist look and a mild smell, not a strong odor. Packages of frozen fish should be solidly frozen, tightly sealed and free of freezer burn and odor.

rita reinke
WAUWATOSA, WISCONSIN

I found this recipe in a cookbook for diabetics. My family really enjoys the honey flavor. The sweetness comes through when I use the leftovers in casseroles and soups, too.

honey-apple turkey breast

PREP: 10 min. | BAKE: 2 hours + standing

> 3/4 cup thawed apple juice concentrate
> 1/3 cup honey
> 1 tablespoon ground mustard
> 1 bone-in turkey breast (6 to 7 pounds)

In a small saucepan, combine the apple juice concentrate, honey and mustard. Cook over low heat for 2-3 minutes or just until blended, stirring occasionally.

Place turkey breast on a rack in a foil-lined shallow roasting pan; pour honey mixture over the top.

Bake, uncovered, at 325° for 2 to 2-1/2 hours or until a thermometer reads 170°, basting with pan juices every 30 minutes. (Cover loosely with foil if turkey browns too quickly.) Cover and let stand for 15 minutes before carving.

YIELD: 12-14 servings.

margaret allen
ABINGDON, VIRGINIA

Here's a one-dish meal that pleases the meat-and-potato lovers in my family. I appreciate that they're also getting their veggies.

herbed shepherd's pie

PREP: 45 min. | BAKE: 10 min.

> 1 pound ground beef
> 1 can (14-1/2 ounces) beef broth, *divided*
> 3 to 4 bay leaves
> 2 whole cloves
> 1/2 teaspoon pepper
> 1/8 teaspoon dried thyme
> 1 pound potatoes, peeled and cubed
> 1/4 to 1/2 cup milk
> 2 tablespoons butter
> 1 tablespoon minced chives
> 1 teaspoon salt, *divided*

> 1 cup (4 ounces) shredded part-skim mozzarella cheese
> 2 medium onions, sliced
> 2 celery ribs, diced
> 1 large carrot, sliced
> 1 cup frozen corn, thawed
> 2 tablespoons all-purpose flour

In a large skillet, cook beef over medium heat until no longer pink; drain. Stir in 1 cup broth, bay leaves, cloves, pepper and thyme. Bring to a boil. Reduce heat; cover and simmer for 30 minutes.

Meanwhile, place potatoes in a large saucepan; cover with water. Bring to a boil. Reduce heat. Cover; cook 15-20 minutes or until tender. Drain. Mash potatoes with milk, butter, chives and 1/2 teaspoon salt. Stir in cheese; keep warm.

Add vegetables and remaining salt to the beef mixture. Cover and simmer for 10 minutes. In a small bowl, whisk flour and remaining broth until smooth. Gradually stir into beef mixture. Bring to a boil; cook and stir for 1-2 minutes or until thickened. Remove from the heat. Discard bay leaves and cloves.

Transfer beef mixture to a greased 11-in. x 7-in. baking dish. Top with mashed potatoes. Bake, uncovered, at 375° for 10 minutes or until heated through.

YIELD: 4-6 servings.

french onion pizza au gratin

PREP: 30 min. | **BAKE:** 10 min.

- 1 large onion, sliced
- 2 tablespoons brown sugar
- 2 tablespoons olive oil, *divided*
- 3 tablespoons balsamic vinegar
- 3 garlic cloves, minced
- 1 tablespoon bourbon, optional
- 1 cup sliced fresh mushrooms
- 1/4 pound thickly sliced deli roast beef, coarsely chopped
- 1 prebaked 12-inch pizza crust
- 3/4 cup French onion dip
- 3/4 cup shredded part-skim mozzarella cheese
- 1 medium sweet red pepper, chopped
- 3/4 cup shredded Gruyere *or* Swiss cheese
- 1 teaspoon minced fresh rosemary

In a large skillet, saute the onion with brown sugar in 1 tablespoon oil until softened. Reduce the heat to medium-low; cook, stirring occasionally, for 30 minutes or until deep golden brown. Stir in the vinegar and garlic. Remove from the heat; add bourbon if desired. Continue cooking until liquid is nearly evaporated.

In another skillet, saute mushrooms in remaining oil until tender; add roast beef and heat through.

Place crust on a pizza pan; spread with French onion dip. Layer with mozzarella cheese, onion mixture, red pepper, mushroom mixture and Gruyere cheese.

Bake at 425° for 10-15 minutes or until cheese is melted. Sprinkle with rosemary.

YIELD: 8 slices.

bonnie long
LAKEWOOD, OHIO

I love a hot bowl of French onion soup and am also a big fan of pizza. I combined the two classics into an unforgettable dinner!

linda foreman
LOCUST GROVE, OKLAHOMA

Champagne, brown sugar and honey make a beautiful glaze for ham that is worthy of any celebration.

champagne baked ham

PREP: 10 min. | **BAKE:** 3 hours + standing

1 boneless fully cooked ham (9 pounds)
1-1/2 cups Champagne
3/4 cup packed brown sugar
4-1/2 teaspoons honey
3/4 teaspoon ground ginger
3/4 teaspoon ground mustard

Place ham on a rack in a shallow roasting pan. Score the surface of the ham, making diamond shapes 1/2 in. deep. Bake, uncovered, at 325° for 2-1/2 hours.

Meanwhile, in a small saucepan, combine the remaining ingredients. Bring to a boil; cook until glaze is reduced by half. Remove from the heat.

Baste ham with glaze; bake 30 minutes longer or until a thermometer reads 140°, basting twice with glaze. Let stand for 10 minutes before slicing. Serve with remaining glaze.

YIELD: 18 servings.

best chicken 'n' biscuits

PREP/TOTAL TIME: 30 min.

6 individually frozen biscuits

1 can (49-1/2 ounces) chicken broth, *divided*

1-1/2 pounds boneless skinless chicken breasts, cubed

5 medium carrots, coarsely chopped

2 celery ribs, chopped

1/2 cup chopped onion

1/2 cup frozen corn

3 teaspoons dried basil

1/4 teaspoon pepper

1 cup all-purpose flour

3/4 teaspoon browning sauce, optional

Bake biscuits according to package directions. Meanwhile, in a Dutch oven, combine 4 cups broth, chicken, carrots, celery, onion, corn, basil and pepper.

Bring to a boil. Reduce heat; cover and simmer for 7-10 minutes or until vegetables are tender.

In a small bowl, combine flour and remaining broth until smooth. Stir into chicken mixture. Bring to a boil; cook and stir for 2 minutes or until thickened. Stir in browning sauce if desired. Split biscuits; top with chicken mixture.

YIELD: 6 servings.

judith whitford
EAST AURORA, NEW YORK

Quick and comforting, here is an oven-fresh dish that's filled with chicken, colorful veggies and spoonfuls of creamy flavor. It's guaranteed to warm your family to their toes!

---

roasted chicken with rosemary

PREP: 20 min. | **BAKE:** 2 hours + standing

1/2 cup butter, cubed

4 tablespoons minced fresh rosemary *or* 2 tablespoons dried rosemary, crushed

2 tablespoons minced fresh parsley

3 garlic cloves, minced

1 teaspoon salt

1/2 teaspoon pepper

1 whole roasting chicken (5 to 6 pounds)

6 small red potatoes, halved

6 medium carrots, halved lengthwise and cut into 2-inch pieces

2 medium onions, quartered

In a small saucepan, melt butter; stir in the seasonings. Place chicken breast side up on a rack in a shallow roasting pan; tie drumsticks together with kitchen string. Spoon half of the butter mixture over chicken. Place the potatoes, carrots and onions around chicken. Drizzle remaining butter mixture over vegetables.

Cover and bake at 350° for 1-1/2 hours, basting chicken every 30 minutes. Uncover; bake 30-60 minutes longer or until a thermometer reads 180°, basting occasionally.

Cover with foil and let stand for 10-15 minutes before carving. Serve with vegetables.

YIELD: 9 servings.

isabel zienkosky
SALT LAKE CITY, UTAH

Herbs, garlic and butter give this hearty meal-in-one a classic flavor. It's a lot like pot roast, only it uses chicken instead of beef.

sylvia dirks
CLEARBROOK,
BRITISH COLUMBIA

With two small children, I appreciate meals that can be easily assembled and put into the oven. I always keep the ingredients for Chicken Parmesan on hand.

BUTTERMILK SUBSTITUTE

For each cup of buttermilk called for in the recipe, you can substitute 1 tablespoon of white vinegar or lemon juice plus enough milk to measure 1 cup. Stir, then let stand for 5 minutes before using.

audrey thibodeau
GILBERT, ARIZONA

What a great way to use up leftover turkey! This casserole bakes up delicious and bubbly for a wonderful main course.

chicken parmesan

PREP: 10 min. | BAKE: 1 hour

3/4 cup grated Parmesan cheese
3/4 cup toasted wheat germ
1-1/4 teaspoons salt
1/2 teaspoon *each* garlic powder, onion powder and dried oregano
1/2 teaspoon dried rosemary, crushed
1/4 teaspoon pepper
1 broiler/fryer chicken (3-1/2 to 4 pounds), cut up
1 cup buttermilk

In a large resealable plastic bag, combine the cheese, wheat germ and seasonings. Dip chicken pieces in buttermilk, then add to bag, a few pieces at a time, and shake to coat.

Place in a greased 13-in. x 9-in. baking dish. Bake, uncovered, at 350° for 1 hour or until chicken juices run clear.

YIELD: 4 servings.

turkey tetrazzini

PREP: 15 min. | BAKE: 50 min.

1 package (1 pound) linguine
6 tablespoons butter
6 tablespoons all-purpose flour
1/2 teaspoon salt
1/4 teaspoon pepper
1/8 teaspoon cayenne pepper
3 cups chicken broth

1 cup heavy whipping cream
4 cups cubed cooked turkey
1 cup sliced fresh mushrooms
1 jar (4 ounces) diced pimientos, drained
1/4 cup chopped fresh parsley
4 to 5 drops hot pepper sauce
1/3 cup grated Parmesan cheese

Cook pasta according to package directions. In a large saucepan, melt butter over medium heat. Stir in the flour, salt, pepper and cayenne until smooth. Gradually add broth. Bring to a boil; cook and stir for 2 minutes or until thickened. Remove from the heat; stir in cream.

Drain linguine; add 2 cups sauce and toss to coat. Transfer to a greased 13-in. x 9-in. baking dish. Make a well in center of pasta, making a space about 6 in. x 4 in.

To the remaining sauce, add the turkey, mushrooms, pimientos, parsley and pepper sauce; mix well. Pour into the center of the dish. Sprinkle with the cheese.

Cover and bake at 350° for 30 minutes. Uncover; bake 20-30 minutes longer or until bubbly and heated through.

YIELD: 8-10 servings.

roadside diner cheeseburger quiche

PREP: 20 min. | BAKE: 50 min. + standing

- 1 sheet refrigerated pie pastry
- 3/4 pound ground beef
- 2 plum tomatoes, seeded and chopped
- 1 medium onion, chopped
- 1/2 cup dill pickle relish
- 1/2 cup crumbled cooked bacon
- 5 eggs
- 1 cup heavy whipping cream
- 1/2 cup 2% milk
- 2 teaspoons prepared mustard
- 1 teaspoon hot pepper sauce
- 1/2 teaspoon salt
- 1/4 teaspoon pepper
- 1-1/2 cups (6 ounces) shredded cheddar cheese
- 1/2 cup shredded Parmesan cheese
- Optional garnishes: mayonnaise, additional pickle relish, crumbled cooked bacon, and chopped onion and tomato

Unroll pastry into a 9-in. deep-dish pie plate; flute edges and set aside. In a large skillet, cook beef over medium heat until no longer pink; drain. Stir in the tomatoes, onion, relish and bacon. Transfer to prepared pastry.

In a large bowl, whisk the eggs, cream, milk, mustard, pepper sauce, salt and pepper. Pour over beef mixture. Sprinkle with cheeses.

Bake at 375° for 50-60 minutes or until a knife inserted near the center comes out clean. Cover edges with foil during the last 15 minutes to prevent overbrowning if necessary.

Let stand for 10 minutes before cutting. Garnish with optional ingredients if desired.

YIELD: 8 servings.

good

barbie miller
OAKDALE, MINNESOTA

Here is an unforgettable quiche that tastes just like its burger counterpart. Easy and appealing, it's perfect for guests and fun for the whole family.

jenny staniec
OAK GROVE, MINNESOTA

What could be better than pizza and mac 'n' cheese combined into one meal? Kids will love it! To make it super-easy, use a can of pizza sauce instead of mixing the tomato sauce, oregano and basil.

macaroni & cheese pizza

PREP: 25 min. | **BAKE:** 10 min.

- 1 package (7-1/4 ounces) macaroni and cheese dinner mix
- 2 eggs, lightly beaten
- 1/2 pound bulk Italian sausage
- 1/4 cup chopped onion
- 1 can (8 ounces) tomato sauce
- 1 teaspoon dried basil
- 1 teaspoon dried oregano
- 1 can (4 ounces) mushroom stems and pieces, drained
- 1 cup (4 ounces) shredded part-skim mozzarella cheese

Prepare macaroni and cheese according to package directions; stir in eggs. Spread onto a greased 12-in. pizza pan. Bake at 375° for 10 minutes or until a thermometer reads 160°.

Meanwhile, in a large skillet, cook sausage and onion over medium heat until meat is no longer pink; drain.

In a small bowl, combine the tomato sauce, basil and oregano. Spread over macaroni mixture. Layer with sausage mixture, mushrooms and cheese. Bake for 10 minutes or until cheese is melted.

YIELD: 8 servings.

turkey biscuit bake

PREP/TOTAL TIME: 30 min.

1 can (10-3/4 ounces) condensed cream of chicken soup, undiluted
1 cup diced cooked turkey *or* chicken
1 can (4 ounces) mushroom stems and pieces, drained
1/2 cup frozen peas
1/4 cup milk
Dash *each* ground cumin, dried basil and thyme
1 tube (12 ounces) refrigerated biscuits

In a large bowl, combine soup, turkey, mushrooms, peas, milk, cumin, basil and thyme. Pour into a greased 8-in. square baking dish. Arrange biscuits over the top.

Bake, uncovered, at 350° for 20-25 minutes or until biscuits are golden brown.

YIELD: 5 servings.

andy zinkle
MT. PLEASANT, IOWA

As a college student, I appreciate stick-to-your-ribs foods that are also easy on the budget. I often make a double batch so that I have plenty of leftovers.

sausage-corn bake

PREP: 20 min. | **BAKE:** 30 min.

1-1/2 pounds bulk pork sausage
1 medium green pepper, chopped
1 medium onion, chopped
4 tablespoons butter, *divided*
3 tablespoons all-purpose flour
1/2 teaspoon salt
1/2 teaspoon white pepper
1-1/2 cups milk
1 can (14-3/4 ounces) cream-style corn
3-1/2 cups (10 ounces) egg noodles, cooked and drained
1/4 cup shredded cheddar cheese
1/2 cup dry bread crumbs

In a large skillet, cook the sausage, green pepper and onion over medium heat until sausage is no longer pink; drain and set aside.

In a large saucepan, melt 3 tablespoons butter over medium heat. Stir in the flour, salt and pepper. Gradually add milk. Bring to a boil; cook and stir for 2 minutes or until thickened. Stir in corn. Add noodles and corn mixture to the sausage mixture. Fold in the cheese.

Transfer to a greased 13-in. x 9-in. baking dish. Melt remaining butter; stir in bread crumbs. Sprinkle over casserole. Bake, uncovered, at 325° for 30-40 minutes or until heated through.

YIELD: 6-8 servings.

bernice morris
MARSHFIELD, MISSOURI

This is true comfort food: creamy and loaded with noodles and pork sausage. It smells fantastic while it bakes.

ellen benninger
GREENVILLE, PENNSYLVANIA

Tender ham balls smothered in a delicious brown sugar sauce are hard to resist. Here's a marvelous way to use up leftover Easter ham.

HOT HAM SALAD

I mix ground leftover ham with chopped olives and green pepper, shredded cheddar cheese, Dijon mustard and mayonnaise. Stuffed into hard rolls and warmed in the oven, these are tasty sandwiches.
—MARION S.
JOSEPH, OREGON

rhonda hampton
COOKEVILLE, TENNESSEE

My family loves garlic...the more the better. Ever since I came up with this recipe, they've been requesting it often for Sunday dinner.

ham balls

PREP: 20 min. | **BAKE:** 1 hour

2 eggs
3/4 cup milk
2/3 cup crushed bite-sized Shredded Wheat
1 pound ground fully cooked ham
1 pound ground pork
SAUCE:
1-1/2 cups packed brown sugar
2/3 cup water
1/3 cup white vinegar
3/4 teaspoon ground mustard

In a large bowl, combine the eggs, milk and cereal; crumble ham and pork over mixture and mix well. Shape into 1-1/2-in. to 2-in. balls; place in a greased 13-in. x 9-in. baking dish.

In a large saucepan, combine sauce ingredients; bring to a boil over medium heat. Reduce heat; simmer, uncovered, for 4 minutes. Pour over ham balls. Bake, uncovered, at 350° for 60-70 minutes or until a thermometer reads 160°.

YIELD: 8 servings.

garlic pot roast

PREP: 20 min. | **BAKE:** 2-1/2 hours

1 boneless beef chuck roast (3 pounds)
4 garlic cloves, peeled and halved
3 teaspoons garlic powder
3 teaspoons Italian salad dressing mix
1/2 teaspoon pepper
1 tablespoon canola oil
3 cups water
1 envelope onion soup mix
1 teaspoon reduced-sodium beef bouillon granules
5 medium potatoes, peeled and quartered
1 pound fresh baby carrots
1 large onion, cut into 1-inch pieces

Using the point of a sharp knife, make eight slits in the roast. Insert garlic into slits. Combine the garlic powder, salad dressing mix and pepper; rub over roast. In a Dutch oven, brown roast in oil on all sides; drain if necessary.

Combine the water, onion soup mix and bouillon; pour over the roast. Cover and bake at 325° for 1-1/2 hours.

Add the potatoes, carrots and onion. Cover and bake 1 hour longer or until meat and vegetables are tender. Thicken pan juices if desired.

YIELD: 8 servings.

turkey potpies *really good*

PREP: 30 min. | **BAKE:** 20 min.

1 small onion, chopped
1 medium carrot, chopped
1/2 cup diced peeled potato
1/4 cup chopped celery
1/4 cup butter, cubed
1/3 cup all-purpose flour
1/2 teaspoon salt
1/2 teaspoon dried parsley flakes
1/4 teaspoon dried rosemary, crushed
1/4 teaspoon rubbed sage
1/4 teaspoon pepper
1 cup 2% milk
1 cup chicken broth
2 cups cubed cooked turkey
1/2 cup frozen peas
1 sheet refrigerated pie pastry

In a large saucepan, saute the onion, carrot, potato and celery in butter until tender. Add the flour and seasonings until blended; gradually add milk and broth. Bring to a boil; cook and stir for 2 minutes or until thickened. Stir in turkey and peas; divide mixture among four ungreased 5-in. pie plates.

Divide pastry into quarters. On a lightly floured surface, roll each quarter into a 6-in. circle; place over filling. Trim, seal and flute edges; cut slits to vent.

Cover and freeze two potpies for up to 3 months. Bake the remaining potpies at 375° for 18-22 minutes or until golden brown. Let stand for 10 minutes before serving.

TO USE FROZEN POTPIES: Remove from the freezer 30 minutes before baking. Cover edges of crusts loosely with foil; place on a baking sheet. Bake at 375° for 30 minutes. Remove foil; bake 15-20 minutes longer or until golden brown and the filling is bubbly.

YIELD: 4 servings.

taste of home test kitchen

Some days, comfort-food cravings don't jive with busy schedules. The solution: whip up a batch of these rich and creamy potpies. Enjoy two tonight and tuck the other two in the freezer for another time. When your busy night hits, you'll have a home-cooked meal on hand that's loaded with comfort and classic taste.

delma snyder

MCCOOK, NEBRASKA

My sister served tortilla pie at the hunting and fishing lodge she used to operate in Colorado. It was a sure bet to win compliments from the men who came in cold and hungry after spending the day tramping through the woods.

layered tortilla pie

PREP: 20 min. | **BAKE:** 20 min.

- 1 pound ground beef
- 1 medium onion, chopped
- 1 can (8 ounces) tomato sauce
- 1 garlic clove, minced
- 1 tablespoon chili powder
- 1/2 teaspoon salt
- 1/4 teaspoon pepper
- 1 can (2-1/4 ounces) sliced ripe olives, drained, optional
- 1 tablespoon butter
- 6 corn tortillas (6 inches)
- 2 cups (8 ounces) shredded cheddar cheese
- 1/4 cup water

In a large skillet, cook beef and onion until meat is no longer pink; drain. Add the tomato sauce, garlic, chili powder, salt, pepper and olives if desired. Bring to a boil. Reduce heat; simmer for 5 minutes or until mixture is thickened.

Lightly butter tortillas on one side; place one tortilla, buttered side down, in a 2-qt. round casserole. Top with about 1/2 cup meat mixture and 1/3 cup cheese. Repeat layers, ending with cheese.

Pour water around the sides of casserole (not over top). Cover and bake at 400° for 20 minutes or until heated through. Let stand for 5 minutes before cutting.

YIELD: 4-6 servings.

lasagna casserole

PREP: 15 min. | **BAKE:** 1 hour + standing

- 1 pound ground beef
- 1/4 cup chopped onion
- 1/2 teaspoon salt
- 1/2 teaspoon pepper, *divided*
- 1 pound medium pasta shells, cooked and drained
- 4 cups (24 ounces) shredded part-skim mozzarella cheese, *divided*
- 3 cups (24 ounces) 4% cottage cheese
- 2 eggs, lightly beaten
- 1/3 cup grated Parmesan cheese
- 2 tablespoons dried parsley flakes
- 1 jar (26 ounces) meatless spaghetti sauce

In a large skillet, cook beef and onion over medium heat until meat is no longer pink; drain. Sprinkle with salt and 1/4 teaspoon pepper; set aside.

In a large bowl, combine the pasta, 3 cups mozzarella cheese, cottage cheese, eggs, Parmesan cheese, parsley and remaining pepper. Transfer to a greased shallow 3-qt. baking dish. Top with beef mixture and spaghetti sauce (dish will be full).

Cover and bake at 350° for 45 minutes. Sprinkle with remaining mozzarella cheese. Bake, uncovered, for 15 minutes longer or until bubbly and cheese is melted. Let stand for 10 minutes before serving.

YIELD: 6-8 servings.

deb morrison
SKIATOOK, OKLAHOMA

Growing up, this was the meal I always wanted on my birthday. Mother made the sauce from scratch, but I use store-bought spaghetti sauce to save time. Replace the ground beef with Italian sausage for more spice.

chicken noodle casserole

PREP: 15 min. | **BAKE:** 40 min.

- 1 can (10-3/4 ounces) condensed cream of chicken soup, undiluted
- 1/2 cup mayonnaise
- 2 tablespoons lemon juice
- 2 cups cubed cooked chicken
- 1 small onion, chopped
- 1/4 cup chopped green pepper
- 1/4 cup chopped sweet red pepper
- 1 cup (4 ounces) shredded Monterey Jack cheese, *divided*
- 1 cup (4 ounces) shredded sharp cheddar cheese, *divided*
- 12 ounces egg noodles, cooked and drained

In a large bowl, combine the soup, mayonnaise and lemon juice. Stir in the chicken, onion, peppers, 1/2 cup Monterey Jack cheese and 1/2 cup cheddar cheese. Add noodles and toss to coat.

Transfer to a greased 2-qt. baking dish. Bake, uncovered, at 350° for 30-35 minutes. Sprinkle with remaining cheeses. Bake 10 minutes longer or until vegetables are tender and cheese is melted.

YIELD: 6 servings.

kay pederson
YELLVILLE, ARKANSAS

Everyone who tries my casserole asks for the recipe. It's actually so simple to make that sometimes I feel like I'm cheating.

jerri moror
RIO RANCHO, NEW MEXICO

My mother frequently made Chicken Tortilla Bake when I was growing up. The corn tortillas, cheddar cheese and zesty green chilies are a classic, comforting mix.

chicken tortilla bake

PREP: 20 min. | BAKE: 30 min.

3 cups shredded cooked chicken

2 cans (4 ounces *each*) chopped green chilies

1 cup chicken broth

1 can (10-3/4 ounces) condensed cream of mushroom soup, undiluted

1 can (10-3/4 ounces) condensed cream of chicken soup, undiluted

1 small onion, finely chopped

12 corn tortillas, warmed

2 cups (8 ounces) shredded cheddar cheese, *divided*

In a large bowl, combine the chicken, chilies, broth, soups and onion; set aside. Layer half of the tortillas in a greased 13-in. x 9-in. baking dish, cutting to fit pan if desired. Top with half of the chicken mixture and half of the cheese. Repeat layers.

Bake, uncovered, at 350° for 30 minutes or until heated through.

YIELD: 6-8 servings.

jone furlong
SANTA ROSA, CALIFORNIA

The first time I made this dish, my uncle asked for seconds even though tuna casseroles are not usually his favorite. The green beans add nice texture, color and flavor.

tuna mushroom casserole

PREP: 30 min. | BAKE: 25 min.

1/2 cup water

1 teaspoon chicken bouillon granules

1 package (9 ounces) frozen cut green beans

1 cup chopped onion

1 cup sliced fresh mushrooms

1/4 cup chopped celery

1 garlic clove, minced

1/2 teaspoon dill weed

1/2 teaspoon salt

1/8 teaspoon pepper

4 teaspoons cornstarch

1-1/2 cups cold milk

1/2 cup shredded Swiss cheese

1/4 cup mayonnaise

2-1/2 cups egg noodles, cooked and drained

1 can (12 ounces) light tuna in water, drained and flaked

1/3 cup dry bread crumbs

1 tablespoon butter

In a large saucepan, bring the water and bouillon to a boil; stir until bouillon is dissolved. Add the next eight ingredients; bring to a boil. Reduce heat; cover and simmer for 5 minutes or until the vegetables are tender.

In a small bowl, combine cornstarch and milk until smooth; gradually add to vegetable mixture. Bring to a boil; cook and stir for 2 minutes or until thickened. Remove from the heat; stir in cheese and mayonnaise until cheese is melted. Fold in noodles and tuna.

Pour into a greased 2-1/2-qt. baking dish. In a small skillet, brown bread crumbs in butter; sprinkle over casserole. Bake, uncovered, at 350° for 25-30 minutes or until heated through.

YIELD: 4-6 servings.

malibu chicken bundles

PREP: 25 min. | **BAKE:** 45 min.

- 4 boneless skinless chicken breast halves (4 ounces each)
- 1/2 cup honey Dijon mustard, *divided*
- 4 thin slices deli ham
- 4 slices reduced-fat Swiss cheese
- 1 can (8 ounces) unsweetened crushed pineapple, well drained
- 1-1/2 cups panko (Japanese) bread crumbs
- 1/4 teaspoon salt
- 1/4 teaspoon pepper

SAUCE:

- 1 can (10-3/4 ounces) reduced-fat reduced-sodium condensed cream of chicken soup, undiluted
- 1/4 cup reduced-fat sour cream
- 1/8 teaspoon dried tarragon

Flatten chicken breasts to 1/4-in. thickness. Spread 1 tablespoon mustard over each; layer with ham, cheese and pineapple. Fold chicken over pineapple; secure with toothpicks. Brush bundles with remaining mustard.

In a shallow bowl, combine the bread crumbs, salt and pepper. Roll bundles in bread crumb mixture; place in an 11-in. x 7-in. baking dish coated with cooking spray. Bake, uncovered, at 350° for 45-50 minutes or until a thermometer reads 170°. Discard toothpicks.

Meanwhile, in a small saucepan, combine the sauce ingredients. Cook, stirring occasionally, until heated through. Serve with chicken.

YIELD: 4 servings.

beverly norris
EVANSTON, WYOMING

These rich-tasting bundles are surprisingly light. Dijon, Swiss and ham are a delightful combination.

lauren versweyveld
DELAVAN, WISCONSIN

I switched up the ingredients in the mac 'n' cheese that my mother makes, and she agrees that my version is rich and heavenly. Just pop it in the oven and dinner will be ready shortly!

marvelous shells 'n' cheese

PREP: 25 min. | BAKE: 30 min.

1 package (16 ounces) medium pasta shells

1 package (8 ounces) process cheese (Velveeta), cubed

1/3 cup 2% milk

2 cups (16 ounces) 2% cottage cheese

1 can (10-3/4 ounces) condensed cream of onion soup, undiluted

3 cups (12 ounces) shredded Mexican cheese blend

2/3 cup dry bread crumbs

1/4 cup butter, melted

Cook pasta according to package directions. Meanwhile, in a large saucepan, combine process cheese and milk; cook and stir over low heat until melted. Remove from the heat. Stir in cottage cheese and soup.

Drain pasta and add to cheese sauce; stir until coated. Transfer to a greased 13-in. x 9-in. baking dish. Sprinkle with Mexican cheese blend. Toss bread crumbs with butter; sprinkle over the top.

Bake, uncovered, at 350° for 30-35 minutes or until heated through.

YIELD: 6 servings.

tasty onion chicken

PREP/TOTAL TIME: 30 min.

1/2 cup butter, melted
1 tablespoon Worcestershire sauce
1 teaspoon ground mustard
1 can (2.8 ounces) French-fried onions, crushed
4 boneless skinless chicken breast halves (4 ounces *each*)

In a shallow bowl, combine butter, Worcestershire sauce and mustard. Place the onions in another shallow bowl. Dip the chicken in butter mixture, then coat with onions.

Place in a greased 11-in. x 7-in. baking dish; drizzle with remaining butter mixture. Bake, uncovered, at 400° for 20-25 minutes or until a thermometer reads 170°.

YIELD: 4 servings.

jennifer hoeft
THORNDALE, TEXAS

French-fried onions are the secret to a yummy, crunchy coating that keeps this chicken juicy and tender. It's perfect served with green beans and hot buttermilk biscuits.

traditional lasagna *great*

PREP: 45 min. | **BAKE:** 50 min. + standing

9 lasagna noodles
1-1/4 pounds bulk Italian sausage
3/4 pound ground beef
1 medium onion, diced
3 garlic cloves, minced
2 cans (one 28 ounces, one 15 ounces) crushed tomatoes
2 cans (6 ounces *each*) tomato paste
2/3 cup water
2 to 3 tablespoons sugar
3 tablespoons plus 1/4 cup minced fresh parsley, *divided*
2 teaspoons dried basil
3/4 teaspoon fennel seed
3/4 teaspoon salt, *divided*
1/4 teaspoon coarsely ground pepper
1 egg, lightly beaten
1 carton (15 ounces) ricotta cheese
4 cups (16 ounces) shredded part-skim mozzarella cheese
3/4 cup grated Parmesan cheese

Cook noodles according to package directions. Meanwhile, in a large saucepan, cook the sausage, beef and onion over medium heat until meat is no longer pink. Add garlic; cook 1 minute longer. Drain.

Stir in the tomatoes, tomato paste, water, sugar, 3 tablespoons parsley, basil, fennel seed, 1/2 teaspoon salt and pepper. Bring to a boil. Reduce heat; simmer, uncovered, for 30 minutes, stirring occasionally. In a small bowl, combine the egg, ricotta, and remaining parsley and salt.

Drain noodles. Spread 2 cups meat sauce into an ungreased 13-in. x 9-in. baking dish. Layer with three noodles and a third of the ricotta mixture. Sprinkle with 1 cup mozzarella cheese and 2 tablespoons Parmesan cheese. Repeat layers twice. Top with remaining meat sauce and cheeses.

Cover and bake at 375° for 25 minutes. Uncover; bake 25 minutes longer or until bubbly and a thermometer reads 160°. Let stand for 15 minutes before cutting.

YIELD: 12 servings.

pam thompson
GIRARD, ILLINOIS

For a casual holiday meal, you can't go wrong with a rich and meaty lasagna. My sons and daughter-in-law request it for their birthdays, too.

taryn kuebelbeck
PLYMOUTH, MINNESOTA

Have a delicious steak-and-potatoes dinner tonight! Baking the round steak for an extended amount of time guarantees tender results.

ABOUT ROUND STEAK

Round steak is a less tender cut of beef that is best cooked slowly with liquid in a covered pan until tender. You can also tenderize round steak by pounding it with a meat mallet prior to cooking.

round steak with potatoes

PREP: 20 min. | **BAKE:** 2-1/2 hours

 2 pounds beef top round steak
 1 teaspoon salt
 1/2 teaspoon pepper
 2 tablespoons canola oil
 1 can (10-3/4 ounces) condensed golden mushroom soup, undiluted
 1-1/4 cups water
 1 cup chopped celery
 1 cup chopped sweet red pepper
 1/2 cup chopped onion
 1/4 teaspoon dried thyme
 12 small red potatoes

Cut steak into six pieces; sprinkle with salt and pepper. In an ovenproof Dutch oven, brown meat in oil on both sides. Stir in the soup, water, celery, red pepper, onion and thyme. Cover and bake at 350° for 1 hour.

Add potatoes; cover and bake 1-1/2 hours longer or until steak and vegetables are tender.

YIELD: 6 servings.

kathy kittell
LENEXA, KANSAS

This may not be a true Reuben, but the taste is still fantastic and it's easy to make. I like to serve this with homemade soup.

reuben crescent bake

PREP: 20 min. | **BAKE:** 15 min.

 2 tubes (8 ounces *each*) refrigerated crescent rolls
 1 pound sliced Swiss cheese, divided
 1-1/4 pounds sliced deli corned beef

 1 can (14 ounces) sauerkraut, rinsed and well drained
 2/3 cup Thousand Island salad dressing
 1 egg white, lightly beaten
 3 teaspoons caraway seeds

Unroll one tube of crescent dough into one long rectangle; seal seams and perforations. Press onto the bottom of a greased 13-in. x 9-in. baking dish. Bake at 375° for 8-10 minutes or until crust is light golden brown.

Layer with half of the cheese and all of the corned beef. Combine sauerkraut and salad dressing; spread over beef. Top with the remaining cheese slices.

On a lightly floured surface, press or roll second tube of crescent dough into a 13-in. x 9-in. rectangle, sealing seams and perforations. Place over cheese. Brush with egg white; sprinkle with caraway seeds.

Bake for 12-16 minutes or until heated through and crust is golden brown. Let stand for 5 minutes before cutting.

YIELD: 8 servings.

italian shepherd's pie

PREP: 20 min. | **BAKE:** 50 min.

- 1 unbaked pastry shell (9 inches)
- 1 pound bulk Italian sausage
- 1 cup (8 ounces) cream-style cottage cheese
- 1 egg
- 1-1/2 cups warm mashed potatoes (without added milk and butter)
- 1/4 cup sour cream
- 1/2 teaspoon dried oregano
- 1/2 to 3/4 teaspoon salt
- 1/8 teaspoon pepper
- 2 teaspoons butter, melted
- 1 cup (4 ounces) shredded cheddar cheese

Cherry tomatoes, quartered
Minced fresh parsley, optional

Line unpricked pastry shell with a double thickness of heavy-duty foil. Bake at 450° for 7 minutes. Remove from the oven and remove foil; set aside. Reduce heat to 350°.

In a large skillet, cook sausage until no longer pink; drain well on paper towels. Place cottage cheese and egg in a blender; cover and process until smooth. Transfer to a large bowl; stir in potatoes, sour cream, oregano, salt and pepper.

Place sausage in pastry shell; top with potato mixture. Drizzle with butter. Bake for 50-60 minutes or until a thermometer reads 160°. Sprinkle with cheese; let stand until melted. Garnish with tomatoes tossed with minced parsley if desired.

YIELD: 6-8 servings.

cindy gage
BLAIR, NEBRASKA

For a filling main dish that's deliciously different, give this pie a try! Shepherd's pie gets a new twist with Italian sausage and a pastry crust. My family is always glad to see me make it.

gina harris
SENECA, SOUTH CAROLINA

Here's a hearty, homey casserole that will please the whole family. You can easily substitute frozen meatballs to make it even faster.

good meatball sub casserole

PREP: 40 min. | BAKE: 30 min.

1/3 cup chopped green onions
1/4 cup seasoned bread crumbs
3 tablespoons grated Parmesan cheese
1 pound ground beef
1 loaf (1 pound) Italian bread, cut into 1-inch slices
1 package (8 ounces) cream cheese, softened
1/2 cup mayonnaise
1 teaspoon Italian seasoning
1/4 teaspoon pepper
2 cups (8 ounces) shredded part-skim mozzarella cheese
3-1/2 cups spaghetti sauce
1 cup water
2 garlic cloves, minced

In a large bowl, combine the onions, bread crumbs and Parmesan cheese. Crumble beef over mixture and mix well. Shape into 1-in. balls; place on a greased rack in a shallow baking pan. Bake at 400° for 15-20 minutes or until no longer pink.

Meanwhile, arrange bread in a single layer in an ungreased 13-in. x 9-in. baking dish (all of the bread might not be used). Combine the cream cheese, mayonnaise, Italian seasoning and pepper; spread over the bread. Sprinkle with 1/2 cup mozzarella.

Combine the spaghetti sauce, water and garlic; add meatballs. Pour over cheese mixture; sprinkle with remaining mozzarella. Bake, uncovered, at 350° for 30 minutes or until heated through.

YIELD: 6 servings.

the **ULTIMATE COMFORT FOOD** cookbook

cheesy vegetable egg dish

PREP: 20 min. | **BAKE:** 35 min.

- 1 medium zucchini, diced
- 1 medium onion, chopped
- 1 can (4 ounces) mushroom stems and pieces, drained
- 1/4 cup chopped green pepper
- 1/2 cup butter, cubed
- 1/2 cup all-purpose flour
- 1 teaspoon baking powder
- 1/2 teaspoon salt
- 10 eggs, lightly beaten
- 2 cups (16 ounces) 4% cottage cheese
- 4 cups (16 ounces) shredded Monterey Jack cheese

In a large skillet, saute zucchini, onion, mushrooms and green pepper in butter until tender. Stir in the flour, baking powder and salt until blended.

In a large bowl, combine eggs and cottage cheese. Stir in vegetables and Monterey Jack cheese until blended.

Transfer to a greased 2-1/2-qt. baking dish. Bake, uncovered, at 350° for 35-45 minutes or until a thermometer reads 160°.

YIELD: 8-10 servings.

elsie campbell
DULZURA, CALIFORNIA

I'm a cook at a Bible camp, and this is one of my most popular recipes with the youngsters. What touched me the most was when a 10-year-old boy asked me for the recipe so his mother could make it at home.

turkey day bake

PREP: 10 min. | **BAKE:** 30 min.

- 4 cups cooked stuffing
- 2-1/2 cups cubed cooked turkey
- 2 cups cooked broccoli florets
- 2 cups turkey gravy
- 4 slices process American cheese, halved

Press the stuffing onto the bottom of a greased 2-1/2-qt. baking dish. Top with turkey and broccoli. Pour gravy over all.

Bake, uncovered, at 350° for 25-30 minutes or until edges are bubbly. Top with cheese; bake 2-4 minutes longer or until cheese is melted.

YIELD: 6-8 servings.

lisa stepanski
MUNNSVILLE, NEW YORK

After Thanksgiving, make room in your fridge by putting together a hearty casserole with the leftovers. A jar of prepared gravy works fine if you are out of homemade gravy.

italian pinwheel meat loaf

PREP: 25 min. | **BAKE:** 1-1/4 hours + standing

- 2 eggs, lightly beaten
- 3/4 cup seasoned bread crumbs
- 1/2 cup spaghetti sauce *or* ketchup
- 1 tablespoon minced fresh parsley
- 1 garlic clove, minced
- 1/2 teaspoon dried oregano
- 1/4 teaspoon onion powder
- 1/4 teaspoon salt
- 1/4 teaspoon pepper
- 2 pounds lean ground beef (90% lean)
- 16 slices part-skim mozzarella cheese, *divided*
- 4 ounces deli ham

Additional spaghetti sauce, warmed, optional

In a large bowl, combine the first nine ingredients. Crumble beef over mixture and mix well.

On a piece of heavy-duty foil, pat beef mixture into a 12-in. x 10-in. rectangle. Layer with six cheese slices, ham and six more cheese slices.

Roll up jelly roll-style, starting with a short side and peeling foil away while rolling. Seal seam and ends. Place seam side down in a greased 13-in. x 9-in. baking dish.

Bake, uncovered, at 350° for 70 minutes or until no pink remains and a thermometer reads 160°. Top with remaining cheese; bake 5 minutes longer or until cheese is melted. Let stand for 10 minutes before slicing. Serve with additional spaghetti sauce if desired.

YIELD: 8 servings.

gail buss
BEVERLY HILLS, FLORIDA

I have been making this special meat loaf for decades. The cheesy filling and saucy topping make it impossible to resist. I assemble it early in the day and just pop it in the oven when I'm ready.

linda mcginty
PARMA, OHIO

We often requested my mother's wonderful Swiss steak when I was growing up. Mom took pride in preparing scrumptious, hearty meals like this for our family. Now it's a favorite in my house, too.

so-tender swiss steak

PREP: 30 min. | **BAKE:** 2 hours

1/4 cup all-purpose flour
1/2 teaspoon salt
1/4 teaspoon pepper
2 pounds beef top round steak, cut into serving-size pieces
2 tablespoons canola oil
1 medium onion, thinly sliced
2 cups water
2 tablespoons Worcestershire sauce

GRAVY:

1/4 cup all-purpose flour
1/4 teaspoon salt
1/8 teaspoon pepper
1-1/4 cups beef broth *or* water
Hot cooked noodles *or* mashed potatoes, optional

In a large resealable plastic bag, combine the flour, salt and pepper. Add steak, a few pieces at a time, and shake to coat. Remove meat from bag and pound with a mallet to tenderize.

In an ovenproof Dutch oven, brown steak in oil on both sides. Arrange onion slices between layers of meat. Add water and Worcestershire sauce.

Cover and bake at 325° for 2 to 2-1/2 hours or until meat is very tender. Remove to a serving platter and keep warm.

In a small bowl, combine the flour, salt, pepper and broth until smooth; stir into pan juices. Bring to a boil over medium heat; cook and stir for 2 minutes or until thickened. Serve steak and gravy with noodles or mashed potatoes if desired.

YIELD: 8 servings.

maureen brand
SOMERS, IOWA

With a spicy coating and creamy horseradish sauce, roast beef is sure to be the star of any meal, whether it's a sit-down dinner or serve-yourself potluck.

peppery roast beef

PREP: 15 min. | **BAKE:** 2-1/2 hours + standing

1 tablespoon olive oil
1 tablespoon seasoned pepper
2 garlic cloves, minced
1/2 teaspoon dried thyme
1/4 teaspoon salt
1 boneless beef eye round roast (4 to 5 pounds)

HORSERADISH SAUCE:

1 cup (8 ounces) sour cream
2 tablespoons lemon juice
2 tablespoons 2% milk
2 tablespoons prepared horseradish
1 tablespoon Dijon mustard
1/4 teaspoon salt
1/8 teaspoon pepper

In a small bowl, combine the oil, seasoned pepper, garlic, thyme and salt; rub over roast. Place fat side up on a rack in a shallow roasting pan.

Bake, uncovered, at 325° for 2-1/2 to 3 hours or until meat reaches desired doneness (for medium-rare, a thermometer should read 145°; medium, 160°; well-done, 170°). Let stand for 10 minutes before slicing.

In a small bowl, combine the sauce ingredients. Serve with roast.

YIELD: 10-12 servings.

lemon basil chicken

PREP: 15 min. | BAKE: 1-1/4 hours + standing

1 medium lemon
2 garlic cloves, peeled, *divided*
1/4 cup minced fresh basil, *divided*
1 broiler/fryer chicken (3 to 4 pounds)
2 tablespoons butter, melted
1/2 teaspoon salt
1/4 teaspoon pepper

Finely grate enough peel from lemon to measure 2 teaspoons. Cut lemon in half; squeeze juice from one half. Set aside. Slice one garlic clove; place sliced garlic, 2 tablespoons basil and the remaining lemon half in the chicken cavity.

Place on a rack in a shallow roasting pan; rub with reserved lemon juice. Mince remaining garlic; combine with butter and reserved lemon peel. Rub mixture over chicken. Sprinkle with salt, pepper and remaining basil.

Bake, uncovered, at 375° for 1-1/4 to 1-1/2 hours or until a thermometer reads 180°. Let stand for 15 minutes before carving.

YIELD: 6 servings.

marguerite marshall
CARENCRO, LOUISIANA

For Sunday dinner or any time, a simply seasoned roast chicken is really special. Fresh basil makes all the difference.

paula petersen
GRANITE CITY, ILLINOIS

These tiny loaves are great when you are craving meat loaf but don't want to wait a long time for a full-sized loaf to bake. My husband and I love them served with au gratin or fried potatoes.

little cheddar meat loaves

PREP/TOTAL TIME: 30 min.

1 egg, lightly beaten
1/3 cup quick-cooking oats
2 tablespoons ketchup
1 tablespoon dried minced onion
1/2 pound lean ground beef (90% lean)

TOPPING:
4 teaspoons ketchup
4 tablespoons shredded cheddar cheese

In a large bowl, combine the egg, oats, ketchup and onion. Crumble beef over mixture and mix well. Coat four muffin cups with cooking spray; fill three-fourths full with meat mixture. Spread ketchup over the loaves.

Bake at 400° for 15 minutes. Sprinkle with cheese. Bake 5 minutes longer or until no pink remains and a thermometer reads 160°. Let stand 5 minutes before removing from muffin cups.

YIELD: 2 servings.

macaroni taco bake

PREP: 30 min. | **BAKE:** 15 min.

- 2 packages (7-1/4 ounces *each*) macaroni and cheese dinner mix
- 1 pound ground beef
- 1 cup chunky salsa
- 2 cups crushed tortilla chips
- 1 can (2-1/4 ounces) sliced ripe olives, drained
- 2 cups (8 ounces) shredded Mexican cheese blend

Sour cream, optional

Prepare macaroni and cheese according to package directions. Meanwhile, in a large skillet, cook beef until no longer pink; drain. Stir in salsa; set aside.

Spread macaroni into a greased 13-in. x 9-in. baking dish. Layer with beef mixture, chips and olives; sprinkle with cheese.

Bake, uncovered, at 350° for 15-20 minutes or until heated through. Top each serving with sour cream if desired.

YIELD: 8 servings.

elizabeth king
DULUTH, MINNESOTA

Comforting mac and cheese with a touch of taco flavoring and tortilla-chip crunch...no wonder everyone loves it! You will love that it's ready in no time flat and isn't expensive to make.

SPRUCED-UP MAC 'N' CHEESE

I prepare a box of macaroni and cheese and dress it up with a can of tuna, peas, dried onion and ground black pepper to taste.
—JEANNETTE C.
DRACUT, MASSACHUSETTS

honey mustard chicken

PREP: 15 min. | **BAKE:** 45 min.

- 1/2 cup honey
- 1/4 cup prepared mustard
- 1 envelope ranch salad dressing mix
- 1 tablespoon dried parsley flakes
- 1-1/2 teaspoons Italian seasoning
- 1/2 teaspoon dried basil
- 1/2 teaspoon chili powder
- 1/4 teaspoon garlic powder
- 1/4 teaspoon pepper
- 6 chicken drumsticks
- 6 bone-in chicken thighs

For sauce, in a small bowl, combine the first nine ingredients. Set aside 1/2 cup for serving. Place chicken in a greased 15-in. x 10-in. x 1-in. baking pan; drizzle with remaining sauce.

Bake, uncovered, at 350° for 45-50 minutes or until a thermometer reads 180°, basting occasionally with pan juices. Warm the reserved sauce; serve with chicken.

YIELD: 6 servings.

richard gallop
PUEBLO, COLORADO

Moist and flavorful, this chicken is a real treat. With just 15 minutes of prep time, you'll be out of the kitchen quick! Experiment with different mustards like Dijon, sweet hot, or even Chinese mustard to find your favorite.

jeri millhouse
ASHLAND, OHIO

A terrific recipe for moms with young kids and busy lives, these little cups take just a short time. Best of all, kids will go absolutely crazy for these darling dinner bites!

cheeseburger cups

PREP/TOTAL TIME: 30 min.

    1 pound ground beef
    1/2 cup ketchup
    2 tablespoons brown sugar
    1 tablespoon prepared mustard
    1-1/2 teaspoons Worcestershire sauce
    1 tube (12 ounces) refrigerated buttermilk biscuits
    1/2 cup cubed process cheese (Velveeta)

In a large skillet, cook beef over medium heat until no longer pink; drain. Stir in the ketchup, brown sugar, mustard and Worcestershire sauce. Remove from the heat; set aside.

Press each biscuit onto the bottom and up the sides of a greased muffin cup. Spoon beef mixture into cups; top with cheese cubes. Bake at 400° for 14-16 minutes or until golden brown.

YIELD: 5 servings.

sharon rawlings
TAMPA, FLORIDA

I always wanted to learn to make Greek gyros at home, but I was intimidated. Then I tried this recipe, and they were great. I slice leftover meat into individual portions and freeze for any time I crave a gyro.

meat loaf gyros

PREP: 30 min. | BAKE: 1 hour + chilling

    1 egg, lightly beaten
    6 garlic cloves, minced
    3 tablespoons dried oregano
    1-1/4 teaspoons salt
    1 teaspoon pepper
    1 pound ground lamb
    1 pound ground beef
TZATZIKI SAUCE:
    1 cup (8 ounces) plain yogurt
    1 medium cucumber, peeled, seeded and chopped
    2 tablespoons lemon juice
    2 garlic cloves, minced
    1/2 teaspoon salt
    1/4 teaspoon pepper
GYROS:
    8 whole pita breads
    3 tablespoons olive oil, *divided*
    16 slices tomato
    8 slices sweet onion, halved

In a large bowl, combine the egg, garlic, oregano, salt and pepper. Crumble lamb and beef over mixture; mix well.

Pat into an ungreased 9-in. x 5-in. loaf pan. Bake, uncovered, at 350° for 60-70 minutes or until no pink remains and a thermometer reads 160°. Cool meat loaf completely on a wire rack, then refrigerate for 1-2 hours.

For sauce, in a small bowl, combine the yogurt, cucumber, lemon juice, garlic, salt and pepper. Cover and refrigerate until serving.

Brush pita breads with 1 tablespoon oil; heat on a lightly greased griddle for 1 minute on each side. Keep warm. Cut meat loaf into very thin slices. In a large skillet, fry meat loaf in remaining oil in batches until crisp.

On each pita bread, layer the tomato, onion and meat loaf slices; top with some tzatziki sauce. Gently fold pitas in half. Serve with remaining sauce.

YIELD: 8 servings.

ham mac and cheese

PREP: 30 min. | **BAKE:** 35 min.

1 package (7-1/4 ounces) macaroni and cheese dinner mix

3/4 cup soft bread crumbs

2 tablespoons grated Parmesan cheese

1 tablespoon minced fresh parsley

1 tablespoon butter, melted

1 cup cubed fully cooked ham

1 cup (8 ounces) cream-style cottage cheese

1/2 cup sour cream

2 tablespoons sliced green onion

1 tablespoon diced pimientos, optional

1/4 teaspoon salt

1/4 teaspoon ground mustard

Prepare macaroni and cheese according to package directions. Meanwhile, in a small bowl, combine the bread crumbs, Parmesan cheese, parsley and butter; set aside.

In a large bowl, combine the macaroni and cheese, ham, cottage cheese, sour cream, green onion, pimientos if desired, salt and mustard. Pour into a greased 1-1/2 qt. baking dish. Sprinkle with bread crumb mixture.

Bake, uncovered, at 350° for 35-40 minutes or until heated through.

YIELD: 4 servings.

susan taul
BIRMINGHAM, ALABAMA

You can switch up this family-pleasing dish in many ways. I sometimes use turkey or chicken instead of ham, and I like to use different types and flavors of mac and cheese. It's always popular with the kids.

helen lipko
MARTINSBURG, PENNSYLVANIA

My mother's meat loaf, served with scalloped potatoes, was my favorite meal growing up. You'll be amazed by all the flavor you can get from just a handful of pantry ingredients!

mom's meat loaf

PREP: 10 min. | **BAKE:** 40 min.

1 egg, lightly beaten
1 can (5-1/2 ounces) V8 juice
1/2 cup seasoned bread crumbs
1 envelope onion soup mix
1/4 cup grated Parmesan cheese
1/4 teaspoon garlic powder
1-1/2 pounds ground beef
1/3 cup ketchup

In a large bowl, combine the egg, V8 juice, bread crumbs, soup mix, cheese and garlic powder. Crumble beef over mixture and mix well. Pat into an ungreased 9-in. x 5-in. loaf pan.

Bake, uncovered, at 350° for 30 minutes. Spread ketchup over top; bake 10 minutes longer or until no pink remains and a thermometer reads 160°.

YIELD: 8 servings.

the **ULTIMATE COMFORT FOOD** cookbook

pretzel-crusted drumsticks

PREP: 10 min. | BAKE: 50 min.

1/2 cup butter, melted
1 teaspoon cayenne pepper
1/8 teaspoon garlic powder
1 cup finely crushed pretzels
1/4 cup chopped pecans
1/2 teaspoon pepper
1-1/2 to 2 pounds chicken drumsticks

In a shallow bowl, combine the butter, cayenne and garlic powder. In another shallow bowl, combine the pretzels, pecans and pepper. Dip chicken in butter mixture, then roll in pretzel mixture.

Place in a greased 13-in. x 9-in. baking dish. Bake chicken, uncovered, at 350° for 50-55 minutes or until a thermometer reads 180°, turning once.

YIELD: 5 servings.

joann frazier hensley
MCGAHEYSVILLE, VIRGINIA

With their crunchy pretzel coating, these drumsticks seem to satisfy everyone's appetites. I'm sure you'll agree—they're yummy!

ham with ruby-red glaze

PREP: 5 min. | BAKE: 2 hours + standing

1 boneless fully cooked ham (about 4 pounds)
3/4 cup packed brown sugar
3/4 cup creamy French salad dressing

Place the ham on a rack in a shallow roasting pan. Bake, uncovered, at 350° for 1-1/2 hours.

Meanwhile, in a small microwave-safe bowl, combine the brown sugar and salad dressing. Cover and microwave on high for 30-60 seconds or until sugar is dissolved. Pour 1/4 cup over the ham.

Bake, uncovered, 30-40 minutes longer or until a thermometer reads 140°. Let meat stand for 10 minutes before slicing. Serve with remaining glaze.

YIELD: 8-10 servings.

EDITOR'S NOTE: This recipe was tested in a 1,100-watt microwave.

beverly payne
EL SOBRANTE, CALIFORNIA

I have used this recipe for over 40 years and it is still a favorite with my family. My grandchildren love the glaze on mashed potatoes.

TASTY MAPLE HAM

I like to fry sliced ham with a little maple syrup until the ham is lightly browned. Turn the slices often to make sure they're well-coated with the syrup, which gives the ham a candied flavor.

—ALFRED S. JR.
FERGUS FALLS, MINNESOTA

linda foreman
LOCUST GROVE, OKLAHOMA

My mother, grandson and I came up with our version of oven-fried chicken. We tweaked the ingredients until the gravy was tasty and the chicken was nicely browned and tender.

CHICKEN QUARTERS DEFINED

The leg quarter of a chicken contains the drumstick, thigh and portion of the back. A breast quarter contains the breast, wing and portion of the back.

chicken with country gravy

PREP: 15 min. | **BAKE:** 50 min.

2 tablespoons butter
2 tablespoons canola oil
1/4 cup all-purpose flour
1/4 teaspoon paprika
Dash *each* seasoned salt, garlic powder, salt and pepper
2 chicken leg quarters

GRAVY:

1 tablespoon all-purpose flour
2/3 cup milk
1/4 teaspoon salt
1/4 tablespoon pepper

Place butter and oil in a large ovenproof skillet. Place in a 425° oven for 5 minutes. Meanwhile, in a large resealable plastic bag, combine flour and seasonings; add chicken, one piece at a time, and shake to coat.

Carefully place chicken, skin side down, in hot skillet. Bake, uncovered, for 30 minutes. Turn the pieces over; bake 20-30 minutes longer or until a thermometer reads 180°. Remove from pan; cover and keep warm.

Transfer 1 tablespoon of drippings from the skillet to a small saucepan; stir in flour until smooth. Gradually stir in the milk, salt and pepper. Bring to a boil; cook and stir for 2 minutes or until thickened. Serve with chicken.

YIELD: 2 servings.

steven espinosa
SALT LAKE CITY, UTAH

I'm asked to make my signature meat loaf at least once a month during the winter, especially for birthday dinners. Garlic mashed potatoes and braised asparagus are terrific accompaniments.

tortilla-salsa meat loaf

Prep: 15 min. | **BAKE:** 1-1/4 hours

2 slices day-old white bread
2 eggs, lightly beaten
1 cup salsa
1/2 cup crushed tortilla chips
1/2 cup *each* chopped green pepper, onion and celery
1 jalapeno pepper, seeded and chopped
6 garlic cloves, minced
1 teaspoon pepper
1/2 teaspoon Italian seasoning
1/4 teaspoon seasoned salt
1 pound ground beef
1 pound ground pork

Place bread in an ungreased 9-in. x 5-in. loaf pan; set aside. In a large bowl, combine the eggs, salsa, tortilla chips, green pepper, onion, celery, jalapeno, garlic, pepper, Italian seasoning and seasoned salt. Crumble beef and pork over mixture and mix well. Pat into prepared pan.

Bake, uncovered, at 375° for 1-1/4 to 1-1/2 hours or until a thermometer reads 160°. Invert meat loaf onto a serving platter; discard bread. Let stand for 5 minutes before slicing.

YIELD: 8 servings.

EDITOR'S NOTE: Wear disposable gloves when cutting hot peppers; the oils can burn skin. Avoid touching your face.

zucchini red pepper lasagna

PREP: 20 min. | **BAKE:** 55 min. + standing

- 1 carton (15 ounces) ricotta cheese
- 1-1/2 cups (6 ounces) shredded part-skim mozzarella cheese, *divided*
- 2 eggs
- 3 tablespoons prepared pesto
- 2 cups sliced zucchini
- 2 cups sliced baby portobello mushrooms
- 2 tablespoons canola oil
- 2 jars (one 24 ounces, one 14 ounces) meatless spaghetti sauce
- 9 no-cook lasagna noodles
- 1 jar (12 ounces) roasted sweet red peppers, drained

In a small bowl, combine the ricotta cheese, 1/2 cup mozzarella cheese, eggs and pesto; set aside. In a large skillet, saute zucchini and mushrooms in oil for 5 minutes or until crisp-tender; set aside.

Spread 1 cup spaghetti sauce in a 13-in. x 9-in. baking dish coated with cooking spray. Top with three noodles; spread 1 cup sauce to edges of noodles. Layer with half of the zucchini mixture, red peppers and cheese mixture. Top with three more noodles and another cup of sauce. Layer with remaining zucchini mixture, peppers, cheese mixture, noodles and sauce.

Cover and bake at 375° for 45 minutes or until a thermometer reads 160°. Uncover; sprinkle with remaining mozzarella cheese. Bake 10 minutes longer or until cheese is melted. Let stand for 15 minutes before cutting.

YIELD: 12 servings.

**taste of home
test kitchen**

No-cook lasagna noodles, prepared pesto and roasted red peppers make this gourmet-tasting dish a snap to prepare. No one will guess that you put it together so quickly!

vivian manary
NEPEAN, ONTARIO

Tiny and tender bay scallops take center stage in these miniature dishes. They're reminiscent of potpies, very creamy and packed with flavorful veggies in every bite.

mini scallop casseroles

PREP: 30 min. | **BAKE:** 20 min.

3 celery ribs, chopped
1 cup sliced fresh mushrooms
1 medium green pepper, chopped
1 small onion, chopped
2 tablespoons butter
1/3 cup all-purpose flour
1/4 teaspoon salt
1/4 teaspoon pepper
2 cups fat-free milk
1 pound bay scallops

TOPPING:
1 cup soft bread crumbs
1 tablespoon butter, melted
1/4 cup shredded cheddar cheese

In a large skillet, saute the celery, mushrooms, green pepper and onion in butter until tender. Stir in the flour, salt and pepper until blended; gradually add milk. Bring to a boil; cook and stir for 2 minutes or until thickened.

Reduce heat; add scallops. Cook, stirring occasionally, for 3-4 minutes or until scallops are firm and opaque.

Divide mixture among four 10-oz. ramekins or custard cups. In a small bowl, combine crumbs and butter; sprinkle over scallop mixture.

Bake, uncovered, at 350° for 15-20 minutes or until bubbly. Sprinkle with cheese; bake 5 minutes longer or until cheese is melted.

YIELD: 4 servings.

poppy seed creamed chicken

PREP: 10 min. | **BAKE:** 30 min.

    2 cups cubed cooked chicken
    1 can (10-3/4 ounces) condensed cream
      of chicken soup, undiluted
    1/2 cup sour cream
    1 teaspoon poppy seeds
    3/4 cup crushed butter-flavored crackers
      (about 18 crackers)
    2 tablespoons butter
Hot cooked noodles

In a large bowl, combine the chicken, soup, sour cream and poppy seeds. Pour mixture into a greased shallow 3-cup baking dish. In a small bowl, combine cracker crumbs and butter; sprinkle over top.

Bake, uncovered, at 350° for 30-35 minutes or until bubbly. Serve with noodles.

YIELD: 2 servings.

june sheaffer
FREDERICKSBURG,
PENNSYLVANIA

A dear friend gave me this recipe, and it's been so popular with my family that I also want to pass it along. A few years back, it won a blue ribbon in a chicken recipe contest.

steak potpie

PREP: 20 min. | **BAKE:** 20 min.

    1-1/4 pounds beef top sirloin steak, cut into
      1/2-inch cubes
    2 tablespoons butter
    1/4 teaspoon pepper
    1 package (16 ounces) frozen vegetables
      for stew
    2 tablespoons water
    1/2 teaspoon dried thyme
    1 jar (12 ounces) mushroom *or* beef gravy
    1 tube (8 ounces) refrigerated crescent
      rolls

In a large ovenproof skillet, brown beef in butter. Remove beef; season with pepper and keep warm. In the same skillet, combine the vegetables, water and thyme. Stir in the gravy. Bring to a boil. Reduce heat; simmer, uncovered, until the vegetables are thawed. Stir in beef; remove from the heat.

Separate crescent dough into eight triangles. Starting from the wide end of each triangle, roll up a third of the length and place over beef mixture with pointed ends toward the center.

Bake, uncovered, at 375° for 16-18 minutes or until golden brown.

YIELD: 4-6 servings.

kristin shaw
CASTLETON, NEW YORK

On cold winter nights, nothing hits the spot like a hot, homemade potpie. You will love how quickly this one comes together.

CHAPTER FOUR

from the slow cooker

margaret thiel
LEVITTOWN, PENNSYLVANIA

Before putting it in the slow cooker, trim the roast of any fat to avoid greasy gravy. If your roast weighs 3 or more pounds, cut it in half to ensure even cooking.

picante beef roast

PREP: 15 min. | COOK: 8 hours

- 1 beef rump roast *or* bottom round roast (3 pounds), trimmed
- 1 jar (16 ounces) picante sauce
- 1 can (15 ounces) tomato sauce
- 1 envelope taco seasoning
- 3 tablespoons cornstarch
- 1/4 cup cold water

Cut roast in half; place in a 5-qt. slow cooker. In a large bowl, combine the picante sauce, tomato sauce and taco seasoning; pour over roast.

Cover and cook on low for 8-9 hours or until meat is tender.

Remove meat to a serving platter; keep warm. Skim fat from cooking juices; transfer 3 cups to a small saucepan. Bring liquid to a boil.

Combine cornstarch and water until smooth. Gradually stir into pan. Bring to a boil; cook and stir for 2 minutes or until thickened. Slice roast; serve with gravy.

YIELD: 8 servings.

allan stackhouse jr.
JENNINGS, LOUISIANA

These ribs are finger-lickin' good and fall-off-the-bone tender! I've made them for a lot of my buddies— including my preacher— and some have even suggested that I try bottling my sauce and selling it to the public.

lazy man's ribs

PREP: 20 min. | COOK: 5 hours

- 2-1/2 pounds pork baby back ribs, cut into eight pieces
- 2 teaspoons Cajun seasoning
- 1 medium onion, sliced
- 1 cup ketchup
- 1/2 cup packed brown sugar
- 1/3 cup orange juice
- 1/3 cup cider vinegar
- 1/4 cup molasses
- 2 tablespoons Worcestershire sauce
- 1 tablespoon barbecue sauce
- 1 teaspoon stone-ground mustard
- 1 teaspoon paprika
- 1/2 teaspoon garlic powder
- 1/2 teaspoon Liquid Smoke, optional

Dash salt
- 5 teaspoons cornstarch
- 1 tablespoon cold water

Rub ribs with Cajun seasoning. Layer ribs and onion in a 5-qt. slow cooker. In a small bowl, combine the ketchup, brown sugar, orange juice, vinegar, molasses, Worcestershire sauce, barbecue sauce, mustard, paprika, garlic powder, Liquid Smoke if desired and salt. Pour over ribs. Cover and cook on low for 5-6 hours or until meat is tender.

Remove ribs and keep warm. Strain cooking juices and skim fat; transfer to a small saucepan. Combine cornstarch and water until smooth; stir into juices. Bring to a boil; cook and stir for 2 minutes or until thickened. Serve with ribs.

YIELD: 4 servings.

baked potato soup

PREP: 35 min. | COOK: 6 hours

2 large onions, chopped
3 tablespoons butter
2 tablespoons all-purpose flour
2 cups water, *divided*
4 cups chicken broth
2 medium potatoes, peeled and diced
1-1/2 cups mashed potato flakes
1/2 pound sliced bacon, cooked and crumbled
3/4 teaspoon pepper
1/2 teaspoon salt
1/2 teaspoon dried basil
1/8 teaspoon dried thyme

1 cup half-and-half cream
1/2 cup shredded cheddar cheese
2 green onions, sliced

In a large skillet, saute onions in butter until tender. Stir in flour. Gradually stir in 1 cup water. Bring to a boil; cook and stir for 2 minutes or until thickened. Transfer to a 5-qt. slow cooker.

Add the broth, potatoes, potato flakes, bacon, pepper, salt, basil, thyme and remaining water. Cover and cook on low for 6-8 hours or until potatoes are tender. Stir in cream; heat through. Garnish with cheese and green onions.

YIELD: 10 servings.

barbara bleigh
COLONIAL HEIGHTS, VIRGINIA

The only thing that beats the comforting flavor of this thick and hearty potato soup is possibly the idea that it simmers on its own all day.

jackie kohn
DULUTH, MINNESOTA

My son shared his favorite goulash recipe with me many years ago. You will love how easily this slow-cooked version of a beloved ethnic dish comes together.

hungarian goulash

PREP: 15 min. | COOK: 8 hours

2 pounds beef top round steak, cut into 1-inch cubes

1 cup chopped onion

2 tablespoons all-purpose flour

1-1/2 teaspoons paprika

1 teaspoon garlic salt

1/2 teaspoon pepper

1 can (14-1/2 ounces) diced tomatoes, undrained

1 bay leaf

1 cup (8 ounces) sour cream
Hot cooked noodles

Place beef and onion in a 3-qt. slow cooker. Combine the flour, paprika, garlic salt and pepper; sprinkle over beef and stir to coat. Stir in tomatoes; add bay leaf. Cover and cook on low for 8-10 hours or until meat is tender.

Discard bay leaf. Just before serving, stir in sour cream; heat through. Serve with noodles.

YIELD: 6-8 servings.

pork burritos

PREP: 25 min. | **COOK:** 8 hours

1 boneless pork shoulder butt roast (3 to 4 pounds)
1 can (14-1/2 ounces) diced tomatoes with mild green chilies, undrained
1/4 cup chili powder
3 tablespoons minced garlic
2 tablespoons lime juice
2 tablespoons honey
1 tablespoon chopped seeded jalapeno pepper
1 teaspoon salt
10 flour tortillas (8 inches), warmed
Sliced avocado and sour cream, optional

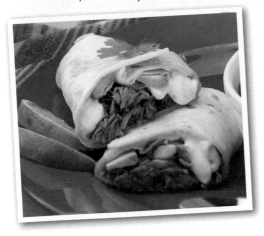

Cut roast in half; place in a 5-qt. slow cooker. In a blender, combine the tomatoes, chili powder, garlic, lime juice, honey, jalapeno and salt; cover and process until smooth. Pour over pork. Cover and cook on low for 8-10 hours or until meat is tender.

Remove roast; cool slightly. Shred pork with two forks and return to slow cooker. Using a slotted spoon, place about 1/2 cup pork mixture down the center of each tortilla; top with avocado and sour cream if desired. Fold sides and ends over filling and roll up.

YIELD: 10 burritos.

EDITOR'S NOTE: Wear disposable gloves when cutting hot peppers; the oils can burn skin. Avoid touching your face.

kelly gengler
THERESA, WISCONSIN

As a working mother, I depend on my slow cooker to help feed my family. We all love the spicy but slightly sweet flavor of these tender, scrumptious burritos.

SOFT TORTILLAS

If your tortillas are too stiff to roll into burritos, place them between two damp paper towels and microwave them. Check every few seconds and remove when they are soft and pliable.

—KAREN B.
GOVE, KANSAS

santa fe chili

PREP: 20 min. | **COOK:** 4 hours

2 pounds ground beef
1 medium onion, chopped
2 cans (16 ounces *each*) kidney beans, rinsed and drained
2 cans (15 ounces *each*) black beans, rinsed and drained
2 cans (15 ounces *each*) pinto beans, rinsed and drained
3 cans (7 ounces *each*) white *or* shoepeg corn, drained
1 can (14-1/2 ounces) diced tomatoes, undrained
1 can (10 ounces) diced tomatoes and green chilies
1 can (11-1/2 ounces) V8 juice
2 envelopes ranch salad dressing mix
2 envelopes taco seasoning
Sour cream, shredded cheddar cheese and corn chips, optional

In a large skillet, cook the ground beef and onion over medium heat until meat is no longer pink; drain. Transfer to a 5- or 6-qt. slow cooker. Stir in the beans, corn, tomatoes, juice, salad dressing mix and taco seasoning.

Cover and cook on high for 4-6 hours or until heated through. Serve with sour cream, cheese and corn chips if desired.

YIELD: 16 servings (4 quarts).

laura manning
LILBURN, GEORGIA

Here's a colorful and hearty chili that's perfect for get-togethers. My family has been enjoying it for years.

jennifer seidel
MIDLAND, MICHIGAN

This recipe is one of my husband's favorites. It only calls for four ingredients, and we try to have them on hand regularly so we can enjoy a delicious and cozy dinner any time!

maple mustard chicken

PREP: 5 min. | COOK: 3 hours

6 boneless skinless chicken breast halves (6 ounces *each*)
1/2 cup maple syrup
1/3 cup stone-ground mustard
2 tablespoons quick-cooking tapioca
Hot cooked brown rice

Place chicken in a 3-qt. slow cooker. In a small bowl, combine the syrup, mustard and tapioca; pour over chicken. Cover and cook on low for 3-4 hours or until meat is tender. Serve with rice.

YIELD: 6 servings.

ann huseby
LAKEVILLE, MINNESOTA

Here's a comforting small-batch soup that's a perfect treat on wintry days. It's so satisfying, you might wish there were leftovers!

savory cheese soup

PREP: 10 min. | COOK: 5-3/4 hours

1 can (14-1/2 ounces) chicken broth
1/4 cup chopped carrot
1/4 cup chopped celery
1 tablespoon chopped onion
1 tablespoon chopped sweet red pepper
2 teaspoons butter
1/8 to 1/4 teaspoon pepper
2 tablespoons all-purpose flour
2 tablespoons cold water
1 package (3 ounces) cream cheese, cubed and softened
3/4 cup shredded cheddar cheese
1/3 cup beer *or* additional chicken broth
Croutons, crumbled cooked bacon and sliced green onions, optional

In a 1-1/2-qt. slow cooker, combine the first seven ingredients. Cover and cook on low for 5-6 hours or until vegetables are tender.

Combine flour and water until smooth; stir into soup. Cover and cook on high for 30 minutes or until thickened.

Stir in cream cheese and cheddar cheese until blended. Stir in beer. Cover and cook on low for 15 minutes or until heated through. Top with croutons, bacon and green onions if desired.

YIELD: 2 servings.

pork chops with sauerkraut

PREP: 15 min. | **COOK:** 3 hours

- 4 bone-in center-cut pork loin chops (8 ounces *each*)
- 2 tablespoons canola oil
- 1 jar (32 ounces) sauerkraut, undrained
- 3/4 cup packed brown sugar
- 1 medium green pepper, sliced
- 1 medium onion, sliced

In a large skillet over medium heat, brown pork chops in oil for 3-4 minutes on each side; drain. In a 5-qt. slow cooker, combine the sauerkraut and brown sugar. Top with the pork chops, green pepper and onion.

Cover and cook on low for 3 to 4 hours or until meat is tender. Serve with a slotted spoon.

YIELD: 4 servings.

stephanie miller
OMAHA, NEBRASKA

I pair tender pork chops with tangy sauerkraut in a classic main dish. It's so easy to put together.

jane bone
CAPE CORAL, FLORIDA

Italian sausage makes these meatballs extra flavorful and tender. This recipe rose quickly to the top of my husband's "most-requested" list.

GLOVES KEEP HANDS CLEAN

Whenever I have a hands-on job like forming meatballs or skinning chicken breasts, I wear disposable gloves. It's quick and easy to change tasks, because my hands are still clean.

—PAUL V.

WHITING, NEW JERSEY

spicy meatballs with sauce

PREP: 30 min. | **COOK:** 5 hours

1 egg, lightly beaten
3/4 cup crushed seasoned salad croutons
1/2 cup finely chopped onion
1/4 cup finely chopped green pepper
1 teaspoon garlic powder
1 teaspoon ground cumin
1 teaspoon dried oregano
1 teaspoon pepper
1 pound ground turkey
1 pound bulk Italian sausage

SAUCE:

3 tablespoons cornstarch
1 tablespoon sugar
3/4 cup beef broth
2 cans (28 ounces *each*) crushed tomatoes
3 medium carrots, diced
1 can (6 ounces) tomato paste

1 envelope onion soup mix
3 garlic cloves, minced
1 teaspoon dried basil
1/2 teaspoon crushed red pepper flakes

Hot cooked pasta

In a large bowl, combine the egg, croutons, onion, green pepper, garlic powder, cumin, oregano and pepper. Crumble turkey and sausage over mixture and mix well. Shape into 1-in. balls. Place in a 5-qt. slow cooker.

In a large bowl, combine the cornstarch, sugar and broth until smooth; stir in the tomatoes, carrots, tomato paste, soup mix, garlic, basil and pepper flakes. Pour over meatballs. Cover and cook on low for 5-6 hours. Serve with pasta.

YIELD: 8 servings.

veggie-sausage cheese soup

PREP: 55 min. | **COOK:** 6-1/2 hours

2 medium onions, finely chopped
1 *each* medium green and sweet red peppers, chopped
2 celery ribs, chopped
1 tablespoon olive oil
4 garlic cloves, minced
1 pound smoked kielbasa *or* Polish sausage, cut into 1/4-inch slices
2 medium potatoes, diced
1 can (14-3/4 ounces) cream-style corn
1 can (14-1/2 ounces) chicken broth
1 can (10-3/4 ounces) condensed cream of mushroom soup, undiluted
2 medium carrots, sliced
1 cup whole kernel corn
1 cup sliced fresh mushrooms
1 tablespoon Worcestershire sauce
1 tablespoon Dijon mustard
1 tablespoon dried basil
1 tablespoon dried parsley flakes
1/2 teaspoon pepper
2 cups (8 ounces) shredded sharp cheddar cheese
1 can (12 ounces) evaporated milk

In a large skillet, saute the onions, peppers and celery in oil until tender. Add garlic and cook 1 minute longer.

Transfer to a 5-qt. slow cooker. Stir in the sausage, potatoes, cream-style corn, broth, soup, carrots, corn, mushrooms, Worcestershire sauce, Dijon mustard and seasonings. Cover and cook on low for 6-8 hours or until vegetables are tender.

Stir in cheese and milk. Cook on low 30 minutes longer or until cheese is melted. Stir until blended.

YIELD: 16 servings (4 quarts).

richard grant
HUDSON, NEW HAMPSHIRE

I took this soup to a potluck at work, where it was well-received...and was the only dish prepared by a guy! The combination of textures and flavors had everyone asking for the recipe.

creamy beef and pasta

PREP: 15 min. | **COOK:** 6 hours

2 cans (10-3/4 ounces *each*) condensed cream of mushroom soup, undiluted
2 cups (8 ounces) shredded cheddar cheese *or* 8 ounces shredded part-skim mozzarella cheese
1 pound ground beef, cooked and drained
2 cups uncooked small pasta
2 cups milk
1/2 to 1 teaspoon onion powder
1/2 to 1 teaspoon salt
1/4 to 1/2 teaspoon pepper

In a 3-qt. slow cooker, combine all the ingredients. Cover and cook on low for 6-8 hours or until pasta is tender.

YIELD: 4-6 servings.

carol losier
BALDWINSVILLE, NEW YORK

When my children were young, I often made this set-it-and-forget-it meal when my husband and I went out for date night. Even the baby-sitters commented how much they liked it.

no-fuss swiss steak

PREP: 10 min. | **COOK:** 6 hours

3 pounds beef top round steak, cut into serving-size pieces
2 tablespoons canola oil
2 medium carrots, sliced
2 celery ribs, sliced
1-3/4 cups water
1 can (11 ounces) condensed tomato rice soup, undiluted
1 can (10-1/2 ounces) condensed French onion soup, undiluted
1/2 teaspoon pepper
1 bay leaf

In a large skillet, brown the beef in oil over medium-high heat; drain. Transfer to a 5-qt. slow cooker. Add carrots and celery. Combine the remaining ingredients; pour over meat and vegetables.

Cover and cook on low for 6-8 hours or until meat is tender. Discard bay leaf. Thicken cooking juices if desired.

YIELD: 8-10 servings.

sharon morrell
PARKER, SOUTH DAKOTA

I make Swiss steak often because my kids love the savory steak, tangy gravy and fork-tender veggies.

lisa ann panzino dinunzio
VINELAND, NEW JERSEY

I give an Italian treatment to chicken by slow-cooking it in a zesty tomato sauce and serving it over spaghetti. It's great for company because it frees up time to spend with guests.

mushroom chicken cacciatore

PREP: 20 min. | COOK: 4 hours

4 boneless skinless chicken breast halves (about 1-1/2 pounds)
2 tablespoons canola oil
1 can (15 ounces) tomato sauce
2 cans (4 ounces *each*) sliced mushrooms, drained
1 medium onion, chopped
1/4 cup red wine *or* chicken broth
2 garlic cloves, minced
1-1/4 teaspoons dried oregano
1/2 teaspoon dried thyme
1/8 to 1/4 teaspoon salt
1/8 teaspoon pepper
Hot cooked spaghetti

In a large skillet, brown the chicken in oil on both sides. Transfer to a 3-qt. slow cooker. In a bowl, combine the tomato sauce, mushrooms, onion, wine, garlic, oregano, thyme, salt and pepper; pour over chicken.

Cover and cook on low for 4-5 hours or until meat is tender. Serve with spaghetti.

YIELD: 4 servings.

sue jurack
MEQUON, WISCONSIN

When herbs are plentiful in my garden, I prepare this recipe. The turkey stays moist in the slow cooker and is bursting with herb flavors. When I served this to our Bible study potluck group, everyone wanted the recipe!

slow-cooked herbed turkey

PREP: 15 min. + marinating | COOK: 4 hours + standing

2 cans (14-1/2 ounces *each*) chicken broth
1 cup lemon juice
1/2 cup packed brown sugar
1/2 cup minced fresh sage
1/2 cup minced fresh thyme
1/2 cup lime juice
1/2 cup cider vinegar
1/2 cup olive oil
2 envelopes onion soup mix
1/4 cup Dijon mustard
2 tablespoons minced fresh marjoram
3 teaspoons paprika
2 teaspoons garlic powder
2 teaspoons pepper
1 teaspoon salt
2 boneless skinless turkey breast halves (3 pounds *each*)

In a blender, combine the first 15 ingredients; cover and process until blended. Place turkey breasts in a gallon-size resealable plastic bag; add half of marinade. Seal bag and turn to coat; seal and refrigerate overnight. Pour remaining marinade into a bowl; cover and refrigerate.

Drain and discard marinade from turkey. Transfer turkey breasts to a 5-qt. slow cooker. Add reserved marinade; cover and cook on high for 4-5 hours or a thermometer reads 170°. Let stand for 10 minutes before slicing.

YIELD: 14-16 servings.

split pea soup

PREP: 15 min. | **COOK:** 8 hours

  1 can (49-1/2 ounces) chicken broth

1-1/2 pounds smoked ham hocks

  2 cups *each* chopped onions, celery and carrots

  1 package (16 ounces) dried green split peas

  2 bay leaves

Salad croutons, optional

In a 4- or 5-qt. slow cooker, combine the broth, ham hocks, vegetables, peas and bay leaves. Cover and cook on low for 8-10 hours or until the ham hocks and peas are tender.

Discard bay leaves. Remove meat from bones when cool enough to handle; cut ham into small pieces and set aside. Cool soup slightly.

In a blender, cover and process soup in batches until smooth. Return soup to slow cooker; stir in reserved ham. Heat through. Garnish with croutons if desired.

YIELD: 7 servings (about 2-1/4 quarts).

taste of home test kitchen

Slow cook your split pea soup while you are out for the afternoon and a delicious dinner will be ready when you arrive home! This is a stick-to-your ribs dinner. The ham hocks lend a smoky flavor.

carol losier
BALDWINSVILLE, NEW YORK

On hot summer days, this cooks without heating up the kitchen while I work on the rest of the meal. It's easy to double or triple for crowds, and if there are any leftovers, you can freeze them to enjoy later!

slow cooker sloppy joes

PREP: 20 min. | COOK: 3 hours

1-1/2 pounds ground beef
1 cup chopped celery
1/2 cup chopped onion
1 bottle (12 ounces) chili sauce
2 tablespoons brown sugar
2 tablespoons sweet pickle relish
1 tablespoon Worcestershire sauce
1 teaspoon salt
1/8 teaspoon pepper
8 hamburger buns, split

In a large skillet, cook the beef, celery and onion over medium heat until meat is no longer pink; drain. Transfer to a 3-qt. slow cooker.

Stir in the chili sauce, brown sugar, pickle relish, Worcestershire sauce, salt and pepper. Cover and cook on low for 3-4 hours or until flavors are blended. Just before serving, spoon 1/2 cup beef mixture onto each bun.

YIELD: 8 servings.

french beef stew

PREP: 15 min. | **COOK:** 9 hours

- 3 medium potatoes, peeled and cut into 1/2-inch cubes
- 2 pounds beef stew meat
- 4 medium carrots, sliced
- 2 medium onions, sliced
- 3 celery ribs, sliced
- 2 cups tomato juice
- 1 cup water
- 1/3 cup quick-cooking tapioca
- 1 tablespoon sugar
- 1 tablespoon salt
- 1 teaspoon dried basil
- 1/2 teaspoon pepper

Place the potatoes in a greased 5-qt. slow cooker. Top with the beef, carrots, onions and celery. In a large bowl, combine the remaining ingredients. Pour over the vegetables.

Cover and cook on low for 9-10 hours or until beef is tender.

YIELD: 8-10 servings.

iola egle
BELLA VISTA, ARKANSAS

When it comes to making a classic, thick and hearty beef stew, I let my slow cooker do the work. Then I simply toss together a green salad and dinner is ready.

TOMATO SOUP ADDS RICH FLAVOR

To add flavor and richness to my beef stew when I make it in the slow cooker, I stir in a can of tomato soup at the start of cooking.
—CAROL F.
LANDERS, CALIFORNIA

green chili beef burritos

PREP: 20 min. | **COOK:** 8 hours

- 2 beef sirloin tip roasts (3 pounds *each*)
- 4 cans (4 ounces *each*) chopped green chilies
- 1 medium onion, chopped
- 3 medium jalapeno peppers, seeded and chopped
- 3 garlic cloves, sliced
- 3 teaspoons chili powder
- 1-1/2 teaspoons ground cumin
- 1 teaspoon salt-free seasoning blend, optional
- 1 cup reduced-sodium beef broth
- 24 fat-free flour tortillas (8 inches), warmed

Chopped tomatoes, shredded lettuce and shredded reduced-fat cheddar cheese, optional

Trim fat from roasts; cut meat into large chunks. Place in a 5-qt. slow cooker. Top with the chilies, onion, jalapenos, garlic, chili powder, cumin and seasoning blend if desired. Pour broth over all. Cover and cook on low for 8-9 hours or until meat is tender.

Remove beef; cool slightly. Shred with two forks. Cool cooking liquid slightly; skim fat. In a blender, cover and process cooking liquid in small batches until smooth.

Return liquid and beef to slow cooker; heat through. Place 1/3 cup beef mixture on each tortilla. Top with tomatoes, lettuce and cheese if desired. Fold in ends and sides.

YIELD: 2 dozen.

EDITOR'S NOTE: Wear disposable gloves when cutting hot peppers; the oils can burn skin. Avoid touching your face.

shirley davidson
THORNTON, COLORADO

Recipes that are lower in fat and calories—like the one for these delicious burritos—helped me lose 30 pounds! Everyone will enjoy these, whether they're watching their diets or not.

lee bremson
KANSAS CITY, MISSOURI

It's wonderful to have a satisfying chowder hot and ready for wintertime guests. They'll think you labored for hours perfecting it.

creamy ham chowder

PREP: 30 min. | **COOK:** 3-1/2 hours

4 cups cubed peeled potatoes
2 tablespoons chopped onion
1/2 cup butter
3/4 cup all-purpose flour
1/4 teaspoon salt
1/4 teaspoon pepper
Pinch ground nutmeg
4 cups chicken broth
4 cups half-and-half cream
2 cups (8 ounces) shredded cheddar cheese
3 cups cubed fully cooked ham
1 package (16 ounces) frozen broccoli cuts, thawed and drained

Place potatoes in a large saucepan and cover with water. Bring to a boil. Reduce heat; cover and cook for 10-15 minutes or until tender.

Meanwhile, in another large saucepan, cook onion in butter over medium heat for 2 minutes. Stir in the flour, salt, pepper and nutmeg; gradually add broth. Bring to a boil; cook and stir for 2 minutes or until thickened. Stir in cream and cheese.

Transfer to a 5-qt. slow cooker. Drain potatoes; add to slow cooker. Stir in the ham. Cover and cook on low for 3-4 hours.

Stir in the broccoli. Cover and cook 30 minutes longer or until heated through.

YIELD: 12 servings (about 3-1/2 quarts).

tatina smith
SAN ANGELO, TEXAS

Chuck roast makes delicious sandwiches after simmering in a rich homemade sauce all day. The meat is tender and juicy and takes minutes to prepare for easy entertaining or a potluck.

barbecued beef sandwiches

PREP: 20 min. | **COOK:** 8-1/4 hours

1 boneless beef chuck roast (3 pounds)
1-1/2 cups ketchup
1/4 cup packed brown sugar
1/4 cup barbecue sauce
2 tablespoons Worcestershire sauce
2 tablespoons Dijon mustard
1 teaspoon Liquid Smoke, optional
1/2 teaspoon salt
1/4 teaspoon garlic powder
1/4 teaspoon pepper
12 sandwich buns, split
Sliced onions, dill pickles and pickled jalapenos, optional

Cut roast in half and place in a 3- or 4-qt. slow cooker. In a small bowl, combine the ketchup, brown sugar, barbecue sauce, Worcestershire sauce, mustard, Liquid Smoke if desired and seasonings. Pour over beef.

Cover and cook on low for 8-10 hours or until meat is tender. Remove meat; cool slightly. Skim fat from cooking liquid.

Shred beef with two forks; return to the slow cooker. Cover and cook for 15 minutes or until heated through. Using a slotted spoon, place 1/2 cup on each bun. Serve with onions, pickles and jalapenos if desired.

YIELD: 12 servings.

tex-mex chili

PREP: 20 min. | COOK: 6 hours

3 pounds beef stew meat
1 tablespoon canola oil
3 garlic cloves, minced
3 cans (16 ounces *each*) kidney beans, rinsed and drained
3 cans (15 ounces *each*) tomato sauce
1 can (14-1/2 ounces) diced tomatoes, undrained
1 cup water
1 can (6 ounces) tomato paste
3/4 cup salsa verde
1 envelope chili seasoning
2 teaspoons dried minced onion
1 teaspoon chili powder
1/2 teaspoon crushed red pepper flakes
1/2 teaspoon ground cumin
1/2 teaspoon cayenne pepper
Shredded cheddar cheese and minced fresh cilantro

In a large skillet, brown the stew meat in oil in batches. Add garlic; cook 1 minute longer. Transfer to a 6-qt. slow cooker.

Stir in the beans, tomato sauce, tomatoes, water, tomato paste and salsa verde and seasonings. Cover and cook on low for 6-8 hours or until meat is tender. Garnish with cheese and cilantro.

YIELD: 12 servings (1-1/3 cups each).

eric hayes
ANTIOCH, CALIFORNIA

Hearty and spicy, this is a man's chili for sure. You can also simmer it on the stove—the longer you cook it, the better!

yvonne mckim
VANCOUVER, WASHINGTON

Here is my favorite slow cooker recipe. The delicious, slightly spicy sauce will win you over, too!

tropical bbq chicken

PREP: 15 min. | COOK: 3 hours

> 2 chicken leg quarters (8 ounces *each*), skin removed
>
> 3 tablespoons ketchup
>
> 2 tablespoons orange juice
>
> 1 tablespoon brown sugar
>
> 1 tablespoon red wine vinegar
>
> 1 tablespoon olive oil
>
> 1 teaspoon minced fresh parsley
>
> 1/2 teaspoon Worcestershire sauce
>
> 1/4 teaspoon garlic salt
>
> 1/8 teaspoon pepper
>
> 2 teaspoons cornstarch
>
> 1 tablespoon cold water

With a sharp knife, cut leg quarters at the joints if desired; place in a 1-1/2-qt. slow cooker. In a small bowl, combine the ketchup, orange juice, brown sugar, vinegar, oil, parsley, Worcestershire sauce, garlic salt and pepper; pour over chicken.

Cover and cook on low for 3-4 hours or until meat is tender. Remove chicken to a serving platter; keep warm.

Skim fat from cooking juices; transfer 1/2 cup juices to a small saucepan. Bring to a boil. Combine cornstarch and water until smooth. Gradually stir into the pan. Bring to a boil; cook and stir for 2 minutes or until thickened. Serve with chicken.

YIELD: 2 servings.

beef and three-bean chili

PREP: 20 min. | **COOK:** 5 hours

1-1/2 pounds beef stew meat, cut into 1-inch pieces
2 teaspoons chili powder
1-1/3 cups chopped onion
2 tablespoons canola oil
1 can (16 ounces) kidney beans, rinsed and drained
1 can (15 ounces) white kidney *or* cannellini beans, rinsed and drained
1 can (15 ounces) black beans, rinsed and drained
2 cans (14-1/2 ounces *each*) diced tomatoes, undrained
1 cup beef broth
1 can (6 ounces) tomato paste
2 jalapeno peppers, seeded and chopped
1 tablespoon brown sugar
2 teaspoons minced garlic
1/2 teaspoon salt
1/2 teaspoon pepper
1/4 teaspoon ground cumin
Sour cream, optional

Sprinkle beef with chili powder. In a large skillet over medium heat, brown beef and onion in oil.

Meanwhile, in a 5-qt. slow cooker coated with cooking spray, combine the beans, tomatoes, broth, tomato paste, jalapenos, brown sugar, garlic, salt, pepper and cumin. Stir in the stew meat, onion and drippings.

Cover and cook on low for 5-6 hours or until meat is tender. Serve with sour cream if desired.

YIELD: 9 servings.

EDITOR'S NOTE: Wear disposable gloves when cutting hot peppers; the oils can burn skin. Avoid touching your face.

nancy whitford
EDWARDS, NEW YORK

Here is a wonderful chili that will make your kitchen smell so good as it cooks! We love eating it with homemade bread or corn bread.

REFRIED BEANS MAKE HEARTY CHILI

For a nice thick pot of chili, I stir in a can of refried beans. No one seems to notice my secret ingredient, but they definitely enjoy my chili's extra-hearty texture.
—KARA K.
KALAMAZOO, MICHIGAN

busy day beef stew

PREP: 10 min. | **COOK:** 10 hours

1 boneless beef chuck roast (1 to 1-1/2 pounds)
1 envelope onion soup mix
2 teaspoons browning sauce, optional
1/2 teaspoon salt
1/2 teaspoon pepper
6 cups water
2 cups cubed peeled potatoes (1/2-inch pieces)
6 to 8 medium carrots, cut into chunks
1 medium onion, chopped
1 cup frozen peas, thawed
1 cup frozen corn, thawed, optional
5 tablespoons cornstarch
6 tablespoons cold water

Place roast in a 5-qt. slow cooker; sprinkle with soup mix, browning sauce if desired, salt and pepper. Pour water over meat. Cover and cook on low for 8-10 hours or until meat is tender.

Remove roast to a cutting board; let stand for 5 minutes. Add vegetables to slow cooker. Cube beef and return to slow cooker. Cover and cook on low for 1-1/2 hours or until vegetables are tender.

Combine cornstarch and cold water until smooth; stir into stew. Cover and cook on high for 30-45 minutes or until thickened.

YIELD: 8-10 servings.

beth wyatt
PARIS, KENTUCKY

Here's an old-fashioned classic beef stew that simmers for hours in the slow cooker. I call it my lazy stew because it's so easy to make on busy days.

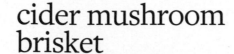

colleen weston
DENVER, COLORADO

Apple juice and gingersnaps give an autumn feel to tender, slow-cooked brisket. It's quick to prep, and the pleasing aromas linger.

BRISKET SANDWICHES

One of our favorite sandwiches is leftover beef brisket with sauteed onion and green pepper on a toasted sandwich roll. I top it with Swiss cheese and broil for a tasty Philly-style sandwich.
—DONNA H.
WILLARD, MISSOURI

loy acerra crane
JACKSON, TENNESSEE

Pork chops simmer to perfection in a sauce that comes together easily with a can of soup, an onion and some parsley flakes. You couldn't ask for a better weeknight meal.

cider mushroom brisket

PREP: 10 min. | COOK: 6 hours

    1 fresh beef brisket (6 pounds)
    2 jars (12 ounces *each*) mushroom gravy
    1 cup apple cider *or* juice
    1 envelope onion mushroom soup mix
    6 gingersnap cookies, crushed

Cut the brisket into thirds; place meat in a 5- or 6-qt. slow cooker. In a large bowl, combine the gravy, cider, soup mix and cookie crumbs; pour over beef. Cover and cook on low for 6-8 hours or until the meat is tender.

   Thinly slice meat across the grain. Skim fat from cooking juices; thicken if desired.

YIELD: 12 servings.

EDITOR'S NOTE: This recipe calls for fresh beef brisket, not corned beef.

old-fashioned pork chops

PREP: 20 min. | COOK: 5 hours

    1/2 cup all-purpose flour
1-1/2 teaspoons ground mustard
    1/2 teaspoon garlic salt
    1/2 teaspoon pepper
      6 boneless pork loin chops (5 ounces each)

      2 tablespoons canola oil
      1 can (10-1/2 ounces) condensed chicken with rice soup, undiluted
      1 medium onion, quartered
1-1/2 teaspoons dried parsley flakes

In a large resealable plastic bag, combine the flour, mustard, garlic salt and pepper. Add pork, a few pieces at a time, and shake to coat.

   In a large skillet, brown chops in oil on each side. Transfer to a 3-qt. slow cooker. Top with soup, onion and parsley. Cover and cook on low for 5-6 hours or until meat is tender.

YIELD: 6 servings.

white chili

PREP: 20 min. | COOK: 6 hours

- 3 medium onions, chopped
- 1 tablespoon olive oil
- 2 garlic cloves, minced
- 4 cups cubed cooked chicken *or* turkey
- 2 cans (15 ounces *each*) white kidney *or* cannellini beans, rinsed and drained
- 1 can (15 ounces) garbanzo beans *or* chickpeas, rinsed and drained
- 2 cups chicken broth
- 1 can (4 ounces) chopped green chilies
- 2 teaspoons ground cumin
- 1/2 teaspoon dried oregano
- 1/4 teaspoon salt
- 1/4 teaspoon cayenne pepper
- 1/4 cup minced fresh cilantro
- Corn chips, shredded Monterey Jack cheese and sour cream

In a large skillet, saute the onions in oil until tender. Add garlic; cook 1 minute longer. Transfer to a 3-qt. slow cooker. Stir in the chicken, beans, broth, green chilies, cumin, oregano, salt and cayenne.

Cover and cook on low for 6-8 hours or until bubbly. Stir in cilantro. Serve over corn chips; top with cheese and sour cream.

YIELD: 8 servings (2 quarts).

shari meissner
CHESTER, MONTANA

White chili may be a little different from what you're used to, but it's sure to warm you up on a cold night. Cilantro and cumin give this comforting chili an authentic Mexican flair.

sarah newman
MAHTOMEDI, MINNESOTA

Staying at home with a young child makes preparing dinner a challenge, but a slow cooker helps me easily make a low-fat meal. The chicken is so tender in these fajitas, and the veggies and beans provide a dose of fiber!

busy mom's chicken fajitas

PREP: 15 min. | COOK: 5 hours

1 pound boneless skinless chicken breast halves

1 can (16 ounces) kidney beans, rinsed and drained

1 can (14-1/2 ounces) diced tomatoes with mild green chilies, drained

1 *each* medium green, sweet red and yellow peppers, julienned

1 medium onion, halved and sliced

2 teaspoons ground cumin

2 teaspoons chili powder

1 garlic clove, minced

1/4 teaspoon salt

6 flour tortillas (8 inches), warmed

Shredded lettuce and chopped tomatoes, optional

In a 3-qt. slow cooker, combine the chicken, beans, tomatoes, peppers, onion and seasonings. Cover and cook on low for 5-6 hours or until chicken is tender.

Remove chicken; cool slightly. Shred chicken and return to the slow cooker; heat through.

Spoon about 3/4 cup chicken mixture down the center of each tortilla. Top with lettuce and tomatoes if desired.

YIELD: 6 servings.

chinese pork ribs

PREP: 10 min. | COOK: 6 hours

1/4 cup reduced-sodium soy sauce

1/3 cup orange marmalade

3 tablespoons ketchup

2 garlic cloves, minced

3 pounds bone-in country-style pork ribs

In a small bowl, combine the soy sauce, marmalade, ketchup and garlic. Pour half of mixture into a 5-qt. slow cooker. Top with the ribs; drizzle with the remaining sauce.

Cover and cook on low for 6-8 hours or until meat is tender. Thicken cooking juices if desired.

YIELD: 4 servings.

june ross

BELMONT, NORTH CAROLINA

Here is one of the few dishes that both of my sons agree on—they love these tasty ribs and always come back for seconds.

pork chops & acorn squash

PREP: 15 min. | COOK: 4 hours

6 boneless pork loin chops (4 ounces *each*)

2 medium acorn squash, peeled and cubed

1/2 cup packed brown sugar

2 tablespoons butter, melted

1 tablespoon orange juice

3/4 teaspoon salt

1/2 teaspoon grated orange peel

3/4 teaspoon browning sauce, optional

Place pork chops in a 5-qt. slow cooker; add squash. In a small bowl, combine the brown sugar, butter, orange juice, salt, orange peel and browning sauce if desired; pour over squash. Cover and cook on low for 4-6 hours or until meat is tender.

YIELD: 6 servings.

mary johnson

COLOMA, WISCONSIN

My husband and I can never get enough of the fresh acorn squash from our garden. These chops cook up sweet and tender in the slow cooker and the marvelous comforting flavor doesn't take a whole day to prepare.

three beans and sausage

PREP: 15 min. | COOK: 4 hours

1-1/2 pounds smoked sausage, cut into 1-inch pieces

1 can (16 ounces) kidney beans, rinsed and drained

1 can (15-1/2 ounces) great northern beans, rinsed and drained

1 can (15 ounces) black beans, rinsed and drained

1 cup chopped onion

1 cup water

1 can (8 ounces) tomato sauce

2/3 cup chopped celery

1 teaspoon chicken bouillon granules

1 teaspoon minced garlic

1 bay leaf

1/2 teaspoon pepper

1/4 teaspoon dried oregano, optional

1/4 teaspoon dried thyme, optional

Hot cooked rice

In a 5-qt. slow cooker, combine first 12 ingredients. Sprinkle with oregano and thyme if desired. Cover and cook on low for 4-5 hours or until heated through. Discard bay leaf. Serve mixture with rice.

YIELD: 8 servings.

judy sumner

RIVERTON, UTAH

For a stick-to-your-ribs meal, try this hearty combination of beans and sausage. Because it calls for several canned items, it's easy to prepare and inexpensive to serve.

jennifer foos-furer
MARYSVILLE, OHIO

Here is a heartwarming and classic way to serve ham. Apple cider and mustard perfectly accent the ham's rich, smoky flavor.

cider-glazed ham

PREP: 15 min. | **COOK:** 4 hours

1 boneless fully cooked ham (3 pounds)
1-3/4 cups apple cider *or* juice
1/4 cup packed brown sugar
1/4 cup Dijon mustard
1/4 cup honey
2 tablespoons cornstarch
2 tablespoons cold water

Place ham in a 5-qt. slow cooker. In a small bowl, combine the cider, brown sugar, mustard and honey; pour over ham. Cover and cook on low for 4-5 hours or until heated through. Remove ham and keep warm.

Pour cooking juices into a small saucepan. Combine cornstarch and water until smooth; stir into cooking juices. Bring to a boil; cook and stir for 2 minutes or until thickened. Serve with ham.

YIELD: 8 servings.

BAKED CIDER-GLAZED HAM: Place ham on a rack in a shallow roasting pan. Score the surface of the ham, making diamond shapes 1/2 in. deep. Pour cider over ham. Combine the brown sugar, mustard and honey; spread over ham. Cover and bake at 325° for 45 minutes. Uncover; bake 15-30 minutes longer or until a meat thermometer reads 140°, basting occasionally. Serve as directed.

ORANGE-GLAZED HAM: Substitute orange juice for the apple cider.

amy chop
OAK GROVE, LOUISIANA

Cumin and chili powder give spark to black bean soup. If you have leftover meat—smoked sausage, browned ground beef or a cooked roast—toss it in during the last 30 minutes of cooking.

hearty black bean soup

PREP: 10 min. | **COOK:** 9 hours

3 medium carrots, halved and thinly sliced
2 celery ribs, thinly sliced
1 medium onion, chopped
4 garlic cloves, minced
1 can (30 ounces) black beans, rinsed and drained
2 cans (14-1/2 ounces *each*) chicken *or* vegetable broth
1 can (15 ounces) crushed tomatoes
1-1/2 teaspoons dried basil
1/2 teaspoon dried oregano
1/2 teaspoon ground cumin
1/2 teaspoon chili powder
1/2 teaspoon hot pepper sauce
Hot cooked rice

In a 3-qt. slow cooker, combine first 12 ingredients. Cover; cook on low for 9-11 hours or until vegetables are tender. Serve with rice.

YIELD: 8 servings.

cheryl martinetto
GRAND RAPIDS, MINNESOTA

My slow cooker is like a reliable friend when I work long shifts. It's wonderful coming home to these saucy, well-seasoned ribs at 6 o'clock. My mother used to make them for her family, and now I do.

braised beef short ribs

PREP: 15 min. | **COOK:** 6 hours

4 pounds bone-in beef short ribs
2 tablespoons canola oil
2-1/2 cups sliced onions
1-1/2 cups beef broth
1-1/2 cups chili sauce
2/3 cup cider vinegar
1 tablespoon brown sugar
2 teaspoons paprika
1-1/2 teaspoons curry powder
1 teaspoon minced garlic
1 teaspoon salt
1/2 teaspoon ground mustard
1/2 teaspoon pepper

In a large skillet, brown ribs in oil in batches. Transfer to a 5-qt. slow cooker; add onions. Combine the remaining ingredients; pour over ribs. Cover and cook on low for 6-8 hours or until meat is tender.

YIELD: 4 servings.

sweet 'n' tangy chicken

PREP: 15 min. | COOK: 4 hours

1 medium onion, chopped
1-1/2 teaspoons minced garlic
1 broiler/fryer chicken (3 pounds), cut up, skin removed
2/3 cup ketchup
1/3 cup packed brown sugar
1 tablespoon chili powder
1 tablespoon lemon juice
1 teaspoon dried basil
1/2 teaspoon salt
1/4 teaspoon pepper
1/8 teaspoon hot pepper sauce
2 tablespoons cornstarch
3 tablespoons cold water

In a 3-qt. slow cooker, combine onion and garlic; top with chicken. In a small bowl, combine the ketchup, brown sugar, chili powder, lemon juice, basil, salt, pepper and pepper sauce; pour over chicken. Cover and cook on low for 4-5 hours or until meat is tender. Remove chicken to a serving platter and keep warm.

Skim fat from cooking juices; transfer to a small saucepan. Bring liquid to a boil. Combine cornstarch and water until smooth. Gradually stir into the pan. Bring to a boil; cook and stir for 2 minutes or until thickened. Serve with chicken.

YIELD: 4 servings.

joan airey
RIVERS, MANITOBA

My slow cooker comes in handy during the haying and harvest seasons. We're so busy that if supper isn't prepared by the time we sit down for lunch, it doesn't seem to get done on time. This recipe is hearty, delicious and fuss-free.

sandy alexander

FAYETTEVILLE,
NORTH CAROLINA

No one ever believes how little effort it takes to make these juicy ribs. The slightly sweet and tangy sauce penetrates through the meat as the ribs simmer.

sesame pork ribs

PREP: 15 min. | COOK: 5 hours

3/4 cup packed brown sugar
1/2 cup reduced-sodium soy sauce
1/2 cup ketchup
1/4 cup honey
  2 tablespoons white wine vinegar
  3 garlic cloves, minced
  1 teaspoon salt
  1 teaspoon ground ginger
1/4 to 1/2 teaspoon crushed red pepper flakes
  5 pounds bone-in country-style pork ribs

  1 medium onion, sliced
  2 tablespoons sesame seeds, toasted
  2 tablespoons chopped green onions

In a large bowl, combine the first nine ingredients. Add ribs and turn to coat. Place the onion in a 5-qt. slow cooker; top with ribs and sauce. Cover and cook on low for 5-6 hours or until meat is tender.

Place ribs on a serving platter; sprinkle with sesame seeds and green onions.

YIELD: 5 servings.

the **ULTIMATE COMFORT FOOD** cookbook

taco meat loaf

PREP: 10 min. | COOK: 8 hours

1 egg
1/2 cup sour cream
1/3 cup salsa
2 to 4 tablespoons taco seasoning
1 cup crushed tortilla chips
1/2 cup shredded cheddar cheese
2 pounds lean ground beef (90% lean)
Optional toppings: sour cream, salsa, shredded cheddar cheese, shredded lettuce, sliced ripe olives

In a large bowl, combine the first six ingredients. Crumble beef over mixture and mix well. Pat into a 3-qt. slow cooker.

Cover and cook on low for 8 hours or until no pink remains and a thermometer reads 160°. Top with the sour cream, salsa, cheese, lettuce and olives if desired.

YIELD: 8 servings.

diane essinger
FINDLAY, OHIO

Our children think there are three basic food groups—pizza, tacos and burgers! They love Taco Meat Loaf, especially when they doctor it up with their favorite toppings.

big red soup

PREP: 20 min. | COOK: 8 hours

2 pounds beef stew meat, cut into 1-inch cubes
2 tablespoons canola oil
3/4 cup chopped onion
2 cloves garlic, minced
2 cans (14-1/2 ounces each) diced tomatoes in sauce
1 can (10-1/2 ounces) condensed beef broth, undiluted
1 can (10-1/2 ounces) condensed chicken broth, undiluted
1 can (10-3/4 ounces) condensed tomato soup, undiluted
1/4 cup water
1 teaspoon ground cumin
1 teaspoon chili powder
1 teaspoon salt
1/2 teaspoon lemon-pepper seasoning
2 teaspoons Worcestershire sauce
1/3 cup picante sauce
8 corn tortillas, cut into quarters
1 cup (4 ounces) shredded cheddar cheese

In a large skillet, brown beef in oil. Transfer to a 5-qt. slow cooker; add the remaining ingredients except for tortillas and cheese. Cover and cook on low for 8-10 hours or until meat is tender.

To serve, place enough tortilla quarters to cover bottom of each bowl. Pour soup over tortilla pieces; sprinkle with cheese.

YIELD: 10-12 servings.

shelly korell
BAYARD, NEBRASKA

We're Nebraska Cornhusker football fans, and on the days when the "Big Red" team is playing, I stir up a big pot of this soup. The whole family gathers around the television set to eat it while watching the game!

melt-in-your-mouth sausages

PREP: 10 min. | COOK: 4 hours

8 Italian sausage links (2 pounds)
1 jar (26 ounces) meatless spaghetti sauce
1/2 cup water
1 can (6 ounces) tomato paste
1 large green pepper, thinly sliced
1 large onion, thinly sliced
1 tablespoon grated Parmesan cheese
1 teaspoon dried parsley flakes
8 brat buns, split
Additional Parmesan cheese, optional

Place the sausages in a large skillet; cover with water. Bring to a boil. Reduce heat; cover and simmer for 10 minutes or until a thermometer reads 140°; drain well.

Meanwhile, in a 3-qt. slow cooker, combine the spaghetti sauce, water, tomato paste, green pepper, onion, cheese and parsley. Add sausages. Cover and cook on low for 4-5 hours or until vegetables are tender. Serve in buns. Sprinkle with additional cheese if desired.

YIELD: 8 servings.

ilean schultheiss
COHOCTON, NEW YORK

My family loves this recipe. It's such a good all-around dish, either for sandwiches like these or served with hot cooked spaghetti.

barbara gordon
ROSWELL, GEORGIA

This sweet and tangy side dish uses canned goods, so it's a snap to throw together. It's nice to serve at a picnic. You can also bake the beans, covered, in a 350° oven for 40 minutes. Remove the cover and cook 10 minutes longer.

ranch beans

PREP: 10 min. | **COOK:** 3 hours

- 1 can (16 ounces) kidney beans, rinsed and drained
- 1 can (15-3/4 ounces) pork and beans, undrained
- 1 can (15 ounces) lima beans, rinsed and drained
- 1 can (14-1/2 ounces) cut green beans, drained
- 1 bottle (12 ounces) chili sauce
- 3/4 cup packed brown sugar
- 1 small onion, chopped

In a 3-qt. slow cooker, combine all the ingredients. Cover and cook on high for 3-4 hours or until beans are heated through.

YIELD: 8-10 servings.

sandy mullen
GAGE, OKLAHOMA

It doesn't get much easier than a hearty, all-in-one meal you can prep in just 10 minutes. And it doesn't get much tastier, either!

country pork chop supper

PREP: 10 min. | **COOK:** 5 hours

- 6 boneless pork loin chops (1/2 inch thick and 4 ounces *each*)
- 2 jars (12 ounces *each*) pork gravy
- 1 can (10-3/4 ounces) condensed cream of mushroom soup, undiluted
- 2 tablespoons ketchup
- 1 tablespoon minced chives
- 1 teaspoon pepper
- 1 teaspoon soy sauce
- 1/2 teaspoon seasoned salt
- 3 medium potatoes, peeled and quartered
- 1 package (16 ounces) frozen mixed vegetables

Place pork chops in a greased 5-qt. slow cooker. In a large bowl, combine the gravy, soup, ketchup, chives, pepper, soy sauce and seasoned salt; pour over pork.

Stir in potatoes; cover and cook on low for 4-5 hours. Stir in vegetables and cook 1 hour longer or until meat and potatoes are tender.

YIELD: 6 servings.

turkey with cranberry sauce

PREP: 15 min. **Bake:** 4 hours

- 2 boneless skinless turkey breast halves (3 pounds *each*)
- 1 can (14 ounces) jellied cranberry sauce
- 1/2 cup plus 2 tablespoons water, *divided*
- 1 envelope onion soup mix
- 2 tablespoons cornstarch

Place turkey breasts in a 5-qt. slow cooker. In a large bowl, combine the cranberry sauce, 1/2 cup water and soup mix. Pour over turkey. Cover and cook on low for 4-6 hours or until meat is tender. Remove turkey and keep warm.

Transfer cooking juices to a large saucepan. Combine the cornstarch and remaining water until smooth. Bring cranberry mixture to a boil; gradually stir in cornstarch mixture until smooth. Cook and stir for 2 minutes or until thickened. Slice turkey; serve with cranberry sauce. Leftovers may be frozen for up to 3 months.

YIELD: 15 servings.

marie ramsden
FAIRGROVE, MICHIGAN

Here is a very tasty and easy way to cook a turkey breast in the slow cooker. Ideal for holiday potlucks, the sweet cranberry sauce perfectly complements the succulent turkey.

sharon delaney-chronis

SOUTH MILWAUKEE, WISCONSIN

Serve up the flavors of the bayou! You'll leave the table feeling satisfied, as this gumbo is brimming with veggies and sausage. For a more authentic Cajun flavor, use andouille instead of Polish sausage.

smoked sausage gumbo

PREP: 20 min. | **COOK:** 4 hours

2 celery ribs, chopped

1 medium onion, chopped

1 medium green pepper, chopped

1 medium carrot, chopped

2 tablespoons olive oil

1/4 cup all-purpose flour

1 cup chicken broth

1 pound smoked kielbasa *or* Polish sausage, cut into 1/2-inch pieces

1 can (14-1/2 ounces) diced tomatoes, undrained

2 teaspoons dried oregano

2 teaspoons dried thyme

1/8 teaspoon cayenne pepper

Hot cooked rice

In a large skillet, saute the celery, onion, green pepper and carrot in oil until tender. Stir in flour until blended; gradually add broth. Bring to a boil. Cook and stir for 2 minutes or until thickened.

Transfer to a 3-qt. slow cooker. Stir in the sausage, tomatoes, oregano, thyme and cayenne. Cover and cook on low for 4-5 hours or until heated through. Serve with rice.

YIELD: 5 servings.

barbecues for the bunch

PREP: 25 min. | COOK: 6 hours

- 2 pounds beef top sirloin steak, cubed
- 1-1/2 pounds boneless pork loin roast, cubed
- 2 large onions, chopped
- 3/4 cup chopped celery
- 1 can (6 ounces) tomato paste
- 1/2 cup packed brown sugar
- 1/4 cup cider vinegar
- 1/4 cup chili sauce
- 2 tablespoons Worcestershire sauce
- 1 tablespoon ground mustard
- 16 hamburger buns, split

In a 5-qt. slow cooker, combine the beef, pork, onions and celery. In a small bowl, combine the tomato paste, brown sugar, vinegar, chili sauce, Worcestershire sauce and mustard. Pour over the meat mixture.

Cover and cook on high for 6-8 hours or until meat is very tender. Shred meat in the slow cooker with two forks. With a slotted spoon, serve 1/2 cup meat mixture on each bun.

YIELD: 16 servings.

louise watkins
LONG KEY, FLORIDA

Here is an easy way to have a party-perfect meal ready for your gang. Just add chips and your favorite picnic foods.

SLOW COOKER CARRIER

I use a milk crate to transport my slow cooker to potlucks. I line the crate with a towel, leave the lid at home, and cover the slow cooker with foil instead. I set the cooker in the crate with my serving utensil. The crate keeps the pot from tipping and catches any drips. And when I leave, I don't have to look for my lid!
—HELEN P.
HORSEHEADS, NEW YORK

slow cooker lasagna

PREP: 25 min. | COOK: 4 hours

- 1 pound ground beef
- 1 large onion, chopped
- 2 garlic cloves, minced
- 1 can (29 ounces) tomato sauce
- 1 cup water
- 1 can (6 ounces) tomato paste
- 1 teaspoon salt
- 1 teaspoon dried oregano
- 1 package (8 ounces) no-cook lasagna noodles
- 4 cups (16 ounces) shredded part-skim mozzarella cheese
- 1-1/2 cups (12 ounces) 4% cottage cheese
- 1/2 cup grated Parmesan cheese

In a skillet, cook beef and onion over medium heat until meat is no longer pink. Add garlic; cook 1 minute longer. Drain. Stir in the tomato sauce, water, tomato paste, salt and oregano.

Spread a fourth of the meat sauce in an ungreased 5-qt. slow cooker. Arrange a third of the noodles over sauce (break the noodles if necessary). Combine the cheeses; spoon a third of the mixture over noodles. Repeat layers twice. Top with remaining meat sauce.

Cover and cook on low for 4-5 hours or until noodles are tender.

YIELD: 6-8 servings.

lisa micheletti
COLLIERVILLE, TENNESSEE

Convenient no-cook lasagna noodles take the work out of a traditional favorite adapted for the slow cooker. We like our lasagna with Parmesan bread or garlic cheese toast.

lori piatt
DANVILLE, ILLINOIS

You'll need just five ingredients to feed a crowd with these great sandwiches. On weekends, I start the roast the night before so I can shred it in the morning.

italian beef hoagies

PREP: 25 min. | COOK: 8 hours

1 beef sirloin tip roast (4 pounds), halved
2 envelopes Italian salad dressing mix
2 cups water
1 jar (16 ounces) mild pickled pepper rings, undrained
18 hoagie buns, split

Place the roast in a 5-qt. slow cooker. Combine the salad dressing mix and water; pour over the roast. Cover and cook on low for 8-10 hours or until meat is tender.

Remove meat; shred with two forks and return to the slow cooker. Add pepper rings; heat through. Spoon 1/2 cup meat mixture onto each bun.

YIELD: 18 servings.

susan dalrymple
MARATHON, FLORIDA

I couldn't bear the thought of going to the supermarket one day, and I was truly determined to come up with something for dinner from what I had. I created this comforting chicken mix, and my husband loved it!

chicken with veggies 'n' gravy

PREP: 10 min. | COOK: 4 hours

3 medium carrots, chopped
2 celery ribs, chopped
1 medium onion, chopped
2 boneless skinless chicken breast halves (5 ounces each)
1/8 teaspoon pepper

1 can (10-3/4 ounces) condensed cream of chicken soup, undiluted
2/3 cup water
1/4 cup white wine or chicken broth
2 individually frozen biscuits

Place the carrots, celery and onion in a 1-1/2-qt. slow cooker; top with chicken. Sprinkle with pepper.

In a small bowl, combine the soup, water and wine; pour over chicken. Cover and cook on low for 4-5 hours or until meat and vegetables are tender.

If desired, thicken cooking juices. Meanwhile, bake biscuits according to package directions. Serve with chicken and gravy.

YIELD: 2 servings.

slow-cooked pepper steak

PREP: 10 min. | COOK: 6-1/2 hours

1-1/2 pounds beef top round steak
   2 tablespoons canola oil
   1 cup chopped onion
1/4 cup reduced-sodium soy sauce
   1 garlic clove, minced
   1 teaspoon sugar
1/2 teaspoon salt
1/4 teaspoon ground ginger
1/4 teaspoon pepper
   4 medium tomatoes, cut into wedges *or* 1
      can (14-1/2 ounces) diced tomatoes,
      undrained
   1 large green pepper, cut into strips
   1 tablespoon cornstarch

1/2 cup cold water
Hot cooked noodles *or* rice

Cut beef into 3-in. x 1-in. strips. In a large skillet, brown beef in oil. Transfer to a 3-qt. slow cooker. Combine the onion, soy sauce, garlic, sugar, salt, ginger and pepper; pour over beef. Cover and cook on low for 5-6 hours or until meat is tender. Add tomatoes and green pepper; cook on low 1 hour longer or until vegetables are tender.

Combine cornstarch and cold water until smooth; gradually stir into slow cooker. Cover and cook on high for 20-30 minutes until thickened. Serve with noodles or rice.

YIELD: 6 servings.

sue gronholz
BEAVER DAM, WISCONSIN

After a long day in our greenhouse raising bedding plants for sale, I appreciate coming in to this hearty beef dish for supper.

tyler sherman
WILLIAMSBURG, VIRGINIA

Although I don't consider myself much of a cook, my turkey-portobello meat loaf is delicious. It's tender and moist, and the sauce has a nice zip to it. Mushrooms and ground turkey are a nice combination.

turkey-portobello meat loaf

PREP: 30 min. | COOK: 3-1/4 hours

2	eggs, lightly beaten
1-1/3	cups soft bread crumbs
1/2	pound large portobello mushrooms, stems removed, finely chopped
1	small onion, finely chopped
2	garlic cloves, minced
3/4	teaspoon salt
1/2	teaspoon dried thyme
1/4	teaspoon pepper
1	pound lean ground turkey
1/4	cup chili sauce
2	teaspoons stone-ground mustard
1/8	teaspoon cayenne pepper

Cut three 20-in. x 3-in. strips of heavy-duty foil; crisscross so they resemble spokes of a wheel. Place strips on the bottom and up the sides of a 3-qt. slow cooker. Coat strips with cooking spray.

In a large bowl, combine the eggs, bread crumbs, mushrooms, onion, garlic, salt, thyme and pepper. Crumble turkey over mixture and mix well. Shape into a 7-1/2-in. x 4-in. loaf.

Place the meat loaf in the center of the strips. Cover and cook on low for 3-4 hours or until no pink remains and a thermometer reads 160°

Combine the chili sauce, mustard and cayenne; pour over meat. Cover and cook 15 minutes longer or until heated through. Using foil strips as handles, remove the meat loaf to a platter.

YIELD: 6 servings.

polynesian roast beef

PREP: 15 min. | **COOK:** 7 hours

1 beef top round roast (3-1/4 pounds)
2 tablespoons browning sauce, optional
1/4 cup all-purpose flour
1 teaspoon salt
1/4 teaspoon pepper
1 medium onion, sliced
1 can (8 ounces) unsweetened sliced pineapple
1/4 cup packed brown sugar
2 tablespoons cornstarch
1/4 teaspoon ground ginger
1/2 cup beef broth
1/4 cup reduced-sodium soy sauce
1/2 teaspoon minced garlic
1 medium green pepper, sliced

Cut roast in half; brush with browning sauce if desired. Combine the flour, salt and pepper; rub over meat. Place onion in a 3-qt. slow cooker; top with roast.

Drain pineapple, reserving juice; refrigerate the pineapple. In a small bowl, combine the brown sugar, cornstarch and ginger; whisk in the broth, soy sauce, garlic and reserved pineapple juice until smooth. Pour over meat. Cover and cook on low for 6-8 hours.

Add pineapple and green pepper. Cook 1 hour longer or until meat is tender.

YIELD: 10-11 servings.

annette mosbarger
PEYTON, COLORADO

This easy and delicious recipe of my sister's has been a family favorite for years. Pineapple and peppers add perfect contrast to the rich and savory beef.

chicken noodle soup

PREP: 20 min. | **COOK:** 5-1/2 hours

12 fresh baby carrots, cut into 1/2-inch pieces
4 celery ribs, cut into 1/2-inch pieces
3/4 cup finely chopped onion
1 tablespoon minced fresh parsley
1/2 teaspoon pepper
1/4 teaspoon cayenne pepper
1-1/2 teaspoons mustard seed
2 garlic cloves, peeled and halved
1-1/4 pounds boneless skinless chicken breast halves
1-1/4 pounds boneless skinless chicken thighs
4 cans (14-1/2 ounces *each*) chicken broth
1 package (9 ounces) refrigerated linguine

In a 5-qt. slow cooker, combine the first six ingredients. Place mustard seed and garlic on a double thickness of cheesecloth; bring up corners of cloth and tie with kitchen string to form a bag. Place in slow cooker. Add chicken and broth. Cover and cook on low for 5-6 hours or until the chicken is tender.

Discard spice bag. Remove chicken; cool slightly. Stir linguine into soup; cover and cook on high for 30 minutes or until tender. Cut chicken into pieces and return to soup; heat through.

YIELD: 12 servings (3 quarts).

norma reynolds
OVERLAND PARK, KANSAS

Here is a homemade soup brimming with vegetables, chicken and noodles. The recipe came from my father-in-law, but I made some adjustments to give it my own spin.

THYME MAKES TASTY SOUP

My grandmother's chicken soup had terrific flavor, but when I made my own batch, it just didn't taste the same. Grandma told me her secret is a healthy pinch of fresh thyme stirred in toward the very end of cooking.

—SHARRON S.
SEWICKLEY, PENNSYLVANIA

dianne joy richardson
COLORADO SPRINGS,
COLORADO

*I found this recipe in one of
our local publications. It's
great for casual wintertime
entertaining, since the meat
cooks all day without
needing any attention.*

french dip sandwiches

PREP: 15 min. | COOK: 10 hours

- 1 beef sirloin tip roast (3 to 4 pounds)
- 1/2 cup reduced-sodium soy sauce
- 1 teaspoon beef bouillon granules
- 1 bay leaf
- 3 to 4 whole peppercorns
- 1 teaspoon dried crushed rosemary
- 1 teaspoon dried thyme
- 1 teaspoon garlic powder

Hard rolls, split

Cut roast in half. Combine the soy sauce, bouillon and seasonings; pour over roast. Add water to almost cover roast. Cover and cook on low for 10-12 hours or until meat is very tender.

Remove roast; cool slightly. Discard bay leaf. Shred meat with two forks and return to slow cooker; heat through. Serve on rolls with broth.

YIELD: 12 sandwiches.

diane hixon
NICEVILLE, FLORIDA

*Tender steak is sliced into
appetizing spirals for
serving, and extra stuffing
cooks conveniently in a foil
packet on top of the meat.
Here's a fuss-free meal
that's great for company.*

stuffed flank steak

PREP: 25 min. | COOK: 6 hours

- 1 package (8 ounces) crushed corn bread stuffing
- 1 cup chopped onion
- 1 cup chopped celery
- 1/4 cup minced fresh parsley
- 1/2 cup egg substitute
- 1-1/4 cups beef broth
- 1/3 cup butter, melted
- 1/2 teaspoon seasoned salt
- 1/2 teaspoon pepper
- 1 beef flank steak (1-1/2 pounds)

In a large bowl, combine the stuffing, onion, celery and parsley. In a small bowl, beat the egg substitute; stir in broth and butter. Pour over stuffing mixture. Sprinkle with seasoned salt and pepper; stir well.

Pound steak to 1/2-in. thickness. Spread 1-1/2 cups stuffing mixture over steak. Roll up, starting with a short side; tie with string. Place in a 5-qt. slow cooker. Remaining stuffing can be wrapped tightly in foil and placed over the rolled steak.

Cover and cook on low for 6-8 hours or until a thermometer inserted in stuffing reads 160° and meat is tender. Remove string before slicing.

YIELD: 6 servings.

EDITOR'S NOTE: No liquid is added to the slow cooker. The moisture comes from the meat.

slow-cooked meat loaf

PREP: 15 min. | **COOK:** 5 hours

1 can (10-3/4 ounces) condensed cream
   of celery soup, undiluted
1-1/4 cups water
1 egg
1/4 cup dry bread crumbs
2 tablespoons grated Parmesan cheese
1-1/2 teaspoons dried parsley flakes
1/2 teaspoon garlic powder
1/4 teaspoon onion powder
1/8 teaspoon salt, optional
1/8 teaspoon pepper
1/2 pound lean ground beef (90% lean)
Hot mashed potatoes, optional

In a small bowl, combine soup and water until blended. Pour half into a 1-1/2-qt. slow cooker. Cover and refrigerate remaining soup mixture.

In a small bowl, combine the egg, bread crumbs, cheese, parsley, garlic powder, onion powder, salt if desired and pepper. Crumble beef over mixture and mix well.

Shape into a loaf; place in slow cooker. Cover and cook on low for 5-6 hours or until meat is no longer pink and a thermometer reads 160°.

For gravy, place reserved soup mixture in a small saucepan; cook over low heat until heated through. Serve the meat loaf and gravy with mashed potatoes if desired.

YIELD: 2 servings.

ginger cortese
HOLLSOPPLE, PENNSYLVANIA

My husband and I both work late, so it's great to come home to a classic homemade meat loaf with mashed potatoes and veggies on the side. It reminds me of a supper that my mom would make.

CHAPTER FIVE

side dishes

PICTURED LEFT TO RIGHT: GREEN BEAN CASSEROLE FOR 2, PAGE 176 • ITALIAN BASIL PASTA SALAD, PAGE 173
CORN AND BROCCOLI IN CHEESE SAUCE, PAGE 197 • REUBEN BAKED POTATOES, PAGE 205

denise baumert
DALHART, TEXAS

This traditional salad is one of my mother-in-law's favorites. It's fun to eat because of its crunchy texture, and the raisins give it a slightly sweet flavor.

carrot raisin salad

PREP/TOTAL TIME: 10 min.

    4 cups shredded carrots (about 4 large)
    3/4 to 1-1/2 cups raisins
    1/4 cup mayonnaise
    2 tablespoons sugar
    2 to 3 tablespoons 2% milk

Place carrots and raisins in a large bowl. In a small bowl, combine the mayonnaise, sugar and enough milk to achieve dressing consistency. Pour over carrot mixture; toss to coat.

YIELD: 8 servings.

kim kreider
MOUNT JOY, PENNSYLVANIA

My homemade corn bread dressing has a full-flavored rustic feel, even though it's made with less fat and sodium. It's a healthier version of a classic.

makeover best corn bread dressing

PREP: 45 min. + cooling | BAKE: 45 min.

    1-1/4 cups all-purpose flour
    3/4 cup yellow cornmeal
    1/4 cup sugar
    2 teaspoons baking powder
    1/2 teaspoon salt
    1 egg
    1 cup fat-free milk
    2 tablespoons canola oil
    2 tablespoons unsweetened applesauce

DRESSING:

    6 cups cubed day-old bread (1/2-inch cubes)
    2 celery ribs, finely chopped
    1 large onion, finely chopped
    1/2 cup chopped pecans
    1/2 cup reduced-fat butter
    2 eggs, beaten
    1-1/2 teaspoons poultry seasoning
    3/4 teaspoon salt
    1/2 teaspoon pepper
    2-1/4 to 2-3/4 cups reduced-sodium chicken broth

In a large bowl, combine the first five ingredients. Combine the egg, milk, oil and applesauce; stir into dry ingredients just until moistened. Transfer to a 9-in. square baking pan coated with cooking spray.

Bake at 400° for 15-18 minutes or until a toothpick inserted near the center comes out clean. Cool on a wire rack. Place cubed bread on baking sheets; bake for 5-7 minutes or until lightly browned. Cool on a wire rack. Cut corn bread into 1/2-in. cubes; set aside.

In a large skillet, saute the celery, onion and pecans in butter until vegetables are tender. Transfer to a large bowl. Stir in the corn bread, cubed bread, eggs, seasonings and enough broth to reach desired moistness (about 2-1/2 cups).

Transfer to a 13-in. x 9-in. baking dish coated with cooking spray. Cover and bake at 350° for 35 minutes. Uncover; bake 8-10 minutes longer or until a thermometer reads 160° and top is lightly browned.

YIELD: 12 servings.

italian basil pasta salad

PREP: 30 min. + chilling

- 1 package (16 ounces) bow tie pasta
- 2 cups grape tomatoes
- 7 ounces fresh mozzarella cheese, cubed
- 1 medium sweet yellow pepper, chopped
- 1 small red onion, chopped
- 1/2 cup pickled banana pepper rings
- 1 can (2-1/4 ounces) sliced ripe olives, drained
- 4 thin slices hard salami, diced
- 1/2 cup fresh basil leaves, thinly sliced

DRESSING:

- 3/4 cup olive oil
- 3/4 cup red wine vinegar
- 1 garlic clove, minced
- 1 teaspoon salt
- 1/2 teaspoon pepper
- 1/4 teaspoon dried basil

Cook pasta according to package directions; drain and rinse in cold water. In a large bowl, combine the pasta, tomatoes, cheese, yellow pepper, onion, pepper rings, olives, salami and basil.

In a small bowl, whisk the dressing ingredients. Pour over the salad and toss to coat. Cover and refrigerate for at least 1 hour before serving.

YIELD: 18 servings.

charlotte gehle
BROWNSTOWN, MICHIGAN

Ready for a big bite of summertime? Pass around this garden-fresh pasta salad. I suggest serving it at your next barbecue, potluck or luncheon.

stacey meyer
MERCED, CALIFORNIA

My sister gave me this fluffy salad recipe that whips up in a jiffy. Unlike many gelatin recipes, the salad doesn't have to set for hours, so it's great for unexpected company.

orange fluff salad

PREP/TOTAL TIME: 15 min.

1 cup (8 ounces) sour cream
1 package (3 ounces) lemon gelatin
2 cans (11 ounces *each*) mandarin oranges, drained
1 can (21 ounces) pineapple tidbits, drained
1 carton (8 ounces) frozen whipped topping, thawed
Pastel miniature marshmallows, optional

Place sour cream in a large bowl. Sprinkle with gelatin and stir until blended. Fold in the oranges, pineapple and whipped topping. Sprinkle with marshmallows if desired.

YIELD: 8 servings.

onion yorkshire puddings

PREP: 20 min. | **BAKE:** 30 min.

- 1/2 pound yellow onions, thinly sliced
- 1 teaspoon salt, *divided*
- 1/4 teaspoon pepper
- 2 tablespoons butter
- 3/4 cup plus 2 tablespoons all-purpose flour
- 2 eggs
- 3/4 cup water
- 3/4 cup 2% milk

In a large skillet, saute the onions, 1/2 teaspoon salt and pepper in butter until tender but not browned. Divide among eight 6-oz. ramekins or custard cups. Place on a baking sheet.

In a large bowl, combine the flour and remaining salt. Whisk the eggs, water and milk; then whisk into the flour mixture just until blended. Pour 1/4 cup into each ramekin.

Bake at 400° for 30-35 minutes or until puffed and golden brown. Serve immediately.

YIELD: 8 servings.

emily chaney
BLUE HILL, MAINE

A cross between traditional Yorksire pudding and popovers, this easy recipe makes a great complement to prime rib. We also like it with beef stew and steak. Make more than you think you'll need because everyone loves them.

cheddar twice-baked potatoes

PREP: 1-1/4 hours | **BAKE:** 20 min.

- 6 large baking potatoes
- 8 tablespoons butter, *divided*
- 1/4 pound sliced bacon, diced
- 1 medium onion, finely chopped
- 1/2 cup 2% milk
- 1 egg
- 1/2 teaspoon salt
- 1/8 teaspoon white pepper
- 1 cup (4 ounces) shredded cheddar cheese

Scrub and pierce potatoes; rub each with 1 teaspoon butter. Place on a baking sheet. Bake at 375° for 1 hour or until tender.

Meanwhile, in a small skillet, cook bacon over medium heat until crisp. Remove to paper towels; drain, reserving 1 tablespoon drippings. In the drippings, saute onion until tender; set aside.

When potatoes are cool enough to handle, cut a thin slice off the top of each and discard. Scoop out pulp, leaving a thin shell. In a small bowl, mash pulp with remaining butter. Stir in the milk, egg, salt and pepper. Stir in the cheese, bacon and onion.

Spoon into the potato shells. Place shells on a baking sheet. Bake at 375° for 20-25 minutes or until heated through.

YIELD: 6 servings.

heather ahrens
COLUMBUS, OHIO

Our family rarely has steak without these easy-to-fix potatoes. They're creamy and loaded with bacon, cheese and onion. What's not to love?

rosemary beaudoin
PLAINVILLE, CONNECTICUT

Here's a scaled-down version of the casserole so many families love. You can replace the green beans with any other frozen veggies. I like a mixture of carrots, broccoli and cauliflower.

YUMMY GREEN BEAN CASSEROLE

Along with the mushroom soup, I flavor my green bean casserole with shredded cheddar cheese and a little horseradish.

—OLIVE S., HAYDENVILLE, MASSACHUSETTS

green bean casserole for 2

PREP: 10 min. | **BAKE:** 25 min.

- 1/2 cup condensed cream of mushroom soup, undiluted
- 1 ounce cream cheese, softened
- 1-3/4 cups frozen French-style green beans
- 5 tablespoons shredded Italian cheese blend, *divided*
- 5 tablespoons french-fried onions, *divided*
- 1/4 cup sour cream

In a small bowl, beat soup and cream cheese until blended. Stir in the green beans, 4 tablespoons cheese, 4 tablespoons onions and sour cream. Transfer to a 3-cup baking dish coated with cooking spray. Sprinkle with remaining cheese and onions.

Bake, uncovered, at 350° for 25-30 minutes or until bubbly and cheese is melted.

YIELD: 2 servings.

lucille terry
FRANKFORT, KENTUCKY

I have a thriving country garden and try a lot of recipes using my squash. It's a pleasure to make this beautiful casserole for special meals.

calico squash

PREP: 20 min. | **BAKE:** 30 min.

- 2 cups sliced yellow summer squash (1/4 inch thick)
- 1 cup sliced zucchini (1/4 inch thick)
- 1 medium onion, chopped
- 1/4 cup sliced green onions
- 1 cup water
- 1 teaspoon salt, *divided*

- 2 cups crushed butter-flavored crackers
- 1/2 cup butter, melted
- 1 can (10-3/4 ounces) condensed cream of chicken soup, undiluted
- 1 can (8 ounces) sliced water chestnuts, drained
- 1 large carrot, shredded
- 1/2 cup mayonnaise
- 1 jar (2 ounces) diced pimientos, drained
- 1 teaspoon rubbed sage
- 1/2 teaspoon white pepper
- 1 cup (4 ounces) shredded sharp cheddar cheese

In a large saucepan, combine first five ingredients; add 1/2 teaspoon salt. Cover and cook until squash is tender, about 6 minutes. Drain well; set aside.

Combine crumbs and butter; spoon half into a greased shallow 1-1/2-qt. baking dish. In a large bowl, combine soup, water chestnuts, carrot, mayonnaise, pimientos, sage, pepper and remaining salt; fold in squash mixture. Spoon over crumbs.

Sprinkle with cheese and the remaining crumb mixture. Bake, uncovered, at 350° for 30 minutes or until lightly browned.

YIELD: 8 servings.

oven fries

PREP: 10 min. | **BAKE:** 40 min.

4 medium potatoes
1 tablespoon olive oil
2-1/2 teaspoons paprika
3/4 teaspoon salt
3/4 teaspoon garlic powder

Cut each potato into 12 wedges. In a large bowl, combine the oil, paprika, salt and garlic powder. Add potatoes; toss to coat.

Transfer to a 15-in. x 10-in. x 1-in. baking pan coated with cooking spray. Bake at 400° for 40-45 minutes or until tender, turning once.

YIELD: 4 servings.

heather byers
PITTSBURGH, PENNSYLVANIA

I jazz up my fries with paprika and garlic powder. Something about the combination of spices packs a heck of a punch. Everyone loves them. We even enjoy the leftovers cold!

delores nickerson
MUSKOGEE, OKLAHOMA

I put a light spin on a Thanksgiving classic with this festive recipe. It captures the flavors of sweet potatoes and marshmallows, but leaves out the extra calories!

mallow sweet potato bake

PREP: 70 min. | **BAKE:** 40 min.

6 large sweet potatoes

3 tablespoons butter

1 can (8 ounces) unsweetened crushed pineapple, undrained

1/2 cup dried cranberries, *divided*

1/3 cup orange juice

3/4 teaspoon salt

2/3 cup miniature marshmallows

1/3 cup chopped pecans

Scrub and pierce sweet potatoes. Bake at 400° for 45-55 minutes or until tender.

Cut sweet potatoes in half; scoop out pulp and place in a large bowl. Stir in butter until melted. Stir in the pineapple, 1/4 cup cranberries, orange juice and salt.

Transfer to an 11-in. x 7-in. baking dish coated with cooking spray. Cover casserole and bake at 350° for 30 minutes.

Uncover; sprinkle with marshmallows, pecans and remaining cranberries. Bake 8-10 minutes longer or just until marshmallows are puffed and lightly browned.

YIELD: 12 servings.

cheddar tot casserole

PREP: 15 min. | **BAKE:** 30 min.

  1 can (12 ounces) evaporated milk
  1 can (10-3/4 ounces) condensed cream of chicken soup, undiluted
  1 cup (8 ounces) sour cream
  1/2 cup butter, melted
  1 teaspoon onion powder
  1 teaspoon garlic powder
  1 package (32 ounces) frozen Tater Tots
1-1/2 cups (6 ounces) shredded cheddar cheese
  1 cup crushed potato chips

In a large bowl, combine the first six ingredients. Gently stir in Tater Tots. Transfer to a greased 13-in. x 9-in. baking dish. Sprinkle cheese and potato chips over the top.

Bake, uncovered, at 350° for 30-35 minutes or until bubbly and heated through.

YIELD: 10 servings.

jessica salts
CORPUS CHRISTI, TEXAS

This rich, amazing dish is fun and popular at parties and potlucks. Kids love it!

fried onion rings

PREP/TOTAL TIME: 25 min.

  1/2 cup all-purpose flour
  1/2 cup water
  1 egg, lightly beaten
  1 teaspoon seasoned salt
  1/2 teaspoon baking powder
  1 large onion, very thinly sliced
Oil for deep-fat frying

In a shallow bowl, whisk the first five ingredients. Separate onion slices into rings. Dip rings into batter. In a deep-fat fryer, heat 1 in. of oil to 375°. Fry onion rings in batches for 1 to 1-1/2 minutes on each side or until golden brown. Drain on paper towels. Serve immediately.

YIELD: 12 servings.

taste of home test kitchen

Use these crispy burger toppers to add an extra element to already fantastic burgers. They're also perfect for giving your salads a little crunch.

garlic mashed potatoes

PREP/TOTAL TIME: 30 min.

  5 large potatoes, peeled and cut into 1/2-inch cubes
 15 garlic cloves, peeled and halved
  2 teaspoons salt, *divided*
  1/2 cup butter, softened
  1/2 cup heavy whipping cream

Place the potatoes, garlic and 1 teaspoon salt in a large saucepan and cover with water. Bring to a boil. Reduce heat; cover and cook for 10-15 minutes or until potatoes are tender. Drain.

Transfer potato mixture to a large bowl; mash. Add the butter, cream and remaining salt; beat until mixture is smooth.

YIELD: 6 servings.

myra innes
AUBURN, KANSAS

Garlic is boiled and then mashed right along with the potatoes to give my side dish extraordinary flavor.

jane everett
PINEHURST, NORTH CAROLINA

As they grew up, my children loved all vegetables, but they often requested spinach served this way. Through the years, this recipe has remained a popular request.

HOW TO DRAIN SPINACH

Drain cooked spinach in a colander with fine holes. With clean hands, press the water out of the spinach. If the spinach was cooked, allow it to cool before handling.

spinach casserole for 2

PREP/TOTAL TIME: 30 min.

- 1 package (10 ounces) frozen chopped spinach
- 5 tablespoons butter, *divided*
- 1/2 teaspoon salt
- 1/4 teaspoon pepper
- 1/2 cup shredded cheddar cheese
- 2 eggs, lightly beaten
- 1/2 cup milk
- 1/2 cup soft bread crumbs

Cook spinach according to package directions; drain well. Add 4 tablespoons butter, salt, pepper, cheese, eggs and milk.

Spoon mixture into two greased ramekins. Melt remaining butter; add crumbs. Sprinkle over tops. Bake at 350° for 25 minutes or just until set.

YIELD: 2 servings.

EDITOR'S NOTE: A shallow 1-qt. baking dish can be used instead of two ramekins. Bake for 25-30 minutes.

lea ann anderson
TULSA, OKLAHOMA

Here's an easy recipe familiar to anyone who's attended reunions and other large gatherings. Sweet and hearty, it includes three kinds of beans and plenty of beef and bacon.

family-favorite baked beans

PREP: 20 min. | **BAKE:** 1 hour

- 1/2 pound ground beef
- 1/2 pound bacon strips, diced
- 1 small onion, chopped
- 1/2 cup ketchup
- 1/2 cup barbecue sauce

- 1/3 cup packed brown sugar
- 2 tablespoons molasses
- 1 can (16 ounces) kidney beans, rinsed and drained
- 1 can (15-3/4 ounces) pork and beans
- 1 can (16 ounces) butter beans, rinsed and drained

In a Dutch oven, cook beef over medium heat until no longer pink; drain and set aside. In the same pan, cook bacon until crisp; drain.

Return beef to the pan. Add the onion, ketchup, barbecue sauce, brown sugar and molasses. Stir in the beans.

Transfer to a greased 3-qt. baking dish. Cover and bake at 350° for 1 hour or until beans reach desired thickness.

YIELD: 8 servings.

roasted vegetable medley

PREP: 25 min. | BAKE: 30 min.

- 3 Yukon Gold potatoes, cut into small wedges
- 2 medium sweet red peppers, cut into 1-inch pieces
- 1 small butternut squash, peeled and cubed
- 1 medium sweet potato, peeled and cubed
- 1 medium red onion, cut into wedges
- 3 tablespoons olive oil
- 2 tablespoons balsamic vinegar
- 2 tablespoons minced fresh rosemary or 2 teaspoons dried rosemary, crushed
- 1 tablespoon minced fresh thyme or 1 teaspoon dried thyme
- 1 teaspoon salt
- 1/2 teaspoon pepper

In a large bowl, combine the potatoes, red peppers, squash, sweet potato and onion. In a small bowl, whisk the oil, vinegar and seasonings. Pour over vegetables and toss to coat.

Transfer to two greased 15-in. x 10-in. x 1-in. baking pans. Bake, uncovered, at 425° for 30-40 minutes or until tender, stirring occasionally.

YIELD: 7 servings.

shirley beauregard
GRAND JUNCTION, COLORADO

Rich-tasting roasted veggies are good with any meat, but I especially like them with pork. Because the vegetables can be prepared in advance, I have more time to spend with my dinner guests.

merle dyck
ELKFORD, BRITISH COLUMBIA

Making this colorful salad a day ahead gives it plenty of time to marinate. We love its tangy sweet dressing.

mixed bean salad

PREP: 15 min. + chilling

1/2 cup sugar
1/3 cup cider vinegar
1/3 cup canola oil
1/2 teaspoon salt
1/8 teaspoon pepper
1 can (16 ounces) kidney beans, rinsed and drained
1 can (14-1/2 ounces) cut wax beans, drained
1 can (14-1/2 ounces) cut green beans, drained
3 celery ribs, sliced
1/2 medium green pepper, chopped
1/4 cup chopped onion

In a small saucepan, combine the sugar, vinegar, oil, salt and pepper. Cook and stir over medium heat until sugar is dissolved. Remove from the heat and cool slightly.

In a large salad bowl, combine the remaining ingredients. Drizzle with dressing; toss to coat. Cover and refrigerate overnight. Serve with a slotted spoon.

YIELD: 8 servings.

broccoli rice casserole

PREP: 15 min. | **BAKE:** 30 min.

- 1-1/2 cups water
- 1/2 cup butter, cubed
- 1 tablespoon dried minced onion
- 2 cups uncooked instant rice
- 1 package (16 ounces) frozen chopped broccoli, thawed
- 1 can (10-3/4 ounces) condensed cream of mushroom soup, undiluted
- 1 jar (8 ounces) process cheese sauce

In a large saucepan, bring the water, butter and onion to a boil. Stir in rice. Remove from the heat; cover and let stand for 5 minutes or until water is absorbed.

Stir in broccoli, soup and cheese sauce. Transfer to a greased 2-qt. baking dish. Bake, uncovered, at 350° for 30-35 minutes or until bubbly.

YIELD: 8 servings.

jennifer fuller
BALLSTON SPA, NEW YORK

When I was little, serving this dish was the only way my mother could get me to eat broccoli. It's an excellent recipe and especially good with poultry.

FRIED RICE

When I have extra rice and leftover meat, I make a fast fried rice. Just cook an onion in butter, then add the rice and chopped meat. Season with garlic powder, salt and pepper and cook until heated through.
—GINGER C.
JONESVILLE, LOUISIANA

homemade noodles

PREP: 45 min. + standing | **COOK:** 15 min.

- 4 cups all-purpose flour
- 1/2 cup whole wheat flour
- 2-1/4 teaspoons salt, *divided*
- 4 eggs
- 1/2 cup plus 4 quarts water, *divided*
- 2 tablespoons olive oil
- 3 tablespoons butter
- 1/2 teaspoon pepper

In a large bowl, combine the flours and 2 teaspoons salt. Make a well in the center. Whisk the eggs, 1/2 cup water and oil; pour into well. Stir together, forming a dough. Cover the dough and let rest for 10 minutes.

Turn the dough onto a floured surface; knead 8-10 times. Divide into fourths. Roll each portion into a 14-in. x 12-in. rectangle. Cut widthwise into 1/2-in. strips; cut strips into 6-in. lengths. Let noodles rest on a clean towel for at least 1 hour.

In a Dutch oven, bring remaining water to a rapid boil. Add noodles; cook for 8-10 minutes or until tender. Drain.

In the same pan, cook the butter over medium heat for 3-4 minutes or until golden brown. Add the noodles, pepper and remaining salt; toss to coat.

YIELD: 12 servings.

paula young
TIFFIN, OHIO

Whole wheat flour pumps up the nutrition in these buttery noodles. They taste so special.

michelle beran
CLAFLIN, KANSAS

It wouldn't be summer if Mom didn't make lots of these creamy cucumbers. Just a handful of simple ingredients—mayonnaise, sugar, vinegar and salt— dress up slices of this crisp garden vegetable.

cucumbers with dressing

PREP: 10 min. + chilling

    1 cup mayonnaise
    1/4 cup sugar
    1/4 cup white vinegar
    1/4 teaspoon salt
    4 cups sliced cucumbers

In a large bowl, combine the mayonnaise, sugar, vinegar and salt. Add cucumbers; toss to coat. Cover and refrigerate for 2 hours.

YIELD: 6-8 servings.

jean winfree
WAUSAU, WISCONSIN

This satisfying dish is welcome at any meal in our house, especially during the holidays. Tart apple slices taste so good when they're baked along with the mild-tasting sweet potatoes.

sweet potatoes with apples

PREP: 40 min. | BAKE: 35 min.

    3 to 3-1/2 pounds sweet potatoes
    2 tart apples, peeled, cored and cut into
      1/4-inch rings
    1/2 cup orange juice
    1/4 cup packed brown sugar
    1/4 teaspoon ground ginger
    1/4 teaspoon ground cinnamon
    2 tablespoons butter

Place sweet potatoes in a large saucepan and cover with water. Bring to a boil. Reduce heat; cover and cook for 30 minutes or until just tender. Drain and cool slightly. Peel and cut into 1/4-in. slices.

In a greased 13-in. x 9-in. baking dish, alternately layer potatoes and apples. Pour the orange juice over top. Combine the brown sugar, ginger and cinnamon; sprinkle over the potatoes and apples. Dot with butter.

Bake, uncovered, at 350° for 35-45 minutes or until apples are tender.

YIELD: 8 servings.

pizza salad

PREP/TOTAL TIME: 25 min.

  2 prebaked mini pizza crusts

1/2 cup Western, Catalina *or* French salad
    dressing

  1 tablespoon minced fresh basil *or*
    oregano

  1 package (10 ounces) torn romaine
    lettuce (8 cups)

  1 cup sliced pepperoni *or* chopped
    Canadian bacon

  1 cup (4 ounces) shredded part-skim
    mozzarella cheese *or* cheese blend

  1 can (2-1/4 ounces) sliced ripe olives,
    drained

Bake pizza crusts at 400° for 8-10 minutes or grill over medium heat until desired crispness. When cool enough to handle, tear crusts into bite-size pieces; set aside.

In a small bowl, combine salad dressing and basil; set aside. In a salad bowl, combine the lettuce, pizza crusts, pepperoni, cheese and olives. Toss to mix ingredients. Drizzle each serving with dressing.

YIELD: 8 servings.

**taste of home
cooking school**

*If your family loves pizza,
let it inspire you to make a
tempting salad! Be sure to
include your own favorite
pizza toppings.*

lorie verkuyl
RIDGECREST, CALIFORNIA

Here's a delicious and unique stuffing that is so good with turkey! I also halve the recipe and use it when I bake a chicken.

artichoke stuffing

PREP: 30 min. | BAKE: 35 min.

1 loaf (1 pound) sourdough bread, cut into 1-inch cubes

1/2 pound sliced fresh mushrooms

2 celery ribs, chopped

1 medium onion, chopped

2 tablespoons butter

3 to 4 garlic cloves, minced

2 jars (6-1/2 ounces *each*) marinated artichoke hearts, drained and chopped

1/2 cup grated Parmesan cheese

1 teaspoon poultry seasoning

1 egg

1 can (14-1/2 ounces) chicken broth

Place bread cubes in two ungreased 15-in. x 10-in. x 1-in. baking pans. Bake at 350° for 15 minutes or until lightly browned.

In a large skillet, saute the mushrooms, celery and onion in butter until tender. Add the garlic; cook 1 minute longer. Stir in the artichokes, cheese and poultry seasoning. Transfer to a large bowl; stir in bread cubes.

In a small bowl, whisk the egg and broth until blended. Pour over bread mixture and mix well.

Transfer to a greased 3-qt. baking dish (dish will be full). Cover and bake at 350° for 30 minutes. Uncover; bake 5-15 minutes longer or until a thermometer reads 160°.

YIELD: 14 cups.

cranberry gelatin salad

PREP: 10 min. + chilling

- 1 package (6 ounces) cherry gelatin
- 1-1/2 cups boiling water
- 1 can (20 ounces) crushed pineapple, undrained
- 1 can (14 ounces) whole-berry cranberry sauce
- 1-1/2 cups seedless red grapes, halved
- 1/4 cup chopped pecans

In a large bowl, dissolve gelatin in water. Stir in pineapple and cranberry sauce. Refrigerate for 30 minutes. Stir in grapes and pecans. Pour into a 2-qt. serving bowl. Refrigerate until firm.

YIELD: 8-10 servings.

betty claycomb
ALVERTON, PENNSYLVANIA

Since it keeps well, I make my gelatin salad a day ahead for our Christmas dinner. It's also a good choice to take to a holiday potluck. Even people who aren't fond of cranberries think it's yummy. I got the recipe from a friend at church who likes to cook and bake as much as I do.

slow-cooked mac 'n' cheese

PREP: 25 min. | COOK: 2-3/4 hours

- 2 cups uncooked elbow macaroni
- 1 can (12 ounces) evaporated milk
- 1-1/2 cups milk
- 1/2 cup egg substitute
- 1/4 cup butter, melted
- 1 teaspoon salt
- 2-1/2 cups (10 ounces) shredded cheddar cheese
- 2-1/2 cups (10 ounces) shredded sharp cheddar cheese, *divided*

Cook macaroni according to package directions; drain and rinse in cold water. In a large bowl, combine the evaporated milk, milk, egg substitute, butter and salt. Stir in the cheddar cheese, 2 cups sharp cheddar cheese and macaroni.

Transfer to a greased 3-qt. slow cooker. Cover and cook on low for 2-3 hours or until center is set, stirring once. Sprinkle with the remaining sharp cheddar cheese.

YIELD: 9 servings.

shelby molina
WHITEWATER, WISCONSIN

Slow-Cooked Mac 'n' Cheese—the words alone are enough to make mouths water. Here is comfort food at its best, rich and extra-cheesy. And because it's made in the slow cooker, it's very easy.

hot bacon asparagus salad

PREP/TOTAL TIME: 20 min.

- 7 bacon strips, diced
- 1 pound fresh asparagus, trimmed
- 1/3 cup white vinegar
- 1 tablespoon sugar
- 1/2 teaspoon ground mustard
- 1/4 teaspoon pepper
- 4 cups torn salad greens
- 1/2 cup sliced almonds
- 2 hard-cooked eggs, sliced

In a large skillet, cook bacon over medium heat until crisp. Using a slotted spoon, remove to paper towels to drain, reserving 2-3 tablespoons drippings. Cut asparagus into 1-1/2-in. pieces; saute in drippings until crisp-tender. Add the vinegar, sugar, mustard, pepper and bacon. Cook and stir for 1-2 minutes or until heated through.

In a large salad bowl, combine salad greens and almonds. Add the asparagus mixture; toss gently. Arrange eggs over the salad.

YIELD: 6 servings.

paulette balda
PROPHETSTOWN, ILLINOIS

This salad is so simple to fix when I get home from work, but it looks like I spent an hour preparing it. It's divine with warm rolls.

alicia quadrozzi
ESCONDIDO, CALIFORNIA

Whenever there's a picnic or cookout, I'm asked to bring my potato salad. It's tangy and a little different.

honey-mustard potato salad

PREP: 40 min. + chilling

5 pounds red potatoes
2 cups chopped celery
1 cup chopped sweet red pepper
4 hard-cooked eggs, chopped
2 green onions, chopped
1/2 cup mayonnaise
1/2 cup honey mustard
1/2 cup prepared mustard
1/4 cup sour cream
3/4 teaspoon salt
1/4 teaspoon pepper

Place potatoes in a saucepan and cover with water. Bring to a boil. Reduce heat; cover and cook for 15-20 minutes or until tender. Drain and cool.

Cut potatoes into quarters; place in a large bowl. Add the celery, red pepper, hard-cooked eggs and onions. In a small bowl, combine the remaining ingredients. Pour over potato mixture and toss to coat. Cover and refrigerate for at least 1 hour.

YIELD: 16 servings.

krista collins
CONCORD, NORTH CAROLINA

Any entree only gets better with a side of veggie-filled pasta salad. I especially like serving it with hamburgers, hot dogs or sloppy joes.

ranch pasta salad

PREP/TOTAL TIME: 25 min.

3 cups uncooked tricolor spiral pasta
1 cup chopped fresh broccoli florets
3/4 cup chopped seeded peeled cucumber
1/2 cup seeded chopped tomato
1 bottle (8 ounces) ranch salad dressing
1/2 cup shredded Parmesan cheese

Cook pasta according to package directions; drain and rinse in cold water. In a large bowl, combine the pasta, broccoli, cucumber and tomato. Drizzle with salad dressing; toss to coat. Sprinkle with cheese.

YIELD: 8 servings.

pamela rickman
VALDOSTA, GEORGIA

When my husband and I were newlyweds and far from family, we invited some friends over for a Thanksgiving feast. I searched for dressing recipes and combined several to create this pleasing one.

deluxe corn bread dressing

PREP: 20 min. | BAKE: 55 min.

6 cups crumbled corn bread
2 cups white bread cubes, toasted
1 cup chopped pecans
1/4 cup minced fresh parsley
1 teaspoon dried thyme
1/2 teaspoon rubbed sage
1/2 teaspoon salt
1/2 teaspoon pepper
1 pound bulk pork sausage
2 tablespoons butter
2 large tart apples, diced
1 cup diced celery
1 medium onion, finely chopped
1-3/4 to 2-1/4 cups chicken broth

In a large bowl, combine the bread, pecans and seasonings; set aside. Crumble sausage into a large skillet; cook over medium heat until no longer pink; remove with a slotted spoon to drain on paper towels.

Add butter to drippings; saute the apples, celery and onion until tender. Add to bread mixture. Stir in sausage and enough broth to moisten.

Spoon into a greased 3-qt. baking dish; cover and bake at 350° for 45 minutes. Uncover and bake for 10 minutes or until light golden brown, or use to stuff a turkey.

YIELD: 10-12 servings.

fruited coleslaw

PREP: 10 min. + chilling

2 cups coleslaw mix
1 snack-size cup (4 ounces) mandarin oranges, drained
1/2 cup chopped apple
1/4 cup mayonnaise
2 teaspoons honey
1/4 teaspoon poppy seeds

In a small bowl, combine the coleslaw mix, oranges and apple. Combine the remaining ingredients; pour over coleslaw mixture and toss to coat. Cover and refrigerate for at least 2 hours before serving.

YIELD: 3 servings.

linda stevens
MADISON, ALABAMA

We all need to get more fruits and vegetables into our diets, and this is a great-tasting way to do it.

leigh gallagher
ASOTIN, WASHINGTON

I knew this spinach salad was something special when my picky husband asked for seconds! The sweet-tart bacon dressing with a hint of honey is a real treat.

spinach-onion salad with hot bacon dressing

PREP/TOTAL TIME: 25 min.

4 bacon strips, chopped
1 medium red onion, chopped, *divided*
1/4 cup balsamic vinegar
5 teaspoons honey
1/4 teaspoon salt
1/8 teaspoon pepper
1/4 cup canola oil
1 package (6 ounces) fresh baby spinach
1/2 cup crumbled feta cheese

In a large skillet, cook bacon and half of the onion over medium heat until bacon is crisp. Stir in the vinegar, honey, salt and pepper; heat through. Transfer to a small bowl; gradually whisk in oil.

Place spinach in a large bowl. Drizzle warm dressing over spinach and toss to coat. Sprinkle with cheese and remaining onion.

YIELD: 6 servings.

family-favorite dressing

PREP: 25 min. | **BAKE:** 45 min.

1 package (14 ounces) seasoned stuffing cubes

1-1/2 cups boiling water

1/2 pound fresh mushrooms, coarsely chopped

2 cups finely chopped celery

1 cup finely chopped onion

1 can (10-3/4 ounces) reduced-fat reduced-sodium condensed cream of chicken soup, undiluted

2 eggs, beaten

1 teaspoon poultry seasoning

Pepper to taste

1/4 cup butter, melted

Paprika

Minced fresh parsley

In a large bowl, combine the stuffing cubes and boiling water; stir until water is absorbed. Add the mushrooms, celery and onion. In a small bowl, combine the soup, eggs, poultry seasoning and pepper until blended. Add to stuffing mixture; mix well.

Transfer to a 13-in. x 9-in. baking dish coated with cooking spray. Drizzle with the butter; sprinkle with paprika. Cover and bake at 350° for 45 minutes or until a thermometer reads 160°. Sprinkle with parsley.

YIELD: 12 servings.

mary tallman

ARBOR VITAE, WISCONSIN

This delightful dressing is a must-have holiday dish with my family. Leftovers freeze well, too.

comforting carrot casserole

PREP: 15 min. | **BAKE:** 20 min.

4 cups sliced fresh carrots

1 cup cubed process cheese (Velveeta)

2 tablespoons dried minced onion

1/4 cup butter, melted

1 cup crushed potato chips

Place 1 in. of water in a large saucepan; add carrots. Bring to a boil. Reduce heat; cover and simmer for 7-9 minutes or until crisp-tender. Drain.

Place carrots in a greased shallow 2-qt. baking dish. Top with cheese and onion. Drizzle with butter; sprinkle with potato chips.

Cover and bake at 350° for 20-25 minutes or until bubbly.

YIELD: 8 servings.

caroline hoyt

SCRANTON, IOWA

Creamy cheese and crunchy chips add unusual taste to my rich baked carrots. And they are so easy to make!

mom's pickled beets

PREP: 15 min. + chilling

3/4 cup sugar

3/4 cup white vinegar

3/4 cup water

1-1/2 teaspoons salt

3/4 to 1 teaspoon pepper

1 large onion, thinly sliced

2 cans (13-1/4 ounces *each*) sliced beets, undrained

Sliced green onions, optional

In a large saucepan, combine the first six ingredients; bring to a boil. Reduce heat; cover and simmer for 5 minutes. Remove from the heat; add beets. let stand at room temperature for 1 hour. Transfer to a large bowl.

Cover and chill 6 hours or overnight. Garnish with green onions if desired.

YIELD: 6 servings.

mildred sherrer

FORT WORTH, TEXAS

Zesty and fresh-tasting, these bright, beautiful beets add spark to any meal. I have fond memories of how wonderful they tasted when Mother prepared them.

sandy mckenzie
BRAHAM, MINNESOTA

We love the combination of parsley and spices with a lemony butter sauce in this classic side dish.

schelby thompson
CAMDEN WYOMING, DELAWARE

This salad perks up any spring or summer meal. The robust dressing provides a fresh burst of flavor with each bite.

lemon-butter new potatoes

PREP/TOTAL TIME: 30 min.

12 small red potatoes
1/3 cup butter, cubed
3 tablespoons lemon juice
1 teaspoon salt
1 teaspoon grated lemon peel
1/4 teaspoon pepper
1/8 teaspoon ground nutmeg
2 tablespoons minced fresh parsley

Peel a strip from around each potato. Place potatoes in a large saucepan and cover with water. Bring to a boil. Reduce heat; cover and cook for 15-20 minutes or just until tender.

Meanwhile, in small saucepan, melt butter. Stir in the lemon juice, salt, lemon peel, pepper and nutmeg. Drain potatoes and place in a serving bowl. Pour butter mixture over potatoes; toss gently to coat. Sprinkle with parsley.

YIELD: 4 servings.

caesar salad

PREP/TOTAL TIME: 10 min.

1 large bunch romaine, torn
3/4 cup olive oil
3 tablespoons red wine vinegar
1 teaspoon Worcestershire sauce
1/2 teaspoon salt
1/4 teaspoon ground mustard
1 large garlic clove, minced
1/2 fresh lemon
Dash pepper
1/4 to 1/2 cup shredded Parmesan cheese
Caesar-flavored *or* garlic croutons

Place lettuce in a large salad bowl. Combine the next six ingredients in a blender; process until smooth. Pour over lettuce and toss to coat.

Squeeze lemon over the lettuce. Sprinkle with pepper, cheese and croutons.

YIELD: 6-8 servings.

layered veggie tortellini salad

PREP/TOTAL TIME: 30 min.

- 1 package (16 ounces) frozen cheese tortellini
- 2 cups fresh broccoli florets
- 2 cups cherry tomatoes, quartered
- 2 celery ribs, finely chopped
- 1 can (2-1/4 ounces) sliced ripe olives, drained
- 1 cup (4 ounces) shredded cheddar cheese

PARMESAN DRESSING:

- 3/4 cup mayonnaise
- 3 tablespoons grated Parmesan cheese
- 2 tablespoons lemon juice
- 2 tablespoons heavy whipping cream
- 1 teaspoon dried thyme

Cook tortellini according to package directions; drain and rinse in cold water. In a 2-1/2-qt. glass bowl, layer the tortellini, broccoli, tomatoes, celery, olives and cheddar cheese.

In a small bowl, whisk the dressing ingredients; spoon over the salad. Cover salad and refrigerate until serving.

YIELD: 10 servings.

dennis vitale
NEW PRESTON, CONNECTICUT

Tortellini and a Parmesan dressing give this layered salad an unexpected twist. It's an impressive addition to any potluck.

kenda burgett
RATTAN, OKLAHOMA

Whenever my husband is cooking meat on the grill, you can bet I'll be in the kitchen preparing these mushrooms. I got the recipe from a friend back when we were in nursing school.

steakhouse mushrooms

PREP/TOTAL TIME: 20 min.

  1 pound medium fresh mushrooms
1/4 cup butter
  2 teaspoons dried basil
1/2 teaspoon dried oregano
1/2 teaspoon seasoned salt
1/4 teaspoon garlic powder
  1 teaspoon browning sauce, optional

In a large skillet, saute the mushrooms in butter until tender. Stir in seasonings and the browning sauce If desIred. Reduce heat; cover and cook, stirring occasionally, for 3-5 minutes to allow the flavors to blend.

YIELD: 4 servings.

mushroom wild rice

PREP: 25 min. | **COOK:** 1 hour

4 cups chicken broth
1-1/2 cups uncooked wild rice
1/2 teaspoon salt
1/4 teaspoon pepper
3 bacon strips, cut into 1/2-inch pieces
2 cups sliced fresh mushrooms
1 small onion, chopped
1/2 cup sliced almonds

In a large saucepan, bring broth to a boil. Stir in the rice, salt and pepper. Reduce heat to low; cover and simmer for 55 minutes or until the rice is tender. Remove from the heat.

Meanwhile, in a large skillet, cook bacon over medium heat until crisp. Using a slotted spoon, remove bacon to paper towels to drain. Saute the mushrooms, onion and almonds in bacon drippings until vegetables are tender; stir into rice mixture. Add bacon.

YIELD: 10 servings.

virginia peter
WINTER, WISCONSIN

With its nutty texture and visual appeal, this hearty side is an easy upgrade when your menu calls for rice. I've learned to make enough so I can send leftovers home with guests.

new england butternut squash

PREP/TOTAL TIME: 30 min.

1 medium butternut squash
1/4 cup butter, melted
1/4 cup maple syrup
3/4 teaspoon ground cinnamon
1/4 teaspoon ground nutmeg

Cut squash in half lengthwise; discard seeds. Place cut side down in a microwave-safe dish; add 1/2 in. of water. Cover and microwave on high for 15-20 minutes or until very tender; drain.

When cool enough to handle, scoop out the pulp and mash. Stir in the butter, syrup, cinnamon and nutmeg.

YIELD: 5 servings.

EDITOR'S NOTE: This recipe was tested in a 1,100-watt microwave oven.

linda massicotte-black
COVENTRY, CONNECTICUT

This traditional fall treat is a favorite because it's delicious and has a hint of sweetness. Microwaving the squash makes it ready in a snap!

velma jenness
MARCUS, IOWA

I predict that once you try this delicious pasta medley, it'll become a staple. Team it up with soups or your favorite grilled meats for a quick and casual dinner.

blt in a bowl

PREP: 20 min. + chilling

- 1/4 cup uncooked elbow macaroni
- 3 tablespoons mayonnaise
- 4 teaspoons chili sauce
- 1-1/2 teaspoons lemon juice
- 1/2 teaspoon sugar
- 1/2 teaspoon chicken bouillon granules
- 1 plum tomato, chopped
- 2 tablespoons chopped red onion
- 1 cup torn iceberg lettuce
- 1 bacon strip, cooked and crumbled

Cook macaroni according to package directions; drain and rinse in cold water. In a small bowl, combine the mayonnaise, chili sauce, lemon juice, sugar and bouillon; stir in the macaroni, tomato and onion.

Refrigerate until chilled. Serve in a lettuce-lined bowl; sprinkle with bacon.

YIELD: 2 servings.

priscilla gilbert
INDIAN HARBOR BEACH, FLORIDA

Baby spinach in a creamy Parmesan cheese sauce is topped with crispy croutons for a wonderful crunch.

creamy parmesan spinach

PREP/TOTAL TIME: 20 min.

- 2 packages (6 ounces *each*) fresh baby spinach, coarsely chopped
- 2 tablespoons water
- 2 teaspoons butter
- 1/2 cup heavy whipping cream
- 2 teaspoons grated lemon peel
- 1/2 teaspoon minced garlic
- 1/8 teaspoon crushed red pepper flakes
- 1/2 cup grated Parmesan cheese
- 2/3 cup onion and garlic salad croutons, crushed

Place spinach and water in a Dutch oven; cover and cook for 3 minutes or until wilted. Drain spinach and set aside.

In the same pan, melt butter. Stir in the cream, lemon peel, garlic and pepper flakes; bring to a gentle boil. Reduce heat; simmer, uncovered, for 5 minutes or until slightly reduced. Stir in cheese and spinach; heat through. Sprinkle with croutons.

YIELD: 3 servings.

corn and broccoli in cheese sauce

PREP: 10 min. | **COOK:** 3 hours

- 1 package (16 ounces) frozen corn, thawed
- 1 package (16 ounces) frozen broccoli florets, thawed
- 4 ounces reduced-fat process cheese (Velveeta), cubed
- 1/2 cup shredded cheddar cheese
- 1 can (10-1/4 ounces) reduced-fat reduced-sodium condensed cream of chicken soup, undiluted
- 1/4 cup fat-free milk

In a 4-qt. slow cooker, combine the corn, broccoli and cheeses. In a small bowl, combine soup and milk; pour over vegetable mixture. Cover and cook on low for 3-4 hours or until heated through. Stir before serving.

YIELD: 8 servings.

joyce johnson
UNIONTOWN, OHIO

I usually make this savory side dish in the slow cooker, but it's simple to prepare in the oven, too. Sometimes I add a little ham to make it a main dish.

teri lindquist
GURNEE, ILLINOIS

When I needed a speedy salad for a luncheon, I used what I had available and everyone loved the results! Light, fluffy and full of fruit, this salad could double as a healthy dessert. You can also tuck it into the kids' lunch boxes for a fun school-day treat.

tropical fruit salad

PREP/TOTAL TIME: 15 min.

2 cans (15-1/4 ounces *each*) mixed tropical fruit, drained

1 can (11 ounces) mandarin oranges, drained

1 medium banana, sliced

1 cup miniature marshmallows

1-1/2 cups (12 ounces) vanilla yogurt

1/4 cup flaked coconut

1/4 cup slivered almonds, toasted

In a large salad bowl, combine the tropical fruit, oranges, banana and marshmallows. Add yogurt; toss gently to coat. Sprinkle with coconut and almonds. Refrigerate until serving.

YIELD: 6 servings.

parmesan peas 'n' rice

PREP/TOTAL TIME: 25 min.

- 1/3 cup uncooked long grain rice
- 1 green onion, chopped
- 1 tablespoon butter
- 1 cup chicken broth
- 1/8 teaspoon pepper
- 2/3 cup frozen peas, thawed
- 1 tablespoon grated Parmesan cheese

In a small saucepan, saute rice and onion in butter until onion is tender. Stir in the broth and pepper. Bring to a boil. Reduce heat; cover and simmer for 10 minutes.

Add peas; cover and cook 5-6 minutes longer or until the liquid is absorbed and rice is tender. Stir in the cheese.

YIELD: 2 servings.

inge schermerhorn
KINGSTON, NEW HAMPSHIRE

My husband, John, likes rice but isn't crazy about peas, and I'm just the opposite. This compromise works for us! It's a wonderful complement to any meal.

GRATED PARMESAN

To grate your own Parmesan cheese, use the finest section on your grating tool. You can also use a blender or food processor. Simply cut the cheese into 1-inch cubes and process 1 cup at a time until finely grated.

grilled vegetable medley

PREP: 15 min. | GRILL: 20 min.

- 1/4 cup olive oil
- 1 teaspoon salt
- 1 teaspoon dried parsley flakes
- 1 teaspoon dried basil
- 3 large ears fresh corn on the cob, cut into 3-inch pieces
- 2 medium zucchini, cut into 1/4-inch slices
- 1 medium yellow summer squash, cut into 1/4-inch slices
- 1 medium sweet onion, sliced
- 1 large green pepper, diced
- 10 cherry tomatoes
- 1 jar (4-1/2 ounces) whole mushrooms, drained
- 1/4 cup butter

In a large bowl, combine the oil, salt, parsley and basil. Add vegetables and toss to coat. Place on a double thickness of heavy-duty foil (about 28 in. x 18 in.). Dot with butter. Fold foil around vegetables and seal tightly.

Grill vegetables, covered, over medium heat for 20-25 minutes or until corn is tender, turning once. Open carefully to allow steam to escape.

YIELD: 8 servings.

lori daniels
BEVERLY, WEST VIRGINIA

This is our favorite way to fix summer vegetables. They go from garden to table in under an hour, and since the veggies cook in foil, cleanup is a breeze.

krista frank

RHODODENDRON, OREGON

With pina colada yogurt and toasted coconut, my fruit salad brings a hint of the tropics to the table. It's delicious with deli sandwiches or even alongside grilled chicken.

island fruit salad

PREP/TOTAL TIME: 15 min.

- 2 medium ripe bananas, sliced
- 1 medium mango, peeled and cubed
- 4 kiwifruit, peeled and cubed
- 1 can (20 ounces) unsweetened pineapple tidbits, drained
- 3/4 cup (6 ounces) reduced-fat pina colada yogurt
- 1/2 cup flaked coconut, toasted

In a large serving bowl, combine bananas, mango, kiwi, pineapple and yogurt; toss to coat. Sprinkle with coconut. Serve with a slotted spoon.

YIELD: 8 servings.

sandra matteson

WESTHOPE, NORTH DAKOTA

My friend Peggy brought this coleslaw to one of our picnics, and everyone liked it so much that we all had to have the recipe.

macaroni coleslaw

PREP: 25 min. + chilling

- 1 package (7 ounces) ring macaroni *or* ditalini
- 1 package (14 ounces) coleslaw mix
- 2 medium onions, finely chopped
- 2 celery ribs, finely chopped
- 1 medium cucumber, finely chopped
- 1 medium green pepper, finely chopped
- 1 can (8 ounces) whole water chestnuts, drained and chopped

DRESSING:
- 1-1/2 cups Miracle Whip Light
- 1/3 cup sugar
- 1/4 cup cider vinegar
- 1/2 teaspoon salt
- 1/4 teaspoon pepper

Cook macaroni according to package directions; drain and rinse in cold water. Transfer to a large bowl; add coleslaw mix, onions, celery, cucumber, green pepper and water chestnuts.

In a small bowl, whisk the dressing ingredients. Pour over salad; toss to coat. Cover and refrigerate for at least 1 hour.

YIELD: 16 servings.

colorful tomato 'n' mozzarella salad

PREP: 20 min. + standing

1 cup fresh baby spinach
2 medium yellow tomatoes, sliced
2 medium red tomatoes, sliced
4 ounces fresh mozzarella cheese, sliced
2 tablespoons thinly sliced fresh basil
  leaves
1/4 teaspoon salt
1/4 teaspoon pepper

1 tablespoon balsamic vinegar
2 teaspoons olive oil

Arrange spinach on a platter; top with tomato and cheese slices. Sprinkle with basil, salt and pepper. Drizzle with vinegar and oil. Let stand for 15 minutes before serving.

YIELD: 4 servings.

tari ambler
SHOREWOOD, ILLINOIS

Here's my twist on the popular tomato-mozzarella salad. Since the rest of the salad is so light, you can afford to splurge with the fresh mozzarella!

hash browns with ham

PREP: 15 min. | COOK: 3-1/4 hours

- 1 package (32 ounces) frozen cubed hash brown potatoes, thawed
- 1 cup cubed fully cooked ham
- 1 small onion, chopped
- 2 cups (8 ounces) shredded cheddar cheese, *divided*
- 1 can (14-3/4 ounces) condensed cream of chicken soup, undiluted
- 1/2 cup butter, melted
- 1 cup (8 ounces) sour cream

In a 3-qt. slow cooker, combine the potatoes, ham, onion and 1 cup cheese. Combine soup and butter; pour over potato mixture. Cover and cook on low for 3-4 hours or until potatoes are tender.

Stir in sour cream. Sprinkle with remaining cheese. Cover and cook for 15 minutes or until cheese is melted.

YIELD: 8 servings.

green beans with bacon

PREP/TOTAL TIME: 20 min.

- 4 bacon strips, diced
- 1/2 cup chopped onion
- 8 cups fresh green beans, trimmed
- 1/4 teaspoon salt
- 1/8 teaspoon pepper

In a large skillet, cook bacon and onion over medium heat until bacon is crisp and onion is tender.

Meanwhile, place beans in a large saucepan and cover with water. Bring to a boil. Cook, uncovered, for 8-10 minutes or until crisp-tender; drain well. Add to bacon mixture. Sprinkle with salt and pepper; toss to coat.

YIELD: 8 servings.

mari anne warren
MILTON, WISCONSIN

Bits of bacon and onion dress up the green beans in this quick side dish. It lends crisp, fresh flavor to any entree from steak to chicken.

garden macaroni salad

PREP: 30 min. + chilling

- 1 cup uncooked elbow macaroni
- 1 cup fresh broccoli florets
- 1 small onion, chopped
- 1 medium carrot, thinly sliced
- 1/2 cup chopped peeled cucumber
- 1/2 cup frozen peas, thawed
- 1/2 cup sliced radishes
- 4 ounces Swiss cheese, cubed
- 1 cup mayonnaise
- 2 tablespoons prepared mustard
- 1 tablespoon sugar
- 4-1/2 teaspoons snipped fresh dill *or* 1-1/2 teaspoons dill weed

Cook macaroni according to package directions; drain and rinse in cold water. In a large bowl, combine the macaroni, broccoli, onion, carrot, cucumber, peas, radishes and cheese.

In a small bowl, combine mayonnaise, mustard, sugar and dill. Pour over macaroni mixture; toss to coat. Cover and refrigerate for at least 2 hours before serving.

YIELD: 8 servings.

anne wamsley
GARFIELD, ARKANSAS

Mustard and dill give my colorful salad a wonderful flavor that's different from other macaroni salads.

doris thomas
SCOTTSVILLE, NEW YORK

My family adores this golden home-style casserole, and if you love corn, you will, too!

scalloped corn

PREP: 20 min. | **BAKE:** 25 min.

- 1/2 cup chopped green pepper
- 1/4 cup chopped onion
- 5 tablespoons butter, *divided*
- 2 cups soft bread crumbs
- 2 cans (8-1/2 ounces *each*) cream-style corn
- 1 can (11 ounces) whole kernel corn, drained
- 2 eggs, lightly beaten
- 1/4 cup dry bread crumbs

In a large skillet, saute green pepper and onion in 4 tablespoons butter until tender. Stir in the soft bread crumbs, corn and eggs. Transfer to a greased 8-in. square baking dish.

Melt the remaining butter; toss with dry bread crumbs. Sprinkle over casserole. Bake, uncovered, at 350° for 25-30 minutes or until a thermometer reads 160°.

YIELD: 5 servings.

mary ulrick
BACONTON, GEORGIA

Can't decide whether to cook vegetables or pasta for a side dish? Try combining them in a medley instead. People will really go for this at potlucks.

cheesy vegetable medley

PREP: 25 min. | **BAKE:** 30 min.

- 3 cups fresh broccoli florets
- 3 cups fresh cauliflowerets
- 2 cups julienned carrots
- 1 small onion, diced
- 1/2 teaspoon garlic powder
- 1/2 teaspoon Italian seasoning
- 1/8 teaspoon salt
- 1/8 teaspoon pepper
- 8 ounces elbow macaroni, cooked and drained
- 2 cups (8 ounces) shredded part-skim mozzarella cheese
- 2 cups (8 ounces) shredded cheddar cheese
- 8 ounces process cheese (Velveeta), sliced
- 3/4 cup half-and-half cream
- 3/4 cup seasoned bread crumbs
- 1/4 cup butter
- 1/2 cup grated Parmesan cheese

Place broccoli and cauliflower in a steamer basket. Place in a saucepan over 1 in. of water; bring to a boil. Cover and steam for 5-8 minutes or until crisp-tender. Rinse in cold water; drain and set aside. Repeat with carrots and onion, steaming for 4-5 minutes or until tender.

Place vegetables in a large bowl; add the garlic powder, Italian seasoning, salt and pepper. Stir in macaroni. Spoon half into a greased 3-qt. baking dish. Sprinkle with half of the mozzarella, cheddar and process cheese. Repeat layers.

Pour half-and-half-cream over the top. Sprinkle with the bread crumbs; dot with butter. Top with Parmesan cheese. Bake, uncovered, at 350° for 30-40 minutes or until bubbly.

YIELD: 12-14 servings.

reuben baked potatoes

PREP: 1 hour | **BAKE:** 25 min.

4 large baking potatoes

2 cups finely diced cooked corned beef

1 can (14 ounces) sauerkraut, rinsed,
   well drained and finely chopped

1/2 cup shredded Swiss cheese

3 tablespoons sliced green onions

1 garlic clove, minced

1 tablespoon prepared horseradish

1 teaspoon caraway seeds

1 package (3 ounces) cream cheese,
   softened

3 tablespoons grated Parmesan cheese

Paprika

Scrub and pierce potatoes. Bake them at 425° for 50-55 minutes or until tender. In a large bowl, combine the corned beef, sauerkraut, Swiss cheese, onions, garlic, horseradish and caraway; set aside.

When potatoes are cool enough to handle, cut a thin slice off the top of each potato and discard. Cut each potato in half lengthwise. Scoop out the pulp, leaving thin shells.

In a large bowl, mash potato pulp with cream cheese; stir in the corned beef mixture. Mound potato mixture into potato shells. Place potatoes on a baking sheet.

Bake at 375° for 20 minutes. Sprinkle potatoes with Parmesan cheese and paprika. Bake 5 minutes longer or until cheese is melted.

YIELD: 8 servings.

erika antolic
VANCOUVER, WASHINGTON

When I was a girl during the Depression, we had enough cabbages to sink a ship! My mother came up with some creative ways to use them, including this comforting specialty.

cynthia edmiston
SULLIVAN'S ISLAND,
SOUTH CAROLINA

Every year, I am asked to take this dish to the family's Thanksgiving gathering. We can't imagine the holiday without it.

broccoli mushroom casserole

PREP: 20 min. | BAKE: 35 min.

2 cups water
1/2 pound sliced fresh mushrooms
3 cups chopped fresh broccoli
1 small onion, chopped
1 can (10-3/4 ounces) reduced-fat reduced-sodium condensed cream of mushroom soup, undiluted
3/4 cup shredded Swiss cheese
1/2 cup reduced-fat mayonnaise
2 egg whites
1 egg
1 teaspoon ground mustard
1/4 teaspoon pepper
1-1/4 cups (5 ounces) shredded reduced-fat cheddar cheese, *divided*
1 cup crushed baked potato chips

In a large saucepan, combine the water, mushrooms, broccoli and onion. Bring to a boil. Reduce heat; cover and simmer for 6-8 minutes or until vegetables are crisp-tender.

Meanwhile, in a large bowl, combine the soup, Swiss cheese, mayonnaise, egg whites, egg, mustard, pepper and 3/4 cup of the cheddar cheese. Drain vegetables; stir into soup mixture.

Transfer to an 11-in. x 7-in. baking dish coated with cooking spray. Sprinkle with potato chips and remaining cheddar cheese. Bake, uncovered, at 350° for 35-40 minutes or until a thermometer reads 160°.

YIELD: 6 servings.

homemade potato salad

PREP/TOTAL TIME: 30 min.

1 tablespoon sugar
2 teaspoons all-purpose flour
1/4 teaspoon ground mustard
Pinch salt
1 egg, lightly beaten

1/3 cup water
1 tablespoon white vinegar
3/4 cup mayonnaise
5 large potatoes, cooked, peeled and cubed
4 hard-cooked eggs, chopped
1 cup chopped celery
1/4 cup chopped green onions
Salt and pepper to taste

In a small saucepan, combine sugar, flour, mustard and salt. Combine the egg, water and vinegar; stir into dry ingredients until smooth. Cook and stir until mixture reaches 160° and coats the back of a metal spoon. Remove from the heat; cool slightly. Stir in mayonnaise.

In a large bowl, combine the potatoes, hard-cooked eggs, celery, onions, salt and pepper. Add the dressing; toss gently to coat. Refrigerate salad until serving.

YIELD: 8-10 servings.

patricia kile
ELIZABETHTOWN,
PENNSYLVANIA

Creamy potato salad is a perfect side dish on a night when you're grilling out. With homemade dressing, it really feels special.

DRESSED-UP POTATO SALAD

I add crumbled cooked bacon and stuffed olives to my favorite potato salad. It's an unexpected treat that sets it apart.

—KARLA H.
LENOX, MASSACHUSETTS

makeover corn pudding

PREP: 15 min. | BAKE: 50 min.

1/3 cup all-purpose flour
2 tablespoons sugar
1 cup fat-free milk
3/4 cup egg substitute
1 tablespoon butter, melted
1 teaspoon salt
8 cups frozen corn, thawed
1 can (14-3/4 ounces) cream-style corn
1 cup (4 ounces) shredded sharp cheddar cheese

In a large bowl, combine flour and sugar. Whisk in the milk, egg substitute, butter and salt. Stir in the corn, cream-style corn and cheese.

Pour into a 13-in. x 9-in. baking dish coated with cooking spray. Bake, uncovered, at 375° for 50-55 minutes or until a knife inserted near the center comes out clean.

YIELD: 12 servings.

arlene spencer
OCONOMOWOC,
WISCONSIN

Our corn pudding was a cherished family tradition at holidays and special gatherings. This lightened version has less than half the fat, sodium and cholesterol of the original, so we can keep serving it up for generations to come!

lora billmire
SPOKANE, WASHINGTON

Dried cranberries give this appealing recipe a splash of color. It makes such a pretty side dish for Thanksgiving or Christmas.

confetti rice

PREP/TOTAL TIME: 30 min.

  2 tablespoons chopped onion
  2 tablespoons chopped celery
  2 teaspoons canola oil
  2/3 cup chicken broth
  1/3 cup uncooked long grain rice
  1/4 teaspoon salt
Dash pepper
  2 tablespoons slivered almonds
  2 tablespoons dried cranberries

In a small saucepan, saute onion and celery in oil until tender. Add the broth, rice, salt and pepper. Bring to a boil, stirring occasionally. Reduce heat; cover and simmer for 10 minutes. Add almonds and cranberries.

  Cover and simmer 9-11 minutes longer or until rice is tender. Fluff with a fork. Serve warm.

YIELD: 2 servings.

julianne johnson
GROVE CITY, MINNESOTA

I loved it when my mom prepared these classic beans. Now I make them for my family. Everyone enjoys the old-fashioned flavor. I often take them to potlucks and picnics. They're wonderful with summertime dinners.

picnic baked beans

PREP: 15 min. + standing | BAKE: 2 hours

  3 cups dried navy beans
  4 quarts cold water, *divided*
  1 medium onion, chopped
  1 cup ketchup
  1 cup packed brown sugar
  2 tablespoons molasses
  1 tablespoon salt

  2 teaspoons ground mustard
  1/4 pound bacon, cooked and crumbled

Place beans in a Dutch oven with 2 qts. water. Bring to a boil; reduce heat and simmer for 3 minutes. Remove from heat and let stand for 1 hour.

  Drain and rinse. Return beans to Dutch oven; add remaining water. Bring to a boil. Reduce heat; cover and simmer for 1 hour or until the beans are almost tender. Drain and reserve liquid.

  Transfer beans to an ungreased 3-qt. baking dish, add the remaining ingredients and 1-1/2 cups of reserved liquid; stir to combine.

  Cover and bake at 300° for 2 to 2-1/2 hours or until beans are tender and reach desired consistency, stirring every 30 minutes. Add reserved liquid as needed.

YIELD: 16 servings.

creamy noodles

PREP/TOTAL TIME: 25 min.

    8 ounces uncooked thin spaghetti
    3 garlic cloves, minced
    3 tablespoons butter, *divided*
    6 ounces fat-free cream cheese, cubed
    3 tablespoons reduced-fat sour cream
    3 tablespoons fat-free milk
    3/4 teaspoon salt
    1/2 teaspoon onion powder
    1/4 teaspoon Cajun seasoning
    1/4 teaspoon white pepper
    4-1/2 teaspoons minced fresh parsley

Cook spaghetti according to package directions. Meanwhile, in a large saucepan, saute the garlic in 1 tablespoon butter for 1 minute. Add the cream cheese, sour cream, milk, salt, onion powder, Cajun seasoning, pepper and remaining butter. Cook and stir over low heat just until smooth (do not boil). Remove from the heat.

Drain spaghetti; toss with cream sauce. Sprinkle with parsley.

YIELD: 6 servings.

brenda nolen
FOLSOM, LOUISIANA

Fresh garlic flavor gives these comforting noodles lots of punch. I like this dish with grilled chicken, but it works well with just about any entree.

**taste of home
test kitchen**

*A lighter version of classic
white sauce coats yummy
cauliflower in this dish. It's
perfect for a buffet.*

cauliflower au gratin

PREP: 30 min. | BAKE: 30 min.

3 packages (16 ounces *each*) frozen
  cauliflower, thawed

1 large onion, chopped

1/3 cup butter, cubed

1/3 cup all-purpose flour

1/2 teaspoon salt

1/4 teaspoon ground mustard

1/4 teaspoon pepper

2 cups fat-free milk

1/2 cup grated Parmesan cheese

TOPPING:

1/2 cup soft whole wheat bread crumbs

2 tablespoons butter, melted

1/4 teaspoon paprika

Place 1 in. of water in a Dutch oven; add cauliflower.
Bring to a boil. Reduce heat; cover and cook for 4-6
minutes or until crisp-tender. Drain and pat dry.

Meanwhile, in a large saucepan, saute onion in
butter until tender. Stir in the flour, salt, mustard
and pepper until blended; gradually add milk. Bring
mixture to a boil; cook and stir for 1-2 minutes or
until thickened. Remove from the heat. Add cheese;
stir until melted.

Place cauliflower in a 13-in. x 9-in. baking dish
coated with cooking spray. Pour sauce over top.

For topping, combine the bread crumbs, butter
and paprika. Sprinkle over sauce. Bake, uncovered,
at 350° for 30-35 minutes or until bubbly.

YIELD: 12 servings.

honey-glazed carrots

PREP/TOTAL TIME: 10 min.

- 1 package (16 ounces) baby carrots
- 1 tablespoon water
- 2 tablespoons butter
- 2 tablespoons honey
- 1 tablespoon lemon juice

Place carrots and water in a 1-1/2-qt. microwave-safe dish. Cover and microwave on high for 3-5 minutes or until crisp-tender.

Meanwhile, melt butter in a skillet; stir in honey and lemon juice. Cook butter mixture over low heat for 3-1/2 minutes, stirring constantly. Add carrots; cook and stir for 1 minute or until glazed.

YIELD: 4 servings.

EDITOR'S NOTE: This recipe was tested in a 1,100-watt microwave oven.

judie anglen
RIVERTON, WYOMING

My mother used sugar in this recipe, but a local man who keeps bees on our farm shares honey with us, so I use that instead.

loaded mashed potatoes

PREP: 20 min. | **BAKE:** 30 min.

- 5 pounds potatoes, peeled and cubed
- 3/4 cup sour cream
- 1/2 cup milk
- 3 tablespoons butter
- Salt and pepper to taste
- 3 cups (12 ounces) shredded cheddar cheese blend, *divided*
- 1/2 pound sliced bacon, cooked and crumbled
- 3 green onions, sliced

Place potatoes in a Dutch oven and cover with water. Bring to a boil. Reduce heat; cover and simmer for 10-15 minutes or until tender. Drain and place in a large bowl. Add the sour cream, milk, butter, salt and pepper. Beat on medium-low speed until the mixture is fluffy. Stir in 2 cups cheese, bacon and onions.

Transfer the potato mixture to a greased 3-qt. baking dish. Top potatoes with remaining cheese. Bake, uncovered, at 350° for 30 minutes or until heated through and the cheese is melted.

YIELD: 14 servings.

dawn reuter
OXFORD, WISCONSIN

Tired of the same old mashed potatoes, I whipped up this new family favorite. We can't get enough of them at our house. Often, I'll prepare the casserole ahead and refrigerate it until I'm ready to make dinner.

jaki allen
IRONS, MICHIGAN

No family gathering would be complete without these classic baked beans. The recipe has been in our family for as long as anyone can remember.

four-bean supreme

PREP: 15 min. | BAKE: 1 hour

- 1 can (16 ounces) kidney beans, rinsed and drained
- 1 can (16 ounces) pork and beans, undrained
- 1 can (15-1/2 ounces) great northern beans, rinsed and drained
- 1 can (15 ounces) black beans, rinsed and drained
- 1 medium onion, chopped
- 1/3 cup packed brown sugar
- 1 teaspoon sugar
- 1 teaspoon salt
- 1 teaspoon lemon juice
- 1/2 to 1 teaspoon hot pepper sauce
- 1/4 teaspoon *each* dried basil, dried oregano, ground cumin, garlic powder, onion powder and pepper
- 3 bacon strips, cut into 2-inch pieces

In a large bowl, combine beans. In another bowl, combine the onion, sugars, salt, lemon juice, hot pepper sauce and seasonings. Stir into beans.

Pour into a greased 2-qt. baking dish. Top with bacon pieces. Bake, uncovered, at 350° for 1 hour or until heated through.

YIELD: 8-10 servings.

suzanne mckinley
LYONS, GEORGIA

Here's an easy way to season fresh corn on the cob. Try it with steaks or your favorite grilled sausages. Your family will enjoy the change of pace.

parmesan corn on the cob

PREP/TOTAL TIME: 30 min.

- 1/4 cup butter, melted
- 1/4 cup grated Parmesan cheese
- 1/2 teaspoon Italian seasoning
- 4 ears corn on the cob
- 1/4 cup water

Salt to taste

In a small bowl, combine the butter, cheese and Italian seasoning; set aside.

Remove husks and silk from corn; place in a shallow microwave-safe dish. Add water. Cover and microwave on high for 7-10 minutes, turning once. Let stand for 5 minutes; drain. Brush with butter mixture; sprinkle with salt.

YIELD: 4 servings.

EDITOR'S NOTE: This recipe was tested in a 1,100-watt microwave oven.

taste of home test kitchen

We're betting you won't find a faster way to dress up crisp sugar snap peas than with this scrumptious recipe. It pairs well with a variety of entrees and is pretty enough to serve when you have company.

roasted sugar snap peas

PREP/TOTAL TIME: 15 min.

- 1 package (8 ounces) fresh sugar snap peas
- 1 tablespoon chopped shallot
- 2 teaspoons olive oil
- 1/2 teaspoon Italian seasoning
- 1/8 teaspoon salt

Place peas in an ungreased shallow baking pan. Combine the shallot, oil, Italian seasoning and salt; drizzle over peas and toss to coat.

Bake, uncovered, at 400° for 8-10 minutes or until crisp-tender, stirring once.

YIELD: 2 servings.

roasted harvest vegetables

PREP: 20 min. | **BAKE:** 30 min.

8 small red potatoes, quartered

2 small onions, quartered

1 medium zucchini, halved and sliced

1 medium yellow summer squash, halved and sliced

1/2 pound fresh baby carrots

1 cup fresh cauliflowerets

1 cup fresh broccoli florets

1/4 cup olive oil

1 tablespoon garlic powder

1-1/2 teaspoons dried rosemary, crushed

1/2 teaspoon dried thyme

1/4 teaspoon salt

1/4 teaspoon pepper

Place vegetables in a large bowl. In a small bowl, whisk remaining ingredients; drizzle over vegetables and toss to coat.

Transfer to two greased 15-in. x 10-in. x 1-in. baking pans. Bake, uncovered, at 400° for 30-35 minutes or until tender, stirring occasionally.

YIELD: 9 servings.

amy logan

MILL CREEK, PENNSYLVANIA

Want to know my favorite side dish to serve when we have company? This is it! I like to serve it with any kind of roasted meat.

CHAPTER SIX

bakeshop favorites

PICTURED LEFT TO RIGHT: APRICOT ALMOND TORTE, PAGE 218 • LARA'S TENDER GINGERSNAPS, PAGE 219
CLOVERLEAF ROLLS, PAGE 233 • BANANA CREAM ECLAIRS, PAGE 237

trisha kruse
EAGLE, IDAHO

My mom taught me this easy recipe, which is great for feeding a crowd. There is never a crumb left over. Mom used her own bread dough, but using frozen dough is my shortcut.

parmesan-ranch pan rolls

PREP: 30 min. + rising | **BAKE:** 20 min.

- 2 loaves (1 pound *each*) frozen bread dough, thawed
- 1 cup grated Parmesan cheese
- 1/2 cup butter, melted
- 1 envelope buttermilk ranch salad dressing mix
- 1 small onion, finely chopped

On a lightly floured surface, divide dough into 18 portions; shape each portion into a ball. In a small bowl, combine the cheese, butter and ranch dressing mix.

Roll balls in cheese mixture; arrange in two greased 9-in. square baking pans. Sprinkle with onion. Cover and let rise in a warm place until doubled, about 45 minutes.

Bake at 350° for 20-25 minutes or until golden brown. Remove from pans to wire racks.

YIELD: 1-1/2 dozen.

mattie carter
ROCK HILL, SOUTH CAROLINA

With peach orchards just a couple of miles from home, it's easy to treat my family to this traditional dessert.

south carolina cobbler

PREP: 10 min. | **BAKE:** 50 min.

- 4 cups sliced peeled fresh *or* frozen peaches, thawed
- 1 cup sugar, *divided*
- 1/2 teaspoon almond extract
- 1/3 cup butter, melted
- 3/4 cup all-purpose flour
- 2 teaspoons baking powder
- Pinch salt
- 3/4 cup milk
- Vanilla ice cream, optional

In a large bowl, gently toss peaches, 1/2 cup sugar and extract; set aside. Pour butter into a shallow 2-qt. baking dish.

In a small bowl, combine the flour, baking powder, salt and remaining sugar; stir in milk until smooth. Pour evenly over butter (do not stir). Top with peach mixture.

Bake at 350° for 50-55 minutes or until golden brown and bubbly. Serve with ice cream if desired.

YIELD: 8 servings.

florida citrus meringue pie

PREP: 30 min. | **BAKE:** 15 min. + chilling

Pastry for single-crust pie (9 inches)
1 cup sugar
5 tablespoons cornstarch
1/2 teaspoon salt
1 cup water
1 cup orange juice
4 egg yolks, lightly beaten
1/2 cup lemon juice
2 tablespoons butter
1 teaspoon grated lemon peel
1 teaspoon grated orange peel

MERINGUE:
3 egg whites
1 teaspoon vanilla extract
6 tablespoons sugar

Roll out pastry to fit a 9-in. pie plate. Transfer pastry to pie plate. Trim pastry to 1/2 in. beyond edge of plate; flute edges. Line unpricked pastry with a double thickness of heavy-duty foil.

Bake at 450° for 8 minutes. Remove foil; bake 5-7 minutes longer or until lightly browned. Cool on a wire rack. Reduce heat to 350°.

Meanwhile, in a large saucepan, combine the sugar, cornstarch and salt. Gradually stir in water and orange juice until smooth. Cook and stir over medium-high heat until thickened and bubbly. Reduce heat; cook and stir 2 minutes longer (mixture will be thick).

Remove from the heat. Stir a small amount of hot mixture into egg yolks; return all to the pan, stirring constantly. Bring to a gentle boil; cook and stir 2 minutes longer. Remove from the heat. Gently stir in the lemon juice, butter, and lemon and orange peels. Pour into prepared crust.

In a large bowl, beat egg whites and vanilla on medium speed until soft peaks form. Gradually beat in sugar, 1 tablespoon at a time, on high until stiff glossy peaks form and sugar is dissolved. Spread over hot filling, sealing edges to crust.

Bake at 350° for 12-15 minutes or until meringue is golden brown. Cool on a wire rack for 1 hour. Refrigerate for at least 3 hours before serving. Store leftovers in the refrigerator.

YIELD: 8 servings.

barbara carlucci
ORANGE PARK, FLORIDA

Why limit a great dessert to just one kind of citrus fruit? Thanks to orange and lemon, this lovely pie packs a bold sweet-tart flavor!

trisha kruse
EAGLE, IDAHO

This pretty cake takes a bit of time, so I like to prepare the layers ahead of time and assemble the day of serving, making it an easier option for entertaining.

apricot almond torte

PREP: 45 min. | **BAKE:** 25 min. + cooling

        3 eggs
1-1/2 cups sugar
        1 teaspoon vanilla extract
1-3/4 cups all-purpose flour
        1 cup ground almonds, toasted
        2 teaspoons baking powder
    1/2 teaspoon salt
1-1/2 cups heavy whipping cream, whipped

FROSTING:

        1 package (8 ounces) cream cheese, softened
        1 cup sugar
    1/8 teaspoon salt
        1 teaspoon almond extract
1-1/2 cups heavy whipping cream, whipped
        1 jar (10 to 12 ounces) apricot preserves
    1/2 cup slivered almonds, toasted

In a large bowl, beat the eggs, sugar and vanilla on high speed until mixture is thick and lemon-colored. Combine the flour, almonds, baking powder and salt; gradually fold into egg mixture alternately with whipped cream.

Transfer to two greased and floured 9-in. round baking pans. Bake at 350° for 22-28 minutes or until a toothpick inserted near the center comes out clean. Cool for 10 minutes before removing from pans to wire racks to cool completely.

In a large bowl, beat the cream cheese, sugar and salt until smooth. Beat in extract. Fold in whipped cream.

Cut each cake horizontally into two layers. Place bottom layer on a serving plate; spread with 1 cup frosting. Top with another cake layer; spread with half of the preserves. Repeat layers. Frost sides of cake; decorate the top edge with remaining frosting. Sprinkle with almonds.

YIELD: 12 servings.

lara's tender gingersnaps

PREP: 15 min. + chilling | **BAKE:** 10 min./batch

1 cup packed brown sugar
3/4 cup butter, melted
1 egg
1/4 cup molasses
2-1/4 cups all-purpose flour
1-1/2 teaspoons ground ginger
1 teaspoon baking soda
1 teaspoon ground cinnamon
1/2 teaspoon ground cloves
1/4 cup sugar

In a large bowl, beat brown sugar and butter until blended. Beat in egg and molasses. Combine the flour, ginger, baking soda, cinnamon and cloves; gradually add to brown sugar mixture and mix well (dough will be stiff). Cover and refrigerate for at least 2 hours.

Shape dough into 1 in. balls. Roll in sugar. Place 2 in. apart on baking sheets coated with cooking spray.

Bake at 350°; for 9-11 minutes or until set. Cool for 1 minute before removing from pans to wire racks.

YIELD: 3 dozen.

lara pennell
MAULDIN, SOUTH CAROLINA

Soft gingersnaps embody the tastes and smells of the Christmas season, so they're also perfect for any fall or winter gathering. I enjoy the warm, cozy flavors of cloves, cinnamon and ginger blended into one delicious cookie.

LIGHT & DARK BROWN SUGAR

Choosing whether to use light or dark brown sugar is frequently a matter of preference. Dark brown sugar contains more molasses, which gives the sugar its darker color and a hint of bittersweet flavor. Unless the recipe specifies a type, use what you prefer.

frosted cinnamon rolls

PREP: 35 min. + rising | **BAKE:** 20 min.

1 cup warm milk (70° to 80°)
1/4 cup water (70° to 80°)
1/4 cup butter, softened
1 egg
1 teaspoon salt
4 cups bread flour
1/4 cup instant vanilla pudding mix
1 tablespoon sugar
1 tablespoon active dry yeast

FILLING:
1/4 cup butter, softened
1 cup packed brown sugar
2 teaspoons ground cinnamon

FROSTING:
4 ounces cream cheese, softened
1/4 cup butter, softened
1-1/2 cups confectioners' sugar
1-1/2 teaspoons milk
1/2 teaspoon vanilla extract

In bread machine pan, place first nine ingredients in order suggested by manufacturer. Select dough setting (check dough after 5 minutes of mixing; add 1 to 2 tablespoons water or flour if needed).

When cycle is completed, turn dough onto lightly floured surface. Roll into a 17-in. x 10-in. rectangle. Spread with butter; sprinkle with brown sugar and cinnamon. Roll up, jelly-roll style, starting from a long side; pinch the seam to seal. Cut the roll into 21 slices.

Place 12 rolls, cut side down, in a greased 13-in. x 9-in. baking pan and nine rolls in a 9-in. square baking pan. Cover; let rise in a warm place until doubled, about 45 minutes.

Bake at 350° for 20-25 minutes or until golden brown. Cool for 10 minutes before removing from pans to wire racks to cool.

In a large bowl, beat frosting ingredients until smooth. Frost warm rolls. Store in refrigerator.

YIELD: 21 rolls.

EDITOR'S NOTE: We recommend you do not use a bread machine's time-delay feature for this recipe.

velma horton
LAGRANGE, CALIFORNIA

These pretty cinnamon rolls are absolutely marvelous and taste just like the ones sold at the mall. Topped with a sweet cream cheese frosting, they're best served warm with steaming cups of coffee. Or reheat leftover rolls in the microwave and enjoy them any time of day.

gloria huey
PORT ALLEGANY,
PENNSYLVANIA

*Because the dough doesn't
require kneading, this is a
very easy bread to make.
The tender loaf has a
pleasant dill flavor. I serve
it with soups, salads and
many entrees.*

dill-onion batter bread

PREP: 15 min. + rising | BAKE: 30 min. + cooling

1 package (1/4 ounce) active dry yeast
1/4 cup warm water (110° to 115°)
1 cup warm 2% milk (110° to 115°)
2 tablespoons butter, softened
2 tablespoons sugar
1 egg
2 teaspoons dill seed
2 teaspoons dried minced onion
1/2 teaspoon salt
3 cups all-purpose flour

In a large bowl, dissolve yeast in warm water. Add the milk, butter, sugar, egg, dill seed, onion, salt and 1-1/2 cups flour. Beat on medium speed for 3 minutes. Stir in remaining flour (batter will be sticky). Do not knead. Cover and let rise in a warm place until doubled, about 1 hour.

Stir batter down. Spoon into a greased 9-in. x 5-in. loaf pan. Cover and let rise until nearly doubled, about 45 minutes.

Bake at 350° for 30-35 minutes or until golden brown (cover loosely with foil if top browns too quickly). Cool for 10 minutes before removing from pan to a wire rack.

YIELD: 1 loaf (16 slices).

rhonda knight
HECKER, ILLINOIS

*Folks who love chocolate
chip cookies will enjoy the
same homey flavor in these
golden bars. They can be
mixed up in a jiffy and still
taste wonderful—perfect for
when you need a yummy
treat in a hurry.*

chocolate chip blondies

PREP: 10 min. | BAKE: 20 min. + cooling

1-1/2 cups packed brown sugar
1/2 cup butter, melted
2 eggs, lightly beaten
1 teaspoon vanilla extract
1-1/2 cups all-purpose flour
1/2 teaspoon baking powder
1/2 teaspoon salt
1 cup (6 ounces) semisweet chocolate chips

In a large bowl, combine the brown sugar, butter, eggs and vanilla just until blended. Combine the flour, baking powder and salt; add to brown sugar mixture. Stir in chocolate chips.

Spread into a greased 13-in. x 9-in. baking pan. Bake at 350° for 18-20 minutes or until a toothpick inserted near the center comes out clean. Cool on a wire rack. Cut into bars.

YIELD: 3 dozen.

ambrosia cupcakes

PREP: 25 min. | BAKE: 20 min./batch + cooling

1/2 cup butter, softened
1/2 cup butter-flavored shortening
2 cups sugar
5 eggs, *separated*
1 teaspoon rum extract
1/2 cup sour cream
1/2 cup apricot nectar
1/4 cup pineapple preserves
1/4 cup apricot preserves
2 cups cake flour
1 teaspoon baking powder
1/2 teaspoon salt
1/4 teaspoon baking soda
1 cup chopped pecans

FROSTING:

1/2 cup butter, softened
1 package (3 ounces) cream cheese, softened
1/2 teaspoon coconut extract
1/2 teaspoon almond extract
1/4 cup pineapple preserves
1/4 cup apricot preserves

3-3/4 cups confectioners' sugar
1 cup flaked coconut
36 maraschino cherries with stems

In a large bowl, cream butter, shortening and sugar until light and fluffy. Add egg yolks, one at a time, beating well after each addition. Beat in extract.

In another bowl, whisk the sour cream, apricot nectar and preserves. Combine the flour, baking powder, salt and baking soda; add to creamed mixture alternately with sour cream mixture. Beat just until blended. Stir in pecans. Beat egg whites until stiff peaks form; fold into batter.

Fill paper-lined muffin cups three-fourths full. Bake at 350° for 18-22 minutes or until a toothpick inserted near the center comes out clean. Cool for 10 minutes before removing from pans to wire racks to cool completely.

In a large bowl, cream the butter, cream cheese and extracts until light and fluffy. Beat in preserves. Gradually beat in confectioners' sugar until blended. Frost cupcakes; garnish with coconut and cherries.

YIELD: 3 dozen.

zan brock
JASPER, ALABAMA

These unbeatable cupcakes are just like the classic Southern salad, only sweeter! Pineapple, apricot, coconut...your taste buds will be dancing! A buttery, rich batter guarantees a moist, tender crumb. Yum!

gail long
PELHAM, ALABAMA

My family just loves this wonderful and easy cake that's as pretty as it is tasty! It's perfect for birthdays with its gorgeous pink color. No one will guess that it's lightened up.

makeover strawberry cake

PREP: 20 min. | BAKE: 20 min. + cooling

- 1 package (18-1/4 ounces) white cake mix
- 1 package (.3 ounce) sugar-free strawberry gelatin
- 4 egg whites
- 1/3 cup canola oil
- 1 cup frozen unsweetened strawberries, thawed
- 1/2 cup water

ICING:

- 1/3 cup butter, softened
- 2-1/3 cups confectioners' sugar

Line two 9-in. round baking pans with waxed paper. Coat pans with cooking spray and sprinkle with flour; set aside. In a large bowl, combine the cake mix and gelatin. Add egg whites and oil; beat until well blended.

In a small bowl, mash strawberries in their juice. Set aside 3 tablespoons for icing. Add water and remaining berries to the batter; mix well.

Pour into the prepared pans. Bake at 350° for 20-25 minutes or until a toothpick inserted near the center comes out clean. Cool the cakes for 10 minutes before removing from the pans to wire racks to cool completely.

For icing, in a small bowl, combine the butter and reserved strawberries. Gradually beat in the confectioners' sugar until light and fluffy. Place one cake layer on a serving platter; top with half of the icing. Repeat layers.

YIELD: 16 servings.

yankee corn muffins

PREP/TOTAL TIME: 25 min.

1 cup all-purpose flour
3/4 cup yellow cornmeal
3 tablespoons sugar
2 teaspoons baking powder
1 teaspoon salt
1 egg
1 cup milk
1/4 cup canola oil

In a large bowl, combine the flour, cornmeal, sugar, baking powder and salt. In a small bowl, beat the egg, milk and oil. Stir into the dry ingredients just until moistened.

Fill greased or paper-lined muffin cups two-thirds full. Bake at 400° for 16-18 minutes or until a toothpick inserted near the center comes clean. Cool for 5 minutes before removing from pan to a wire rack. Serve warm.

YIELD: 8 muffins.

barb marshall
PICKERINGTON, OHIO

Traditional corn muffins are perfect alongside chili or casseroles, but they really complement any meal. Topped with a little butter, fresh-from-the-oven treats like these never last too long around our house.

raspberry coffee cake

PREP: 25 min. | **BAKE:** 35 min. + cooling

1-1/2 cups all-purpose flour
1/2 cup sugar
1-1/2 teaspoons baking powder
1/2 teaspoon salt
1/2 teaspoon ground cinnamon
1/8 teaspoon ground mace, optional
1/2 cup cold butter, cubed
1 egg
1/2 cup 2% milk
1/2 teaspoon vanilla extract

FILLING:
1/2 cup sugar
2 tablespoons cornstarch
6 tablespoons water
1 cup fresh raspberries
1-1/2 teaspoons lemon juice

TOPPING:
1/3 cup all-purpose flour
3 tablespoons sugar
4-1/2 teaspoons cold butter
3 tablespoons chopped walnuts

In a large bowl, combine the first five ingredients. Add mace if desired. Cut in butter until mixture resembles coarse crumbs. Whisk the egg, milk and vanilla; stir into crumb mixture just until moistened. Spoon into a 9-in. x 5-in. loaf pan coated with cooking spray.

In a small saucepan, combine sugar and cornstarch; stir in water until smooth. Add raspberries and lemon juice. Bring to a boil; cook and stir for 1-2 minutes or until thickened. Pour over batter; cut through with a knife to swirl.

In a small bowl, combine flour and sugar. Cut in butter until crumbly. Sprinkle over batter; top with nuts. Bake at 350° for 35-40 minutes or until a toothpick inserted near the center comes out clean. Cool on a wire rack.

YIELD: 6 servings.

mary ross
WASHBURN, WISCONSIN

Swirled with a fresh raspberry filling, this fuss free coffee cake has a crunchy crumb topping. You could use cherries, blackberries or blueberries instead of raspberries; I like to use whatever I happened to pick that day.

kathleen specht
CLINTON, MONTANA

This rich dessert is my own original creation, and I'm very proud of it. It's easy enough to make on weeknights but special enough to serve guests or take to a potluck.

turtle praline tart

PREP: 35 min. + chilling

      1 sheet refrigerated pie pastry
    36 caramels
      1 cup heavy whipping cream, *divided*
3-1/2 cups pecan halves
   1/2 cup semisweet chocolate chips, melted

Unroll pastry on a lightly floured surface. Transfer to an 11-in. fluted tart pan with removable bottom; trim edges.

Line unpricked pastry shell with a double thickness of heavy-duty foil. Bake at 450° for 8 minutes. Remove foil; bake 5-6 minutes longer or until light golden brown. Cool on a wire rack.

In a large saucepan, combine the caramels and 1/2 cup cream. Cook and stir them over medium-low heat until caramels are melted. Stir in pecans. Spread filling evenly into crust. Drizzle with the melted chocolate.

Cover and refrigerate for 30 minutes or until set. Whip remaining cream; serve with tart.

YIELD: 16 servings.

**taste of home
test kitchen**

Instead of turning to a boxed cake mix, why not try your hand at this easy recipe for a basic yellow cake? You just can't beat the homemade goodness!

yellow layer cake

PREP: 10 min. | BAKE: 25 min. + cooling

   2/3 cup butter, softened
1-3/4 cups sugar
      2 eggs
1-1/2 teaspoons vanilla extract
2-1/2 cups all-purpose flour
2-1/2 teaspoons baking powder
   1/2 teaspoon salt
1-1/4 cups 2% milk
2-1/2 cups frosting of your choice

In a large bowl, cream butter and sugar until light and fluffy. Add the eggs, one at a time, beating well after each addition. Beat in the vanilla. Combine the flour, baking powder and salt; add to the creamed mixture alternately with milk, beating well after each addition.

Pour into two greased and floured 9-in. round baking pans. Bake at 350° for 25-30 minutes or until a toothpick inserted near the center comes out clean. Cool for 10 minutes before removing from pans to wire racks to cool completely.

Spread frosting between layers and over the top and sides of cake.

YIELD: 12 servings.

CHOCOLATE CHIP CAKE: Fold 2/3 cup miniature semisweet chocolate chips into the batter.

YELLOW NUT CAKE: Fold 1 cup chopped nuts (almonds, pecans, walnuts, hazelnuts or macadamia) into the batter.

swedish tea ring

PREP: 30 min. + rising | **BAKE:** 20 min. + cooling

elsie epp
NEWTON, KANSAS

This showstopper will add a special touch to any holiday spread, but it's absolutely spectacular no matter when you serve it!

    1 tablespoon active dry yeast
1-1/2 cups warm water (110° to 115°)
    1/4 cup sugar
    1/4 cup canola oil
      2 egg whites, lightly beaten
1-1/4 teaspoons salt
5-1/2 to 6 cups all-purpose flour
    1/2 cup chopped walnuts
    1/2 cup chopped maraschino cherries, patted dry
    1/4 cup packed brown sugar
      1 teaspoon ground cinnamon
      2 tablespoons butter, melted

ICING:

      1 cup confectioners' sugar
      1 to 2 tablespoons fat-free milk

In a large bowl, dissolve yeast in warm water. Add the sugar, oil, egg whites, salt and 1 cup flour; beat until smooth. Stir in enough remaining flour to form a soft dough.

Turn onto a lightly floured surface; knead until smooth, about 6-8 minutes. Place in a bowl coated with cooking spray, turning once to coat the top. Cover and let rise until doubled, about 1 hour.

Combine the walnuts, cherries, brown sugar and cinnamon; set aside. Punch dough down; roll into an 18-in. x 12-in. rectangle. Brush with butter; sprinkle with nut mixture to within 1/2 in. of edges. Roll up jelly-roll style, starting with a long side; pinch seam to seal.

Place seam side down on a 14-in. pizza pan coated with cooking spray; pinch ends together to form a ring. With scissors, cut from outside edge two-thirds of the way toward center of ring at scant 1-in. intervals. Separate strips slightly; twist to allow filling to show. Cover and let rise until doubled, about 40 minutes.

Bake at 400° for 20-25 minutes or until golden brown. Remove from pan to a wire rack to cool.

In a small bowl, combine confectioners' sugar and enough milk to achieve desired consistency; drizzle over warm tea ring.

YIELD: 1 ring (24 slices).

ORGANIZED BRUNCH

The day before your event, iron linens, set the table and put out serving dishes and utensils. Put refrigerated condiments (such as butter, jam and cream cheese) on the same shelf so you can quickly reach for them. Prepare foods that will store well in advance.

classic chocolate layer cake

PREP: 25 min. | BAKE: 25 min. + cooling

  2 cups sugar
  1 cup canola oil
  1 cup milk
  1 cup brewed coffee, room temperature
  2 eggs
  1 teaspoon vanilla extract
  2 cups all-purpose flour
3/4 cup baking cocoa
  2 teaspoons baking soda
  1 teaspoon baking powder
  1 teaspoon salt
BUTTERCREAM FROSTING:
  1 cup butter, softened
  8 cups confectioners' sugar
  2 teaspoons vanilla extract
1/2 to 3/4 cup milk

In a large bowl, beat the sugar, oil, milk, coffee, eggs and vanilla until well blended. Combine the flour, cocoa, baking soda, baking powder and salt; gradually beat into sugar mixture until blended.

Pour into two greased and floured 9-in. round baking pans. Bake at 325° for 25-30 minutes or until a toothpick inserted near the center comes out clean. Cool in pans for 10 minutes before removing to wire racks to cool completely.

For frosting, in a small bowl, cream butter and confectioners' sugar until light and fluffy. Beat in vanilla. Add enough milk until frosting reaches desired consistency. Spread frosting between layers and over top and sides of cake.

YIELD: 12 servings.

morning crispies

PREP: 30 min. + rising | **BAKE:** 15 min.

1 package (1/4 ounce) active dry yeast
1/2 cup warm water (110° to 115°)
1 cup warm milk (110° to 115°)
2 cups sugar, *divided*
1/2 cup canola oil
1-1/4 teaspoons salt
2 eggs
1-1/2 teaspoons lemon extract
5-1/2 to 6 cups all-purpose flour
6 tablespoons butter, softened, *divided*
1 tablespoon ground cinnamon

In a large bowl, dissolve yeast in water; let stand for 5 minutes. Add the milk, 1/2 cup sugar, oil, salt, eggs, extract and 2 cups flour; beat well. Stir in enough remaining flour to make a soft dough.

Turn onto a floured surface; knead until smooth and elastic, about 6-8 minutes. Place in a greased bowl, turning once to grease top. Cover and let rise in a warm place until doubled, about 1 hour.

Punch the dough down. Turn onto a floured surface, roll out into a 1/4-in.-thick rectangle. Spread with 2 tablespoons butter and sprinkle with 1/3 cup of the remaining sugar. Fold dough in half lengthwise; roll out to 1/4-in. thickness. Spread with 2 tablespoons butter and sprinkle with 1/3 cup sugar.

Fold in half widthwise; roll to 1/4-in. thickness. Spread with remaining butter and sprinkle with 1/3 cup sugar. Fold in half lengthwise; roll out to an 18-in. x 10-in. rectangle. Combine the cinnamon and remaining sugar; sprinkle half over the dough to within 1/4 in. of all edges.

Roll up jelly-roll style, starting with a short side; pinch seams to seal. Cut into 1/2-in. slices and place on greased baking sheets (four to six slices per sheet). Cover with waxed paper and flatten with palm of hand. Sprinkle with remaining cinnamon-sugar. Let stand for 30 minutes.

Bake at 400° for 12-15 minutes or until golden brown. Remove from pans to wire racks to cool.

YIELD: about 1-1/2 dozen.

emily goad
FRANKLIN, INDIANA

These large cinnamon-sugar pastries make quite an impression on the table. Serve them with brunch or as an afternoon treat.

chocolate lover's dream cookies

PREP: 15 min. | **BAKE:** 15 min./batch

6 tablespoons canola oil
1/4 cup butter, softened
3/4 cup packed brown sugar
1/2 cup sugar
2 eggs
1 teaspoon vanilla extract
1-1/4 cups all-purpose flour
1/2 cup baking cocoa
1/4 teaspoon baking powder
1 cup white baking chips
1 cup (6 ounces) semisweet chocolate chips

In a large bowl, beat the oil, butter and sugars until well blended. Add eggs, one at a time, beating well after each addition. Beat in vanilla. Combine the flour, cocoa and baking powder; gradually add to oil mixture and mix well. Stir in chips.

Drop by rounded tablespoonfuls 2 in. apart onto ungreased baking sheets. Bake at 350° for 12-15 minutes or until edges begin to brown. Cool for 1 minute before removing from pans to wire racks.

YIELD: 3-1/2 dozen.
CHOCOLATE PECAN COOKIES: Omit white baking chips. Stir in 1 cup chopped pecans along with the semisweet chips.

paula zsiray
LOGAN, UTAH

My daughter won first prize in the cookie division of a local chocolate festival with these —beating out a number of adult bakers. The sweet chocolate cookies with white chocolate chips are scrumptious.

carolyn ruch
NEW LONDON, WISCONSIN

Here's a dessert any busy hostess will love! It goes together in minutes, yet looks and tastes like you really fussed.

easy dutch apple pie

PREP: 15 min. | BAKE: 50 min. + cooling

    1 can (21 ounces) apple pie filling
    1 unbaked pastry shell (9 inches)
  1/2 teaspoon ground cinnamon
    4 tablespoons butter, *divided*
1-1/2 to 2 cups crushed pecan shortbread cookies

Pour pie filling into pastry shell. Sprinkle with cinnamon and dot with 1 tablespoon butter. Melt remaining butter. Place cookie crumbs in a small bowl; stir in butter until coarse crumbs form. Sprinkle over filling. Cover edges of pastry loosely with foil.

Bake at 450° for 10 minutes. Reduce heat to 350°; remove foil and bake for 40-45 minutes or until crust is golden brown and filling is bubbly. Cool on a wire rack for at least 2 hours.

YIELD: 6-8 servings.

joan ort
MILFORD, NEW JERSEY

Slices of warm cinnamon bread and cups of hot tea are the perfect treat for drop-in visitors to our home during the holidays.

cinnamon raisin bread

PREP: 25 min. + rising | BAKE: 45 min. + cooling

  2 packages (1/4 ounce *each*) active dry yeast
  2 cups warm water (110° to 115°)
  1 cup sugar, *divided*
1/4 cup canola oil
  2 teaspoons salt
  2 eggs
  6 to 6-1/2 cups all-purpose flour
  1 cup raisins
Additional canola oil
  3 teaspoons ground cinnamon

In a large bowl, dissolve yeast in warm water. Add 1/2 cup sugar, oil, salt, eggs and 4 cups flour. Beat until smooth. Stir in enough remaining flour to form a soft dough.

Turn onto a floured surface; knead until smooth and elastic, about 6-8 minutes. Place in a greased bowl, turning once to grease top. Cover and let rise in a warm place or until doubled, about 1 hour.

Punch dough down. Turn onto a lightly floured surface; divide in half. Knead 1/2 cup raisins into each; roll each portion into a 15-in. x 9-in. rectangle. Brush with additional oil. Combine cinnamon and remaining sugar; sprinkle to within 1/2 in. of edges.

Tightly roll up, jelly-roll style, starting with a short side; pinch seam to seal. Place seam side down in two greased 9-in. x 5-in. loaf pans. Cover and let rise until doubled, about 30 minutes.

Brush with additional oil. Bake at 375° for 45-50 minutes or until golden brown. Remove from pans to wire racks to cool.

YIELD: 2 loaves (16 slices each).

gingerbread cookies

PREP: 30 min. + chilling | **BAKE:** 10 min./batch + cooling

3/4 cup butter, softened
1 cup packed brown sugar
1 egg
3/4 cup molasses
4 cups all-purpose flour
2 teaspoons ground ginger
1-1/2 teaspoons baking soda
1-1/2 teaspoons ground cinnamon
3/4 teaspoon ground cloves
1/4 teaspoon salt
Vanilla frosting of your choice
Red and green paste food coloring

In a large bowl, cream butter and brown sugar until light and fluffy. Add egg and molasses. Combine the flour, ginger, baking soda, cinnamon, cloves and salt; gradually add to creamed mixture and mix well. Cover and refrigerate dough for 4 hours or until easy to handle.

On a lightly floured surface, roll dough to 1/8-in. thickness. Cut with floured 2-1/2-in. cookie cutters. Place 1 in. apart on ungreased baking sheets.

Bake at 350° for 8-10 minutes or until edges are firm. Remove to wire racks to cool. Tint some of the frosting red and some green. Decorate cookies.

YIELD: 5 dozen.

christy thelen
KELLOGG, IOWA

Our two boys linger around the kitchen when these aromatic cookies are baking. I make them throughout the year using a variety of cookie cutters.

valerie belley
ST. LOUIS, MISSOURI

A can of pie filling and a few tubes of crescent rolls help me assemble this sweet treat. It's the perfect addition to hot coffee and good conversation.

cherry crescent coffee cake

PREP: 25 min. | BAKE: 15 min.

- 1 package (8 ounces) cream cheese, softened
- 3/4 cup confectioners' sugar, *divided*
- 1 egg
- 1/2 teaspoon vanilla extract
- 2 tubes (8 ounces *each*) refrigerated crescent rolls
- 1 can (21 ounces) cherry pie filling
- 2 to 3 teaspoons milk

In a small bowl, beat cream cheese and 1/4 cup confectioners' sugar until smooth. Beat in egg and vanilla just until combined; set aside.

Unroll crescent dough and separate into triangles. Set four triangles aside. Place remaining triangles on a greased 14-in. pizza pan, forming a ring with wide ends facing outer edge of pan and pointed ends toward the center; leave a 3-in. hole in the center. Lightly press seams together.

Spread cream cheese mixture over dough to within 1/2 in. of edges. Top with pie filling to within 1/2 in. of cream cheese edges. Cut reserved triangles into thirds, starting at the wide end and ending at the point. Arrange over pie filling with points facing outer edge of pan, forming spokes. Press ends at center and outer edge to seal.

Bake at 375° for 15-20 minutes or until golden brown. Cool on a wire rack. Combine remaining confectioners' sugar and enough milk to achieve drizzling consistency; drizzle the icing over warm coffee cake.

YIELD: 12 servings.

apple crisp

PREP: 20 min. | **BAKE:** 1 hour

1 cup all-purpose flour
3/4 cup rolled oats
1 cup packed brown sugar
1 teaspoon ground cinnamon
1/2 cup butter
4 cups chopped peeled apples
1 cup sugar
2 tablespoons cornstarch
1 cup water
1 teaspoon vanilla extract
Vanilla ice cream, optional

In a large bowl, combine first four ingredients. Cut in butter until crumbly. Press half into a greased 2-1/2-qt. baking dish or a 9-in. square baking pan. Cover with apples.

In a small saucepan, combine the sugar, cornstarch, water and vanilla. Bring to a boil; cook and stir for 2 minutes or until thick and clear. Pour over apples. Sprinkle with remaining crumb mixture.

Bake at 350° for 60-65 minutes or until apples are tender. Serve warm, with ice cream if desired.

YIELD: 8 servings.

gertrude bartnick
PORTAGE, WISCONSIN

I live in apple country, and a delicious apple crisp is one good way to use them that doesn't take a lot of time to make. It is so tasty.

SHORTCUT FOR CUTTING IN BUTTER

I always grate cold butter before cutting it into my favorite cobbler recipe. Grating makes uniform pieces that cut in faster.
—CHERYL A.
OREGON, WISCONSIN

jumbo chocolate chip cookies

PREP: 20 min. | **BAKE:** 15 min. + cooling

1/2 cup butter, softened
1/2 cup sugar
1/2 cup packed brown sugar
1 egg
1 teaspoon vanilla extract
1-1/4 cups all-purpose flour
1/2 teaspoon baking soda
1/2 teaspoon baking powder
1/2 teaspoon salt
1-1/3 cups flaked coconut
1/2 cup semisweet chocolate chips
1/4 cup milk chocolate chips
2-1/2 ounces white candy coating, chopped, optional

In a large bowl, cream butter and sugars until light and fluffy. Beat in egg and vanilla. Combine flour, baking soda, baking powder and salt; gradually add to creamed mixture and mix well. Stir in coconut and chips. Shape 3 tablespoonfuls of dough into a ball; repeat with remaining dough.

Place balls 3 in. apart on ungreased baking sheets. Bake at 350° for 12-18 minutes or until lightly browned. Remove to wire racks to cool.

In a microwave, melt candy coating if desired. Dip one end of cooled cookies in candy coating. Allow excess to drip off. Place on waxed paper; let stand until set.

YIELD: 1 dozen.

jackie ruckwardt
COTTAGE GROVE, OREGON

These cookies are sure to impress anyone to whom you serve them. The white candy coating adds a wonderful flavor and makes them look so special.

dee davis
SUN CITY, ARIZONA

These cookies are great for the little ones, and they keep adults guessing as to how they can be made with only five ingredients.

peanut butter kiss cookies

PREP: 20 min. | BAKE: 10 min. + cooling

- 1 cup peanut butter
- 1 cup sugar
- 1 egg
- 1 teaspoon vanilla extract
- 24 milk chocolate kisses

In a large bowl, cream peanut butter and sugar until light and fluffy. Add egg and vanilla; beat until mixture is well blended.

Roll into 1-1/4-in. balls. Place 2 in. apart on ungreased baking sheets. Bake at 350° for 10-12 minutes or until tops are slightly cracked.

Immediately press one chocolate kiss into the center of each cookie. Cool for 5 minutes before removing from pans to wire racks.

EDITOR'S NOTE: This recipe does not contain flour. Reduced-fat or generic brands of peanut butter are not recommended for this recipe.

YIELD: 2 dozen.

janis plageman
LYNDEN, WASHINGTON

I packed chocolate chips, raisins, nuts and cinnamon into my oatmeal cookies. Our kids love them!

chewy oatmeal cookies

PREP: 15 min. | BAKE: 10 min./batch + cooling

- 1 cup butter, softened
- 1 cup sugar
- 1 cup packed brown sugar
- 2 eggs
- 1 tablespoon molasses
- 2 teaspoons vanilla extract
- 2 cups all-purpose flour
- 2 cups quick-cooking oats
- 1-1/2 teaspoon baking soda
- 1 teaspoon ground cinnamon
- 1/2 teaspoon salt
- 1 cup *each* raisins and chopped pecans
- 1 cup (6 ounces) semisweet chocolate chips

In a large bowl, cream butter and sugars until light and fluffy. Add the eggs, molasses and vanilla; beat well. Combine the flour, oats, baking soda, cinnamon and salt; gradually add to creamed mixture and mix well. Stir in the raisins, pecans and chocolate chips. Drop by tablespoonfuls 2 in. apart onto greased baking sheets.

Bake at 350° for 9-10 minutes or until lightly browned. Cool on pans for 2 minutes before removing to wire racks.

YIELD: about 5 dozen.

cloverleaf rolls

PREP: 25 min. + rising | BAKE: 15 min.

1 package (1/4 ounce) active dry yeast
1-1/4 cups warm milk (110° to 115°)
1/4 cup butter, softened
1 egg
3 tablespoons sugar
1 teaspoon salt
4 to 4-1/2 cups all-purpose flour
Additional butter, melted

In a large bowl, dissolve yeast in warm milk. Add the butter, egg, sugar, salt and 3 cups flour. Beat until smooth. Stir in enough remaining flour to form a soft dough.

Turn onto a floured surface; knead until smooth and elastic, about 6-8 minutes. Place in a greased bowl, turning once to grease top. Cover and let rise in a warm place until doubled, about 1 hour.

Punch the dough down and divide in half. Divide each half into 36 pieces and shape into balls. Place three balls each in greased muffin cups. Cover and let rise until doubled, about 30 minutes. Brush with additional butter.

Bake at 375° for 15-18 minutes or until lightly browned. Remove to wire racks. Serve warm.

YIELD: 2 dozen.

brenda dufresne
MIDLAND, MICHIGAN

When I was little, my mom would most often rely on traditional from-scratch recipes like this one. My sister and I ate more than our share of these beautiful golden rolls.

noelle myers
GRAND FORKS,
NORTH DAKOTA

You can make this pie without the nuts if you prefer, and it is still very delicious. Servings are great with a scoop of vanilla ice cream on the side.

apple praline pie

PREP: 30 min. | BAKE: 1 hour + cooling

  1-3/4 cups all-purpose flour
    1 teaspoon sugar
  1/2 teaspoon salt
    1 cup cold butter, cubed
    1 teaspoon cider vinegar
    4 to 6 tablespoons cold water

FILLING:

    6 cups thinly sliced peeled tart apples
    1 tablespoon ginger ale
    1 teaspoon lemon juice
    1 teaspoon vanilla extract
  3/4 cup sugar
  1/4 cup all-purpose flour
    3 teaspoons ground cinnamon
  1/4 teaspoon ground nutmeg
    2 tablespoons butter

TOPPING:

  1/4 cup butter, cubed
  1/2 cup packed brown sugar
  2/3 cup pecan halves
    2 tablespoons heavy whipping cream
  1/2 teaspoon vanilla extract

In a large bowl, combine the flour, sugar and salt; cut in butter until crumbly. Sprinkle with vinegar. Gradually add water, tossing with a fork until dough forms a ball.

Divide dough in half so that one portion is slightly larger than the other. Roll out larger portion to fit a 9-in. pie plate. Transfer pastry to pie plate. Trim pastry even with edge.

In a large bowl, toss apples with the ginger ale, lemon juice and vanilla. Combine the sugar, flour, cinnamon and nutmeg; add to apple mixture and toss to coat. Spoon into crust; dot with butter.

Roll out the remaining pastry to fit top of pie. Place over filling. Trim, seal and flute edges. Cut slits in pastry.

Bake at 400° for 55-65 minutes or until the crust is golden brown and filling is bubbly. Cover the edges with foil during the last 30 minutes to prevent overbrowning if necessary.

Meanwhile, in a small saucepan over medium heat, melt butter. Stir in brown sugar; cook and stir until mixture comes to a boil and sugar is dissolved. Stir in pecans; cook 1 minute longer. Remove from the heat; stir in cream and vanilla. Immediately pour over pie. Bake 3-5 minutes longer or until topping is bubbly. Cool on a wire rack.

YIELD: 8 servings.

cheesecake pumpkin muffins

PREP: 25 min. | **BAKE:** 15 min.

- 3 cups all-purpose flour
- 2 cups sugar
- 2 teaspoons baking soda
- 2 teaspoons baking powder
- 1 teaspoon salt
- 1 teaspoon ground cinnamon
- 4 eggs
- 1 can (15 ounces) solid-pack pumpkin
- 1-1/2 cups canola oil

CREAM CHEESE FILLING:

- 1 package (8 ounces) cream cheese, softened
- 1/2 cup sugar
- 1 egg
- 1 tablespoon all-purpose flour

PRALINE TOPPING:

- 2/3 cup chopped pecans
- 1/3 cup packed brown sugar
- 2 tablespoons sour cream

In a large bowl, combine the first six ingredients. In another bowl, whisk the eggs, pumpkin and oil. Stir into dry ingredients just until moistened. Fill 24 greased or paper-lined muffin cups one-third full.

For filling, beat the cream cheese, sugar, egg and flour until smooth. Drop by tablespoonfuls into center of each muffin. Top with remaining batter.

For topping, in a small bowl, combine the pecans, brown sugar and sour cream; spoon over batter. Bake at 400° for 15-18 minutes or until a toothpick inserted in the muffin portion comes out clean. Cool for 5 minutes before removing from pans to wire racks. Refrigerate leftovers.

YIELD: 2 dozen.

lisa powelson
SCOTT CITY, KANSAS

My mother-in-law came up with these tender treats by combining a few of her favorite muffin recipes. Chock-full of pumpkin, they feature both a sweet cream cheese filling and crunchy praline topping.

maple sticky buns

PREP: 30 min. + chilling | **BAKE:** 25 min.

- 2 packages (1/4 ounce *each*) active dry yeast
- 2 cups warm water (110° to 115°)
- 1/4 cup shortening
- 1/2 cup sugar
- 1 egg
- 2 teaspoons salt
- 6 to 6-1/2 cups all-purpose flour
- 6 tablespoons butter, softened
- 3/4 cup packed brown sugar
- 1 tablespoon ground cinnamon
- 3/4 cup chopped walnuts
- 1-1/2 cup maple syrup
- Additional brown sugar

In a large bowl, dissolve yeast in water. Add the shortening, sugar, egg, salt and 5 cups flour. Beat until smooth. Add enough remaining flour to form a soft dough. Cover and refrigerate overnight or up to 24 hours.

Punch dough down. Turn onto a floured surface; knead until smooth and elastic, about 6-8 minutes, adding more flour if needed. Divide into thirds. Roll each portion into a 16-in. x 10-in. rectangle.

On each rectangle, spread 2 tablespoons butter and sprinkle with 1/4 cup brown sugar, 1 teaspoon cinnamon and 1/4 cup walnuts. Pour syrup into three greased 9-in. round baking pans. Sprinkle with additional brown sugar.

Tightly roll up each rectangle, jelly-roll style, starting with the short side. Slice each roll into 10 pieces; place over syrup. Cover and let rise until doubled, about 30 minutes.

Bake at 350° for 25-30 minutes or until golden brown. Cool in pans for 5 minutes; invert onto serving plates.

YIELD: 2-1/2 dozen.

priscilla rossi
EAST BARRE, VERMONT

My family has a small sugaring operation in our backyard. This recipe makes good use of the maple syrup we make. It's a family tradition to serve these sticky buns on Thanksgiving every year.

dawn berg
BUDD LAKE, NEW JERSEY

Shortly after we married, my husband asked if I would bake up a pan of brownies for him to take to work. I said, "Sure—I have the best recipe." He liked to cook, too, and said he had the best recipe. To settle the matter, we each baked a batch and let his coworkers decide. My recipe won!

glazed chocolate chip brownies

PREP: 25 min. + chilling | **BAKE:** 30 min.

2/3 cup butter, melted and cooled
2 eggs, lightly beaten
1 teaspoon vanilla extract
2 cups sugar
1-1/3 cups all-purpose flour
3/4 cup baking cocoa
1/2 teaspoon baking soda
1/4 teaspoon salt
1/2 cup water
1 cup (6 ounces) semisweet chocolate chips

GLAZE:

3/4 cup semisweet chocolate chips
2 tablespoons butter
1/4 cup 2% milk
1-1/4 cups confectioners' sugar
1 teaspoon vanilla extract

In a large bowl, combine the butter, eggs and vanilla. Combine dry ingredients; add to butter mixture. Stir in water and chocolate chips until blended.

Pour the batter into a greased 13-in. x 9-in. baking pan. Bake at 350° for 30-35 minutes or until brownies pull away from the sides of the pan. Cool on a wire rack.

In a microwave-safe bowl, melt the chips and butter with milk; stir until smooth. Whisk in the confectioners' sugar and vanilla until smooth. Refrigerate for 20 minutes or until mixture reaches a spreading consistency; frost brownies.

YIELD: 4 dozen.

eddie lennon
NEWPORT, TENNESSEE

White baking chips and macadamia nuts are a delightful duo in these splendid, buttery cookies. They just might become your new favorite.

white chocolate macadamia cookies

PREP: 10 min. | **BAKE:** 10 min./batch

1/2 cup butter, softened
2/3 cup sugar
1 egg
1 teaspoon vanilla extract

1 cup plus 2 tablespoons all-purpose flour
1/2 teaspoon baking soda
1 jar (3-1/2 ounces) macadamia nuts, chopped
1 cup vanilla *or* white chips

In a large bowl, cream butter and sugar until light and fluffy. Beat in egg and vanilla. Combine flour and baking soda; gradually add to creamed mixture and mix well. Stir in nuts and vanilla chips.

Drop by heaping teaspoonfuls 2 in. apart onto ungreased baking sheets. Bake at 350° for 10-12 minutes or until golden brown. Cool for 1 minute before removing to wire racks to cool completely.

YIELD: about 4-1/2 dozen.

banana cream eclairs

PREP: 40 min. | **BAKE:** 25 min. + cooling

1 cup water
1/2 cup butter, cubed
1/4 cup sugar
1/2 teaspoon salt
1 cup all-purpose flour
4 eggs

FILLING:

2-1/2 cups heavy whipping cream
3 tablespoons sugar
1 teaspoon vanilla extract
3 to 4 medium firm bananas

GLAZE:

1/2 cup confectioners' sugar
2 tablespoons baking cocoa
2 tablespoons butter, melted
1 teaspoon vanilla extract
1 to 2 tablespoons boiling water
1/2 cup finely chopped pecans

In a large saucepan, bring the water, butter, sugar and salt to a boil. Add flour all at once and stir until a smooth ball forms. Remove from the heat; let stand for 5 minutes. Add eggs, one at a time, beating well after each addition. Continue beating until dough is smooth and shiny.

Insert a 3/4-in. round tip into a pastry bag; add dough. Pipe 3-in. strips about 3 in. apart on greased baking sheets. Bake at 400° for 25-30 minutes or until golden brown. Remove to wire racks. Immediately split puffs open; remove tops and set aside. Discard soft dough from inside. Cool puffs.

In a large bowl, beat cream until it begins to thicken. Add sugar and vanilla; beat until stiff peaks form. In another bowl, mash bananas; gently fold in whipped cream. Spoon into eclairs; replace tops.

In a small bowl, combine the confectioners' sugar, cocoa, butter and vanilla. Add enough water to make a thin glaze. Spread over eclairs. Sprinkle with pecans. Refrigerate leftovers.

YIELD: 16 servings.

ruby williams
BOGALUSA, LOUISIANA

To surprise my banana-loving family, I made this dessert for a reunion, where it stood out among the usual potluck fare. These special treats look and taste simply amazing.

bethany eledge
CLEVELAND, TENNESSEE

The inspiration for this cheery-looking cake came from one of my favorite flowers, the sunflower. The yellow Peeps make eye-catching flower petals, and I carefully placed chocolate chips in a circular pattern to resemble the seeds in the middle of a sunflower.

peeps sunflower cake

PREP: 15 min. | BAKE: 30 min. + cooling

- 1 package (18-1/4 ounces) yellow cake mix
- 2 cans (16 ounces *each*) chocolate frosting
- 19 yellow chick Peeps candies
- 1-1/2 cups semisweet chocolate chips

Prepare and bake cake according to package directions, using two greased and waxed paper-lined 9-in. round baking pans. Cool for 10 minutes before removing from pans to wire racks to cool completely; carefully remove waxed paper.

Level tops of cakes. Spread frosting between layers and over the top and sides of cake.

Without separating Peeps and curving slightly to fit, arrange chicks around edge of cake for sunflower petals. For sunflower seeds, arrange chocolate chips in center of cake.

YIELD: 12 servings.

lemon meringue pie

PREP: 30 min. + chilling | **BAKE:** 30 min. + cooling

1-1/2 cups all-purpose flour
1/2 teaspoon salt
1/2 cup shortening
1/4 cup cold water

FILLING:

1-1/2 cups sugar
1/4 cup cornstarch
3 tablespoons all-purpose flour
1/4 teaspoon salt
1-1/2 cups water
3 egg yolks, lightly beaten
2 tablespoons butter
1/3 cup lemon juice
1 teaspoon grated lemon peel
1 teaspoon lemon extract

MERINGUE:

3 egg whites
1/4 teaspoon cream of tartar
6 tablespoons sugar

In a small bowl, combine flour and salt; cut in the shortening until crumbly. Gradually add water, tossing with a fork until dough forms a ball. Roll out pastry to fit a 9-in. pie plate. Transfer pastry to pie plate. Trim pastry to 1/2 in. beyond edge of pie plate; flute edges.

Line with a double thickness of heavy-duty foil. Bake at 450° for 8 minutes or until lightly browned. Remove foil; cool on a wire rack.

For filling, in a small saucepan, combine the sugar, cornstarch, flour and salt. Gradually stir in water. Cook and stir over medium heat until thickened and bubbly, about 2 minutes. Reduce heat; cook and stir 2 minutes longer. Remove from the heat. Gradually stir 1 cup hot filling into egg yolks; return all to pan. Bring to a gentle boil; cook and stir for 2 minutes. Remove from the heat. Stir in the butter, lemon juice, peel and extract until butter is melted. Pour hot filling into crust.

In a small bowl, beat egg whites and cream of tartar on medium speed until soft peaks form. Gradually beat in sugar, 1 tablespoon at a time, on high until stiff glossy peaks form and sugar is dissolved. Spread evenly over hot filling, sealing edges to crust.

Bake at 350° for 12-15 minutes or until the meringue is golden brown. Cool on a wire rack for 1 hour. Refrigerate for at least 3 hours before serving. Store leftovers in the refrigerator.

YIELD: 6-8 servings.

susan jones
BRADFORD, OHIO

My father always wants lemon meringue pie for his birthday. I rely on this recipe, which won first place at our county fair. It has a flaky crust, refreshing filling and soft meringue with pretty golden peaks.

honey whole wheat rolls

PREP: 20 min. + rising | **BAKE:** 20 min.

2 packages (1/4 ounce each) active dry yeast
1 cup warm water (110° to 115°)
1/4 cup butter, melted
1/4 cup honey
1 egg
3/4 cup whole wheat flour
1/2 cup old-fashioned oats
1 teaspoon salt
2-1/4 to 2-3/4 cups all-purpose flour
Additional melted butter

In a large bowl, dissolve yeast in warm water. Stir in the butter, honey, egg, whole wheat flour, oats, salt and 1 cup of all-purpose flour; beat until smooth. Add enough remaining all-purpose flour to form a soft dough.

Turn onto a floured surface; knead dough until smooth and elastic, about 6-8 minutes. Place in a greased bowl and turn once to grease the top. Cover and let rise in a warm place until doubled, about 1 hour.

Punch dough down. Shape into 15 rolls. Place in a greased 13-in. x 9-in. baking pan. Cover and let rise until doubled, about 45 minutes.

Bake at 375° for 20 minutes or until golden brown. Brush with butter.

YIELD: 15 rolls.

celecia stoup
HOBART, OKLAHOMA

Most of the farmers in our area grow wheat, so my recipe definitely represents where I'm from. I bake these rolls often, especially when I'm making soup.

ruth ann stelfox
RAYMOND, ALBERTA

My family's delicious, nutritious cookies use lots of oatmeal. They're crisp on the outside and so sweet and chewy inside.

OATMEAL COOKIE ADDITION

Add an overripe banana to your oatmeal cookie dough, and you'll be rewarded with moister cookies. Add two if the recipe makes a lot.
—EMROSE C.
JOLIET, ILLINOIS

oatmeal chip cookies

PREP: 25 min. + chilling | **BAKE:** 15 min./batch

- 2 cups butter, softened
- 2 cups sugar
- 2 cups packed brown sugar
- 4 eggs
- 2 teaspoons vanilla extract
- 6 cups quick-cooking oats
- 3 cups all-purpose flour
- 2 teaspoons baking soda
- 1 teaspoon salt
- 2 cups (12 ounces) semisweet chocolate chips

In a large bowl, cream butter and sugars until light and fluffy. Beat in eggs and vanilla. Combine the oats, flour, baking soda and salt; gradually add to creamed mixture and mix well. Stir in chocolate chips. Chill dough for 1 hour or until firm.

Roll dough into 1-1/2 in. balls; place on greased baking sheets. Bake at 350° for 11-13 minutes or until lightly browned. Remove from pans to wire racks.

YIELD: about 7 dozen.

laura mcdermott
BIG LAKE, MINNESOTA

I turned biscuit mix into fresh, hot cinnamon rolls one morning because a friend was stopping by. She was so impressed.

cinnamon rolls in a snap

PREP/TOTAL TIME: 20 min.

- 4-1/2 cups biscuit/baking mix
- 1-1/3 cups milk
- **FILLING:**
  - 2 tablespoons butter, softened
- 1/4 cup sugar
- 1 teaspoon ground cinnamon
- 1/3 cup raisins, optional
- **ICING:**
  - 2 cups confectioners' sugar
  - 2 tablespoons milk
  - 2 tablespoons butter, melted
  - 1 teaspoon vanilla extract

In a large bowl, combine biscuit mix and milk. Turn onto a floured surface; knead 8-10 times. Roll the dough into a 12-in. x 10-in. rectangle. Spread with butter. Combine the sugar, cinnamon and raisins if desired; sprinkle over butter.

Roll up from a long side; pinch seam to seal. Cut into 12 slices; place with cut side down on a large greased baking sheet.

Bake at 450° for 10-12 minutes or until golden brown. Meanwhile, combine the icing ingredients; spread over warm rolls. Serve warm.

YIELD: 1 dozen.

chocolate braids

PREP: 40 min. + rising | **BAKE:** 30 min. + cooling

2 packages (1/4 ounce *each*) active
  dry yeast
1/2 cup warm water (110° to 115°)
1/3 cup honey, *divided*
6 tablespoons butter, softened
1 egg
1/2 cup baking cocoa
1/2 teaspoon salt
2-1/2 to 3 cups bread flour

CREAM CHEESE FILLING:
4 ounces cream cheese, softened
1/4 cup sugar
1/4 cup all-purpose flour
1 teaspoon vanilla extract
1/4 teaspoon ground nutmeg

TOPPING:
1/4 cup all-purpose flour
1/4 cup sugar
1/2 teaspoon ground cinnamon
2 tablespoons cold butter
1/4 cup chopped macadamia nuts

ICING:
1-1/2 cups confectioners' sugar
1 tablespoon baking cocoa
1/4 teaspoon vanilla extract
3 to 4 tablespoons milk

In a large bowl, dissolve yeast in warm water. Add 2
teaspoons honey; let stand for 5 minutes. Add the
butter, egg, cocoa, salt, 1-1/2 cups bread flour and
remaining honey. Beat for 2 minutes or until
smooth. Stir in enough remaining bread flour to
form a soft dough.

Turn onto a floured surface; knead until smooth
and elastic, about 6-8 minutes. Place in a greased
bowl, turning once to grease top. Cover and let rise
in a warm place until doubled, about 1 hour.

Punch dough down; divide in half. On a lightly
floured surface, roll out one portion into a 12-in. x
7-in. rectangle.

In a small bowl, beat filling ingredients until
smooth. Spread half of the filling over dough to
within 1 in. of edges. Roll up jelly-roll style, starting
with a long side; pinch seams to seal.

Place seam side down on a large greased baking
sheet. With a sharp knife, cut roll in half lengthwise,
leaving one end intact. Carefully turn cut sides up.
Loosely twist strips around each other, keeping cut
sides up. Pinch ends to seal. Repeat with remaining
dough and filling. Cover and let rise in a warm place
for 30 minutes.

For topping, combine the flour, sugar and
cinnamon in a small bowl; cut in butter until crumbly.
Add nuts. Sprinkle over loaves.

Bake at 350° for 30-35 minutes or until golden
brown. Remove from pans to wire racks to cool. In
a small bowl, combine the confectioner's sugar,
cocoa, vanilla and enough milk to achieve desired
consistency; drizzle over warm loaves.

YIELD: 2 loaves (8 slices each).

erika aylward
CLINTON, MICHIGAN

*Here's a spectacular-looking
bread that gets rave reviews
every time. The recipe is a
little more complicated than
some, but it's worth the
extra effort.*

lemon anise biscotti

PREP: 25 min. | **BAKE:** 40 min. + cooling

carrie sherrill
FORESTVILLE, WISCONSIN

With the growing popularity of gourmet coffees, cappuccino and espresso, I'm finding lots of people enjoy these classic Sicilian dipping cookies.

2 eggs
1 cup sugar
1/4 cup canola oil
1/2 teaspoon lemon extract
1/4 teaspoon vanilla extract
2 cups all-purpose flour
1 teaspoon baking powder
1/2 teaspoon salt
4 teaspoons grated lemon peel
2 teaspoons aniseed, crushed

In a small bowl, beat eggs and sugar for 2 minutes or until thickened. Add oil and extracts; mix well. Combine the flour, baking powder and salt; beat into egg mixture. Stir in lemon peel and aniseed.

Divide dough in half. On a lightly floured surface, shape each portion into a 12-in. x 2-in. rectangle. Transfer to a baking sheet lined with parchment paper. Flatten to 1/2-in. thickness.

Bake at 350° for 30-35 minutes or until golden and tops begin to crack. Carefully remove to wire racks; cool for 5 minutes.

Transfer to a cutting board; cut with a serrated knife into scant 3/4-in. slices. Place cut side down on ungreased baking sheets. Bake for 5 minutes. Turn and bake 5-7 minutes longer or until firm and golden brown. Remove to wire racks to cool. Store in an airtight container.

YIELD: 3 dozen.

eggnog pumpkin pie

PREP: 10 min. | **BAKE:** 1 hour + cooling

1 can (15 ounces) solid-pack pumpkin
1-1/4 cups eggnog

2/3 cup sugar
3 eggs
1-1/2 teaspoons pumpkin pie spice
1/4 teaspoon salt
Pastry for single-crust pie (9 inches)

In a large bowl, combine the pumpkin, eggnog, sugar, eggs, pumpkin pie spice and salt. Pour into pastry shell.

Bake at 375° for 60-65 minutes or until a knife inserted near the center comes out clean. Cool on a wire rack. Refrigerate until serving.

YIELD: 6-8 servings.

EDITOR'S NOTE: This recipe was tested with commercially prepared eggnog.

terri kearns
OKLAHOMA CITY, OKLAHOMA

This pie of my mom's is the absolute best pumpkin pie I have ever tasted. Eggnog is the special ingredient in the creamy custard filling.

carrot cake doughnuts

PREP: 30 min. | **COOK:** 5 min./batch

2 tablespoons butter, softened
1 cup sugar
2 eggs
1 teaspoon grated orange peel
3-1/2 cups all-purpose flour
4 teaspoons baking powder
1-1/2 teaspoons ground cinnamon
1 teaspoon baking soda
3/4 teaspoon *each* salt, ground nutmeg and cloves
1/3 cup milk
1 cup shredded carrots
Oil for deep-fat frying
GLAZE:
1 cup confectioners' sugar
2 tablespoons orange juice
1 tablespoon finely shredded carrot
1/2 teaspoon vanilla extract
1/4 cup finely chopped walnuts

In a large bowl, cream butter and sugar until light and fluffy. Add eggs, one at a time, beating well after each addition. Stir in orange peel. Combine the flour, baking powder, cinnamon, baking soda, salt, nutmeg and cloves; add to creamed mixture alternately with milk. Fold in carrots.

Turn dough onto a lightly floured surface; roll out to 1/2-in. thickness. Cut with a floured 2-1/2-in. doughnut cutter.

In an electric skillet or deep-fat fryer, heat oil to 375°. Fry doughnuts, a few at a time, for 1-1/2 to 2 minutes on each side or until golden brown. Drain on paper towels.

For glaze, combine the confectioners' sugar, orange juice, carrot and vanilla; drizzle over warm doughnuts. Sprinkle with walnuts.

YIELD: 1-1/2 dozen.

tamera danforth
THE DALLES, OREGON

I love carrot cake and wanted to carry its flavor over into a doughnut recipe. My experiments worked and these are now my family's favorite doughnuts. The recipe is easy to make, too.

carol fritz
FULTON, ILLINIOIS

This tender loaf that's dotted with golden raisins is great for any time of year, though it's popular on St. Patrick's Day. It also makes great toast in the morning.

irish soda bread

PREP: 20 min. | **BAKE:** 40 min.

4 cups all-purpose flour
1 tablespoon sugar
1-1/2 teaspoons baking soda
1 teaspoon baking powder
1/2 teaspoon salt
1/4 cup cold butter
1 cup golden raisins
1-3/4 cups buttermilk

In a large bowl, combine the flour, sugar, baking soda, baking powder and salt. Cut in butter until mixture resembles coarse crumbs. Add raisins. Stir in buttermilk just until moistened. Turn onto a lightly floured surface; gently knead 6-8 times.

Place on an ungreased baking sheet; pat into a 7-in. round loaf. Using a sharp knife, cut a 1-in. cross about 1/4 in. deep on top of the loaf. Bake at 375° for 40-45 minutes or until golden brown. Cool bread on a wire rack.

YIELD: 1 loaf (16 slices).

edna hoffman
HEBRON, INDIANA

Here's a pared-down version of this classic old-fashioned dessert. It's perfect when you crave something sweet but do not want leftovers.

mini pineapple upside-down cake

PREP: 15 min. | **BAKE:** 30 min.

1 can (8 ounces) sliced pineapple
1/4 cup packed brown sugar
3 tablespoons butter, melted, *divided*
4 maraschino cherries
4 pecan halves
3/4 cup all-purpose flour
1/3 cup sugar
1 teaspoon baking powder
1/4 teaspoon salt
1/8 teaspoon ground allspice
1 egg, lightly beaten
1/4 cup 2% milk

Drain the pineapple, reserving 1 tablespoon juice. Set pineapple aside. In a small bowl, combine the brown sugar and 2 tablespoons butter; stir until sugar is dissolved.

Pour into an ungreased 6-in. round baking pan. Arrange the pineapple slices in a single layer in pan; place the cherries and pecans in the centers of pineapple slices.

In a small bowl, combine the flour, sugar, baking powder, salt and allspice. Beat in the egg, milk, reserved pineapple juice and remaining butter just until combined. Spoon over pineapple.

Bake at 350° for 30-35 minutes or until cake springs back when lightly touched. Cool for 5 minutes before inverting onto a serving plate. Serve warm.

YIELD: 4 servings.

pecan pumpkin pie

PREP: 10 min. | **BAKE: 55 min. + chilling**

Pastry for single-crust pie (9 inches)
    2 eggs
    1 can (15 ounces) solid-pack pumpkin
    1/2 cup maple syrup
    1/4 cup sugar
    1/4 cup heavy whipping cream
    1 teaspoon ground cinnamon
    1/2 teaspoon ground nutmeg

TOPPING:
    2 eggs, lightly beaten
    1 cup chopped pecans
    1/2 cup sugar
    1/2 cup maple syrup
Whipped topping, optional

Line a 9-in. pie plate with pastry; trim and flute edges. In a large bowl, beat the eggs, pumpkin, syrup, sugar, cream, cinnamon and nutmeg until smooth; pour into pastry.

For the topping, in a large bowl, combine the eggs, pecans, sugar and syrup; spoon over top.

Bake at 425° for 15 minutes. Reduce heat to 350°. Bake 40-45 minutes longer or until crust is golden brown and top of pie is set.

Cool on a wire rack for 1 hour. Refrigerate overnight or until set. Serve with whipped topping if desired.

YIELD: 8 servings.

deborah whitley
NASHVILLE, TENNESSEE

A rich, crispy pecan topping and maple syrup give this creamy pumpkin pie a mouthwatering twist. Yum!

barbara rohlf
SPIRIT LAKE, IOWA

I've have had so many favorable comments from folks who've sampled my cookie-like apricot bars. A sprinkling of coconut makes them feel special!

apricot bars

PREP: 25 min. | **BAKE:** 25 min. + cooling

 1 package (16 ounces) pound cake mix
 4 eggs
1/2 cup butter, melted
 2 teaspoons vanilla extract, *divided*
 1 cup chopped dried apricots
 1 package (8 ounces) cream cheese, softened
 2 cups confectioners' sugar
1/2 cup apricot preserves
3/4 cup flaked coconut
3/4 cup sliced almonds

In a large bowl, combine the cake mix, 2 eggs, butter and 1 teaspoon vanilla; beat until well blended. Fold in dried apricots. Spread into a greased 15-in. x 10-in. x 1-in. baking pan; set aside.

In another bowl, beat the cream cheese, confectioners' sugar, preserves and remaining vanilla. Add remaining eggs; beat on low speed just until combined. Gently spread over cake batter. Sprinkle with coconut and almonds.

Bake at 350° for 25-30 minutes or until golden brown. Cool on a wire rack. Cut into bars. Refrigerate the leftovers.

YIELD: 2 dozen.

nut roll coffee cake

PREP: 40 min. + chilling | **BAKE:** 40 min. + cooling

- 2 packages (1/4 ounce each) active dry yeast
- 1/4 cup warm water (110° to 115°)
- 1 cup butter, melted
- 1/2 cup warm 2% milk (110° to 115°)
- 4 egg yolks
- 2 tablespoons sugar
- 3/4 teaspoon salt
- 2-1/2 cups all-purpose flour

FILLING:

- 3 egg whites
- 1 cup plus 3 tablespoons sugar, *divided*
- 2 cups ground walnuts
- 2 tablespoons 2% milk
- 2 teaspoons ground cinnamon

In a large bowl, dissolve yeast in warm water. Add the butter, milk, egg yolks, sugar, salt and flour. Beat until smooth (mixture will be sticky). Cover and refrigerate overnight.

For filling, in a small bowl, beat egg whites on medium speed until soft peaks form. Gradually beat in 1 cup sugar, about 2 tablespoons at a time, on high until sugar is dissolved. In a large bowl, combine the walnuts, milk, cinnamon and remaining sugar; fold in egg whites.

Divide dough in half. On a well-floured surface, roll each portion into an 18-in. x 12-in. rectangle. Spread filling evenly over each rectangle to within 1/2 in. of edges. Roll up jelly-roll style, starting with a long side; pinch seam to seal.

Place one filled roll seam side up in a greased 10-in. tube pan. Top with second roll, seam side down. Bake at 350° for 40-45 minutes or until golden brown. Cool for 10 minutes before removing from pan to a wire rack.

YIELD: 16 servings.

patricia mele
LOWER BURRELL, PENNSYLVANIA

This beautiful walnut-swirled coffee cake is a great taste to wake up to. As a finishing touch, drizzle it with glaze or add a dusting of confectioners' sugar.

OVERNIGHT YEAST DOUGH

Chilling yeast dough overnight allows for a slow and gentle rising that accommodates your schedule. After rising overnight in the refrigerator, the dough is ready for you to shape and proceed as the recipe directs.

cherry blueberry pie

PREP: 15 min. + standing | **BAKE:** 45 min. + cooling

Pastry for a double-crust pie (9 inches)
- 2 cups pitted sweet cherries
- 2 cups fresh *or* frozen blueberries
- 3/4 cup sugar
- 1/4 cup all-purpose flour
- 1/8 teaspoon ground nutmeg
- 1 tablespoon butter
Additional sugar

Line a 9-in. pie plate with bottom crust; trim pastry even with edge. Set aside.

In a large bowl, gently combine cherries and blueberries. Combine the sugar, flour and nutmeg; stir into fruit. Let stand for 10 minutes. Pour into crust; dot with butter. Roll out remaining pastry; make lattice crust. Seal and flute edges. Sprinkle with additional sugar. Cover edges of pie loosely with foil.

Bake at 425° for 15 minutes. Reduce heat to 350°; bake 30-35 minutes longer or until pastry is golden brown and filling is bubbly. Cool on a wire rack.

YIELD: 6-8 servings.

betty williams
SCOTTS, MICHIGAN

I created a pie that combines cherries and blueberries, two fruits that are abundant here in southwestern Michigan. It's especially good served warm with ice cream.

kim marie van rheenen
MENDOTA, ILLINOIS

To save time when making these bite-size treats, bake the crusts the day before, then cool and store them in an airtight container. Top with your favorite filling just before serving.

tiny shortbread tarts

PREP: 20 min. | BAKE: 20 min./batch + cooling

1 cup butter, softened
1/2 cup confectioners' sugar
2 cups all-purpose flour
1 can (21 ounces) raspberry, cherry *or* strawberry pie filling

In a large bowl, cream butter and confectioners' sugar until light and fluffy. Gradually add flour and mix well.

Shape into 1-in. balls; press onto the bottom and up the sides of greased miniature muffin cups.

Bake at 300° for 17-22 minutes or until set. Cool for 15 minutes before carefully removing from pan

to a wire rack to cool completely. Spoon 1 teaspoon of pie filling into each tart.

YIELD: about 3 dozen.

josie bochek
STURGEON BAY, WISCONSIN

Here's a recipe for a traditional sweet and nutty Greek pastry. It's a tasty end to any meal.

walnut baklava

PREP: 1-1/4 hours | BAKE: 45 min. + cooling

4 cups finely chopped walnuts
1/4 cup sugar
1 tablespoon ground cinnamon
1 cup butter, melted
1 package (16 ounces) frozen phyllo dough, thawed

SYRUP:
1 cup sugar
1/2 cup water
1/4 cup honey
1 teaspoon lemon juice
1 teaspoon vanilla extract

In a small bowl, combine the walnuts, sugar and cinnamon; set aside. Grease a 13-in. x 9-in. baking dish with some of the melted butter. Unroll phyllo dough sheets (keep dough covered with plastic wrap while assembling).

Place one sheet of phyllo in baking dish; brush with butter. Top with a second sheet; brush with butter. Fold long ends under to fit the dish. Sprinkle with about 1/4 cup nut mixture. Repeat 18 times, layering two sheets, brushing with butter and sprinkling with nut mixture. Top with remaining dough; brush with butter. Cut into 2-in. diamonds with a sharp knife.

Bake at 350° for 45-55 minutes or until golden brown. Meanwhile, in a saucepan, combine the syrup ingredients; bring to a boil. Reduce heat; simmer, uncovered, for 10 minutes. Pour over warm baklava. Cool on a wire rack.

YIELD: 3 dozen.

lemon crumb muffins

PREP: 25 min. | **BAKE:** 20 min./batch

6 cups all-purpose flour

4 cups sugar

3/4 teaspoon baking soda

3/4 teaspoon salt

8 eggs

2 cups (16 ounces) sour cream

2 cups butter, melted

3 tablespoons grated lemon peel

2 tablespoons lemon juice

TOPPING:

3/4 cup all-purpose flour

3/4 cup sugar

1/4 cup cold butter, cubed

GLAZE:

1/2 cup sugar

1/3 cup lemon juice

In a large bowl, combine the flour, sugar, baking soda and salt. In another bowl, combine the eggs, sour cream, butter, lemon peel and juice. Stir into dry ingredients just until moistened. Fill greased or paper-lined muffin cups three-fourths full.

In a small bowl, combine flour and sugar; cut in butter until mixture resembles coarse crumbs. Sprinkle over batter.

Bake at 350° for 20-25 minutes or until a toothpick inserted near the center comes out clean. Cool for 5 minutes before removing from pans to wire racks. In a small bowl, whisk glaze ingredients; drizzle over warm muffins. Serve warm.

YIELD: 40 muffins.

claudette brownlee
KINGFISHER, OKLAHOMA

I love to make these muffins for brunch buffets, luncheons and potlucks. They bake up in just 20 minutes and taste delicious warm. Their cake-like texture and pretty topping set them apart.

june mueller
SIOUX CITY, IOWA

I acquired this delicious recipe some 40 years ago, when my husband and I first moved to southern Iowa and had peach trees growing in our backyard. It's been a family favorite since then and always brings back memories of both summer and those happy early years.

peach pie

PREP: 35 min. + standing | **BAKE:** 50 min. + cooling

1/2 cup sugar
1/4 cup packed brown sugar
4-1/2 cups sliced peeled peaches
Pastry for double-crust pie (9 inches)
  3 tablespoons cornstarch
1/4 teaspoon ground nutmeg
1/4 teaspoon ground cinnamon
1/8 teaspoon salt
  2 teaspoons lemon juice
  1 tablespoon butter

In a large bowl, combine sugars; add peaches and toss gently. Cover and let stand for 1 hour. Line a 9-in. pie plate with bottom pastry; trim even with edge. Set aside. Drain peaches, reserving juice.

In a small saucepan, combine the cornstarch, nutmeg, cinnamon and salt; gradually stir in reserved juice. Bring to a boil; cook and stir for 2 minutes or until thickened. Remove from the heat; stir in lemon juice and butter. Gently fold in peaches. Pour into the crust.

Roll out remaining pastry; make a lattice crust. Trim, seal and flute edges. Cover edges loosely with foil. Bake at 400° for 50-60 minutes or until crust is golden brown and filling is bubbly. Cool pie on a wire rack.

YIELD: 6-8 servings.

banana brickle muffins

PREP: 15 min. | **BAKE:** 20 min.

- 2 cups all-purpose flour
- 1/2 cup packed brown sugar
- 1 tablespoon baking powder
- 1 cup mashed ripe bananas
- 1/2 cup milk
- 1/3 cup canola oil
- 1 egg
- 1 package (8 ounces) brickle toffee bits, *divided*

In a large bowl, combine the flour, brown sugar and baking powder. In a small bowl, combine the bananas, milk, oil and egg. Stir into dry ingredients just until moistened. Fold in 1 cup toffee bits.

Fill greased muffin cups three-fourths full. Sprinkle with remaining toffee bits. Bake at 350° for 18-20 minutes or until a toothpick inserted near the center comes out clean. Cool for 5 minutes before removing from pan to a wire rack. Serve warm.

YIELD: 1 dozen.

andra cogan
GROSSE POINTE PARK, MICHIGAN

Toffee bits add great flavor to these delicious banana muffins. Serve them at breakfast, lunch, dinner or as a special snack.

challah

PREP: 30 min. | **BAKE:** 30 min.

- 2 packages (1/4 ounce *each*) active dry yeast
- 1 cup warm water (110° to 115°)
- 1/2 cup canola oil
- 1/3 cup sugar
- 1 tablespoon salt
- 4 eggs
- 6 to 6-1/2 cups all-purpose flour

TOPPING:

- 1 egg
- 1 teaspoon cold water
- 1 tablespoon sesame *or* poppy seeds, optional

In a large bowl, dissolve yeast in warm water. Add the oil, sugar, salt, eggs and 4 cups flour. Beat until smooth. Stir in enough remaining flour to form a firm dough. Turn onto a floured surface; knead until smooth and elastic, about 6-8 minutes. Place in a greased bowl and turn once to grease the top. Cover and let rise in a warm place until doubled, about 1 hour.

Punch dough down. Turn onto a lightly floured surface; divide in half. Divide each portion into thirds. Shape each piece into a 15-in. rope.

Place three ropes on a greased baking sheet and braid; pinch ends to seal and tuck under. Repeat with remaining dough. Cover and let rise until doubled, about 1 hour.

Beat egg and cold water; brush over braids. Sprinkle with sesame or poppy seeds if desired. Bake at 350° for 30-35 minutes or until golden brown. Remove to wire racks to cool.

YIELD: 2 loaves (16 slices each).

taste of home test kitchen
GREENDALE, WISCONSIN

This traditional Jewish bread is often called egg bread because it uses more eggs than most. The attractive golden color and delicious flavor make it hard to resist.

victoria zmarzley-hahn
NORTHAMPTON,
PENNSYLVANIA

My chewy oatmeal cookies are loaded with tasty goodies. Every so often, I add a half-cup of chopped pecans to a batch for something different.

PERFECT DROP COOKIES

Use a small ice cream scoop to make uniform drop cookies. Just scoop the dough, even it with a flat-edged spatula and release it onto a baking sheet. A 1-tablespoon scoop yields a 2-in. cookie.

monica mcgilvray
MUKWONAGO, WISCONSIN

This exceptional cookie features a wonderful, chunky combination of cashews, dried cranberries and white chips. They disappear quickly!

butterscotch raisin cookies

PREP: 20 min. | BAKE: 10 min./batch

1 cup butter, softened
3/4 cup packed brown sugar
1/4 cup sugar
2 eggs
3 cups quick-cooking oats
1-1/2 cups all-purpose flour
1 package (3.4 ounces) instant butterscotch pudding mix
1 teaspoon baking soda
1 cup raisins
1/2 cup butterscotch chips

In a large bowl, cream butter and sugars until light and fluffy. Beat in eggs. Combine the oats, flour, dry pudding mix and baking soda; gradually add to creamed mixture and mix well. Stir in raisins and butterscotch chips (dough will be stiff).

Drop dough by tablespoonfuls 2 in. apart onto ungreased baking sheets. Bake at 375° for 9-11 minutes or until lightly browned. Remove to wire racks to cool.

YIELD: 3-1/2 dozen.

cranberry-cashew drop cookies

PREP: 20 min. | BAKE: 10 min./batch

1 cup butter, softened
1 cup packed brown sugar
1/2 cup sugar
2 eggs
1 teaspoon vanilla extract

2-1/4 cups all-purpose flour
1 teaspoon baking soda
1 teaspoon salt
1 package (10 to 12 ounces) white baking chips
1 cup chopped cashews
1 cup dried cranberries

In a large bowl, cream butter and sugars until light and fluffy. Beat in eggs and vanilla. Combine flour, baking soda and salt; gradually add to creamed mixture and mix well. Stir in chips, cashews and cranberries.

Drop by rounded tablespoonfuls 2 in. apart onto ungreased baking sheets. Bake at 350° for 9-11 minutes or until golden brown. Remove to wire racks to cool.

YIELD: 4-1/2 dozen.

pumpkin spice cupcakes

PREP: 30 min. | **BAKE:** 30 min. + cooling

2 cups sugar

1 can (15 ounces) solid-pack pumpkin

4 eggs

1 cup canola oil

2 cups all-purpose flour

2 teaspoons baking powder

2 teaspoons ground cinnamon

1 teaspoon baking soda

1/2 teaspoon salt

1/2 teaspoon ground ginger

1/4 teaspoon ground cloves

1 cup raisins

CREAM CHEESE FROSTING:

1/3 cup butter, softened

1 package (3 ounces) cream cheese, softened

1 teaspoon vanilla extract

2 cups confectioners' sugar

1/2 cup chopped walnuts

In a large bowl, beat the sugar, pumpkin, eggs and oil until well blended. Combine the flour, baking powder, cinnamon, baking soda, salt, ginger and cloves; gradually beat into pumpkin mixture until blended. Stir in the raisins.

Fill paper-lined muffin cups three-fourths full. Bake at 350° for 28-32 minutes or until a toothpick inserted near the center comes out clean. Cool for 10 minutes before removing from pans to wire racks to cool completely.

For frosting, in a small bowl, beat butter and cream cheese until smooth. Beat in vanilla. Gradually add confectioners' sugar. Frost cupcakes; sprinkle with walnuts. Store in the refrigerator.

YIELD: 20 cupcakes.

amber butzer

GLADSTONE, OREGON

Pumpkin spice cupcakes are a must for our annual Halloween party. I bake them in decorative liners and top them with spooky Halloween-themed sprinkles instead of nuts. If you still want walnuts in your holiday-themed cupcakes, you can stir them into the cupcake batter. These are great year-round.

lois kamps
HUDSONVILLE, MICHIGAN

*When I was searching for a
moist bread that wouldn't
crumble when thinly sliced,
a friend recommended her
grandmother's cherished
recipe. It slices perfectly.*

honey white loaves

PREP: 20 min. + rising | **BAKE:** 25 min.

 2 packages (1/4 ounce *each*) active dry
  yeast
2-1/2 cups warm water (110° to 115°)
 1/2 cup butter, melted
 1/2 cup honey
 2 eggs
 3 teaspoons salt
 8 to 9 cups all-purpose flour

In a large bowl, dissolve yeast in warm water. Add
the butter, honey, eggs, salt and 4 cups flour. Beat
on medium for 3 minutes. Stir in enough remaining
flour to form a soft dough.

Turn onto a floured surface; knead until smooth
and elastic, about 6-8 minutes. Place in a greased
bowl, turning once to grease top. Cover and let rise
in a warm place until doubled; about 1 hour.

Punch the dough down. Divide it into thirds.
Shape thirds into loaves. Place in three greased 8-in.
x 4-in. loaf pans. Cover and let rise until doubled,
about 30 minutes.

Bake at 375° for 25-30 minutes or until golden
brown. Remove from pans to wire racks to cool.

YIELD: 3 loaves (12 slices each).

the **ULTIMATE COMFORT FOOD** cookbook

pull-apart caramel coffee cake

PREP: 10 min. | **BAKE:** 25 min.

- 2 tubes (12 ounces *each*) refrigerated flaky buttermilk biscuits
- 1 cup packed brown sugar
- 1/2 cup heavy whipping cream
- 1 teaspoon ground cinnamon

Cut each biscuit into four pieces; arrange evenly in a 10-in. fluted tube pan coated with cooking spray. Combine the brown sugar, cream and cinnamon; pour over biscuits.

Bake at 350° for 25-30 minutes or until golden brown. Cool for 5 minutes before inverting onto a serving platter.

YIELD: 12 servings.

jaime keeling
KEIZER, OREGON

The first time I made this delightful breakfast treat for a brunch party, it was a huge hit. Now I get requests every time family or friends do anything around the breakfast hour! I always keep the four simple ingredients on hand.

orange cinnamon rolls

PREP: 25 min. + rising | **BAKE:** 15 min.

- 1 loaf (1 pound) frozen bread dough, thawed
- 1/4 cup butter, softened
- 1/2 cup chopped pecans
- 1/4 cup sugar
- 1/4 cup packed brown sugar
- 1 tablespoon grated orange peel
- 1 teaspoon ground cinnamon

ICING:

- 1 cup confectioners' sugar
- 1 tablespoon butter, melted
- 1/2 teaspoon vanilla extract
- 2 to 3 tablespoons orange juice

On a lightly floured surface, roll out the dough into a 14-in. square. Spread with butter. In a small bowl, combine the pecans, sugar, brown sugar, orange peel and cinnamon. Sprinkle over dough to within 1/2 in. of edges.

Roll up jelly-roll style; pinch seams to seal. Cut into 1/2-in. slices. Place cut side down in two greased 9-in. round baking pans. Cover and let rise in a warm place until doubled, about 40 minutes.

Bake at 350° for 14-16 minutes or until golden brown. Combine the confectioners' sugar, butter, vanilla and enough orange juice to achieve desired consistency; drizzle over warm rolls.

YIELD: about 2 dozen.

donna taylor
SOUTHBRIDGE, MASSACHUSETTS

Ready-made bread dough gives a jump-start to these dainty citrus rolls. Bake some of them up in disposable foil pans to share with the neighbors.

sharon pickerd
SPARTA, MICHIGAN

These cookies melt in your mouth...even when they're not frosted. The recipe was handed down years ago from a cousin who first tried the cookies at a children's fund-raiser.

frosted butter cookies

PREP: 30 min. | **BAKE:** 10 min./batch

    2 cups butter, softened
1-3/4 cups sugar
    1 egg yolk
    4 cups all-purpose flour
Prepared vanilla frosting
Food coloring and decorating sprinkles, optional

In a large bowl, cream butter and sugar until light and fluffy. Beat in egg yolk. Gradually add flour and mix well.

Roll into 1-in. balls. Place 2 in. apart on ungreased baking sheets. Flatten with a glass dipped in flour. Bake at 375° for 8-10 minutes or until lightly browned. Remove to wire racks to cool.

Tint frosting with food coloring if desired. Frost cookies. Decorate as desired.

YIELD: 4-1/2 dozen.

rebecca phillips
BURLINGTON, CONNECTICUT

Instead of going to a baker, head to the kitchen and surprise your family with homemade bagels. For variation and flavor, sprinkle the tops with cinnamon-sugar instead of sesame and poppy seeds.

from-scratch bagels

PREP: 30 min. + rising | **BAKE:** 20 min.

    1 teaspoon active dry yeast
1-1/4 cups warm milk (110° to 115°)
    1/2 cup butter, softened
    2 tablespoons sugar
    1 teaspoon salt
    1 egg yolk
3-3/4 to 4-1/4 cups all-purpose flour
Sesame *or* poppy seeds, optional

In a large bowl, dissolve yeast in warm milk. Add the butter, sugar, salt and egg yolk; mix well. Stir in enough flour to form a soft dough.

Turn onto a floured surface; knead until smooth and elastic, about 6-8 minutes. Place in a greased bowl, turning once to grease top. Cover and let rise in a warm place until doubled, about 1 hour.

Punch dough down. Shape into 12 balls. Push thumb through centers to form a 1-1/2-in. hole. Stretch and shape dough to form an even ring. Place on a floured surface. Cover and let rest for 10 minutes; flatten bagels slightly.

Fill a Dutch oven two-thirds full with water; bring to a boil. Drop bagels, two at a time, into boiling water. Cook for 45 seconds; turn and cook 45 seconds longer. Remove with a slotted spoon; drain well on paper towels.

Sprinkle the bagels with sesame or poppy seeds if desired. Place 2 in. apart on greased baking sheets. Bake at 400° for 20-25 minutes or until golden brown. Remove from pans to wire racks to cool.

YIELD: 1 dozen.

rustic autumn fruit tart

PREP: 25 min. + chilling | BAKE: 40 min. + cooling

1/2 cup butter, softened
4 ounces cream cheese, softened
1-1/2 cups all-purpose flour
2 large apples, peeled and thinly sliced
1 medium pear, peeled and thinly sliced
4-1/2 teaspoons cornstarch
1/2 teaspoon ground cinnamon
1/4 teaspoon ground cardamom
1/4 teaspoon ground nutmeg
1/4 cup orange juice
1/3 cup packed brown sugar
1/2 cup apricot jam, warmed

In a small bowl, beat the butter and cream cheese until smooth. Gradually add the flour, beating just until mixture forms a ball. Cover and refrigerate for 1 hour.

In a large bowl, combine the apples and pear. In a small bowl, combine the cornstarch and spices; stir in the orange juice until smooth. Stir in brown sugar until blended. Add to apple mixture and stir gently to coat.

On a lightly floured surface, roll out dough into a 14-in. circle. Transfer to a parchment paper-lined baking sheet. Spoon filling over the pastry to within 2 in. of edges. Fold up edges of pastry over filling, leaving center uncovered.

Bake at 375° for 40-45 minutes or until crust is golden and filling is bubbly. Spread with apricot jam. Using parchment paper, slide tart onto a wire rack to cool.

YIELD: 6 servings.

jennifer wickes
PINE BEACH, NEW JERSEY

Your guests are sure to love this impressive dessert featuring rich, buttery pastry with apple and pear. It's surprisingly easy.

sherri cox
LUCASVILLE, OHIO

Rich coffee flavor accents the filling of these ooey, gooey rolls. The icing goes on while they're still warm. These rolls never last long!

SPECIAL COFFEE

To brew a pot of coffee "deluxe," I place a single bag of spiced tea on top of my grounds in the filter basket. It makes the coffee just a little bit different.
—SHARON J.
CHARLES CITY, VIRGINIA

cappuccino cinnamon rolls

PREP: 45 min. + rising | **BAKE:** 25 min.

1 package (1/4 ounce) active dry yeast
1 cup warm water (110° to 115°)
3/4 cup warm milk (110° to 115°)
1/2 cup buttermilk
3 tablespoons sugar
2 tablespoons butter, softened
1-1/4 teaspoons salt
5-1/2 to 6 cups all-purpose flour

FILLING:
1/4 cup butter, melted
1 cup packed brown sugar
4 teaspoons instant coffee granules
2 teaspoons ground cinnamon

ICING:
1-1/2 cups confectioners' sugar
2 tablespoons butter, softened
1 to 2 tablespoons milk
2 teaspoons cappuccino mix
1/2 teaspoon vanilla extract

In a large bowl, dissolve yeast in warm water. Add the warm milk, buttermilk, sugar, butter, salt and 4 cups flour. Beat on medium speed until smooth. Stir in enough remaining flour to form a soft dough (dough will be sticky).

Turn onto a floured surface; knead until smooth and elastic, about 6-8 minutes. Place in a greased bowl, turning once to grease the top. Cover and let rise in a warm place until doubled, about 1 hour.

Punch dough down; turn onto a floured surface. Roll into an 18-in. x 12-in. rectangle; brush with butter. Combine the brown sugar, coffee granules and cinnamon; sprinkle over dough to within 1/2 in. of edges.

Roll up jelly-roll style, starting with a long side; pinch seam to seal. Cut into 12 slices. Place rolls, cut side down, in a greased 13-in. x 9-in. baking pan. Cover and let rise until doubled, about 30 minutes.

Bake at 350° for 22-28 minutes or until golden brown. Place pan on a wire rack. In a small bowl, beat the icing ingredients until smooth. Spread over warm rolls. Serve warm.

YIELD: 1 dozen.

quick rosemary focaccia

PREP/TOTAL TIME: 25 min.

- 1 loaf (1 pound) frozen bread dough, thawed
- 2 tablespoons olive oil
- 1/4 cup thinly sliced onion
- 1-1/2 teaspoons minced garlic
- 1 cup (4 ounces) shredded part-skim mozzarella cheese
- 2 tablespoons minced fresh rosemary

Press the dough into an ungreased 15-in. x 10-in. x 1-in. baking pan; build up edges slightly. Brush with oil; top with onion, garlic, cheese and rosemary.

Bake at 400° for 15-20 minutes or until golden brown and cheese is melted. Let stand for 5 minutes before slicing.

YIELD: 15 servings.

shelley ross
BOW, WASHINGTON

With fresh rosemary and lots of cheese, these bread squares will make an everyday dinner seem like a festive occasion.

cranberry-topped lemon tarts

PREP: 45 min. + chilling | BAKE: 20 min. + cooling

- 2 cups all-purpose flour
- 3 tablespoons sugar
- 3/4 teaspoon salt
- 1 cup cold butter, cubed

TOPPING:
- 3 cups fresh *or* frozen cranberries
- 1-1/4 cups sugar
- 1/4 cup water

FILLING:
- 5 eggs
- 1-1/2 cups sugar
- 3/4 cup lemon juice
- 4 teaspoons grated lemon peel
- 1/3 cup butter, cubed

GARNISH:
- 1 medium lemon, cut into 1/4-inch slices
- 1/2 cup sugar
- 1/4 cup water

In a large bowl, combine the flour, sugar and salt; cut in butter until mixture resembles coarse crumbs. Stir until dough forms a ball. Divide into eight portions; press each onto the bottom and up the sides of eight 4-in. tart pans.

Cover and refrigerate for 20 minutes. Bake at 350° for 20-25 minutes or until golden brown. Cool on wire racks.

In a large saucepan, combine the cranberries, sugar and water. Cook over medium heat until berries have popped, about 20 minutes.

Meanwhile, in a small heavy saucepan over medium heat, whisk the eggs, sugar, lemon juice and peel until blended. Add butter; cook, whisking constantly, until mixture is thickened and coats the back of a spoon.

Transfer to a small bowl; cool. Cover and refrigerate for 1 hour. Transfer berry topping to another bowl; refrigerate until serving.

Spoon filling into tart shells. Chill, uncovered, until set. For garnish, in a small saucepan, bring lemon slices, sugar and water to a boil. Reduce heat; simmer, uncovered, for 20-25 minutes or until lemon is tender. Cut slices in half; chill.

Just before serving, spoon cranberry topping over tarts. Garnish with lemon slices.

YIELD: 8 servings.

ruth lee
TROY, ONTARIO

The delicious combination of colors and tangy-sweet flavors make individual lemon tarts a really special dessert. You'll receive a ton of compliments on your culinary expertise.

johnnie mcleod
BASTROP, LOUISIANA

Here's a fun and festive way to serve brownies. Family and friends will love topping their slices with whipped cream and strawberries.

fudge brownie pie

PREP: 15 min. | **BAKE:** 25 min.

1/2 cup butter, melted
1 cup sugar
2 eggs
1/2 cup all-purpose flour
1/3 cup baking cocoa
1/4 teaspoon salt
1 teaspoon vanilla extract
1/2 cup chopped pecans
Whipped cream, optional
Strawberries, optional

In a large bowl, beat butter and sugar. Add the eggs and mix well. Add flour, cocoa and salt. Stir in the vanilla and nuts.

Pour into a greased 9-in. pie pan. Bake at 350° for 25-30 minutes or until almost set. Serve with whipped cream and strawberries if desired.

YIELD: 6 servings.

pam cheney
ONALASKA, WASHINGTON

My family and I farm 40 acres of rhubarb, and I love mixing it with different fruits, combining its tart goodness with something sweet. Raspberries and a crumbly streusel topping set my pie apart.

dutch rhubarb pie

PREP: 15 min. | **BAKE:** 35 min.

Pastry for single-crust pie (9 inches)
3 cups chopped fresh *or* frozen rhubarb
2 cups fresh raspberries
3/4 cup sugar
3 tablespoons all-purpose flour
1 teaspoon vanilla extract
1 egg, lightly beaten
1/4 teaspoon ground nutmeg
TOPPING:
1/3 cup all-purpose flour
1/4 cup packed brown sugar
3 tablespoons butter, melted

Line a 9-in. pie plate with pastry. Trim to 1/2 in. beyond edge of plate; flute edges. In a large bowl, combine the rhubarb, raspberries, sugar, flour, vanilla and egg. Pour into crust; sprinkle with nutmeg. In a small bowl, combine the topping ingredients; sprinkle over filling.

Bake at 350° for 35-40 minutes or until filling is set and crust is golden brown (if needed, cover edges loosely with foil during the last 10 minutes to prevent overbrowning). Cool on a wire rack.

YIELD: 6-8 servings.

EDITOR'S NOTE: If using frozen rhubarb, measure rhubarb while still frozen, then thaw completely. Drain in a colander, but do not press liquid out.

apricot tea rings

PREP: 45 min. + rising | BAKE: 25 min. + cooling

4-1/4 cups all-purpose flour

1/4 cup sugar

2 packages (1/4 ounce *each*) active dry yeast

1 teaspoon salt

1/4 teaspoon ground nutmeg

1 cup 2% milk

1/4 cup water

1/4 cup butter, cubed

2 eggs

FILLING:

12 ounces dried apricots, diced

2 cups water

6 tablespoons brown sugar

4 teaspoons orange juice

1/2 cup chopped pecans

GLAZE:

1 cup confectioners' sugar

2 to 3 tablespoons 2% milk

In a large bowl, combine the flour, sugar, yeast, salt and nutmeg. In a small saucepan, heat the milk, water and butter to 120°-130°. Add to dry ingredients; beat until moistened. Beat in eggs until smooth. Cover and refrigerate overnight.

In a large saucepan, combine apricots and water. Cook over medium heat for 30 minutes or until the water is absorbed and apricots are tender. Remove from the heat; stir in the brown sugar, juice and nuts. Cool.

Punch dough down. Turn onto a lightly floured surface; divide in half. Roll one portion into an 18-in. x 12-in. rectangle. Spread half of filling over rectangle to within 1/2 in. of edges. Roll up jelly-roll style, starting with a long side; pinch seam to seal.

Place seam side down on a greased baking sheet; pinch ends together to form a ring. Repeat for second ring. With scissors, cut each from outside edge two-thirds toward center of ring at 1 in. intervals. Separate strips slightly; twist so filling shows, slightly overlapping with previous piece. Cover; let rise in a warm place until doubled, about 1 hour.

Bake at 375° for 25-28 minutes or until golden brown. Remove from pans to wire racks to cool.

In a small bowl, combine confectioners' sugar and enough milk to achieve desired consistency; drizzle over warm tea rings.

YIELD: 2 rings (12 slices each).

dot christiansen
BETTENDORF, IOWA

These tea rings are perfect for entertaining or sharing with friends. They're attractive and delicious and cut like a dream. Sometimes I use canned pie filling when I want a different flavor or if I'm pressed for time.

vicki raatz
WATERLOO, WISCONSIN

These soft cookies have a cake-like texture and lots of banana flavor that folks seem to love.

banana chocolate chip cookies

PREP: 20 min. | **BAKE:** 10 min./batch

1/3 cup butter, softened
1/2 cup sugar
1 egg
1/2 cup mashed ripe banana
1/2 teaspoon vanilla extract
1 cup all-purpose flour
1 teaspoon baking powder
1/4 teaspoon salt
1/8 teaspoon baking soda
1 cup (6 ounces) semisweet chocolate chips

In a small bowl, cream butter and sugar until light and fluffy. Beat in the egg, banana and vanilla. Combine the flour, baking powder, salt and baking soda; gradually add to creamed mixture and mix well. Stir in chocolate chips.

Drop by tablespoonfuls 2 in. apart onto baking sheets coated with cooking spray. Bake at 350° for 9-11 minutes or until edges are lightly browned. Remove to wire racks to cool.

YIELD: 3 dozen.

cranberry nut bagels

PREP: 30 min. + rising | **BAKE:** 20 min.

- 1 cup plus 2 tablespoons water (70° to 80°)
- 2 tablespoons sugar
- 1 teaspoon salt
- 1-1/4 teaspoons ground cinnamon
- 1/4 cup quick-cooking oats
- 3 cups bread flour
- 2-1/2 teaspoons active dry yeast
- 3/4 cup dried cranberries
- 1/4 cup chopped pecans

TOPPING:
- 2 tablespoons brown sugar
- 1 teaspoon ground cinnamon

In bread machine pan, place the first seven ingredients in order suggested by manufacturer. Select dough setting (check dough after 5 minutes of mixing; add 1 to 2 tablespoons of water or flour if needed). Just before the final kneading (your machine may audibly signal this), add the cranberries and pecans.

When cycle is completed, turn the dough onto a lightly floured surface; cover and let rest for 15 minutes. Divide dough into eight balls. Push thumb through the center of each ball to form a 1-in. hole. Place on a lightly floured surface. Cover and let rest for 10 minutes.

Fill a Dutch oven two-thirds full with water; bring to a boil. Drop bagels, one at a time, into boiling water. Cook for 45 seconds; turn and cook 45 seconds longer. Remove with a slotted spoon; drain well on paper towels.

Combine brown sugar and cinnamon; sprinkle mixture over bagels. Place 2 in. apart on greased baking sheets. Bake at 375° for 20-25 minutes or until golden brown. Remove from pan to wire rack to cool.

YIELD: 8 bagels.

john russell
GREENTOWN, INDIANA

Do you love homemade bagels but not the time commitment? This convenient recipe allows you to prepare those delicious baked goods in a lot less time.

old-time cake doughnuts

PREP: 30 min. + chilling | **COOK:** 5 min./batch

- 2 tablespoons butter, softened
- 1-1/2 cups sugar, *divided*
- 3 eggs
- 4 cups all-purpose flour
- 1 tablespoon baking powder
- 3 teaspoons ground cinnamon, *divided*
- 1/2 teaspoon salt
- 1/8 teaspoon ground nutmeg
- 3/4 cup 2% milk
- Oil for deep-fat frying

In a large bowl, beat butter and 1 cup sugar until crumbly, about 2 minutes. Add eggs, one at a time, beating well after each addition.

Combine the flour, baking powder, 1 teaspoon cinnamon, salt and nutmeg; add to butter mixture alternately with milk, beating well after each addition. Cover and refrigerate for 2 hours.

Turn onto a heavily floured surface; pat dough to 1/4-in. thickness. Cut with a floured 2-1/2-in. doughnut cutter. In an electric skillet or deep fryer, heat oil to 375°.

Fry doughnuts, a few at a time, until golden brown on both sides. Drain on paper towels.

Combine remaining sugar and cinnamon; roll warm doughnuts in mixture.

YIELD: about 2 dozen.

alissa stehr
GAU-ODERNHEIM, GERMANY

This tender cake doughnut is a little piece of heaven at breakfast. For a variation, add a little rum extract or 1 tablespoon dark rum for a richer flavor.

kentucky chocolate pecan pie

PREP: 15 min. | **BAKE:** 40 min. + cooling

3 eggs
2 egg yolks
3/4 cup packed brown sugar
2/3 cup light corn syrup
1/3 cup butter, melted
2 tablespoons Kentucky bourbon, optional
1 teaspoon vanilla extract
Dash salt
1 cup coarsely chopped pecans *or* chopped walnuts
1 unbaked pastry shell (9 inches)
1 egg white, lightly beaten
3/4 cup semisweet chocolate chips
1 cup heavy whipping cream
2 tablespoons confectioners' sugar

In a large bowl, whisk the eggs, yolks, brown sugar, corn syrup, butter, bourbon if desired, vanilla and salt. Stir in nuts.

Brush pastry shell with egg white. Sprinkle with chocolate chips. Pour filling over chips. Bake at 350° for 40-45 minutes or until set. Cool on a wire rack.

In a small bowl, beat cream until it begins to thicken. Add confectioners' sugar; beat until stiff peaks form. Dollop on pie just before serving. Refrigerate leftovers.

YIELD: 6-8 servings.

aunt betty's blueberry muffins

PREP: 15 min. | **BAKE:** 20 min.

1/2 cup old-fashioned oats
1/2 cup orange juice
1 egg
1/2 cup canola oil
1/2 cup sugar
1-1/2 cups all-purpose flour
1-1/4 teaspoons baking powder
1/2 teaspoon salt
1/4 teaspoon baking soda
1 cup fresh *or* frozen blueberries

TOPPING:

2 tablespoons sugar
1/2 teaspoon ground cinnamon

In a large bowl, combine oats and orange juice; let stand for 5 minutes. Beat in the egg, oil and sugar until blended. Combine the flour, baking powder, salt and baking soda; stir into oat mixture just until moistened. Fold in blueberries.

Fill greased or paper-lined muffin cups two-thirds full. Combine topping ingredients; sprinkle over batter. Bake at 400° for 20-25 minutes or until a toothpick inserted near the center comes out clean. Cool for 5 minutes before removing from pan to a wire rack. Serve warm.

YIELD: about 1 dozen.

EDITOR'S NOTE: If using frozen blueberries, use without thawing to avoid discoloring the batter.

candy apple pie

PREP: 20 min. | BAKE: 45 min.

    6 cups thinly sliced peeled tart apples
    2 tablespoons lime juice
    3/4 cup sugar
    1/4 cup all-purpose flour
    1/2 teaspoon ground cinnamon
    1/4 teaspoon salt
Pastry for double-crust pie (9 inches)
    2 tablespoons butter
TOPPING:
    1/4 cup butter, cubed
    1/2 cup packed brown sugar
    2 tablespoons heavy whipping cream
    1/2 cup chopped pecans

In a large bowl, toss apples with lime juice. Combine the sugar, flour, cinnamon and salt; add to apples and toss lightly.

Line a 9-in. pie plate with bottom crust and trim even with edge; fill with apple mixture. Dot with butter. Roll out remaining pastry to fit top of pie. Place over filling. Trim, seal and flute edges; cut slits in pastry.

Bake at 400° for 40-45 minutes or until golden brown and apples are tender.

Meanwhile, melt butter in a small saucepan. Stir in brown sugar and cream. Bring mixture to a boil, stirring constantly. Remove from the heat and stir in the pecans.

Pour over top crust. Bake 3-4 minutes longer or until bubbly. Place on a wire rack. Serve warm.

YIELD: 8 servings.

cindy kleweno
BURLINGTON, COLORADO

This is the only apple pie my husband will eat, but that's all right since he makes it as often as I do. A combination of apple and pecan pie, it's a lovely sweet treat that usually tops off our holiday meals from New Year's all the way through Christmas!

gilda lester
MILLSBORO, DELAWARE

Chocolate, pistachios and cranberries are great together, especially during the holiday season! Warm your friends and neighbors with hot drinks and these coffee-house treats.

chocolate pistachio biscotti

PREP: 30 min. | **BAKE:** 30 min. + cooling

1/3 cup butter, softened
1 cup plus 1 tablespoon sugar, *divided*
3 eggs
2 teaspoons vanilla extract
2-3/4 cups all-purpose flour
1/3 cup baking cocoa
2-1/2 teaspoons baking powder
1/2 teaspoon ground cinnamon
1 cup (6 ounces) semisweet chocolate chips
1/2 cup pistachios
1/2 cup dried cranberries

In a large bowl, cream butter and 1 cup sugar until light and fluffy. Add eggs, one at a time, beating well after each addition. Beat in vanilla. Combine the flour, cocoa, baking powder and cinnamon; add to the creamed mixture and mix well (dough will be sticky). Stir in chips, pistachios and cranberries.

Divide dough into four portions. On ungreased baking sheets, shape portions into 10-in. x 2-1/2-in. rectangles. Sprinkle with remaining sugar. Bake at 350° for 20-25 minutes or until set. Carefully remove to wire racks; cool for 5 minutes.

Transfer to a cutting board; cut each rectangle into 10 slices. Place cut side down on ungreased baking sheets. Bake for 5-8 minutes on each side or until lightly browned. Remove to wire racks to cool. Store in an airtight container.

YIELD: 40 cookies.

the **ULTIMATE COMFORT FOOD** cookbook

peachy cheese danish

PREP: 20 min. | **BAKE:** 15 min.

1 tube (8 ounces) refrigerated
  crescent rolls
4 ounces cream cheese, softened
1/4 cup sugar
2 tablespoons lemon juice
8 teaspoons peach preserves *or* flavor
  of your choice

GLAZE:

1/4 cup confectioners' sugar
1/2 teaspoon vanilla extract
1 to 2 teaspoons milk

Separate dough into four rectangles; seal perforations. On a lightly floured surface, roll each into a 7-in. x 3-1/2-in. rectangle. In a small bowl, combine cream cheese, sugar and lemon juice until smooth; spread over rectangles. Roll up from a long side; pinch edges to seal. Holding one end, loosely coil each.

Place on an ungreased baking sheet. Top each coil with 2 teaspoons preserves. Bake at 350° for 15-20 minutes or until golden brown. Remove from pan to wire rack.

For glaze, in a small bowl, combine confectioners' sugar, vanilla and enough milk to achieve desired consistency. Drizzle over warm rolls.

YIELD: 4 servings.

carolyn kyzer
ALEXANDER, ARKANSAS

I've prepared these sweet rolls for late-night snacks and for breakfast when we have guests. It can be your little secret how quickly these gorgeous pastries come together.

CRESCENT PASTRIES

Leftover crescent rolls are a great addition to breakfast. Lightly spritz them with butter-flavored spray , then sprinkle with sugar and cinnamon and heat in the microwave. Yum!
—ROBIN T.
LOS GATOS, CALIFORNIA

cheddar english muffins

PREP: 20 min. + rising | **COOK:** 20 min./batch

3 to 3-1/4 cups bread flour
1 tablespoon sugar
1 package (1/4 ounce) active dry yeast
1 teaspoon salt
3/4 cup warm water (120° to 130°)
2 tablespoons canola oil
1 egg
1 tablespoon cider vinegar
1/2 cup shredded cheddar cheese
4 tablespoons cornmeal, *divided*

Combine 2 cups flour, sugar, yeast and salt. Add water and oil; beat on medium speed for 2 minutes. Add egg and vinegar; beat on high 2 minutes. Stir in cheese and enough remaining flour to form a stiff dough. Turn onto a floured surface; knead until smooth and no longer sticky, about 2 minutes.

Roll dough to about 1/2-in. thickness. Cut with a 3-in. round cutter. Roll scraps if desired. Coat baking sheets with cooking spray and sprinkle with 2 tablespoons cornmeal. Place muffins on pans; sprinkle with remaining cornmeal. Cover and let rise until doubled, about 1 hour. Heat an ungreased griddle or electric skillet to 325°. Cook muffins for 20-25 minutes or until golden brown, turning every 5 minutes. Remove to wire racks to cool. Split with a fork and toast if desired.

YIELD: about 16 muffins.

marge goral
RIDGEFIELD, CONNECTICUT

These chewy English muffins have a scrumptious, mild cheese flavor that intensifies when they're split and toasted. My family really enjoys them at breakfast or brunch.

janet hall
CLINTON, WISCONSIN

In the mood for homemade cookies? These crisp, chewy treats are a delicious way to show someone you care. The treasured recipe is the only one my grandmother wrote down.

peanut butter cookies

PREP/TOTAL TIME: 30 min.

1/3 cup shortening
1/3 cup peanut butter
1/3 cup sugar
1/3 cup packed brown sugar
1 egg
1 cup all-purpose flour
3/4 teaspoon baking soda
1/8 teaspoon salt

In a small bowl, cream the shortening, peanut butter and sugars until light and fluffy. Beat in egg. Combine the flour, baking soda and salt; add to creamed mixture and mix well.

Roll into 1-1/2-in. balls. Place 3 in. apart on an ungreased baking sheet. Flatten with a fork. Bake at 375° for 10-15 minutes or until lightly browned. Remove to a wire rack.

YIELD: 1 dozen.

taste of home test kitchen

Enjoy a gorgeous, made-for-summer pie. Each bite bursts with sweet, juicy berries. It's the perfect way to cap off any warm-weather celebration.

berry patch pie

PREP: 30 min. + cooling

Pastry for single-crust pie (9 inches)
3/4 cup sugar
1/4 cup cornstarch
2 cups halved fresh strawberries

1-1/2 cups fresh raspberries
1 cup fresh blackberries
1 cup fresh blueberries
1 tablespoon lemon juice

On a lightly floured surface, unroll pastry. Transfer to a 9-in. pie plate. Trim pastry to 1/2 in. beyond edge of plate; flute edges. Line unpricked pastry with a double thickness of heavy-duty foil. Bake at 450° for 8 minutes. Remove foil; bake 5-7 minutes longer or until golden brown. Cool on a wire rack.

Meanwhile, in a large saucepan, combine sugar and cornstarch. Stir in berries and lemon juice. Cook, stirring occasionally, over medium heat until mixture just comes to a boil; pour into prepared crust. Cool completely on a wire rack.

YIELD: 8 servings.

cranberry-white chocolate cinnamon rolls

PREP: 45 min. + chilling | **BAKE:** 30 min. + cooling

- 2 packages (1/4 ounce *each*) active dry yeast
- 2 cups warm water (110° to 115°)
- 1 cup butter, melted
- 1/2 cup sugar
- 2 teaspoons salt
- 5 to 6 cups all-purpose flour

FILLING:

- 1 cup butter, softened
- 1/2 cup packed brown sugar
- 2 teaspoons ground cinnamon
- 1 package (10 to 12 ounces) white baking chips
- 1 cup dried cranberries
- 1/2 cup chopped pecans

GLAZE:

- 2 cups confectioners' sugar
- 2 teaspoons vanilla extract
- 5 to 6 tablespoons heavy whipping cream

In a large bowl, dissolve yeast in warm water. Add the butter, sugar, salt and 4 cups flour; beat until smooth. Stir in enough remaining flour to form a soft dough.

Turn onto a floured surface; knead until smooth and elastic, about 6-8 minutes. Place in a greased bowl, turning once to grease the top. Cover and refrigerate overnight.

Punch dough down. On a lightly floured surface, roll into a 24-in. x 12-in. rectangle. For filling, combine the butter, brown sugar and cinnamon; spread over dough to within 1/2 in. of edges. Sprinkle with chips, cranberries and pecans. Roll up jelly-roll style, starting with a long side; pinch seam to seal.

Cut into 16 slices. Place cut side down in two greased 13-in. x 9-in. baking pans. Cover and let rise in a warm place until doubled, about 45 minutes.

Bake at 350° for 30-35 minutes or until golden brown. Meanwhile, in a small bowl, combine the confectioners' sugar, vanilla and enough cream to achieve desired consistency; drizzle over warm rolls. Cool on wire racks.

YIELD: 16 servings.

meg marriott
TACOMA, WASHINGTON

A basket of warm cinnamon rolls is a sure way to impress family and friends. Add cranberries and white chocolate to the ingredient mix, and these treats become irresistible.

nancy roper
ETOBICOKE, ONTARIO

Chopped cranberries and orange peel give this coffee cake bursts of tart flavor, but a cream cheese layer on top sweetens it nicely. It's so lovely, you'll want to serve it when company comes.

CRANBERRIES

Fresh cranberries are in season from early fall through December. Look for shiny, bright red berries. Avoid berries that are bruised, shriveled or have brown spots. Ripe cranberries should bounce when dropped, which is why they are sometimes called bounceberries.

cranberry cream cheese coffee cake

PREP: 15 min. | BAKE: 70 min. + cooling

    2 cups all-purpose flour
    1 cup sugar
1-1/2 teaspoons baking powder
  1/2 teaspoon baking soda
    1 egg
  3/4 cup orange juice
  1/4 cup butter, melted
    1 teaspoon vanilla extract
    2 cups coarsely chopped fresh *or* frozen
      cranberries
    1 tablespoon grated orange peel
CREAM CHEESE LAYER:
    1 package (8 ounces) cream cheese,
      softened
  1/3 cup sugar
    1 egg
    1 teaspoon vanilla extract
TOPPING:
  3/4 cup all-purpose flour
  1/2 cup sugar
  1/2 cup cold butter, cubed

In a large bowl, combine the first four ingredients. Whisk the egg, orange juice, butter and vanilla; stir into dry ingredients until well combined. Fold in the cranberries and orange peel. Pour into a greased 9-in. springform pan.

In a small bowl, beat cream cheese and sugar until smooth. Beat in egg and vanilla. Spread over batter. Combine flour and sugar; cut in butter until the mixture resembles coarse crumbs. Sprinkle over top.

Place pan on a baking sheet. Bake at 350° for 70-75 minutes or until golden brown. Cool on a wire rack for 15 minutes before removing sides of pan.

YIELD: 12 servings.

raspberry streusel muffins

PREP: 15 min. | **BAKE:** 20 min.

MUFFINS:

1-1/2 cups all-purpose flour
1/2 cup sugar
2 teaspoons baking powder
1/2 cup milk
1/2 cup butter, melted
1 egg, lightly beaten
1 cup fresh *or* frozen whole unsweetened raspberries, *divided*

PECAN STREUSEL TOPPING:

1/4 cup chopped pecans
1/4 cup brown sugar
1/4 cup all-purpose flour
2 tablespoons butter, melted

In a large bowl, combine the flour, sugar and baking powder. In a small bowl, combine the milk, butter and egg. Stir milk mixture into flour mixture just until moistened.

Spoon about 1 tablespoon batter into each of 12 greased muffin cups. Divide half of the raspberries among cups; top with remaining batter, then remaining raspberries.

For the topping, combine the ingredients until mixture resembles moist crumbs; sprinkle over muffins. Bake at 375° for 20-25 minutes or until a toothpick inserted near the center comes out clean. Let stand for 5 minutes; carefully remove from pans. Serve warm.

YIELD: 12 muffins.

rosemary smith
FORT BRAGG, CALIFORNIA

These muffins can be made in minutes for unexpected guests or for a quick breakfast. They're also perfect for pairing with afternoon tea.

caramel-pecan sticky buns

PREP: 20 min. + rising | **BAKE:** 30 min.

2 packages (1/4 ounce each) active dry yeast
1 cup warm 2% milk (110° to 115°)
2 eggs
5 tablespoons butter, melted
1/2 cup sugar
1 teaspoon salt
5 cups all-purpose flour

CARAMEL SAUCE:

1 cup butter, cubed
2 cups packed brown sugar
1/4 cup corn syrup
1/2 to 3/4 cup chopped pecans

FILLING:

2 tablespoons butter, melted
1/2 cup sugar
1 teaspoon ground cinnamon

In a large bowl, dissolve yeast in warm milk. Add the eggs, butter, sugar, salt and 3 cups flour. Beat until smooth. Stir in enough remaining flour to form a soft dough.

Turn onto a lightly floured surface; knead until smooth and elastic, about 6-8 minutes. Place in a greased bowl and turn once to grease the top. Cover and let rise in a warm place until doubled, about 1 hour.

Meanwhile, for sauce, melt butter in a large saucepan. Stir in brown sugar and corn syrup. Boil over medium heat for 2 minutes, stirring constantly. Pour into a greased 13-in. x 9-in. baking dish. Sprinkle with pecans; set aside.

Punch the dough down. Turn onto a floured surface. Roll into a 17-in. x 15-in. rectangle. Spread butter to within 1/2 in. of edges. Combine sugar and cinnamon; sprinkle over dough. Roll up jelly-roll style, starting with a long side; pinch seam to seal.

Cut into 15 slices. Place cut side down over caramel sauce. Cover; let rise until doubled, about 30 minutes.

Bake at 350° for 30-35 minutes or until golden brown. Let stand for 5 minutes before inverting onto a serving platter.

YIELD: 15 servings.

lois jacobsen
DALLAS, WISCONSIN

These irresistible rolls are perfect for Easter brunch or any other holiday morning get-together!

sharon knelsen
COALDALE, ALBERTA

I've been cooking since I was a young girl and am always on the lookout for easy yet delicious dishes. This recipe fits the bill.

easy apple betty

PREP: 15 min. | **BAKE:** 40 min.

10 cups sliced peeled tart apples (about 3 pounds)

1/4 cup unsweetened apple juice

1-3/4 cups crushed oatmeal cookies (about 18)

1/4 cup butter, melted

1/2 teaspoon ground cinnamon

Toss apples and apple juice; arrange half in a 13-in. x 9-in. baking dish coated with cooking spray. Combine cookie crumbs, butter and cinnamon; sprinkle half over apples. Repeat layers.

Bake at 375° for 40-45 minutes or until apples are tender and topping is golden brown.

YIELD: 12 servings.

mary wiebe
ALTONA, MANITOBA

Basic cake mix gets a kick start with everybody's favorite chocolate sandwich cookie. And since there's cookie in every bite, kids will love them!

chocolate cookie cupcakes

PREP: 20 min. | **BAKE:** 20 min. + cooling

1 package (18-1/4 ounces) white cake mix

1-1/4 cups water

1/4 cup canola oil

3 egg whites

1 cup coarsely crushed cream-filled chocolate sandwich cookies (about 9 cookies)

1 can (16 ounces) vanilla frosting

Additional crushed cream-filled chocolate sandwich cookies

In a large bowl, combine the cake mix, water, oil and egg whites; beat on low speed for 30 seconds. Beat on high for 2 minutes. Gently fold in cookie crumbs. Fill paper-lined muffin cups two-thirds full.

Bake at 350° for 18-22 minutes or until a toothpick inserted near the center comes out clean. Cool for 10 minutes before removing from pans to wire racks to cool completely. Frost cupcakes; sprinkle with additional cookie crumbs.

YIELD: 2 dozen.

chocolate-peanut butter cupcakes

PREP: 30 min. | **BAKE:** 20 min. + cooling

- 1 package (18-1/4 ounces) chocolate cake mix
- 1-1/4 cups water
- 1/2 cup peanut butter
- 1/3 cup canola oil
- 3 eggs
- 24 miniature peanut butter cups

FROSTING:

- 6 ounces semisweet chocolate, chopped
- 2/3 cup heavy whipping cream
- 1/3 cup peanut butter
- Additional miniature peanut butter cups, chopped

In a large bowl, combine the cake mix, water, peanut butter, oil and eggs; beat on low speed for 30 seconds. Beat on medium for 2 minutes or until batter is smooth.

Fill 24 paper-lined muffin cups half full. Place a peanut butter cup in the center of each cupcake. Cover each with 1 tablespoonful batter.

Bake at 350° for 18-22 minutes or until a toothpick inserted near the center of the cupcake comes out clean. Cool cupcakes for 10 minutes before removing them from pans to wire racks to cool completely.

Place chocolate in a small bowl. In a small saucepan, bring cream just to a boil. Pour over chocolate; whisk until smooth. Stir in peanut butter. Cool, stirring occasionally, to room temperature or until mixture reaches a spreading consistency, about 10 minutes.

Spread over cupcakes; sprinkle with additional peanut butter cups. Let stand until frosting is set.

YIELD: 2 dozen.

EDITOR'S NOTE: Reduced-fat peanut butter is not recommended for this recipe.

taste of home test kitchen

Satisfy your chocolate craving with these cupcakes. The creamy frosting topped with chopped peanut butter cups is the best part.

rich & creamy desserts

PICTURED LEFT TO RIGHT: FUDGE SUNDAE PIE, PAGE 279 • PUMPKIN CREME BRULEE, PAGE 280
CHOCOLATE-COVERED CHEESECAKE SQUARES, PAGE 282 • CREAM-FILLED CHOCOLATE CAKE ROLL, PAGE 294

jana moses
WEST LINN, OREGON

Packed with orange flavor, marshmallow creme and white chocolate chips, this makeover is like eating an orange Creamsicle ice cream bar...in amazing fudge form.

makeover marbled orange fudge

PREP: 30 min. + chilling

- 2-1/2 cups sugar
- 2/3 cup evaporated milk
- 1/2 cup butter, cubed
- 1 package (10 to 12 ounces) white baking chips
- 1 jar (7 ounces) marshmallow creme
- 3 teaspoons orange extract
- 12 drops yellow food coloring
- 9 drops red food coloring

Line a 13-in. x 9-in. pan with foil and coat with cooking spray; set aside. In a small heavy saucepan, combine the sugar, evaporated milk and butter. Cook and stir over low heat until sugar is dissolved. Bring to a boil; cook and stir for 4 minutes. Remove from the heat; stir in chips and marshmallow creme until smooth.

Remove 1 cup and set aside. Add extract and food coloring to the remaining mixture; stir until blended. Pour into prepared pan. Pour reserved marshmallow mixture over the top; cut through mixture with a knife to swirl. Cover and refrigerate until set.

Using foil, lift fudge out of pan. Discard foil; cut fudge into 1-in. squares. Store in an airtight container in the refrigerator.

YIELD: about 2-1/2 pounds.

ruth gordon
LAKEWOOD, NEW YORK

Chocolate lovers will truly appreciate these delectable truffles. For a change of pace, try the cappuccino or orange-flavored variations.

double chocolate truffles

PREP: 20 min. + chilling

- 1-1/3 cups semisweet chocolate chips
- 3 tablespoons butter
- 1/3 cup heavy whipping cream
- 1 teaspoon vanilla extract
- 1 cup white baking chips
- 2 tablespoons shortening, *divided*
- 1 cup milk chocolate chips

In a microwave, melt the semisweet chocolate chips and butter with the cream; stir until smooth. Add vanilla; cool. Refrigerate 1 hour or muntil almost set but still workable.

Shape into 1/2-in. balls. In a microwave, melt white chips and 1 tablespoon shortening; stir until smooth. Dip half of the balls in white chocolate mixture; allow excess to drip off. Place on waxed paper; let stand until set.

Microwave milk chocolate chips and remaining shortening; stir until smooth. Dip remaining balls in milk chocolate mixture; allow excess to drip off. Place on waxed paper; let stand until set.

If desired, drizzle truffles with melted chocolate of opposite color. Store in an airtight container.

YIELD: 2-1/2 dozen.

ORANGE TRUFFLES: Substitute 3/4 teaspoon orange extract for the vanilla extract.

CAPPUCCINO TRUFFLES: Omit vanilla. Dissolve 2 teaspoons instant coffee granules and 1 teaspoon ground cinnamon in 1 tablespoon boiling water; stir into melted semisweet chocolate mixture. Proceed as directed. Coat truffles with melted white and milk chocolate, or roll in a mixture of 3 tablespoons sugar and 1-1/2 teaspoons ground cinnamon.

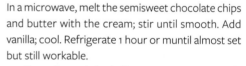

easy tiramisu

PREP/TOTAL TIME: 10 min.

12 vanilla wafers, *divided*
 1 teaspoon instant coffee granules
 2 tablespoons hot water
 2 snack-size cups (3-1/2 ounces *each*)
   vanilla pudding
1/4 cup whipped topping
 1 teaspoon baking cocoa

Set aside two vanilla wafers; coarsely crush remaining wafers. Divide wafer crumbs between two dessert dishes.

In a small bowl, dissolve coffee granules in hot water. Drizzle over wafer crumbs. Spoon pudding into dessert dishes. Top with whipped topping; sprinkle with cocoa. Garnish with reserved wafers.

YIELD: 2 servings.

betty claycomb
ALVERTON, PENNSYLVANIA

Need a great dessert that's ready in a hurry? Here is a fun way to dress up pudding snack cups!

kathy rundle
FOND DU LAC, WISCONSIN

A delectable white chocolate sauce is the crowning touch on servings of sweet cinnamon bread pudding.

white chocolate bread pudding

PREP: 30 min. + standing | **BAKE:** 55 min.

16 slices cinnamon bread, crusts removed, cubed

1 cup dried cranberries

3/4 cup white baking chips

3/4 cup chopped pecans

1/4 cup butter, melted

6 eggs, lightly beaten

4 cups 2% milk

3/4 cup plus 1 tablespoon sugar, *divided*

1 teaspoon vanilla extract

1/4 teaspoon ground cinnamon

1/4 teaspoon ground allspice

SAUCE:

2/3 cup heavy whipping cream

2 tablespoons butter

8 ounces white baking chocolate, chopped

In a greased 13-in. x 9-in. baking dish, layer half of the bread cubes, cranberries, white chips and pecans. Repeat layers. Drizzle with butter.

In a large bowl, whisk the eggs, milk, 3/4 cup sugar, vanilla, cinnamon and allspice until blended; pour over bread mixture. Let mixture stand for 15-30 minutes.

Sprinkle the top with remaining sugar. Bake, uncovered, at 375° for 55-65 minutes or until a knife inserted near the center comes out clean. Cover loosely with foil during the last 15 minutes if the top browns too quickly.

In a small saucepan, bring cream and butter to a boil. Add chocolate and remove from the heat (do not stir). Let stand for 5 minutes; whisk until smooth. Serve with warm bread pudding.

YIELD: 12 servings (1-1/2 cups sauce).

peanut butter parfaits

PREP: 10 min. + cooling

- 1/2 cup packed light brown sugar
- 3 tablespoons milk
- 2 tablespoons light corn syrup
- 2 teaspoons butter
- 2 tablespoons creamy peanut butter
- Vanilla ice cream
- 1/4 cup peanuts

In a small heavy saucepan, combine the brown sugar, milk, corn syrup and butter. Cook and stir over medium heat until sugar is dissolved and mixture is smooth, about 4 minutes.

Remove from the heat; stir in peanut butter until smooth. Cool to room temperature. Spoon half into two parfait glasses; top with ice cream. Repeat layers. Sprinkle with peanuts.

YIELD: 2 servings.

mildred sherrer
FORT WORTH, TEXAS

My husband and I love these parfaits, and they also make an elegant finish to a meal when company comes. You'll receive many enthusiastic compliments!

PRETTY PARFAIT GARNISH

For a pretty garnish, dip the rims of the parfait glasses into a little melted chocolate and then into chopped peanuts or your favorite sprinkles. This is a fun treatment for ice cream sundaes, too!

fudge sundae pie

PREP: 20 min. + freezing

- 1/4 cup plus 3 tablespoons light corn syrup, *divided*
- 3 tablespoons reduced-fat butter
- 2 tablespoons brown sugar
- 2-1/2 cups crisp rice cereal
- 1/4 cup reduced-fat creamy peanut butter
- 1/4 cup fat-free hot fudge ice cream topping, warmed
- 1/4 cup chopped unsalted peanuts
- 4 cups fat-free vanilla frozen yogurt, softened

In a large saucepan, combine 1/4 cup corn syrup, butter and brown sugar. Bring to a boil; cook and stir for 1 minute.

Remove from the heat; stir in cereal until blended. Press the cereal mixture into a greased 9-in. pie plate.

In a small bowl, combine the peanut butter, hot fudge topping and remaining corn syrup. Set aside 1/3 cup for topping. Spread remaining mixture over crust; sprinkle with half of the peanuts. Top with frozen yogurt and remaining peanuts. Cover and freeze for 6 hours or until firm.

Warm reserved peanut butter mixture; drizzle over pie. Let stand at room temperature for 5 minutes before cutting.

YIELD: 8 servings.

EDITOR'S NOTE: This recipe was tested with Land O'Lakes light stick butter.

margaret riley
TALLAHASSEE, FLORIDA

My son always asks for this guilt-free frozen yogurt pie for his birthday. Complete with peanut butter, fudge topping and nuts, it tastes ice cream parlor-good...but it's healthier.

joan jay
FRISCO, TEXAS

My lemony mousse is popular at summer cookouts, but it makes a delicious light finish to hearty winter meals, too. For a pretty presentation, I serve it in individual glass dishes garnished with sliced fresh strawberries.

light lemon mousse

PREP: 20 min. + chilling

- 3/4 cup sugar
- 1/2 cup cornstarch
- 3 cups fat-free milk
- 2/3 cup lemon juice
- 1-1/2 teaspoons grated lemon peel
- 1/4 teaspoon vanilla extract
- 2 cups reduced-fat whipped topping
- 3 drops yellow food coloring, optional

In a large saucepan, combine the sugar and cornstarch; gradually stir in milk until smooth. Bring to a boil over medium heat, stirring constantly. Cook and stir for 2 minutes or until thickened and bubbly. Remove from the heat. Stir in the lemon juice, peel and vanilla.

Set saucepan in ice; stir until mixture reaches room temperature, about 5 minutes. Fold in whipped topping and food coloring if desired.

Spoon into dessert dishes. Refrigerate for at least 1 hour before serving.

YIELD: 10 servings.

tamara leonard merritt
RALEIGH, NORTH CAROLINA

I've never met a creme brulee that I didn't love! I'm not a big pumpkin fan, but this dessert is fantastic.

pumpkin creme brulee

PREP: 20 min. | BAKE: 25 min. + chilling

- 8 egg yolks
- 1/3 cup plus 1/4 cup sugar, *divided*
- 3 cups heavy whipping cream
- 3/4 cup canned pumpkin
- 1-1/2 teaspoons vanilla extract
- 1/2 teaspoon ground cinnamon
- 1/4 teaspoon *each* ground ginger, nutmeg and cloves

In a small bowl, whisk egg yolks and 1/3 cup sugar. In a small saucepan, heat cream over medium heat until bubbles form around sides of pan. Remove from the heat; stir a small amount of hot cream into egg yolk mixture. Return all to the pan, stirring constantly. Stir in the pumpkin, vanilla and spices.

Transfer to eight 6-oz. ramekins or custard cups. Place ramekins in a baking pan; add 1 in. of boiling water to pan. Bake, uncovered, at 325° for 25-30 minutes or until centers are just set (mixture will jiggle). Remove ramekins from water bath; cool for 10 minutes. Refrigerate for at least 4 hours.

If using a creme brulee torch, sprinkle with remaining sugar. Heat sugar with the torch until caramelized. Serve immediately.

If broiling the custards, place ramekins on a baking sheet; let stand at room temperature for 15 minutes. Sprinkle with remaining sugar. Broil 8 in. from the heat for 4-7 minutes or until sugar is caramelized. Refrigerate for 1-2 hours or until firm.

YIELD: 8 servings.

decadent brownie swirl cheesecake

PREP: 30 min. | **BAKE:** 1-1/2 hours + chilling

1 package fudge brownie mix
  (13-inch x 9-inch pan size)

FILLING:

4 packages (8 ounces *each*) cream
  cheese, softened

1 cup sugar

4 eggs, lightly beaten

3 teaspoons vanilla extract *or* 1 teaspoon
  almond extract and 2 teaspoons vanilla
  extract

Fresh raspberries and chocolate curls,
  optional

Prepare brownie mix according to package directions for chewy fudge brownies. Set aside 2/3 cup brownie batter; spread remaining batter into a greased 9-in. springform pan.

Place pan on a double thickness of heavy-duty foil (about 18 in. square). Securely wrap foil around pan. Bake at 350° for 25-28 minutes (brownies will barely test done). Cool for 10 minutes on a wire rack.

In a large bowl, beat cream cheese and sugar until smooth. Beat in eggs and vanilla on low speed just until combined. Stir 1/3 cup into reserved brownie batter; set aside. Spoon half the cheesecake batter into crust; dollop with half of reserved chocolate cheesecake batter. Repeat layers. Cut through batter with a knife to swirl the chocolate cheesecake batter.

Place in a larger baking pan; add 1 in. of hot water to larger pan. Bake at 325° for 1-1/2 hours or until surface is no longer shiny and center is almost set.

Remove pan from water bath and foil. Cool on a wire rack for 10 minutes. Carefully run a knife around the edge of pan to loosen; cool for 1 hour longer. Refrigerate overnight. Remove the sides of the pan. Garnish with raspberries and chocolate curls if desired.

YIELD: 16 servings.

esther neustaeter

LA CRETE, ALBERTA

Satisfy your cheesecake craving with these bite-size delights! They're party favorites and perfect for the holidays when there are so many sweets to choose from.

chocolate-covered cheesecake squares

PREP: 1-1/2 hours + freezing

1 cup graham cracker crumbs
1/4 cup finely chopped pecans
1/4 cup butter, melted

FILLING:

2 packages (8 ounces *each*) cream cheese, softened
1/2 cup sugar
1/4 cup sour cream
2 eggs, lightly beaten
1/2 teaspoon vanilla extract

COATING:

24 ounces semisweet chocolate, chopped
3 tablespoons shortening

Line a 9-in. square baking pan with foil and grease the foil. In a small bowl, combine the graham cracker crumbs, pecans and butter. Press into prepared pan; set aside.

In a large bowl, beat the cream cheese, sugar and sour cream until smooth. Add the eggs; beat on low speed just until combined. Stir in vanilla. Pour over crust.

Bake at 325° for 35-40 minutes or until center is almost set. Cool on a wire rack. Refrigerate until chilled, and then freeze overnight.

In a microwave, melt chocolate and shortening; stir until smooth. Cool slightly.

Using foil, lift cheesecake out of pan. Gently peel off foil; cut into 49 squares. Remove a few pieces at a time for dipping; keep remaining squares refrigerated until ready to dip.

Using a toothpick, completely dip squares, one at a time, in melted chocolate; allow excess to drip off. Place on waxed paper-lined baking sheets; spoon about 1 teaspoon chocolate over each. (Reheat chocolate if needed to finish dipping.) Let stand for 20 minutes or until set. Store in an airtight container in the refrigerator or freezer.

YIELD: 49 squares.

the **ULTIMATE COMFORT FOOD** cookbook

caramel chip malts

PREP/TOTAL TIME: 5 min.

1 cup milk
2 cups chocolate chip ice cream
1/2 cup caramel ice cream topping
3 tablespoons chocolate malted milk powder

In a blender, combine the milk, ice cream, caramel topping and chocolate malted milk powder; cover and process mixture until blended. Pour malts into chilled glasses.

YIELD: 2 servings.

taste of home test kitchen

You can satisfy a sweet tooth in a hurry with a yummy chocolate chip malt that has a sweet hint of caramel. With its thick, creamy texture, it makes a speedy snack or dessert.

butter pecan ice cream

PREP: 20 min. + cooling | PROCESS: 20 min./batch + freezing

2 cups whole milk
2 cups half-and-half cream
1 cup sugar
1/2 cup packed light brown sugar
1/4 teaspoon salt
2 eggs, lightly beaten
1-1/2 teaspoons vanilla extract
1 cup finely chopped pecans
2 tablespoons butter

In a large heavy saucepan, heat the milk, cream, sugars and salt until bubbles form around sides of pan. Whisk a small amount of hot mixture into the eggs. Return all to the pan, whisking constantly.

Cook and stir over low heat until mixture is thickened and coats the back of a spoon. Quickly transfer to a bowl; place in ice water and stir for 2 minutes. Stir in the vanilla. Press waxed paper onto the surface of the custard. Refrigerate for several hours or overnight.

In a small skillet, saute pecans in butter, stirring constantly. Cool.

Fill cylinder of ice cream freezer two-thirds full; freeze according to the manufacturer's directions.

Stir in toasted pecans. Refrigerate remaining mixture until ready to freeze. When ice cream is frozen, transfer to a freezer container; freeze for 2-4 hours before serving.

YIELD: 2 quarts.

connie webb
NEEDHAM, INDIANA

Making homemade ice cream has long been our family's favorite pastime, and this butter pecan recipe is our first choice in fall.

rosanna fowler
BEDFORD, INDIANA

I made these parfaits for my children to take to school on St. Patrick's Day. Everyone loved them. You can make them right before serving or a few hours beforehand.

pistachio pudding parfaits

PREP/TOTAL TIME: 20 min.

- 1 package (8 ounces) cream cheese, softened
- 1 cup confectioners' sugar
- 1-1/2 cups whipped topping
- 1 package (3.4 ounces) instant pistachio pudding mix
- 10 pecan shortbread cookies, coarsely crushed

In a small bowl, beat cream cheese and confectioners' sugar. Fold in whipped topping; set aside. Prepare pudding according to package directions; set aside.

Spoon 1 tablespoon cookie crumbs into each of eight parfait glasses. Top with half of the pudding and whipped topping mixture. Repeat layers. Top with remaining cookie crumbs. Chill until serving.

YIELD: 8 servings.

margaret dechant
NEWBERRY, MICHIGAN

You can whip up this classic dessert on short notice if you keep cooked rice on hand. Cooked rice can be frozen in an airtight container for up to 3 months. Thaw it in the refrigerator, or microwave it and you're good to go.

grandma's rice pudding

PREP: 10 min. | **BAKE:** 45 min.

- 1-1/2 cups cooked rice
- 1/4 cup raisins
- 2 eggs
- 1-1/2 cups milk
- 1/2 cup sugar
- 1/2 teaspoon ground nutmeg

Additional milk, optional

Place rice and raisins in a greased 1-qt. casserole. In a small bowl, whisk the eggs, milk, sugar and nutmeg; pour over rice.

Bake, uncovered, at 375° for 45-50 minutes or until a knife inserted in the center comes out clean. Cool. Pour milk over each serving if desired. Refrigerate leftovers.

YIELD: 4-6 servings.

chocolate and vanilla creme brulee

PREP: 30 min. | **BAKE:** 35 min. + chilling

4 cups heavy whipping cream
9 egg yolks
1 cup sugar, *divided*
1 teaspoon vanilla extract
1/2 cup semisweet chocolate chips

In a large saucepan, heat cream until bubbles form around sides of pan. In a small bowl, whisk egg yolks and 3/4 cup sugar. Remove cream from the heat; stir a small amount of hot cream into egg yolk mixture. Return all to the pan, stirring constantly. Stir in vanilla. Set aside.

In a microwave, melt chocolate chips; stir until smooth. Slowly whisk in 2 cups of cream mixture until smooth. Transfer to eight ungreased 6-oz. ramekins or custard cups.

Slowly pour remaining cream mixture over the back of a small spoon into the ramekins, forming layers. Place ramekins in a baking pan; add 1 in. of boiling water to pan.

Bake, uncovered, at 325° for 35-40 minutes or until centers are just set (mixture will jiggle). Remove ramekins from water bath; cool for 10 minutes. Cover and refrigerate for at least 4 hours.

If using a creme brulee torch, sprinkle custards with the remaining sugar; heat until caramelized. Serve immediately.

If broiling the custards, place ramekins on a baking sheet; let stand at room temperature for 15 minutes. Sprinkle with sugar. Broil 8 in. from the heat for 4-7 minutes or until caramelized. Refrigerate for 1-2 hours or until chilled.

YIELD: 8 servings.

VANILLA CREME BRULEE: Omit chocolate chips.
CHOCOLATE CREME BRULEE: Increase chocolate chips to 1 cup and whisk entire custard mixture into the melted chips.

taste of home cooking school

For a truly delicious dessert that will impress every guest, try this fancy recipe. It tastes so delicious.

elizabeth nelson
MANNING, NORTH DAKOTA

My family loves squash. I often prepare this pretty dessert for an autumn special occasion.

BUY & STORE WINTER SQUASH

Purchase winter squash that are heavy for their size with hard, deep-colored rinds that are free of blemishes. Store unwashed winter squash in a cool, well-ventilated place for up to 1 month.

butternut squash cake roll

PREP: 15 min. | BAKE: 15 min. + chilling

> 3 eggs
> 1 cup sugar
> 2/3 cup mashed cooked butternut squash
> 3/4 cup all-purpose flour
> 1 teaspoon baking soda
> 1/2 teaspoon ground cinnamon
> 1 cup finely chopped walnuts

Confectioners' sugar

FILLING:

> 1 package (8 ounces) cream cheese, softened
> 2 tablespoons butter, softened
> 1 cup confectioners' sugar
> 3/4 teaspoon vanilla extract

Additional confectioners' sugar, optional

Line a 15-in. x 10-in. x 1-in. baking pan with waxed paper; grease and flour the paper and set aside.

In a large bowl, beat eggs for 3 minutes. Gradually add sugar; beat for 2 minutes or until mixture becomes thick and lemon-colored. Stir in squash. Combine the flour, baking soda and cinnamon; fold into squash mixture. Spread batter evenly into prepared pan. Sprinkle with walnuts.

Bake at 375° for 13-15 minutes or until a toothpick inserted near the center comes out clean. Cool on a wire rack for 10 minutes.

Turn cake onto a kitchen towel dusted with confectioners' sugar. Gently peel off waxed paper. Roll up cake in the towel, jelly-roll style, starting with a short side. Cool completely on a wire rack.

In a small bowl, beat the cream cheese, butter, confectioners' sugar and vanilla until smooth. Unroll cake; spread filling evenly over cake to within 1 in. of edges. Roll up again. Cover and refrigerate for 1 hour. Just before serving, dust with confectioners' sugar if desired.

YIELD: 10 servings.

cola floats

PREP/TOTAL TIME: 5 min.

    4 cups cherry cola, chilled
    1 teaspoon vanilla extract
    8 scoops fudge ripple ice cream
    Whipped cream in a can, optional
    4 maraschino cherries

In a pitcher, combine cola and vanilla. Place two scoops of ice cream in each of four chilled glasses. Pour cola over ice cream; top with whipped cream if desired and cherries.

YIELD: 4 servings.

taste of home test kitchen

These thick, frosty floats add fun to any casual meal. Try substituting other soda-ice cream blends for the floats, such as root beer with caramel-swirl vanilla ice cream.

cashew caramel fudge

PREP: 25 min. + cooling

    2 teaspoons plus 1/2 cup butter, softened, *divided*
    1 can (5 ounces) evaporated milk
    2-1/2 cups sugar
    2 cups (12 ounces) semisweet chocolate chips
    1 jar (7 ounces) marshmallow creme
    24 caramels, quartered
    3/4 cup salted cashew halves
    1 teaspoon vanilla extract

Line a 9-in. square pan with foil; butter the foil with 2 teaspoons butter. Set aside.

In a large heavy saucepan, combine the milk, sugar and remaining butter. Cook and stir over medium heat until sugar is dissolved. Bring to a rapid boil; boil for 5 minutes, stirring constantly. Remove from the heat; stir in chocolate chips and marshmallow creme until melted. Fold in the caramels, cashews and vanilla.

Pour into prepared pan. Cool. Using foil, lift fudge out of pan. Discard foil; cut fudge into 1-in. squares. Store in an airtight container.

YIELD: about 3 pounds.

cathy grubelnik
RATON, NEW MEXICO

A pretty plate of yummy fudge makes a great present! I especially enjoy making it for a holiday treat. Cashews and caramel are such a delicious combination.

amber sampson
SOMONAUK, ILLINOIS

One of the nice things about this easy pudding is that you don't have to stand and stir it. It's a must for us year-round! I also make it into a pie with a graham cracker crust that our grandchildren love.

old-fashioned chocolate pudding

PREP: 5 min. | **COOK:** 30 min.

- 2 cups milk
- 2 tablespoons butter
- 2 ounces unsweetened chocolate, chopped
- 2/3 cup sugar
- 1/3 cup all-purpose flour
- 1/4 teaspoon salt
- 2 egg yolks, beaten
- 1/2 teaspoon vanilla extract

Whipped cream, optional

In a double boiler or metal bowl over simmering water, heat the milk, butter and chocolate until the chocolate is melted (chocolate may appear to become curdled).

Combine the sugar, flour and salt. Sprinkle dry mixture over chocolate mixture (do not stir). Cover and cook over medium-low heat for 20 minutes. With a wooden spoon, stir until smooth. Remove from the heat.

Stir a small amount of hot mixture into egg yolks; return all to the pan, stirring constantly. Cook and stir until mixture is thickened and a thermometer reads 160°. Remove from the heat. Stir in vanilla.

Cool for 15 minutes, stirring occasionally. Transfer to dessert dishes.

Cover and refrigerate for 1 hour. Garnish servings with whipped cream if desired.

YIELD: 4 servings.

elisa pellegriti
FLORIDA, NEW YORK

With a rich mocha filling and cute chocolate garnish, here is a yummy pie that's perfect for any time at all.

cappuccino cheesecake pie

PREP: 20 min. | **BAKE:** 40 min. + chilling

- 2 packages (8 ounces *each*) cream cheese, softened
- 1/2 cup sugar
- 1 envelope mocha cappuccino mix (1/4 cup)
- 2 eggs, lightly beaten
- 1/4 cup milk
- 1 extra-servings-size graham cracker crust (9 ounces)

GARNISH:

- 1/4 cup semisweet chocolate chips
- 1/2 teaspoon shortening

In a large bowl, beat the cream cheese, sugar and cappuccino mix until smooth. Add eggs and milk; beat just until combined. Pour into crust.

Bake at 325° for 40-45 minutes or until the center is almost set. Cool on a wire rack for 1 hour. Refrigerate for 3 hours or overnight.

In a microwave, melt chocolate chips and shortening; stir until smooth. Spread into a 4-in. square on a sheet of waxed paper. Let stand at room temperature until set, about 1 hour.

Using a small heart-shaped cookie cutter, cut out eight chocolate hearts. Top each serving with a heart. Refrigerate leftovers.

YIELD: 8 servings.

edna's ho ho cake

PREP/TOTAL TIME: 15 min.

2 tablespoons all-purpose flour
1 cup milk
2/3 cup sugar, *divided*
2/3 cup shortening
1/3 cup butter, softened
3/4 teaspoon vanilla extract
Pinch salt
2 prepared 9-inch round chocolate cakes

GLAZE:
1/4 cup butter, cubed
1/4 cup baking cocoa
3/4 cup confectioners' sugar
2 to 4 tablespoons milk

For filling, in a small saucepan, combine the flour and milk until smooth; stir in 1/3 cup sugar. Bring to a boil over medium heat; cook and stir for 2 minutes or until filling is thickened.

Transfer to a large bowl; cool. Beat in the shortening, butter, vanilla, salt and remaining sugar until smooth. Spread between cake layers.

For glaze, melt the butter and cocoa in a small saucepan. Whisk in the confectioners' sugar and enough milk to achieve a drizzling consistency. Drizzle over top of cake, allowing some to drape down the sides.

YIELD: 12-16 servings.

edna miller
MOUNT HOPE, OHIO

This treat serves up appealing flavor in big fluffy wedges of chocolate and cream. It's like a giant Ho Ho snack cake.

barbara nowakowski
NORTH TONAWANDA,
NEW YORK

A pretty cranberry sauce nicely complements the sweet, fudgy mousse in this holiday-perfect dessert. You can even make it the day before the party for added convenience.

chocolate mousse with cranberry sauce

PREP: 45 min. + chilling

2 cups (12 ounces) semisweet chocolate chips
1/4 cup butter, cubed
1 egg yolk, lightly beaten
1-1/2 cups heavy whipping cream, *divided*
1/3 cup light corn syrup
1 teaspoon vanilla extract

CRANBERRY SAUCE:

1/3 cup cranberry juice
1 teaspoon lime juice
1 cup jellied cranberry sauce

In a large microwave-safe bowl, melt chocolate chips and butter; stir until smooth. In a small heavy saucepan, combine the egg yolk, 1/4 cup cream and corn syrup. Cook and stir over low heat until mixture reaches 160°, about 2 minutes.

Remove from the heat; stir into chocolate mixture. Refrigerate for 20 minutes or until cooled and slightly thickened, stirring occasionally. Line a 1-qt. bowl with plastic wrap; set aside.

In a large bowl, beat remaining cream until it begins to thicken. Add vanilla; beat until soft peaks form. Fold into chocolate mixture. Spoon into prepared bowl. Cover and refrigerate overnight.

Place the sauce ingredients in a blender; cover and process until smooth. Transfer to a small bowl; cover and refrigerate until serving.

Just before serving, invert mousse onto a platter; remove plastic wrap. Cut into wedges; serve with cranberry sauce.

YIELD: 10 servings (about 1 cup sauce).

strawberry cheesecake ice cream

PREP: 20 min. | PROCESS: 20 min./batch + freezing

- 3 cups sliced fresh strawberries
- 6 ounces reduced-fat cream cheese

- 2 cans (12 ounces *each*) fat-free evaporated milk
- 1 can (14 ounces) fat-free sweetened condensed milk
- 1 teaspoon vanilla extract
- 1 cup reduced-fat whipped topping

Place strawberries in a blender; cover and process until smooth. In a large bowl, beat cream cheese until smooth. Beat in the evaporated milk, condensed milk, vanilla and pureed strawberries. Fold in whipped topping.

Fill cylinder of ice cream freezer two-thirds full; freeze according to manufacturer's directions. Refrigerate remaining mixture until ready to freeze. When ice cream is frozen, transfer to a freezer container; freeze for 2-4 hours before serving.

YIELD: 2 quarts.

karen maubach
FAIRBURY, ILLINOIS

I found the recipe for this creamy and refreshing dessert in an old cookbook. We love how it tastes like a berry-topped cheesecake. Family gatherings wouldn't be the same without our favorite treat!

heart's delight eclair

PREP: 30 min. | chilling | BAKE: 15 min.

- 1 package (17.3 ounces) frozen puff pastry, thawed
- 3 cups cold milk
- 1 package (5.1 ounces) instant vanilla pudding mix
- 2 cups heavy whipping cream
- 1 teaspoon vanilla extract, *divided*
- 1 cup confectioners' sugar
- 1 tablespoon water
- 1/4 teaspoon almond extract
- 1/2 cup semisweet chocolate chips
- 1 teaspoon shortening

On a lightly floured surface, roll each puff pastry sheet into a 12-in. square. Using an 11-in. heart pattern, cut each pastry into a heart shape. Place on greased baking sheets. Bake at 400° for 12-15 minutes or until golden brown. Remove to wire racks to cool.

Meanwhile, whisk milk and pudding mix for 2 minutes. Let stand for 2 minutes or until soft-set. In a large bowl, beat cream and 1/2 teaspoon vanilla until stiff peaks form. Carefully fold into pudding.

Split puff pastry hearts in half. Place one layer on a serving plate. Top with a third of the pudding mixture. Repeat twice. Top with remaining pastry.

In a large bowl, combine the confectioners' sugar, water, almond extract and remaining vanilla until smooth. Spread over top. In a microwave, melt chocolate chips and shortening; stir until smooth.

Pipe in diagonal lines in one direction over frosting. Beginning 1 in. from side of heart, use a sharp knife to draw right angles across the piped lines. Refrigerate until set. Refrigerate leftovers.

YIELD: 10-12 servings.

lorene milligan
CHEMAINUS,
BRITISH COLUMBIA

Here is a lovely and luscious surprise that will win the hearts of everyone who takes a bite. If you like, you can skip the step of cutting a heart shape in each pastry sheet and bake them instead as 12-inch squares.

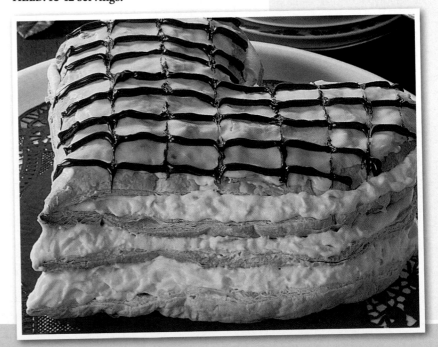

rita sherman

COLEVILLE, CALIFORNIA

Layers of silky white chocolate mousse and sweet cherry sauce alternate in these delectable single-serving desserts. I use a pastry bag to pipe the mousse into pretty dishes handed down from my husband's grandmother.

COOKING WITH CHERRIES

Just to be safe when I'm making cherry desserts, I quickly pinch each cherry to make sure that no pits sneak their way into the dish I'm preparing.

—ARLENE B. MARTIN, NORTH DAKOTA

white chocolate cherry parfaits

PREP: 40 min. + chilling

    1/2 cup sugar
    2 tablespoons cornstarch
    1/2 cup cold water
    2 cups fresh *or* frozen pitted tart cherries
    1/2 teaspoon orange extract
WHITE CHOCOLATE MOUSSE:
    3 tablespoons sugar
    1 teaspoon cornstarch
    1/2 cup milk
    2 egg yolks, lightly beaten
    4 ounces white baking chocolate, chopped
    1/2 teaspoon vanilla extract
  1-1/2 cups heavy whipping cream, whipped

In a small saucepan, combine sugar and cornstarch; stir in water until smooth. Add cherries. Bring to a boil over medium heat; cook and stir for 2 minutes or until thickened. Remove from the heat; stir in extract. Refrigerate until chilled.

In another saucepan, combine the sugar and cornstarch; stir in milk until smooth. Bring to a boil

over medium heat. Reduce heat; cook and stir for 2 minutes. Remove from heat. Whisk a small amount of hot mixture into egg yolks; return all to the pan, whisking constantly. Bring to a gentle boil; cook and stir for 2 minutes.

Remove from the heat. Stir in chocolate and vanilla until chocolate is melted. Cool to room temperature. Fold in whipped cream

Spoon 1/4 cup mousse into each parfait glass. Top with a rounded 1/4 cup of cherry mixture. Repeat layers. Refrigerate until chilled.

YIELD: 6 servings.

nancy mueller

BLOOMINGTON, MINNESOTA

Crushed peanut butter cookies make the crust for this crowd-pleasing dessert. The cream cheese, chocolate pudding and whipped topping layers make it an appealing potluck favorite.

peanut butter icebox dessert

PREP: 20 min. + chilling

  2-1/4 cups crushed peanut butter cookies (about 11 cookies)
    1/4 cup sugar
    1/4 cup butter, melted
    2 packages (3 ounces *each*) cream cheese, softened
    1 cup confectioners' sugar
    1 carton (8 ounces) frozen whipped topping, thawed, *divided*
  2-1/2 cups cold 2% milk
    2 packages (3.9 ounces *each*) instant chocolate pudding mix
Additional peanut butter cookies, broken into pieces

In a large bowl, combine crushed cookies, sugar and butter; press into an ungreased 13-in. x 9-in. baking dish. Bake at 350° for 6-8 minutes or until golden brown; cool on a wire rack.

In a large bowl, beat cream cheese and confectioners' sugar until smooth; fold in 1 cup whipped topping. Spread over cooled crust.

In another large bowl, beat milk and pudding mix on low speed for 2 minutes or until thickened. Spread over cream cheese layer. Top with remaining whipped topping; sprinkle with cookie pieces. Cover and refrigerate for at least 1 hour before serving.

YIELD: 12-15 servings.

strawberry tiramisu trifle

PREP: 30 min. + chilling

1 quart fresh strawberries

1-1/4 cups cold milk

1 package (3.4 ounces) instant vanilla pudding mix

1 package (8 ounces) cream cheese, softened

4 tablespoons strong brewed coffee, room temperature, *divided*

2 cups whipped topping

1 package (3 ounces) ladyfingers, split

6 ounces bittersweet chocolate, grated

Set aside three strawberries for garnish; slice the remaining strawberries. In a large bowl, whisk milk and pudding mix for 2 minutes. Let stand for 2 minutes or until soft-set. In a large bowl, beat cream cheese until smooth; gradually beat in 2 tablespoons coffee. Beat in pudding. Fold in whipped topping.

Brush remaining coffee over ladyfingers. Line the bottom of a 3-qt. trifle or glass serving bowl with half of the ladyfingers. Top with half of the sliced berries, grated chocolate and pudding mixture; repeat layers. Cut reserved berries in half; place on trifle. Cover and refrigerate for at least 4 hours.

YIELD: 12 servings.

tammy irvine
WHITBY, ONTARIO

We do a lot of entertaining, and I like to make this trifle when I want to impress our guests but don't have a lot of time to bake. Berries make it different from a traditional tiramisu.

evalyn pokorny
HAZELHURST, WISCONSIN

Here is a sumptuous dessert that's absolutely divine. The creamy filling, tender cake and rich chocolate glaze come bundled up in a pretty jelly-roll shape.

cream-filled chocolate cake roll

PREP: 25 min. | BAKE: 10 min. + cooling

  2 eggs, *separated*
  4 tablespoons sugar, *divided*
  2 tablespoons water
1/4 teaspoon vanilla extract
  3 tablespoons whole wheat flour
  2 tablespoons all-purpose flour
  2 tablespoons baking cocoa
1/2 teaspoon baking powder
1/8 teaspoon salt

FILLING:

  1 cup heavy whipping cream
1-1/2 teaspoons confectioners' sugar
1-1/2 teaspoons instant chocolate drink mix

GLAZE:

1/4 cup sugar
2-1/4 teaspoons cornstarch
1-1/2 teaspoons baking cocoa
Dash salt
1/4 cup water
1-1/2 teaspoons canola oil
  1 tablespoon butter
1/4 teaspoon vanilla extract

In a small bowl, beat egg yolks until slightly thickened. Gradually add 2 tablespoons sugar, beating until thick and lemon-colored. Stir in water and vanilla.

Combine the flours, cocoa, baking powder and salt; add to yolk mixture and mix well.

In another bowl, beat egg whites on medium speed until soft peaks form. Gradually beat in remaining sugar, 1 tablespoon at a time, on high until stiff glossy peaks form and sugar is dissolved. Fold a fourth of egg whites into the batter, then fold in remaining whites.

Spread into an 11-in. x 7-in. baking dish coated with cooking spray. Bake at 375° for 10-15 minutes or until cake springs back when lightly touched. Cool for 5 minutes. Turn cake onto a kitchen towel dusted with confectioners' sugar. Roll up cake in the towel jelly roll-style, starting with a short side. Cool completely on a wire rack.

For filling, in a small bowl, beat cream and confectioners' sugar until stiff peaks form. Transfer half of the mixture to a small bowl; fold in drink mix. Unroll cake. Spread chocolate whipped cream widthwise over half of the cake to within 1/2 in. of edges. Repeat with plain whipped cream on remaining half. Roll up carefully. Place seam side down on a serving platter.

For glaze, in a small saucepan, combine the sugar, cornstarch, cocoa and salt. Stir in water and oil. Bring to a boil; cook and stir for 1-2 minutes or until thickened. Remove from the heat; stir in butter and vanilla. Spread over cake roll. Refrigerate until serving.

YIELD: 6 servings.

strawberry shakes

PREP/TOTAL TIME: 5 min.

    1/3 cup 2% milk
    1-1/2 cups vanilla ice cream
    1/2 cup frozen unsweetened strawberries
    1 tablespoon strawberry preserves

In a blender, combine all ingredients; cover and process until smooth. Pour into chilled glasses; serve immediately.

YIELD: 2 servings.

taste of home test kitchen

Cool off with a thick and rich treat that will remind you of a malt shoppe!

puff pastry hearts

PREP: 1 hour + chilling | **BAKE:** 10 min./batch + cooling

    3/4 cup sugar
    3 tablespoons cornstarch
    1/4 teaspoon salt
    1-1/2 cups milk
    6 egg yolks, lightly beaten
    1/2 to 1 teaspoon rum extract
    1/2 teaspoon vanilla extract
    1-1/2 cups heavy whipping cream
    2 packages (17.3 ounces *each*) frozen puff pastry, thawed
    1 jar (12 ounces) seedless raspberry preserves
    2 cups fresh raspberries
Confectioners' sugar

In a large saucepan, combine the sugar, cornstarch and salt. Stir in milk until smooth. Cook and stir over medium-high heat until thickened and bubbly. Reduce heat; cook and stir 2 minutes longer. Remove from the heat. Stir a small amount of hot mixture into egg yolks; return all to pan, stirring constantly. Bring to a gentle boil; cook and stir 2 minutes longer.

Remove from the heat. Gently stir in extracts. Cool to room temperature without stirring. Cover and refrigerate for 2-3 hours or until chilled.

In a large bowl, beat cream until soft peaks form. Fold into custard. Cover and refrigerate until serving. Roll out pastry on a lightly floured surface. Cut with a lightly floured 3-1/2-in. heart-shaped cookie cutter.

Place 1 in. apart on parchment paper-lined baking sheets. Bake at 400° for 8-10 minutes or until golden brown. Remove to wire racks to cool.

Just before serving, warm preserves in a small saucepan; drizzle some onto dessert plates. Split puff pastry hearts in half. Place bottom halves on plates; spread each with 2 tablespoons of filling. Replace tops; drizzle with remaining preserves. Garnish with raspberries and confectioners' sugar.

YIELD: 3 dozen.

sarah vasques
MILFORD, NEW HAMPSHIRE

These adorable cream-filled hearts are perfect for Valentine's Day or any time you want to serve a "lovable" treat.

mini raspberry mousse parfaits

PREP: 30 min. + chilling

1-3/4 cups fresh *or* frozen unsweetened
    raspberries, thawed
   3 tablespoons sugar
   2 teaspoons cornstarch
   2 teaspoons orange juice
1-1/3 cups whipped topping
  12 cubes angel food cake (1/2-inch cubes)

Press raspberries through a strainer and discard seeds and pulp. In a small saucepan, combine sugar and cornstarch; stir in raspberry puree. Bring to a boil; cook and stir for 2 minutes or until thickened. Refrigerate until chilled.

   Divide raspberry mixture in half. Stir orange juice into one portion; set aside. Place remaining mixture in a small bowl; fold in whipped topping.

   Divide the angel food cake among four small cocktail glasses or dessert dishes. Layer each with a scant tablespoon of reserved raspberry-orange mixture and 1/3 cup creamy mixture. Refrigerate until serving.

YIELD: 4 servings.

no-bake cherry dessert

PREP/TOTAL TIME: 15 min.

2/3 cup graham cracker crumbs
  2 tablespoons brown sugar
  2 tablespoons butter, melted
  4 ounces cream cheese, softened
  1 tablespoon confectioners' sugar
  1 cup whipped topping
1-1/4 cups cherry pie filling

In a small bowl, combine the cracker crumbs, brown sugar and butter; press into an ungreased 9-in. x 5-in. loaf pan.

   In a large bowl, beat the cream cheese and confectioners' sugar until smooth; fold in whipped topping. Spread over crust. Top with pie filling. Chill until serving.

YIELD: 4 servings.

snowflake pudding

PREP: 20 min. + chilling

1 envelope unflavored gelatin
1-1/4 cups cold milk, *divided*
1/2 cup sugar
1/2 teaspoon salt
1 teaspoon vanilla extract
1-1/3 cups flaked coconut, toasted
1 cup heavy whipping cream, whipped

SAUCE:

1 package (10 ounces) frozen sweetened
    raspberries, thawed
1-1/2 teaspoons cornstarch
1/2 cup red currant jelly

In a small saucepan, sprinkle gelatin over 1/4 cup milk; let stand for 1 minute. Heat over low heat, stirring until gelatin is completely dissolved.

In a large saucepan, combine the sugar, salt and remaining milk; heat just until sugar is dissolved. Remove from the heat; stir in gelatin mixture and vanilla. Refrigerate until partially set. Fold in coconut and whipped cream. Pour into dessert dishes; refrigerate for at least 2 hours.

Meanwhile, strain raspberries to remove seeds. In a small saucepan, combine cornstarch, raspberry puree and currant jelly; stir until smooth. Bring to a boil; cook and stir for 2 minutes or until thickened. Chill for at least 1 hour. Serve with pudding.

YIELD: 6 servings

patricia stratton
MUSKEGON, MICHIGAN

Flakes of coconut give my pudding its snow-like texture—and plenty of flavor besides! The currant-raspberry sauce is delicious and pretty, too.

joanne wright
NILES, MICHIGAN

Trifles are terrific desserts because they're made in advance and feed a crowd. My caramel apple version appeals to kids of all ages.

caramel apple trifle

PREP: 40 min. + chilling

3 tablespoons butter

4 cups chopped peeled tart apples (about 5 medium)

1 cup chopped walnuts

1/2 cup packed brown sugar

1 teaspoon apple pie spice, *divided*

1 package (8 ounces) cream cheese, softened

1 jar (12-1/4 ounces) caramel ice cream topping, *divided*

1 carton (12 ounces) frozen whipped topping, thawed, *divided*

2 loaves (10-3/4 ounces *each*) frozen pound cake, thawed and cut into 1-inch cubes

Additional apple pie spice, optional

In a large skillet, melt butter over medium heat. Stir in the apples, walnuts, brown sugar and 1/2 teaspoon apple pie spice. Cook and stir for 8-10 minutes or until apples are tender.

In a large bowl, beat cream cheese until smooth. Beat in 1/2 cup caramel topping and remaining apple pie spice. Fold in 2 cups whipped topping.

In a 3-1/2-qt. trifle bowl or glass serving bowl, layer a third of the cake cubes, cream cheese mixture and apple mixture. Repeat layers twice. Garnish with remaining whipped topping and drizzle with remaining caramel topping. Sprinkle with additional apple pie spice if desired. Cover and refrigerate for at least 1 hour before serving.

YIELD: 14 servings.

mocha cream puffs

PREP: 25 min. + chilling | **BAKE:** 20 min.

1/4 cup water
2 tablespoons butter
1/8 teaspoon salt
1/4 cup all-purpose flour
1 egg

FILLING:

2/3 cup heavy whipping cream, *divided*
3 tablespoons semisweet chocolate chips
2 teaspoons sugar

Dash salt

1/2 teaspoon vanilla extract
1/2 teaspoon instant coffee granules
Confectioners' sugar

In a small saucepan, bring the water, butter and salt to a boil. Add flour all at once and stir until a smooth ball forms. Remove from the heat; let stand for 5 minutes. Add the egg; beat until mixture is smooth and shiny.

Drop batter into four mounds 3 in. apart on a greased baking sheet. Bake at 425° for 20-25 minutes or until golden brown. Remove puffs to a wire rack. Immediately split puffs open; remove tops and set aside. Discard soft dough from inside. Cool puffs.

For the filling, in a small saucepan, combine 3 tablespoons cream, chocolate chips, sugar and salt. Cook over low heat until the chips are melted; stir until blended. Remove from the heat; gradually stir in the vanilla, coffee and remaining cream.

Transfer mixture to a small bowl. Refrigerate until chilled. Beat the filling until stiff. Fill the cream puffs just before serving; replace tops. Dust with confectioners' sugar.

YIELD: 4 cream puffs.

aimee kirk
JACKSONVILLE, ALABAMA

Looking for a special dessert that's easy to fix? Try these cream puffs with a chocolate and coffee-flavored filling. The recipe makes four pretty servings.

chocolate almond ice cream

PREP: 30 min. + chilling | **PROCESS:** 20 min./batch + freezing

2 envelopes unflavored gelatin
6 tablespoons cold water
3 cups milk
3 cups sugar
1/4 teaspoon salt
3 eggs, lightly beaten
6 to 7 ounces unsweetened chocolate, melted
4 cups heavy whipping cream
2 teaspoons vanilla extract
1 cup sliced *or* slivered almonds, toasted

In a small bowl, sprinkle gelatin over cold water; let stand for at least 2 minutes. In a large heavy saucepan, heat the milk, sugar and salt until bubbles form around sides of pan. Whisk a small amount of hot mixture into the eggs. Return all to the pan, whisking constantly.

Cook and stir over low heat until mixture is thickened and coats the back of a spoon. Remove from the heat. Stir in the gelatin mixture until dissolved; stir in chocolate until blended. Cool quickly by placing pan in a bowl of ice water; stir for 2 minutes. Stir in cream and vanilla. Press plastic wrap onto surface of custard. Refrigerate for several hours or overnight.

Fill cylinder of ice cream freezer two-thirds full with the chilled custard; freeze according to manufacturer's directions. Stir in toasted almonds. Refrigerate remaining mixture until ready to freeze. When ice cream is frozen, transfer to a freezer container; freeze for 2-4 hours before serving.

YIELD: 2-1/2 quarts.

alice hicken
HEBER CITY, UTAH

It wouldn't be the Fourth of July for our family without this special treat. Even though electric models make it easier, I still prefer to hand-crank ice cream.

renee ratcliffe

CHARLOTTE, NORTH CAROLINA

My college roommate gave me this recipe, which I lightened up a little. You can try other pudding flavors, but I think the combination of mint and chocolate is refreshing and perfect for the holidays.

chocolate mint eclair dessert

PREP: 20 min. + chilling

23 whole chocolate graham crackers
3 cups cold fat-free milk
2 packages (3.3 to 3.4 ounces *each*) instant white chocolate *or* vanilla pudding mix
1/2 teaspoon mint *or* peppermint extract
3 to 4 drops green food coloring, optional
1 carton (8 ounces) frozen reduced-fat whipped topping, thawed

CHOCOLATE FROSTING:

1 tablespoon butter
2 tablespoons baking cocoa
2 tablespoons plus 1 teaspoon fat-free milk
1 teaspoon vanilla extract
1 cup confectioners' sugar

Coat a 13-in. x 9-in. dish with cooking spray. Break five of the whole graham crackers in half; line the bottom of the pan with three half crackers and six whole crackers.

In a large bowl, whisk milk and pudding mixes for 2 minutes. Let stand for 2 minutes or until soft-set. Whisk in extract and food coloring if desired. Fold in whipped topping.

Spread half over graham crackers. Top with a another layer of three half and six whole crackers. Top with remaining pudding mixture and graham crackers (save remaining half cracker for another use). Cover and refrigerate for 2 hours.

For frosting, melt the butter in a saucepan. Stir in the cocoa and milk until blended. Remove from the heat; stir in the vanilla and confectioners' sugar until smooth. Spread over dessert. Cover and refrigerate overnight.

YIELD: 15 servings.

karen grant

TULARE, CALIFORNIA

These sweet frozen treats are simple to prepare and guaranteed to bring out the kid in anyone. The chocolate and peanut topping makes them fun.

rocky road fudge pops

PREP: 20 min. + freezing

2-1/2 cups 2% milk
1 package (3.4 ounces) cook-and-serve chocolate pudding mix
1/2 cup chopped peanuts
1/2 cup miniature semisweet chocolate chips
12 disposable plastic cups (3 ounces *each*)
1/2 cup marshmallow creme
12 Popsicle sticks

In a large microwave-safe bowl, whisk milk and pudding mix. Microwave, uncovered, on high for 4-6 minutes or until bubbly and slightly thickened, stirring every 2 minutes. Cool for 20 minutes, stirring several times.

Meanwhile, combine peanuts and chocolate chips; divide among plastic cups. Stir marshmallow creme into pudding; spoon into cups. Insert Popsicle sticks; freeze.

YIELD: 12 servings.

EDITOR'S NOTE: This recipe was tested in a 1,100-watt microwave.

aunt ruth's famous butterscotch cheesecake

PREP: 30 min. | **BAKE:** 65 min. + chilling

- 1-1/2 cups graham cracker crumbs
- 1/3 cup packed brown sugar
- 1/3 cup butter, melted
- 1 can (14 ounces) sweetened condensed milk
- 3/4 cup cold 2% milk
- 1 package (3.4 ounces) instant butterscotch pudding mix
- 3 packages (8 ounces *each*) cream cheese, softened
- 1 teaspoon vanilla extract
- 3 eggs, lightly beaten

Whipped cream and crushed butterscotch candies, optional

Place a greased 9-in. springform pan on a double thickness of heavy-duty foil (about 18 in. square). Securely wrap foil around pan. In a small bowl, combine cracker crumbs and sugar; stir in butter.

Press onto the bottom of prepared pan. Place pan on a baking sheet. Bake at 325° for 10 minutes. Cool on a wire rack.

In a small bowl, whisk the milks and pudding mix for 2 minutes. Let stand for 2 minutes or until soft-set.

Meanwhile, in a large bowl, beat cream cheese until smooth. Beat in pudding and vanilla. Add eggs; beat on low speed just until combined. Pour over crust. Place springform pan in a large baking pan; add 1 in. of hot water to larger pan.

Bake at 325° for 65-75 minutes or until center is almost set and top appears dull. Remove springform pan from water bath. Cool cheesecake on a wire rack for 10 minutes.

Carefully run a knife around edge of pan to loosen; cool 1 hour longer. Refrigerate overnight. Garnish with whipped cream and butterscotch candies if desired.

YIELD: 12 servings.

trisha kruse
EAGLE, IDAHO

Aunt Ruth was our nanny when I was little and made this cheesecake often. It was torture when my sister and I had to wait until the next day to have a piece since it had to chill overnight.

diane lombardo
NEW CASTLE, PENNSYLVANIA

This delicious pie is easy to make and very pretty. Since you can make it in advance, it's ideal for entertaining.

caramel toffee ice cream pie

PREP: 25 min. + freezing

1-1/2 cups chocolate graham cracker crumbs (about 8 whole crackers)

2 tablespoons sugar

1 egg white, beaten

2 tablespoons butter, melted

4 cups fat-free vanilla frozen yogurt, softened, *divided*

2 English toffee candy bars (1.4 ounces each), coarsely chopped, *divided*

1/2 cup caramel ice cream topping, *divided*

In a small bowl, combine cracker crumbs and sugar; stir in egg white and butter. Press onto the bottom and up the sides of a 9-in. pie plate coated with cooking spray. Bake at 375° for 6-8 minutes or until set. Cool completely on a wire rack.

Spread 2-2/3 cups of frozen yogurt into the crust. Sprinkle with half of the toffee bits; drizzle with half of caramel. Repeat layers. Cover and freeze for 8 hours or overnight. Remove from the freezer 15 minutes before serving.

YIELD: 8 servings.

mocha mallow parfaits

PREP: 20 min. + chilling

- 12 large marshmallows
- 1/2 cup water
- 1-1/2 teaspoons instant coffee granules
- 1/2 cup heavy whipping cream, whipped
- 1/3 cup chocolate wafer crumbs

In a small saucepan, combine the marshmallows, water and coffee granules. Cook and stir over medium heat until marshmallows are melted, stirring often. Cool completely. Fold in whipped cream.

Set aside 2 teaspoons wafer crumbs. Spoon about 3 tablespoons of marshmallow mixture into each parfait glass; sprinkle with about 1 tablespoon wafer crumbs. Repeat layers. Top with remaining marshmallow mixture; sprinkle with reserved crumbs. Refrigerate for at least 2 hours before serving.

YIELD: 2 servings.

janice mitchell
AURORA, COLORADO

Mocha is one of my favorite flavors, so I make these parfaits often. It's easy to keep the ingredients on hand, which lets us enjoy these treats any time.

mint-chocolate ice cream cake

PREP: 15 min. + freezing

- 1 package (16 ounces) Suzy Q's
- 3 cups mint chocolate chip ice cream, softened
- 12 cream-filled chocolate sandwich cookies, crushed, *divided*
- 2 cups whipped topping
- 1/2 teaspoon mint extract, optional

Line an 8-in. x 4-in. loaf pan with plastic wrap. Place four Suzy Q's in the pan, completely covering the bottom. Spread ice cream over the Suzy Q's; sprinkle with half of the cookie crumbs. Press the remaining Suzy Q's on top. Cover and freeze for at least 3 hours.

Just before serving, remove from the freezer and invert onto a serving plate. Remove pan and plastic wrap. Combine whipped topping and extract if desired; frost top and sides of cake. Sprinkle with remaining cookie crumbs.

YIELD: 10 servings.

kathy morrow
HUBBARD, OHIO

Here's a simple ice cream cake that's special enough for company. Tint the whipped topping if desired, or try different flavors of ice cream, extracts and cookie or candy crumbs to suit the occasion and what your family loves!

MINTY ICE CREAM TREAT

I give vanilla ice cream a boost with a topping of crushed chocolate mint cookies. It's a simple yet heavenly dessert that my whole family enjoys.
—CATHY W.
BROKEN BOW, NEBRASKA

barbara mccalley
ALLISON PARK, PENNSYLVANIA

A smooth cheesecake layer, a nutty crust, and a praline-like topping make these squares extra-special. I make them often for friends or when my big Italian family gets together.

cheesecake praline squares

PREP: 20 min. | **BAKE:** 35 min. + chilling

2-1/2 cups all-purpose flour
1 cup butter, melted
2/3 cup finely chopped pecans
2 tablespoons confectioners' sugar

FILLING:

3 packages (8 ounces *each*) cream cheese, softened
2/3 cup sugar
1 can (14 ounces) sweetened condensed milk
2 teaspoons vanilla extract
1/2 teaspoon grated lemon peel
4 eggs, lightly beaten

TOPPING:

1 cup packed brown sugar
1 cup heavy whipping cream
1 cup chopped pecans
1-1/2 teaspoons vanilla extract

In a large bowl, combine the flour, butter, pecans and confectioners' sugar. Press into an ungreased 13-in. x 9-in. baking dish. Bake at 350° for 20-24 minutes or until lightly browned. Cool the crust on a wire rack.

In a large bowl, beat cream cheese and sugar until smooth. Add the milk, vanilla and lemon peel. Add eggs; beat on low speed just until combined. Pour over crust.

Bake at 350° for 35-40 minutes or until edges are lightly browned. Cool on a wire rack.

In a small saucepan, combine the brown sugar and cream. Cook and stir over medium heat until the mixture comes to a boil. Reduce the heat; simmer, uncovered, for 10 minutes. Remove from the heat; stir in the pecans and vanilla. Pour over cheesecake. Refrigerate for 4 hours or overnight. Cut into squares.

YIELD: 15 servings.

marye franzen
GOTHENBURG, NEBRASKA

Here's a delightful dessert with the classic flavor of a banana split. It's a cool, creamy treat with no last-minute fuss since you just pull it from the freezer. It always solicits praise from our big family.

banana split supreme

PREP: 30 min. + freezing

3/4 cup butter, *divided*
2 cups confectioners' sugar
1 cup evaporated milk
3/4 cup semisweet chocolate chips
24 cream-filled chocolate sandwich cookies, crushed
3 to 4 medium firm bananas, cut into 1/2-inch slices
2 quarts vanilla ice cream, softened, *divided*
1 can (20 ounces) crushed pineapple, drained
1 jar (10 ounces) maraschino cherries, drained and halved
3/4 cup chopped pecans
Whipped topping

In a large saucepan, combine 1/2 cup butter, sugar, milk and chocolate chips. Bring to a boil over medium heat; cook and stir for 8 minutes. Remove from the heat and cool completely.

Meanwhile, melt the remaining butter; toss with cookie crumbs. Press into a greased 13-in. x 9-in. pan. Freeze for 15 minutes. Arrange banana slices over crust; spread with 1 quart of ice cream. Top with 1 cup of chocolate sauce. Freeze for 1 hour. Refrigerate remaining chocolate sauce. Spread the remaining ice cream over dessert; top with pineapple, cherries and pecans. Cover dessert and freeze overnight.

Remove from the freezer 10 minutes before serving. Reheat the chocolate sauce. Cut dessert into squares; serve with whipped topping and chocolate sauce.

YIELD: 12-15 servings.

lemonade icebox pie

PREP: 15 min. + chilling

- 1 package (8 ounces) cream cheese, softened
- 1 can (14 ounces) sweetened condensed milk
- 3/4 cup thawed lemonade concentrate
- 1 carton (8 ounces) frozen whipped topping, thawed

Yellow food coloring, optional

- 1 graham cracker crust (9 inches)

In a large bowl, beat cream cheese and milk until smooth. Beat in lemonade concentrate. Fold in whipped topping and food coloring if desired. Pour into crust. Cover and refrigerate until set.

YIELD: 8 servings.

ORANGE ICEBOX PIE: Substitute 3/4 cup thawed orange juice concentrate for the lemonade, add 1/2 teaspoon grated orange peel and omit the yellow food coloring.

CREAMY PINEAPPLE PIE: Substitute 1 can (8 ounces) crushed, undrained pineapple and 1/4 cup lemon juice for lemonade. Omit cream cheese and yellow food coloring.

COOL LIME PIE: Substitute 3/4 cup thawed limeade concentrate for lemonade and use green food coloring instead of yellow.

cheryl wilt
EGLON, WEST VIRGINIA

This refreshing lemonade pie is light and fluffy, with a creamy, smooth consistency that we appreciate. It's the dessert that immediately comes to mind when I think of my favorite summer meal.

doreen martin
KITIMAT, BRITISH COLUMBIA

The fluffy filling for these cream puffs has a refreshing citrus flavor and delicate yellow color.

FREEZE CREAM PUFFS FOR FUTURE USE

Unfilled cream puffs can be frozen in an airtight container for up to 2 months. To thaw, let stand at room temperature for 10-15 minutes. Fill with your favorite filling right before serving.

lemon cream puffs

PREP: 20 min. + cooling | **BAKE:** 30 min.

1/2 cup water
1/4 cup butter, cubed
1/2 cup all-purpose flour
2 eggs

LEMON FILLING:

1 egg, beaten
1/3 cup sugar
3 tablespoons lemon juice
2 tablespoons butter, cubed
1 cup heavy whipping cream
2 teaspoons sugar
Confectioners' sugar

In a large saucepan, bring the water and butter to a boil. Add the flour all at once, stirring mixture until a smooth ball forms. Remove from the heat; let stand for 5 minutes. Add the eggs, one at a time, beating well after each addition. Continue beating until mixture is smooth.

Drop by rounded tablespoonfuls 3 in. apart onto greased baking sheets. Bake at 400° for 30-35 minutes or until golden brown. Remove to wire racks. Immediately split puffs and remove tops; discard soft dough from inside. Set puffs and tops aside to cool.

For filling, in a small heavy saucepan, combine the egg, sugar, lemon juice and butter. Bring to a boil over medium heat; cook and stir for 5-7 minutes or until mixture is thick enough to coat the back of a spoon.

Remove from the heat. Cool quickly by placing pan in a bowl of ice water; stir for 2 minutes. Transfer to a bowl; press plastic wrap onto surface of filling. Chill for 1 hour or until partially set.

In a large bowl, beat cream and sugar until stiff peaks form; fold into lemon mixture. Fill cream puffs; replace tops. Dust with confectioners' sugar.

YIELD: 10 servings.

peach ice cream

PREP: 20 min. | **PROCESS:** 20 min./batch + freezing

1 tablespoon unflavored gelatin
2 tablespoons cold water
1-1/2 cups milk
1 cup half-and-half cream
1/2 cup evaporated milk
2 cups sliced peeled ripe peaches
1-3/4 cups sugar, *divided*
1 teaspoon vanilla extract
1/4 teaspoon almond extract
1/8 teaspoon salt

In a small microwave-safe bowl, sprinkle gelatin over cold water; let stand for 1 minute. Microwave on high for 20 seconds; stir. Let stand until gelatin is completely dissolved.

In a large bowl, combine the gelatin, milk, cream and evaporated milk.

In another bowl, mash the peaches with 1 cup sugar. Add the peach mixture, extracts, salt and remaining sugar to the cream mixture; stir until sugar is dissolved.

Fill cylinder of ice cream freezer two-thirds full; freeze according to manufacturer's directions. When ice cream is frozen, transfer to a freezer container; freeze for 2-4 hours before serving.

YIELD: about 1 quart.

linda wallace
HARTSVILLE, SOUTH CAROLINA

South Carolina is one of the leading producers of peaches, and we live just three miles from an orchard. We can hardly wait until the harvest so we can make ice cream.

cream cake dessert

PREP: 30 min. | **BAKE:** 30 min. + cooling

1 package (18-1/4 ounces) yellow cake mix
1 package (3.4 ounces) instant vanilla pudding mix
1/2 cup shortening
1 cup water
4 eggs

FILLING:
5 tablespoons all-purpose flour
1 cup 2% milk
1/2 cup butter, softened
1/2 cup shortening
1 cup sugar
1 teaspoon vanilla extract
1/2 teaspoon salt
Fresh raspberries, optional

In a large bowl, beat the cake mix, dry pudding mix and shortening on low speed until crumbly. Add water and eggs; beat on low speed for 30 seconds.

Beat on medium for 2 minutes. Pour into a greased and floured 13-in. x 9-in. baking pan.

Bake at 350° for 30-35 minutes or until a toothpick inserted near the center comes out clean. Cool for 10 minutes; invert the cake onto a wire rack to cool completely.

Meanwhile, in a small saucepan, combine flour and milk until smooth. Bring to a boil; cook and stir for 2 minutes or until thickened. Cool completely.

In a large bowl, cream the butter, shortening and sugar, until light and fluffy. Beat in the milk mixture, vanilla and salt until smooth.

Cut cake horizontally into two layers. Place bottom layer on a serving plate; top with filling. Top with remaining cake layer. Garnish with raspberries if desired.

YIELD: 16-20 servings.

peggy stott
LOMAX, IOWA

Folks really go for this tender cake with rich ream filling. My son first tried it in high school and asked me to get the recipe. I've used it countless times since for all sorts of occasions. It's easy to transport to a potluck because the cream is on the inside.

sandy hold

SAPULPA, OKLAHOMA

This recipe is a favorite at family get-togethers. Everyone, from my 80-year-old grandmother to my 2-year-old daughter, enjoys it. I usually prepare the mix early in the day, then later everyone gets in on cranking the ice cream.

very cherry ice cream

PREP: 20 min. + chilling | PROCESS: 20 min./batch + freezing

1 pound fresh *or* frozen pitted dark sweet cherries, coarsely chopped (about 1-3/4 cups)

1/2 cup sugar

1 package (3 ounces) cherry gelatin

1 cup boiling water

1 package (3 ounces) cook-and-serve vanilla pudding mix

3-1/2 cups milk

2 cups heavy whipping cream

2 teaspoons vanilla extract

In a large bowl, combine cherries and sugar; set aside. Dissolve gelatin in boiling water; set aside. Cook pudding according to package directions, using 3-1/2 cups milk. Add to cherries. Stir in cream, vanilla and prepared gelatin.

Refrigerate, stirring occasionally, until cold. Fill cylinder of ice cream freezer two-thirds full; freeze according to manufacturer's directions. Refrigerate remaining mixture until ready to freeze. When ice cream is frozen, transfer to a freezer container; freeze for 2-4 hours before serving.

YIELD: 2 quarts.

taste of home test kitchen

Our torte looks fancy, but it uses store-bought ladyfingers and canned mandarin oranges. The filling is so light and fluffy.

orange dream torte

PREP: 20 min. + chilling

1 package (3 ounces) orange gelatin

2/3 cup boiling water

1/2 cup cold water

1 carton (16 ounces) frozen whipped topping, thawed, *divided*

1 package (8 ounces) cream cheese, softened

1/4 cup sugar

1/4 cup milk

1/4 cup graham cracker crumbs

1 package (3 ounces) ladyfingers, split

1 can (11 ounces) mandarin oranges, drained

In a large bowl, dissolve gelatin in boiling water. Stir in cold water. Cover and refrigerate for 30 minutes or until syrupy.

Fold in 3 cups whipped topping; set aside. In a small bowl, beat cream cheese and sugar until smooth; gradually beat in milk. Fold in remaining whipped topping.

Grease the bottom of a 9-in. springform pan; sprinkle with cracker crumbs. Arrange ladyfingers around edge of pan. Set aside 1-1/2 cups of the orange mixture. Alternately spoon the cream cheese mixture and remaining orange mixture into pan. Spread reserved orange mixture over top. Refrigerate for 1 hour or until set.

Remove the sides of the pan. Garnish torte with mandarin oranges.

YIELD: 12 servings.

german chocolate cheesecake

PREP: 30 min. | **BAKE:** 50 min. + chilling

1-1/2 cups chocolate graham cracker crumbs
    (about 8 whole crackers)
2 tablespoons brown sugar
1/4 cup butter, melted

FILLING:

2 packages (8 ounces *each*) cream
    cheese, softened
1 cup (6 ounces) semisweet chocolate
    chips, melted and cooled
2/3 cup packed brown sugar
2 tablespoons baking cocoa
5 eggs, lightly beaten
1 teaspoon almond extract
1 teaspoon vanilla extract

TOPPING:

3/4 cup flaked coconut
3/4 cup chopped walnuts
1/3 cup packed brown sugar
1/3 cup half-and-half cream
5 tablespoons butter, cubed

Place a greased 9-in. springform pan on a double thickness of heavy-duty foil (about 18 in. square). Securely wrap foil around pan. In a small bowl, combine cracker crumbs and brown sugar; stir in butter.

Press onto the bottom and 1 in. up the sides of prepared pan. Place pan on a baking sheet. Bake at 350° for 10 minutes. Cool on a wire rack.

In a large bowl, beat cream cheese until smooth. Beat in the chocolate, brown sugar and cocoa. Add eggs; beat on low speed just until combined. Stir in extracts. Pour into crust.

Place pan in a large baking pan. Fill the larger pan with 1 in. of hot water. Bake at 350° for 50-55 minutes or until the center is just set and the top appears dull. Remove springform pan from water bath. Cool on a wire rack for 10 minutes. Carefully run a knife around edge of pan to loosen; cool 1 hour longer. Refrigerate 4 hours or overnight. Remove sides of pan.

In a large saucepan, bring topping ingredients to a boil over medium heat; cook and stir for 3 minutes. Cool. Spread over cheesecake.

YIELD: 12 servings.

mary bakken
NEW RICHLAND, MINNESOTA

My cheesecake version of German chocolate cake is rich and flavorful. It makes an elegant ending to a special meal.

general recipe index

APPETIZERS

COLD APPETIZERS

Antipasto Platter, 17
Delightful Deviled Eggs, 28
Olive & Roasted Pepper Bruschetta, 29
Pickled Shrimp, 27
Savory Ham Cheesecake, 19
Shrimp Cocktail, 24

DIPS & SPREADS

Creamy Olive-Bacon Dip, 11
Creamy Ranch Dip, 28
Easy Buffalo Chicken Dip, 25
Festive Feta Cheese Ball, 16
French Onion Cheese Fondue, 14
Spinach Artichoke Dip, 27
Taffy Apple Dip, 20
Tomato Nacho Dip, 11

HOT APPETIZERS

Appetizer Pizzas, 20
Brie in Puff Pastry, 16
Brie Phyllo Cups, 15
Cheddar Crab Bites, 23
Chicken Chili Nachos, 31
Cranberry Meatballs, 30
Fat Rascals, 19
Glazed Meatballs, 30
Ham and Cheese Party Calzones, 13
Mexican Chicken Meatballs, 21
Mini BBQ Chicken Pizzas, 23
Orange-Glazed Smokies, 23
Party Time Mini Cheeseburgers, 22
Pigs in a Blanket, 10
Pineapple Ham Pizzas, 11
Pizza Cups, 19
Pizza Egg Rolls, 15
Prosciutto Pinwheels, 24
Saucy Meatballs, 30
Sausage-Stuffed Mushrooms, 26
Seasoned Crab Cakes, 18
Smoky Potato Rounds, 9
Southwest Pretzels, 8
Spicy Chicken Wings, 12
Spinach Artichoke Dip, 27
Stromboli Ladder Loaf, 31
Sweet & Spicy Jalapeno Poppers, 8

SNACK MIX

Fun-on-the-Run Snack Mix, 31

APPLES

Apple Crisp, 231
Apple-Onion Pork Chops, 74
Baked Cider-Glazed Ham, 156
Candy Apple Pie, 265
Caramel Apple Trifle, 298
Cider-Glazed Ham, 156
Cider Mushroom Brisket, 152
Easy Apple Betty, 272
Easy Dutch Apple Pie, 228

Honey-Apple Turkey Breast, 102
Rustic Autumn Fruit Tart, 257
Sweet Potatoes with Apples, 184
Taffy Apple Dip, 20

APRICOTS

Apricot Almond Torte, 218
Apricot Bars, 246
Apricot Ham Steak, 45
Apricot Tea Rings, 261

BACON

Bacon Cheeseburger Pasta, 49
Baked Potato Soup, 137
BLT in a Bowl, 196
Creamy Olive-Bacon Dip, 11
Family-Favorite Baked Beans, 180
Green Beans with Bacon, 203
Hot Bacon Asparagus Salad, 187
Loaded Mashed Potatoes, 211
Pizza Carbonara, 89
Ravioli Carbonara, 66
Spinach-Onion Salad with Hot Bacon
    Dressing, 190
Sweet & Spicy Jalapeno Poppers, 8

BANANAS

Banana Brickle Muffins, 251
Banana Chocolate Chip Cookies, 262
Banana Cream Eclairs, 237
Banana Split Supreme, 304

BEANS

Beef and Three-Bean Chili, 151
Chicken Chili Nachos, 31
Chili Mac, 80
Family-Favorite Baked Beans, 180
Four-Bean Supreme, 212
Hearty Black Bean Soup, 156
Meatless Chili Mac, 57
Mixed Bean Salad, 182
Picnic Baked Beans, 208
Ranch Beans, 160
Santa Fe Chili, 139
Tex-Mex Chili, 149
Three Beans and Sausage, 155
White Chili, 153

BEEF *(ALSO SEE GROUND BEEF)*

MAIN DISHES

Barbecued Beef Sandwiches, 148
Barbecues for the Bunch, 163
Beef and Three-Bean Chili, 151
Bohemian Pot Roast, 38
Braised Beef Short Ribs, 156
Chicken Fried Steak, 73
Cider Mushroom Brisket, 152
Cubed Steak Stroganoff, 50

French Dip Sandwiches, 168
French Onion Pizza au Gratin, 103
Garlic-Butter Steak, 55
Garlic Pot Roast, 110
Green Chili Beef Burritos, 147
Hungarian Goulash, 138
Italian Beef Hoagies, 164
Mushroom Beef Tenderloin, 70
No-Fuss Swiss Steak, 143
Peppered Filets & Balsamic Red Onions, 52
Peppery Roast Beef, 122
Picante Beef Roast, 136
Polynesian Roast Beef, 167
Reuben Crescent Bake, 118
Round Steak with Potatoes, 118
Slow-Cooked Pepper Steak, 165
So-Tender Swiss Steak, 122
Spicy Pepper Steak, 61
Steak and Rice Roll-Ups, 44
Steak Potpie, 133
Stuffed Flank Steak, 168
Super Flatbread Wraps, 76
Swiss Steak with Dumplings, 96

SOUPS, STEWS & CHILI

Beef and Three-Bean Chili, 151
Beef Stew for 2, 79
Big Red Soup, 159
Busy Day Beef Stew, 151
French Beef Stew, 147
Italian Beef Stew, 54
Tex-Mex Chili, 149

BELL PEPPERS

Olive & Roasted Pepper Bruschetta, 29
Prosciutto-Pepper Pork Chops, 59
Roasted Pepper Ravioli, 90
Slow-Cooked Pepper Steak, 165
Spicy Pepper Steak, 61
Zucchini Red Pepper Lasagna, 131

BERRIES

Aunt Betty's Blueberry Muffins, 264
Berry Patch Pie, 268
Cherry Blueberry Pie, 247
Cranberry-Cashew Drop Cookies, 252
Cranberry Cream Cheese Coffee Cake, 270
Cranberry Gelatin Salad, 187
Cranberry Meatballs, 30
Cranberry Nut Bagels, 263
Cranberry-Topped Lemon Tarts, 259
Cranberry-White Chocolate Cinnamon
    Rolls, 269
Dutch Rhubarb Pie, 260
Makeover Strawberry Cake, 222
Mini Raspberry Mousse Parfaits, 296
Pineapple Cranberry Ham, 72
Pork Chops with Cranberry Sauce, 48
Puff Pastry Hearts, 295

the **ULTIMATE COMFORT FOOD** cookbook

Raspberry Coffee Cake, 223
Raspberry Streusel Muffins, 271
Snowflake Pudding, 297
Strawberry Cheesecake Ice Cream, 291
Strawberry Shakes, 295
Strawberry Tiramisu Trifle, 293
Turkey with Cranberry Sauce, 161

BEVERAGES
Caramel Chip Malts, 283
Cola Floats, 287
Strawberry Shakes, 295

BREADS *SEE QUICK BREADS; YEAST BREADS.*

BROCCOLI
Broccoli Mushroom Casserole, 206
Broccoli Rice Casserole, 183
Corn and Broccoli in Cheese Sauce, 197

BURGERS
Change-of-Pace Burgers, 62
Mama Mia Burgers, 69
Mini Burgers with the Works, 12
My Favorite Burger, 83
Party Time Mini Cheeseburgers, 22
Pizzeria Burgers, 69

CARAMEL & BUTTERSCOTCH
Butterscotch Raisin Cookies, 252
Caramel Apple Trifle, 298
Caramel Chip Malts, 283
Caramel-Pecan Sticky Buns, 271
Cashew Caramel Fudge, 287
Pull-Apart Caramel Coffee Cake, 255
Turtle Praline Tart, 224

CARROTS
Carrot Cake Doughnuts, 243
Carrot Raisin Salad, 172
Comforting Carrot Casserole, 191
Honey-Glazed Carrots, 211

CHEESE & CREAM CHEESE
APPETIZERS
Brie in Puff Pastry, 16
Brie Phyllo Cups, 15
Creamy Ranch Dip, 28
Fat Rascals, 19
Festive Feta Cheese Ball, 16
French Onion Cheese Fondue, 14
Ham and Cheese Party Calzones, 13
Mexican Chicken Meatballs, 21
Party Time Mini Cheeseburgers, 22
Savory Ham Cheesecake, 19
Sweet & Spicy Jalapeno Poppers, 8
BREADS, MUFFINS & COFFEE CAKE
Cheddar English Muffins, 267
Cheesecake Pumpkin Muffins, 235
Cranberry Cream Cheese Coffee Cake, 270

Parmesan-Ranch Pan Rolls, 216
Peachy Cheese Danish, 267
DESSERTS
Aunt Ruth's Famous Butterscotch Cheesecake, 301
Cappuccino Cheesecake Pie, 288
Cheesecake Praline Squares, 304
Chocolate-Covered Cheesecake Squares, 282
Cool Lime Pie, 305
Decadent Brownie Swirl Cheesecake, 281
German Chocolate Cheesecake, 309
Lemonade Icebox Pie, 305
Orange Icebox Pie, 305
Strawberry Cheesecake Ice Cream, 291
MAIN DISHES
Bacon Cheeseburger Pasta, 49
Bistro Mac & Cheese, 66
Budget Macaroni and Cheese, 70
Cheeseburger Cups, 126
Cheesy Vegetable Egg Dish, 121
Chicago-Style Stuffed Pizza, 92
Chicken Parmesan, 106
Confetti Mac 'n' Cheese, 43
Crunchy Ham and Cheese, 49
Four-Cheese Baked Ziti, 86
French Onion Pizza au Gratin, 103
Ham Mac and Cheese, 127
Little Cheddar Meat Loaves, 124
Macaroni & Cheese Pizza, 108
Macaroni Taco Bake, 125
Mama Mia Burgers, 69
Marvelous Shells 'n' Cheese, 116
Pizza Carbonara, 89
Pizza Pork Chops, 67
Pizzeria Burgers, 69
Reuben Crescent Bake, 118
Roadside Diner Cheeseburger Quiche, 107
Turkey Reubens, 35
Turkey Scallopini, 46
SALADS
Colorful Tomato 'n' Mozzarella Salad, 201
Layered Veggie Tortellini Salad, 193
SIDE DISHES
Cheddar Tot Casserole, 179
Cheddar Twice-Baked Potatoes, 175
Cheesy Vegetable Medley, 204
Corn and Broccoli in Cheese Sauce, 197
Creamy Parmesan Spinach, 196
Hash Browns with Ham, 202
Loaded Mashed Potatoes, 211
Parmesan Corn on the Cob, 212
Parmesan Peas 'n' Rice, 199
Slow-Cooked Mac 'n' Cheese, 187
SOUPS
Savory Cheese Soup, 140
Veggie-Sausage Cheese Soup, 143

CHERRIES
Cherry Blueberry Pie, 247
Cherry Crescent Coffee Cake, 230
No-Bake Cherry Dessert, 296

Sweet Cherry Pork Chops, 53
Very Cherry Ice Cream, 308

CHICKEN
APPETIZERS
Chicken Chili Nachos, 31
Easy Buffalo Chicken Dip, 25
Mexican Chicken Meatballs, 21
Mini BBQ Chicken Pizzas, 23
Spicy Chicken Wings, 12
MAIN DISHES
Best Chicken 'n' Biscuits, 105
Breaded Chicken Strips, 51
Busy Mom's Chicken Fajitas, 154
Chicken 'n' Corn Bread Dressing, 94
Chicken and Dumpling Casserole, 90
Chicken Caesar Pasta, 64
Chicken Lasagna Rolls, 95
Chicken Noodle Casserole, 113
Chicken Parmesan, 106
Chicken Tortilla Bake, 114
Chicken Vegetable Potpie, 98
Chicken with Country Gravy, 130
Chicken with Veggies 'n' Gravy, 164
Citrus-Baked Cornish Hens, 97
Classic Fried Chicken, 34
Cordon Bleu Casserole, 101
Cornmeal Oven-Fried Chicken, 91
Fried Chicken with Pan Gravy, 39
Herbed Fried Chicken with Gravy, 39
Honey Mustard Chicken, 125
Italian Chicken Pockets, 58
Lemon Basil Chicken, 123
Malibu Chicken Bundles, 115
Maple Mustard Chicken, 140
Mushroom Chicken Cacciatore, 144
Oregano Roasting Chicken, 88
Poppy Seed Creamed Chicken, 133
Pretzel-Crusted Drumsticks, 129
Roasted Chicken with Rosemary, 105
Roasted Chicken with Sausage Stuffing, 99
Southwest Bean and Chicken Pasta, 42
Sweet 'n' Tangy Chicken, 157
Tasty Onion Chicken, 117
Tropical BBQ Chicken, 150
SOUP & CHILI
Chicken Noodle Soup, 167
White Chili, 153

CHOCOLATE (*ALSO SEE WHITE CHOCOLATE*)
Banana Chocolate Chip Cookies, 262
Cappuccino Truffles, 276
Caramel Chip Malts, 283
Cashew Caramel Fudge, 287
Chocolate Almond Ice Cream, 299
Chocolate and Vanilla Creme Brulee, 285
Chocolate Braids, 241
Chocolate Chip Blondies, 220
Chocolate Chip Cake, 224
Chocolate-Covered Cheesecake Squares, 282

CHOCOLATE (*CONTINUED*)

Chocolate Creme Brulee, 285
Chocolate Lover's Dream Cookies, 227
Chocolate Mousse with Cranberry Sauce, 290
Chocolate-Peanut Butter Cupcakes, 273
Chocolate Pecan Cookies, 227
Chocolate Pistachio Biscotti, 266
Classic Chocolate Layer Cake, 226
Cream-Filled Chocolate Cake Roll, 294
Decadent Brownie Swirl Cheesecake, 281
Double Chocolate Truffles, 276
Fudge Brownie Pie, 260
Fudge Sundae Pie, 279
German Chocolate Cheesecake, 309
Glazed Chocolate Chip Brownies, 236
Jumbo Chocolate Chip Cookies, 231
Kentucky Chocolate Pecan Pie, 264
Mint-Chocolate Ice Cream Cake, 303
Oatmeal Chip Cookies, 240
Old-Fashioned Chocolate Pudding, 288
Orange Truffles, 276
Peanut Butter Icebox Dessert, 292
Peanut Butter Kiss Cookies, 232
Peeps Sunflower Cake, 238
Rocky Road Fudge Pops, 300
Turtle Praline Tart, 224

CINNAMON

Cappuccino Cinnamon Rolls, 258
Caramel-Pecan Sticky Buns, 271
Cinnamon Raisin Bread, 228
Cinnamon Rolls in a Snap, 240
Cranberry-White Chocolate Cinnamon
    Rolls, 269
Frosted Cinnamon Rolls, 219
Orange Cinnamon Rolls, 255

COCONUT

Ambrosia Cupcakes, 221
German Chocolate Cheesecake, 309
Island Fruit Salad, 200
Jumbo Chocolate Chip Cookies, 231
Snowflake Pudding, 297
Tropical Fruit Salad, 198

COFFEE

Cappuccino Cheesecake Pie, 288
Cappuccino Cinnamon Rolls, 258
Cappuccino Truffles, 276
Easy Tiramisu, 277
Mocha Cream Puffs, 299
Mocha Mallow Parfaits, 303
Strawberry Tiramisu Trifle, 293

COFFEE CAKE *SEE QUICK BREADS;*
YEAST BREADS.

CORN

Corn and Broccoli in Cheese Sauce, 197
Chicken 'n' Corn Bread Dressing, 94
Grilled Vegetable Medley, 199
Holiday Corn 'n' Turkey Casserole, 97
Makeover Corn Pudding, 207
Parmesan Corn on the Cob, 212
Sausage-Corn Bake, 106
Scalloped Corn, 204

CREAM CHEESE *SEE CHEESE &*
CREAM CHEESE.

DESSERTS
BARS & BROWNIES

Apricot Bars, 246
Chocolate Chip Blondies, 220
Fudge Brownie Pie, 260
Glazed Chocolate Chip Brownies, 236
Walnut Baklava, 248

CAKES

Apricot Almond Torte, 218
Butternut Squash Cake Roll, 286
Chocolate Chip Cake, 224
Classic Chocolate Layer Cake, 226
Cream Cake Dessert, 307
Cream-Filled Chocolate Cake Roll, 294
Edna's Ho Ho Cake, 289
Makeover Strawberry Cake, 222
Mini Pineapple Upside-Down Cake, 244
Mint-Chocolate Ice Cream Cake, 303
Nut Roll Coffee Cake, 247
Orange Dream Torte, 308
Peeps Sunflower Cake, 238
Yellow Layer Cake, 224
Yellow Nut Cake, 224

CANDY

Cappuccino Truffles, 276
Cashew Caramel Fudge, 287
Double Chocolate Truffles, 276
Makeover Marbled Orange Fudge, 276
Orange Truffles, 276

CHEESECAKES

Aunt Ruth's Famous Butterscotch
    Cheesecake, 301
Cappuccino Cheesecake Pie, 288
Cheesecake Praline Squares, 304
Chocolate-Covered Cheesecake Squares, 282
Decadent Brownie Swirl Cheesecake, 281
German Chocolate Cheesecake, 309
No-Bake Cherry Dessert, 296

COOKIES

Banana Chocolate Chip Cookies, 262
Butterscotch Raisin Cookies, 252
Chewy Oatmeal Cookies, 232
Chocolate Lover's Dream Cookies, 227
Chocolate Pecan Cookies, 227
Chocolate Pistachio Biscotti, 266
Cranberry-Cashew Drop Cookies, 252
Frosted Butter Cookies, 256
Gingerbread Cookies, 229
Jumbo Chocolate Chip Cookies, 231
Lara's Tender Gingersnaps, 219
Lemon Anise Biscotti, 242
Oatmeal Chip Cookies, 240
Peanut Butter Cookies, 268
Peanut Butter Kiss Cookies, 232
White Chocolate Macadamia Cookies, 236

CREAM PUFFS & ECLAIRS

Banana Cream Eclairs, 237
Chocolate Mint Eclair Dessert, 300
Heart's Delight Eclair, 291
Lemon Cream Puffs, 306
Mocha Cream Puffs, 299

CRISPS & COBBLERS

Apple Crisp, 231
Easy Apple Betty, 272
South Carolina Cobbler, 216

CUPCAKES

Ambrosia Cupcakes, 221
Chocolate Cookie Cupcakes, 272
Chocolate-Peanut Butter Cupcakes, 273
Pumpkin Spice Cupcakes, 253

ICE CREAM & FROZEN DESSERTS

Banana Split Supreme, 304
Butter Pecan Ice Cream, 283
Caramel Chip Malts, 283
Caramel Toffee Ice Cream Pie, 302
Chocolate Almond Ice Cream, 299
Cola Floats, 287
Fudge Sundae Pie, 279
Mint-Chocolate Ice Cream Cake, 303
Peach Ice Cream, 307
Peanut Butter Parfaits, 279
Rocky Road Fudge Pops, 300
Strawberry Cheesecake Ice Cream, 291
Strawberry Shakes, 295
Very Cherry Ice Cream, 308

PARFAITS & TRIFLES

Caramel Apple Trifle, 298
Mini Raspberry Mousse Parfaits, 296
Mocha Mallow Parfaits, 303
Peanut Butter Parfaits, 279
Pistachio Pudding Parfaits, 284
Strawberry Tiramisu Trifle, 293
White Chocolate Cherry Parfaits, 292

PIES & TARTS

Apple Praline Pie, 234
Berry Patch Pie, 268
Candy Apple Pie, 265
Caramel Toffee Ice Cream Pie, 302
Cherry Blueberry Pie, 247
Cool Lime Pie, 305
Cranberry-Topped Lemon Tarts, 259
Creamy Pineapple Pie, 305
Dutch Rhubarb Pie, 260
Easy Dutch Apple Pie, 228
Eggnog Pumpkin Pie, 243
Florida Citrus Meringue Pie, 217
Fudge Brownie Pie, 260
Kentucky Chocolate Pecan Pie, 264
Lemon Meringue Pie, 239
Lemonade Icebox Pie, 305
Orange Icebox Pie, 305
Peach Pie, 250
Pecan Pumpkin Pie, 245
Rustic Autumn Fruit Tart, 257

Tiny Shortbread Tarts, 248
Turtle Praline Tart, 224
PUDDINGS & CUSTARDS
 Chocolate and Vanilla Creme Brulee, 285
 Chocolate Creme Brulee, 285
 Chocolate Mousse with Cranberry Sauce, 290
 Grandma's Rice Pudding, 284
 Lemon Cream Puffs, 306
 Light Lemon Mousse, 280
 Old-Fashioned Chocolate Pudding, 288
 Puff Pastry Hearts, 295
 Pumpkin Creme Brulee, 280
 Snowflake Pudding, 297
 Vanilla Creme Brulee, 285
 White Chocolate Bread Pudding, 278

DOUGHNUTS
 Carrot Cake Doughnuts, 243
 Old-Time Cake Doughnuts, 263

DRESSING *SEE STUFFING & DRESSING.*

EGGS
 Cheesy Vegetable Egg Dish, 121
 Eggnog Pumpkin Pie, 243
 South-of-the-Border Quiche, 87

FISH & SEAFOOD
APPETIZERS
 Cheddar Crab Bites, 23
 Pickled Shrimp, 27
 Seasoned Crab Cakes, 18
 Shrimp Cocktail, 24
MAIN DISHES
 Dilly Salmon Patties, 37
 Easy Shrimp Scampi, 50
 Homemade Fish Sticks, 101
 Lemon-Batter Fish, 62
 Mini Scallop Casseroles, 132
 Pesto Scallops Vermicelli, 40
 Salmon Cakes, 77
 Salmon Mornay, 60
 Shrimp 'n' Noodle Bowls, 63
 Shrimp Piccata Pasta, 71
 Tuna Alfredo, 74
 Tuna 'n' Pea Casserole, 100
 Tuna Mushroom Casserole, 114
 Tuna Noodle Skillet, 81
 Tuna Veggie Macaroni, 36

FRUIT (*ALSO SEE SALADS; SPECIFIC KINDS*)
 Dutch Rhubarb Pie, 260
 Fruited Coleslaw, 189
 Island Fruit Salad, 200
 Pineapple Cranberry Ham, 72
 Rustic Autumn Fruit Tart, 257
 Tiny Shortbread Tarts, 248
 Tropical Fruit Salad, 198

GARLIC
 Garlic-Butter Steak, 55
 Garlic Mashed Potatoes, 179
 Garlic Pot Roast, 110

GINGER
 Gingerbread Cookies, 229
 Lara's Tender Gingersnaps, 219

GREEN BEANS
 Green Bean Casserole for 2, 176
 Green Beans with Bacon, 203

GROUND BEEF
APPETIZERS
 Cranberry Meatballs, 30
 Easy Meatballs, 28
 Glazed Meatballs, 30
 Mini Burgers with the Works, 12
 Party Time Mini Cheeseburgers, 22
 Pigs in a Blanket, 10
 Saucy Meatballs, 30
CHILI
 Santa Fe Chili, 139
MAIN DISHES
 Bacon Cheeseburger Pasta, 49
 Beef Macaroni Skillet, 34
 Big-Batch Spaghetti 'n' Meatballs, 45
 Change-of-Pace Burgers, 62
 Cheeseburger Cups, 126
 Creamy Beef and Pasta, 143
 Creole Meat Loaf, 89
 Dad's Swedish Meatballs, 73
 Deluxe Macaroni Dinner, 53
 Family-Pleasing Sloppy Joes, 58
 Farmhouse Chili Dogs, 42
 Hamburger Mac Skillet, 78
 Herbed Shepherd's Pie, 102
 Italian Pinwheel Meat Loaf, 121
 Lasagna Casserole, 113
 Layered Tortilla Pie, 112
 Little Cheddar Meat Loaves, 124
 Macaroni Taco Bake, 125
 Mama Mia Burgers, 69
 Meat Loaf Gyros, 126
 Meatball Sub Casserole, 120
 Mini Burgers with the Works, 12
 Mom's Meat Loaf, 128
 My Favorite Burger, 83
 Pizza Joes, 46
 Pizza Spaghetti, 47
 Pizzeria Burgers, 69
 Roadside Diner Cheeseburger Quiche, 107
 Slow-Cooked Meat Loaf, 169
 Slow Cooker Lasagna, 163
 Slow Cooker Sloppy Joes, 146
 Spaghetti 'n' Meatballs for 2, 65
 Stovetop Hamburger Casserole, 82
 Taco Lasagna, 98
 Taco Meat Loaf, 159
 Tacos in a Bowl, 75
 Tortilla-Salsa Meat Loaf, 130

HAM
APPETIZERS
 Ham and Cheese Party Calzones, 13
 Pineapple Ham Pizzas, 11

Prosciutto Pinwheels, 24
Savory Ham Cheesecake, 19
MAIN DISHES
 Apricot Ham Steak, 45
 Baked Cider-Glazed Ham, 156
 Barbecue Ham Sandwiches, 38
 Champagne Baked Ham, 104
 Cider-Glazed Ham, 156
 Cordon Bleu Casserole, 101
 Country Ham and Potatoes, 74
 Crunchy Ham and Cheese, 49
 Ham Balls, 110
 Ham Mac and Cheese, 127
 Ham-Noodle Bake, 93
 Ham with Ruby-Red Glaze, 129
 Orange-Glazed Ham, 156
 Pineapple Cranberry Ham, 72
 Prosciutto-Pepper Pork Chops, 59
SIDE DISH
 Hash Browns with Ham, 202
SOUPS
 Creamy Ham Chowder, 148
 Split Pea Soup, 145

HONEY
 Honey-Apple Turkey Breast, 102
 Honey-Glazed Carrots, 211
 Honey Mustard Chicken, 125
 Honey Mustard Pork, 78
 Honey White Loaves, 254
 Honey Whole Wheat Rolls, 239

HOT PEPPERS
 Green Chili Beef Burritos, 147
 Sweet & Spicy Jalapeno Poppers, 8

LAMB
 Meat Loaf Gyros, 126
 Rosemary Lamb Chops, 65

LASAGNA
 Chicken Lasagna Rolls, 95
 Lasagna Casserole, 113
 Slow Cooker Lasagna, 163
 Taco Lasagna, 98
 Traditional Lasagna, 117
 Zucchini Red Pepper Lasagna, 131

LEMON & LIME
 Citrus-Baked Cornish Hens, 97
 Cool Lime Pie, 305
 Cranberry-Topped Lemon Tarts, 259
 Florida Citrus Meringue Pie, 217
 Lemon Anise Biscotti, 242
 Lemon Basil Chicken, 123
 Lemon-Batter Fish, 62
 Lemon-Butter New Potatoes, 192
 Lemon Cream Puffs, 306
 Lemon Crumb Muffins, 249
 Lemon Meringue Pie, 239
 Lemonade Icebox Pie, 305
 Light Lemon Mousse, 280

MAIN DISHES SEE BACON; BEEF; BURGERS; CHEESE & CREAM CHEESE; CHICKEN; FISH & SEAFOOD; HAM; LASAGNA; MEAT LOAF & MEATBALLS; MEATLESS MAIN DISHES; PASTA & NOODLES; PIZZA; PORK; SANDWICHES; SAUSAGE, PEPPERONI & HOT DOGS; SLOW COOKER; SOUPS, STEWS & CHILI; TURKEY.

MAPLE
Maple-Butter Turkey with Gravy, 94
Maple Mustard Chicken, 140
Maple Sticky Buns, 235

MARSHMALLOWS
Mallow Sweet Potato Bake, 178
Mocha Mallow Parfaits, 303
Tropical Fruit Salad, 198

MEAT LOAF & MEATBALLS
Big-Batch Spaghetti 'n' Meatballs, 45
Cranberry Meatballs, 30
Creole Meat Loaf, 89
Dad's Swedish Meatballs, 73
Easy Meatballs, 28
Glazed Meatballs, 30
Ham Balls, 110
Italian Pinwheel Meat Loaf, 121
Little Cheddar Meat Loaves, 124
Meat Loaf Gyros, 126
Meatball Sub Casserole, 120
Mom's Meat Loaf, 128
Saucy Meatballs, 30
Slow-Cooked Meat Loaf, 169
Spaghetti 'n' Meatballs for 2, 65
Spicy Meatballs with Sauce, 142
Taco Meat Loaf, 159
Tortilla-Salsa Meat Loaf, 130
Turkey-Portobello Meat Loaf, 166

MEATLESS MAIN DISHES
Bistro Mac & Cheese, 66
Budget Macaroni and Cheese, 70
Cheesy Vegetable Egg Dish, 121
Confetti Mac 'n' Cheese, 43
Four-Cheese Baked Ziti, 86
Marvelous Shells 'n' Cheese, 116
Meatless Chili Mac, 57
Roasted Pepper Ravioli, 90
South-of-the-Border Quiche, 87
Zucchini Red Pepper Lasagna, 131

MINT
Chocolate Mint Eclair Dessert, 300
Mint-Chocolate Ice Cream Cake, 303

MUFFINS SEE QUICK BREADS.

MUSHROOMS
Beef Stew for 2, 79
Broccoli Mushroom Casserole, 206
Family-Favorite Dressing, 191
Mushroom Beef Tenderloin, 70
Mushroom Chicken Cacciatore, 144
Mushroom Wild Rice, 195
Pork Chops with Mushroom Gravy, 81
Sausage-Stuffed Mushrooms, 26
Steakhouse Mushrooms, 194
Tuna Mushroom Casserole, 114
Turkey-Portobello Meat Loaf, 166

MUSTARD
Honey Mustard Chicken, 125
Honey Mustard Pork, 78
Honey-Mustard Potato Salad, 188
Malibu Chicken Bundles, 115
Maple Mustard Chicken, 140
Pork in Mustard Sauce, 69

NUTS (ALSO SEE PEANUT BUTTER)
Apricot Almond Torte, 218
Butter Pecan Ice Cream, 283
Butternut Squash Cake Roll, 286
Caramel-Pecan Sticky Buns, 271
Cashew Caramel Fudge, 287
Cheesecake Praline Squares, 304
Chocolate Almond Ice Cream, 299
Chocolate Pecan Cookies, 227
Chocolate Pistachio Biscotti, 266
Cranberry-Cashew Drop Cookies, 252
Cranberry Nut Bagels, 263
Deluxe Corn Bread Dressing, 188
Hot Bacon Asparagus Salad, 187
Kentucky Chocolate Pecan Pie, 264
Nut Roll Coffee Cake, 247
Peanut Butter Parfaits, 279
Pecan Pumpkin Pie, 245
Rocky Road Fudge Pops, 300
Turtle Praline Tart, 224
Walnut Baklava, 248
White Chocolate Macadamia Cookies, 236
Yellow Nut Cake, 224

OATS
Butterscotch Raisin Cookies, 252
Chewy Oatmeal Cookies, 232
Oatmeal Chip Cookies, 240

OLIVES
Antipasto Platter, 17
Creamy Olive-Bacon Dip, 11
Olive & Roasted Pepper Bruschetta, 29

ONIONS
Apple-Onion Pork Chops, 74
Dill-Onion Batter Bread, 220
French Onion Cheese Fondue, 14
French Onion Pizza au Gratin, 103
Fried Onion Rings, 179
Onion Yorkshire Puddings, 175
Peppered Filets & Balsamic Red Onions, 52
Spinach-Onion Salad with Hot Bacon Dressing, 190
Tasty Onion Chicken, 117

ORANGE
Citrus-Baked Cornish Hens, 97
Florida Citrus Meringue Pie, 217
Makeover Marbled Orange Fudge, 276
Orange Cinnamon Rolls, 255
Orange Dream Torte, 308
Orange Fluff Salad, 174
Orange-Glazed Ham, 156
Orange-Glazed Smokies, 23
Orange Icebox Pie, 305
Orange Truffles, 276
Makeover Marbled Orange Fudge, 27
Pork Medallions in Orange Sauce, 68

PASTA & NOODLES (ALSO SEE LASAGNA; SALADS)
MAIN DISHES
Bacon Cheeseburger Pasta, 49
Beef Macaroni Skillet, 34
Big-Batch Spaghetti 'n' Meatballs, 45
Bistro Mac & Cheese, 66
Budget Macaroni and Cheese, 70
Chicken Caesar Pasta, 64
Chicken Lasagna Rolls, 95
Chili Mac, 80
Creamy Beef and Pasta, 143
Cubed Steak Stroganoff, 50
Deluxe Macaroni Dinner, 53
Easy Shrimp Scampi, 50
Four-Cheese Baked Ziti, 86
Gnocchi with Hearty Meat Sauce, 41
Ham-Noodle Bake, 93
Hamburger Mac Skillet, 78
Lasagna Casserole, 113
Macaroni & Cheese Pizza, 108
Macaroni Taco Bake, 125
Marvelous Shells 'n' Cheese, 116
Meatless Chili Mac, 57
Pasta Sausage Supper, 37
Pesto Scallops Vermicelli, 40
Pizza Spaghetti, 47
Poppy Seed Creamed Chicken, 133
Ravioli Carbonara, 66
Roasted Pepper Ravioli, 90
Sausage Mac Supper, 54
Shrimp 'n' Noodle Bowls, 63
Shrimp Piccata Pasta, 71
Smoked Sausage Pasta, 61
Southwest Bean and Chicken Pasta, 42
Spaghetti 'n' Meatballs for 2, 65
Spicy Meatballs with Sauce, 142
Stovetop Hamburger Casserole, 82
Tuna Alfredo, 74
Tuna 'n' Pea Casserole, 100
Tuna Noodle Skillet, 81
Tuna Veggie Macaroni, 36
Turkey Pasta Supreme, 82
Turkey Tetrazzini, 106

SIDE DISHES
- Cheesy Vegetable Medley, 204
- Creamy Noodles, 209
- Homemade Noodles, 183
- Slow-Cooked Mac 'n' Cheese, 187

PEACHES
- Peach Ice Cream, 307
- Peach Pie, 250
- Peachy Cheese Danish, 267
- Peachy Pork Chops, 56
- South Carolina Cobbler, 216

PEANUT BUTTER
- Chocolate-Peanut Butter Cupcakes, 273
- Peanut Butter Cookies, 268
- Peanut Butter Icebox Dessert, 292
- Peanut Butter Kiss Cookies, 232
- Peanut Butter Parfaits, 279

PEAS
- Parmesan Peas 'n' Rice, 199
- Roasted Sugar Snap Peas, 212
- Split Pea Soup, 145
- Tuna 'n' Pea Casserole, 100

PEPPERS *SEE BELL PEPPERS; HOT PEPPERS.*

PINEAPPLE
- Creamy Pineapple Pie, 305
- Mini Pineapple Upside-Down Cake, 244
- Orange Fluff Salad, 174
- Pineapple Cranberry Ham, 72
- Pineapple Ham Pizzas, 11

PIZZA
- Appetizer Pizzas, 20
- Chicago-Style Stuffed Pizza, 92
- French Onion Pizza au Gratin, 103
- German Oktoberfest Pizza, 86
- Macaroni & Cheese Pizza, 108
- Pineapple Ham Pizzas, 11
- Pizza Carbonara, 89
- Pizza Cups, 19

PORK *(ALSO SEE HAM; SAUSAGE, PEPPERONI & HOT DOGS)*
- Apple-Onion Pork Chops, 74
- Barbecues for the Bunch, 163
- Chinese Pork Ribs, 155
- Country Pork Chop Supper, 160
- Cranberry-Dijon Pork, 66
- Dad's Swedish Meatballs, 73
- Glazed Pork Medallions, 57
- Ham Balls, 110
- Honey Mustard Pork, 78
- Lazy Man's Ribs, 136
- Old-Fashioned Pork Chops, 152
- Peachy Pork Chops, 56
- Pizza Pork Chops, 67

- Pork Burritos, 139
- Pork Chops & Acorn Squash, 155
- Pork Chops with Cranberry Sauce, 48
- Pork Chops with Mushroom Gravy, 81
- Pork Chops with Sauerkraut, 141
- Pork in Mustard Sauce, 69
- Pork Medallions in Orange Sauce, 68
- Prosciutto-Pepper Pork Chops, 59
- Sesame Pork Ribs, 158
- Sweet Cherry Pork Chops, 53
- Tortilla-Salsa Meat Loaf, 130

POTATOES *(ALSO SEE SALADS)*
- Baked Potato Soup, 137
- Cheddar Tot Casserole, 179
- Cheddar Twice-Baked Potatoes, 175
- Country Ham and Potatoes, 74
- Fat Rascals, 19
- Garlic Mashed Potatoes, 179
- Hash Browns with Ham, 202
- Herbed Shepherd's Pie, 102
- Italian Shepherd's Pie, 119
- Lemon-Butter New Potatoes, 192
- Loaded Mashed Potatoes, 211
- Oven Fries, 177
- Reuben Baked Potatoes, 205
- Round Steak with Potatoes, 118
- Smoky Potato Rounds, 9

PUMPKIN
- Cheesecake Pumpkin Muffins, 235
- Eggnog Pumpkin Pie, 243
- Pecan Pumpkin Pie, 245
- Pumpkin Creme Brulee, 280
- Pumpkin Spice Cupcakes, 253

QUICK BREADS
COFFEE CAKE
- Cherry Crescent Coffee Cake, 230
- Cranberry Cream Cheese Coffee Cake, 270
- Pull-Apart Caramel Coffee Cake, 255
- Raspberry Coffee Cake, 223
LOAF
- Irish Soda Bread, 244
MUFFINS
- Aunt Betty's Blueberry Muffins, 264
- Banana Brickle Muffins, 251
- Cheesecake Pumpkin Muffins, 235
- Lemon Crumb Muffins, 249
- Raspberry Streusel Muffins, 271
- Yankee Corn Muffins, 223
SWEET ROLLS
- Cinnamon Rolls in a Snap, 240

RAISINS
- Butterscotch Raisin Cookies, 252
- Carrot Raisin Salad, 172
- Cinnamon Raisin Bread, 228

RICE
- Broccoli Rice Casserole, 183
- Confetti Rice, 208

- Grandma's Rice Pudding, 284
- Mushroom Wild Rice, 195
- Parmesan Peas 'n' Rice, 199
- Steak and Rice Roll-Ups, 44

SALADS
FRUIT & GELATIN
- Cranberry Gelatin Salad, 187
- Island Fruit Salad, 200
- Orange Fluff Salad, 174
- Tropical Fruit Salad, 198
LETTUCE & GREENS
- Caesar Salad, 192
- Hot Bacon Asparagus Salad, 187
- Pizza Salad, 185
- Spinach-Onion Salad with Hot Bacon Dressing, 190
PASTA
- BLT in a Bowl, 196
- Garden Macaroni Salad, 203
- Italian Basil Pasta Salad, 173
- Layered Veggie Tortellini Salad, 193
- Macaroni Coleslaw, 200
- Ranch Pasta Salad, 188
POTATO
- Homemade Potato Salad, 207
- Honey-Mustard Potato Salad, 188
VEGETABLE
- Carrot Raisin Salad, 172
- Colorful Tomato 'n' Mozzarella Salad, 201
- Cucumbers with Dressing, 184
- Fruited Coleslaw, 189
- Garden Macaroni Salad, 203
- Hot Bacon Asparagus Salad, 187
- Layered Veggie Tortellini Salad, 193
- Macaroni Coleslaw, 200
- Mixed Bean Salad, 182
- Mom's Pickled Beets, 191

SANDWICHES *(ALSO SEE BURGERS)*
- Barbecue Ham Sandwiches, 38
- Barbecued Beef Sandwiches, 148
- Barbecues for the Bunch, 163
- Crunchy Ham and Cheese, 49
- Family-Pleasing Sloppy Joes, 58
- Farmhouse Chili Dogs, 42
- French Dip Sandwiches, 168
- Italian Beef Hoagies, 164
- Italian Chicken Pockets, 58
- Meat Loaf Gyros, 126
- Melt-in-Your-Mouth Sausages, 159
- Reuben Crescent Bake, 118
- Slow Cooker Sloppy Joes, 146
- Super Flatbread Wraps, 76
- Turkey Reubens, 35

SAUERKRAUT
- Reuben Baked Potatoes, 205
- Reuben Crescent Bake, 118
- Pork Chops with Sauerkraut, 141

SAUSAGE, PEPPERONI & HOT DOGS
APPETIZERS
Antipasto Platter, 17
Orange-Glazed Smokies, 23
Pigs in a Blanket, 10
Pizza Cups, 19
Pizza Egg Rolls, 15
Sausage-Stuffed Mushrooms, 26
MAIN DISHES
Chicago-Style Stuffed Pizza, 92
Farmhouse Chili Dogs, 42
German Oktoberfest Pizza, 86
Gnocchi with Hearty Meat Sauce, 41
Italian Shepherd's Pie, 119
Kielbasa Cabbage Skillet, 41
Macaroni & Cheese Pizza, 108
Mama Mia Burgers, 69
Melt-in-Your-Mouth Sausages, 159
Pasta Sausage Supper, 37
Pizza Pork Chops, 67
Pizza Spaghetti, 47
Pizzeria Burgers, 69
Roasted Chicken with Sausage Stuffing, 99
Sausage-Corn Bake, 106
Sausage Mac Supper, 54
Smoked Sausage Pasta, 61
Spaghetti 'n' Meatballs for 2, 65
Spicy Meatballs with Sauce, 142
Three Beans and Sausage, 155
SOUPS & STEW
Italian Stew, 77
Smoked Sausage Gumbo, 162
Veggie-Sausage Cheese Soup, 143
SALAD
Pizza Salad, 185

SEAFOOD *SEE FISH & SEAFOOD.*

SIDE DISHES *(ALSO SEE SALADS)*
BEANS
Family-Favorite Baked Beans, 180
Four-Bean Supreme, 212
Picnic Baked Beans, 208
PASTA & NOODLES
Creamy Noodles, 209
Homemade Noodles, 183
Slow-Cooked Mac 'n' Cheese, 187
POTATOES
Cheddar Tot Casserole, 179
Cheddar Twice-Baked Potatoes, 175
Garlic Mashed Potatoes, 179
Hash Browns with Ham, 202
Lemon-Butter New Potatoes, 192
Loaded Mashed Potatoes, 211
Oven Fries, 177
Reuben Baked Potatoes, 205
RICE
Broccoli Rice Casserole, 183
Confetti Rice, 208
Mushroom Wild Rice, 195
Parmesan Peas 'n' Rice, 199

STUFFING & DRESSING
Artichoke Stuffing, 186
Deluxe Corn Bread Dressing, 188
Family-Favorite Dressing, 191
Makeover Best Corn Bread Dressing, 172
VEGETABLES
Broccoli Mushroom Casserole, 206
Broccoli Rice Casserole, 183
Calico Squash, 176
Cauliflower au Gratin, 210
Cheesy Vegetable Medley, 204
Comforting Carrot Casserole, 191
Corn and Broccoli in Cheese Sauce, 197
Creamy Parmesan Spinach, 196
Fried Onion Rings, 179
Green Bean Casserole for 2, 176
Green Beans with Bacon, 203
Grilled Vegetable Medley, 199
Honey-Glazed Carrots, 211
Makeover Corn Pudding, 207
Mallow Sweet Potato Bake, 178
New England Butternut Squash, 195
Onion Yorkshire Puddings, 175
Parmesan Corn on the Cob, 212
Parmesan Peas 'n' Rice, 199
Roasted Harvest Vegetables, 213
Roasted Sugar Snap Peas, 212
Roasted Vegetable Medley, 181
Scalloped Corn, 204
Spinach Casserole for 2, 180
Steakhouse Mushrooms, 194
Sweet Potatoes with Apples, 184

SLOW COOKER
MAIN DISHES
Barbecued Beef Sandwiches, 148
Barbecues for the Bunch, 163
Braised Beef Short Ribs, 156
Busy Mom's Chicken Fajitas, 154
Chicken with Veggies 'n' Gravy, 164
Chinese Pork Ribs, 155
Cider-Glazed Ham, 156
Cider Mushroom Brisket, 152
Country Pork Chop Supper, 160
Creamy Beef and Pasta, 143
French Dip Sandwiches, 168
Green Chili Beef Burritos, 147
Hungarian Goulash, 138
Italian Beef Hoagies, 164
Lazy Man's Ribs, 136
Maple Mustard Chicken, 140
Melt-in-Your-Mouth Sausages, 159
Mushroom Chicken Cacciatore, 144
No-Fuss Swiss Steak, 143
Old-Fashioned Pork Chops, 152
Orange-Glazed Ham, 156
Picante Beef Roast, 136
Polynesian Roast Beef, 167
Pork Burritos, 139
Pork Chops & Acorn Squash, 155
Pork Chops with Sauerkraut, 141

Sesame Pork Ribs, 158
Slow-Cooked Herbed Turkey, 144
Slow-Cooked Meat Loaf, 169
Slow-Cooked Pepper Steak, 165
Slow Cooker Lasagna, 163
Slow Cooker Sloppy Joes, 146
Spicy Meatballs with Sauce, 142
Stuffed Flank Steak, 168
Sweet 'n' Tangy Chicken, 157
Taco Meat Loaf, 159
Three Beans and Sausage, 155
Tropical BBQ Chicken, 150
Turkey-Portobello Meat Loaf, 166
Turkey with Cranberry Sauce, 161
SIDE DISHES
Corn and Broccoli in Cheese Sauce, 197
Hash Browns with Ham, 202
Ranch Beans, 160
Slow-Cooked Mac 'n' Cheese, 187
SOUPS, STEWS & CHILI
Baked Potato Soup, 137
Beef and Three-Bean Chili, 151
Big Red Soup, 159
Busy Day Beef Stew, 151
Chicken Noodle Soup, 167
Creamy Ham Chowder, 148
French Beef Stew, 147
Hearty Black Bean Soup, 156
Santa Fe Chili, 139
Savory Cheese Soup, 140
Smoked Sausage Gumbo, 162
Split Pea Soup, 145
Tex-Mex Chili, 149
Veggie-Sausage Cheese Soup, 143

SOUPS, STEWS & CHILI
Baked Potato Soup, 137
Beef and Three-Bean Chili, 151
Beef Stew for 2, 79
Big Red Soup, 159
Busy Day Beef Stew, 151
Chicken Noodle Soup, 167
Creamy Ham Chowder, 148
French Beef Stew, 147
Hearty Black Bean Soup, 156
Italian Beef Stew, 54
Italian Stew, 77
Santa Fe Chili, 139
Savory Cheese Soup, 140
Smoked Sausage Gumbo, 162
Split Pea Soup, 145
Tex-Mex Chili, 149
Veggie-Sausage Cheese Soup, 143
White Chili, 153

SPINACH
Creamy Parmesan Spinach, 196
Spinach Artichoke Dip, 27
Spinach Casserole for 2, 180
Spinach-Onion Salad with Hot Bacon
    Dressing, 190

SQUASH
Butternut Squash Cake Roll, 286
Calico Squash, 176
Grilled Vegetable Medley, 199
New England Butternut Squash, 195
Pork Chops & Acorn Squash, 155
Roasted Vegetable Medley, 181
Zucchini Red Pepper Lasagna, 131

STUFFING & DRESSING
Artichoke Stuffing, 186
Deluxe Corn Bread Dressing, 188
Family-Favorite Dressing, 191
Makeover Best Corn Bread Dressing, 172
Roasted Chicken with Sausage Stuffing, 99
Stuffed Flank Steak, 168

SWEET POTATOES
Mallow Sweet Potato Bake, 178
Sweet Potatoes with Apples, 184

TOFFEE
Banana Brickle Muffins, 251
Caramel Toffee Ice Cream Pie, 302

TOMATOES
BLT in a Bowl, 196
Colorful Tomato 'n' Mozzarella Salad, 201
Layered Veggie Tortellini Salad, 193
Tomato Nacho Dip, 11

TORTILLAS
Busy Mom's Chicken Fajitas, 154
Chicken Tortilla Bake, 114
Green Chili Beef Burritos, 147
Layered Tortilla Pie, 112
Pork Burritos, 139
Taco Lasagna, 98

TURKEY
Chili Mac, 80
Cordon Bleu Casserole, 101
Gnocchi with Hearty Meat Sauce, 41
Holiday Corn 'n' Turkey Casserole, 97
Honey-Apple Turkey Breast, 102
Maple-Butter Turkey with Gravy, 94
Pizza Spaghetti, 47
Slow-Cooked Herbed Turkey, 144
Spicy Meatballs with Sauce, 142
Turkey Biscuit Bake, 109
Turkey Day Bake, 121
Turkey Pasta Supreme, 82
Turkey-Portobello Meat Loaf, 166
Turkey Potpies, 111
Turkey Reubens, 35
Turkey Scallopini, 46
Turkey Tetrazzini, 106
Turkey with Cranberry Sauce, 161

VEGETABLES (*ALSO SEE SALADS; SPECIFIC KINDS*)
Artichoke Stuffing, 186
Beef Stew for 2, 79

Cauliflower au Gratin, 210
Cheesy Vegetable Medley, 204
Chicken Vegetable Potpie, 98
Corn and Broccoli in Cheese Sauce, 197
Grilled Vegetable Medley, 199
Italian Beef Stew, 54
Roasted Harvest Vegetables, 213
Roasted Vegetable Medley, 181
Spinach Artichoke Dip, 27
Tuna Veggie Macaroni, 36
Veggie-Sausage Cheese Soup, 143

VEGETARIAN *SEE MEATLESS MAIN DISHES.*

WHITE CHOCOLATE (*ALSO SEE CHOCOLATE*)
Cranberry-White Chocolate Cinnamon Rolls, 269
Makeover Marbled Orange Fudge, 276
White Chocolate Bread Pudding, 278
White Chocolate Cherry Parfaits, 292
White Chocolate Macadamia Cookies, 236

YEAST BREADS
BREAKFAST BREADS (*ALSO SEE SWEET ROLLS*)
Cheddar English Muffins, 267
Cranberry Nut Bagels, 263
From-Scratch Bagels, 256
Morning Crispies, 227
COFFEE CAKE
Apricot Tea Rings, 261
Nut Roll Coffee Cake, 247
Swedish Tea Ring, 225
LOAVES
Challah, 251
Chocolate Braids, 241
Cinnamon Raisin Bread, 228
Dill-Onion Batter Bread, 220
Honey White Loaves, 254
Quick Rosemary Focaccia, 259
Stromboli Ladder Loaf, 31
ROLLS & INDIVIDUAL BREADS
Cloverleaf Rolls, 233
Honey Whole Wheat Rolls, 239
Parmesan-Ranch Pan Rolls, 216
Southwest Pretzels, 8
Super Flatbread Wraps, 76
SWEET ROLLS
Cappuccino Cinnamon Rolls, 258
Caramel-Pecan Sticky Buns, 271
Cranberry-White Chocolate Cinnamon Rolls, 269
Frosted Cinnamon Rolls, 219
Maple Sticky Buns, 235

ZUCCHINI *SEE SQUASH.*

cooking tips index

Appetizer Party, Planning, 12
Brown Sugar, Types, 219
Brownies, Tasty Addition, 296
Brunch, Preparations, 225
Butter, Cutting In, 231
Buttermilk Substitute, 106
Cabbage, Pointers, 41
Cheese Ball, Shaping, 16
Cherries, Cooking with, 292
Chicken Quarters, 130
Coffee, Special, 258
Cranberries, Dried, 66
Cranberries, Purchasing, 270
Cream Puffs, Freezing, 306
Crescent Rolls, as Breakfast Pastries, 267
Drop Cookies, Uniform, 252
Fish, Mild Flavor, 62
Fish, Purchasing, 101
Garlic, Substitutes, 78
Gloves, Keeping Hands Clean, 142
Green Bean Casserole, 176
Green Onions, Cutting, 50
Ground Beef, Saving Time, 34
Ham Salad, 110
Ham Slices, with Maple Syrup, 129
Holiday Meals, Easy Service, 204
Ice Cream, Minty Treat, 303
Lasagna Noodles, in Soup, 95
Macaroni 'n' Cheese, Stir-In Idea, 125
Nuts, Keeping on Hand, 234
Oatmeal Cookies, Moist, 240
Pan Gravy, 73
Parfait, Garnish, 279
Parmesan, Grated, 199
Pickled Shrimp, Menu Ideas, 27
Pizza, Leftovers in, 89
Pizza Snacks, Freezing, 23
Pork Tenderloin, 57
Potato Salad, Additions, 207
Potatoes, Buyng, 192
Refried Beans, in Chili, 151
Rice, Fried from Leftovers, 183
Round Steak, 118
Slow Cooker, Carrier, 163
Spinach, Draining, 180
Stuffed Shells, 46
Thyme, in Soup, 167
Tomato Soup, in Beef Stew, 147
Tortillas, Softening, 139
Winter Squash, Buying and Storing, 286
Yeast Dough, Overnight, 247
Yeast Dough, Rapid Mixing Method, 8

alphabetical recipe index

A

Ambrosia Cupcakes, 221
Antipasto Platter, 17
Appetizer Pizzas, 20
Apple Crisp, 231
Apple-Onion Pork Chops, 74
Apple Praline Pie, 234
Apricot Almond Torte, 218
Apricot Bars, 246
Apricot Ham Steak, 45
Apricot Tea Rings, 261
Artichoke Stuffing, 186
Aunt Betty's Blueberry Muffins, 264
Aunt Ruth's Famous Butterscotch Cheesecake, 301

B

Bacon Cheeseburger Pasta, 49
Baked Cider-Glazed Ham, 156
Baked Potato Soup, 137
Banana Brickle Muffins, 251
Banana Chocolate Chip Cookies, 262
Banana Cream Eclairs, 237
Banana Split Supreme, 304
Barbecue Ham Sandwiches, 38
Barbecued Beef Sandwiches, 148
Barbecues for the Bunch, 163
Beef and Three-Bean Chili, 151
Beef Macaroni Skillet, 34
Beef Stew for 2, 79
Berry Patch Pie, 268
Best Chicken 'n' Biscuits, 105
Big-Batch Spaghetti 'n' Meatballs, 45
Big Red Soup, 159
Bistro Mac & Cheese, 66
BLT in a Bowl, 196
Bohemian Pot Roast, 38
Braised Beef Short Ribs, 156
Breaded Chicken Strips, 51
Brie in Puff Pastry, 16
Brie Phyllo Cups, 15
Broccoli Mushroom Casserole, 206
Broccoli Rice Casserole, 183
Budget Macaroni and Cheese, 70
Busy Day Beef Stew, 151
Busy Mom's Chicken Fajitas, 154
Butter Pecan Ice Cream, 283
Butternut Squash Cake Roll, 286
Butterscotch Raisin Cookies, 252

C

Caesar Salad, 192
Calico Squash, 176
Candy Apple Pie, 265
Cappuccino Cheesecake Pie, 288
Cappuccino Cinnamon Rolls, 258

Cappuccino Truffles, 276
Caramel Apple Trifle, 298
Caramel Chip Malts, 283
Caramel-Pecan Sticky Buns, 271
Caramel Toffee Ice Cream Pie, 302
Carrot Cake Doughnuts, 243
Carrot Raisin Salad, 172
Cashew Caramel Fudge, 287
Cauliflower au Gratin, 210
Challah, 251
Champagne Baked Ham, 104
Change-of-Pace Burgers, 62
Cheddar Crab Bites, 23
Cheddar English Muffins, 267
Cheddar Tot Casserole, 179
Cheddar Twice-Baked Potatoes, 175
Cheeseburger Cups, 126
Cheesecake Praline Squares, 304
Cheesecake Pumpkin Muffins, 235
Cheesy Vegetable Egg Dish, 121
Cheesy Vegetable Medley, 204
Cherry Blueberry Pie, 247
Cherry Crescent Coffee Cake, 230
Chewy Oatmeal Cookies, 232
Chicago-Style Stuffed Pizza, 92
Chicken 'n' Corn Bread Dressing, 94
Chicken and Dumpling Casserole, 90
Chicken Caesar Pasta, 64
Chicken Chili Nachos, 31
Chicken Fried Steak, 73
Chicken Lasagna Rolls, 95
Chicken Noodle Casserole, 113
Chicken Noodle Soup, 167
Chicken Parmesan, 106
Chicken Tortilla Bake, 114
Chicken Vegetable Potpie, 98
Chicken with Country Gravy, 130
Chicken with Veggies 'n' Gravy, 164
Chili Mac, 80
Chinese Pork Ribs, 155
Chocolate Almond Ice Cream, 299
Chocolate and Vanilla Creme Brulee, 285
Chocolate Braids, 241
Chocolate Chip Blondies, 220
Chocolate Chip Cake, 224
Chocolate Cookie Cupcakes, 272
Chocolate-Covered Cheesecake Squares, 282
Chocolate Creme Brulee, 285
Chocolate Lover's Dream Cookies, 227
Chocolate Mint Eclair Dessert, 300
Chocolate Mousse with Cranberry Sauce, 290
Chocolate-Peanut Butter Cupcakes, 273
Chocolate Pecan Cookies, 227
Chocolate Pistachio Biscotti, 266
Cider-Glazed Ham, 156
Cider Mushroom Brisket, 152

Cinnamon Raisin Bread, 228
Cinnamon Rolls in a Snap, 240
Citrus-Baked Cornish Hens, 97
Classic Chocolate Layer Cake, 226
Classic Fried Chicken, 34
Cloverleaf Rolls, 233
Cola Floats, 287
Colorful Tomato 'n' Mozzarella Salad, 201
Comforting Carrot Casserole, 191
Confetti Mac 'n' Cheese, 43
Confetti Rice, 208
Cool Lime Pie, 305
Cordon Bleu Casserole, 101
Corn and Broccoli in Cheese Sauce, 197
Cornmeal Oven-Fried Chicken, 91
Country Ham and Potatoes, 74
Country Pork Chop Supper, 160
Cranberry-Cashew Drop Cookies, 252
Cranberry Cream Cheese Coffee Cake, 270
Cranberry-Dijon Pork, 66
Cranberry Gelatin Salad, 187
Cranberry Meatballs, 30
Cranberry Nut Bagels, 263
Cranberry-Topped Lemon Tarts, 259
Cranberry-White Chocolate Cinnamon Rolls, 269
Cream Cake Dessert, 307
Cream-Filled Chocolate Cake Roll, 294
Creamy Beef and Pasta, 143
Creamy Ham Chowder, 148
Creamy Noodles, 209
Creamy Olive-Bacon Dip, 11
Creamy Parmesan Spinach, 196
Creamy Pineapple Pie, 305
Creamy Ranch Dip, 28
Creole Meat Loaf, 89
Crunchy Ham and Cheese, 49
Cubed Steak Stroganoff, 50
Cucumbers with Dressing, 184

D

Dad's Swedish Meatballs, 73
Decadent Brownie Swirl Cheesecake, 281
Delightful Deviled Eggs, 28
Deluxe Corn Bread Dressing, 188
Deluxe Macaroni Dinner, 53
Dill-Onion Batter Bread, 220
Dilly Salmon Patties, 37
Double Chocolate Truffles, 276
Dutch Rhubarb Pie, 260

E

Easy Apple Betty, 272
Easy Buffalo Chicken Dip, 25
Easy Dutch Apple Pie, 228
Easy Meatballs, 28

the **ULTIMATE COMFORT FOOD** cookbook

Easy Shrimp Scampi, 50
Easy Tiramisu, 277
Edna's Ho Ho Cake, 289
Eggnog Pumpkin Pie, 243

F

Family-Favorite Baked Beans, 180
Family-Favorite Dressing, 191
Family-Pleasing Sloppy Joes, 58
Family-Style Turkey Potpie, 93
Farmhouse Chili Dogs, 42
Fat Rascals, 19
Festive Feta Cheese Ball, 16
Florida Citrus Meringue Pie, 217
Four-Bean Supreme, 212
Four-Cheese Baked Ziti, 86
French Beef Stew, 147
French Dip Sandwiches, 168
French Onion Cheese Fondue, 14
French Onion Pizza au Gratin, 103
Fried Chicken with Pan Gravy, 39
Fried Onion Rings, 179
From-Scratch Bagels, 256
Frosted Butter Cookies, 256
Frosted Cinnamon Rolls, 219
Fruited Coleslaw, 189
Fudge Brownie Pie, 260
Fudge Sundae Pie, 279
Fun-on-the-Run Snack Mix, 31

G

Garden Macaroni Salad, 203
Garlic-Butter Steak, 55
Garlic Mashed Potatoes, 179
Garlic Pot Roast, 110
German Chocolate Cheesecake, 309
German Oktoberfest Pizza, 86
Gingerbread Cookies, 229
Glazed Chocolate Chip Brownies, 236
Glazed Meatballs, 30
Glazed Pork Medallions, 57
Gnocchi with Hearty Meat Sauce, 41
Grandma's Rice Pudding, 284
Green Bean Casserole for 2, 176
Green Beans with Bacon, 203
Green Chili Beef Burritos, 147
Grilled Vegetable Medley, 199

H

Ham and Cheese Party Calzones, 13
Ham Balls, 110
Ham Mac and Cheese, 127
Ham-Noodle Bake, 93
Ham with Ruby-Red Glaze, 129
Hamburger Mac Skillet, 78
Hash Browns with Ham, 202
Heart's Delight Eclair, 291
Hearty Black Bean Soup, 156
Herbed Fried Chicken with Gravy, 39

Herbed Shepherd's Pie, 102
Holiday Corn 'n' Turkey Casserole, 97
Homemade Fish Sticks, 101
Homemade Noodles, 183
Homemade Potato Salad, 207
Honey-Apple Turkey Breast, 102
Honey-Glazed Carrots, 211
Honey Mustard Chicken, 125
Honey Mustard Pork, 78
Honey-Mustard Potato Salad, 188
Honey White Loaves, 254
Honey Whole Wheat Rolls, 239
Hot Bacon Asparagus Salad, 187
Hungarian Goulash, 138

I

Irish Soda Bread, 244
Island Fruit Salad, 200
Italian Basil Pasta Salad, 173
Italian Beef Hoagies, 164
Italian Beef Stew, 54
Italian Chicken Pockets, 58
Italian Pinwheel Meat Loaf, 121
Italian Shepherd's Pie, 119
Italian Stew, 77

J

Jumbo Chocolate Chip Cookies, 231

K

Kentucky Chocolate Pecan Pie, 264
Kielbasa Cabbage Skillet, 41

L

Lara's Tender Gingersnaps, 219
Lasagna Casserole, 113
Layered Tortilla Pie, 112
Layered Veggie Tortellini Salad, 193
Lazy Man's Ribs, 136
Lemon Anise Biscotti, 242
Lemon Basil Chicken, 123
Lemon-Batter Fish, 62
Lemon-Butter New Potatoes, 192
Lemon Cream Puffs, 306
Lemon Crumb Muffins, 249
Lemon Meringue Pie, 239
Lemonade Icebox Pie, 305
Light Lemon Mousse, 280
Little Cheddar Meat Loaves, 124
Loaded Mashed Potatoes, 211

M

Macaroni & Cheese Pizza, 108
Macaroni Coleslaw, 200
Macaroni Taco Bake, 125
Makeover Best Corn Bread Dressing, 172
Makeover Corn Pudding, 207
Makeover Marbled Orange Fudge, 276
Makeover Strawberry Cake, 222

Malibu Chicken Bundles, 115
Mallow Sweet Potato Bake, 178
Mama Mia Burgers, 69
Maple-Butter Turkey with Gravy, 94
Maple Mustard Chicken, 140
Maple Sticky Buns, 235
Marvelous Shells 'n' Cheese, 116
Meat Loaf Gyros, 126
Meatball Sub Casserole, 120
Meatless Chili Mac, 57
Melt-in-Your-Mouth Sausages, 159
Mexican Chicken Meatballs, 21
Mini BBQ Chicken Pizzas, 23
Mini Burgers with the Works, 12
Mini Pineapple Upside-Down Cake, 244
Mini Raspberry Mousse Parfaits, 296
Mini Scallop Casseroles, 132
Mint-Chocolate Ice Cream Cake, 303
Mixed Bean Salad, 182
Mocha Cream Puffs, 299
Mocha Mallow Parfaits, 303
Mom's Meat Loaf, 128
Mom's Pickled Beets, 191
Morning Crispies, 227
Mushroom Beef Tenderloin, 70
Mushroom Chicken Cacciatore, 144
Mushroom Wild Rice, 195
My Favorite Burger, 83

N

New England Butternut Squash, 195
No-Bake Cherry Dessert, 296
No-Fuss Swiss Steak, 143
Nut Roll Coffee Cake, 247

O

Oatmeal Chip Cookies, 240
Old-Fashioned Chocolate Pudding, 288
Old-Fashioned Pork Chops, 152
Old-Time Cake Doughnuts, 263
Olive & Roasted Pepper Bruschetta, 29
Onion Yorkshire Puddings, 175
Orange Cinnamon Rolls, 255
Orange Dream Torte, 308
Orange Fluff Salad, 174
Orange-Glazed Ham, 156
Orange-Glazed Smokies, 23
Orange Icebox Pie, 305
Orange Truffles, 276
Oregano Roasting Chicken, 88
Oven Fries, 177

P

Parmesan Corn on the Cob, 212
Parmesan Peas 'n' Rice, 199
Parmesan-Ranch Pan Rolls, 216
Party Time Mini Cheeseburgers, 22
Pasta Sausage Supper, 37
Peach Ice Cream, 307

P (CONTINUED)

Peach Pie, 250
Peachy Cheese Danish, 267
Peachy Pork Chops, 56
Peanut Butter Cookies, 268
Peanut Butter Icebox Dessert, 292
Peanut Butter Kiss Cookies, 232
Peanut Butter Parfaits, 279
Pecan Pumpkin Pie, 245
Peeps Sunflower Cake, 238
Peppered Filets & Balsamic Red Onions, 52
Peppery Roast Beef, 122
Pesto Scallops Vermicelli, 40
Picante Beef Roast, 136
Pickled Shrimp, 27
Picnic Baked Beans, 208
Pigs in a Blanket, 10
Pineapple Cranberry Ham, 72
Pineapple Ham Pizzas, 11
Pistachio Pudding Parfaits, 284
Pizza Carbonara, 89
Pizza Cups, 19
Pizza Egg Rolls, 15
Pizza Joes, 46
Pizza Pork Chops, 67
Pizza Salad, 185
Pizza Spaghetti, 47
Pizzeria Burgers, 69
Polynesian Roast Beef, 167
Poppy Seed Creamed Chicken, 133
Pork Burritos, 139
Pork Chops & Acorn Squash, 155
Pork Chops with Cranberry Sauce, 48
Pork Chops with Mushroom Gravy, 81
Pork Chops with Sauerkraut, 141
Pork in Mustard Sauce, 69
Pork Medallions in Orange Sauce, 68
Pretzel-Crusted Drumsticks, 129
Prosciutto-Pepper Pork Chops, 59
Prosciutto Pinwheels, 24
Puff Pastry Hearts, 295
Pull-Apart Caramel Coffee Cake, 255
Pumpkin Creme Brulee, 280
Pumpkin Spice Cupcakes, 253

Q

Quick Rosemary Focaccia, 259

R

Ranch Beans, 160
Ranch Pasta Salad, 188
Raspberry Coffee Cake, 223
Raspberry Streusel Muffins, 271
Ravioli Carbonara, 66
Reuben Baked Potatoes, 205
Reuben Crescent Bake, 118
Roadside Diner Cheeseburger Quiche, 107
Roasted Chicken with Rosemary, 105
Roasted Chicken with Sausage Stuffing, 99
Roasted Harvest Vegetables, 213
Roasted Pepper Ravioli, 90

Roasted Sugar Snap Peas, 212
Roasted Vegetable Medley, 181
Rocky Road Fudge Pops, 300
Rosemary Lamb Chops, 65
Round Steak with Potatoes, 118
Rustic Autumn Fruit Tart, 257

S

Salmon Cakes, 77
Salmon Mornay, 60
Santa Fe Chili, 139
Saucy Meatballs, 30
Sausage-Corn Bake, 106
Sausage Mac Supper, 54
Sausage-Stuffed Mushrooms, 26
Savory Cheese Soup, 140
Savory Ham Cheesecake, 19
Scalloped Corn, 204
Seasoned Crab Cakes, 18
Sesame Pork Ribs, 158
Shrimp 'n' Noodle Bowls, 63
Shrimp Cocktail, 24
Shrimp Piccata Pasta, 71
Slow-Cooked Herbed Turkey, 144
Slow-Cooked Mac 'n' Cheese, 187
Slow-Cooked Meat Loaf, 169
Slow-Cooked Pepper Steak, 165
Slow Cooker Lasagna, 163
Slow Cooker Sloppy Joes, 146
Smoked Sausage Gumbo, 162
Smoked Sausage Pasta, 61
Smoky Potato Rounds, 9
Snowflake Pudding, 297
So-Tender Swiss Steak, 122
South Carolina Cobbler, 216
South-of-the-Border Quiche, 87
Southwest Bean and Chicken Pasta, 42
Southwest Pretzels, 8
Spaghetti 'n' Meatballs for 2, 65
Spicy Chicken Wings, 12
Spicy Meatballs with Sauce, 142
Spicy Pepper Steak, 61
Spinach Artichoke Dip, 27
Spinach Casserole for 2, 180
Spinach-Onion Salad with Hot Bacon
     Dressing, 190
Split Pea Soup, 145
Steak and Rice Roll-Ups, 44
Steak Potpie, 133
Steakhouse Mushrooms, 194
Stovetop Hamburger Casserole, 82
Strawberry Cheesecake Ice Cream, 291
Strawberry Shakes, 295
Strawberry Tiramisu Trifle, 293
Stromboli Ladder Loaf, 31
Stuffed Flank Steak, 168
Super Flatbread Wraps, 76
Swedish Tea Ring, 225
Sweet & Spicy Jalapeno Poppers, 8
Sweet 'n' Tangy Chicken, 157
Sweet Cherry Pork Chops, 53

Sweet Potatoes with Apples, 184
Swiss Steak with Dumplings, 96

T

Taco Lasagna, 98
Taco Meat Loaf, 159
Tacos in a Bowl, 75
Taffy Apple Dip, 20
Tasty Onion Chicken, 117
Tex-Mex Chili, 149
Three Beans and Sausage, 155
Tiny Shortbread Tarts, 248
Tomato Nacho Dip, 11
Tortilla-Salsa Meat Loaf, 130
Traditional Lasagna, 117
Tropical BBQ Chicken, 150
Tropical Fruit Salad, 198
Tuna Alfredo, 74
Tuna 'n' Pea Casserole, 100
Tuna Mushroom Casserole, 114
Tuna Noodle Skillet, 81
Tuna Veggie Macaroni, 36
Turkey Biscuit Bake, 109
Turkey Day Bake, 121
Turkey Pasta Supreme, 82
Turkey-Portobello Meat Loaf, 166
Turkey Potpies, 111
Turkey Reubens, 35
Turkey Scallopini, 46
Turkey Tetrazzini, 106
Turkey with Cranberry Sauce, 161
Turtle Praline Tart, 224

V

Vanilla Creme Brulee, 285
Veggie-Sausage Cheese Soup, 143
Very Cherry Ice Cream, 308

W

Walnut Baklava, 248
White Chili, 153
White Chocolate Bread Pudding, 278
White Chocolate Cherry Parfaits, 292
White Chocolate Macadamia Cookies, 236

Y

Yankee Corn Muffins, 223
Yellow Layer Cake, 224
Yellow Nut Cake, 224

Z

Zucchini Red Pepper Lasagna, 131